Library of
Davidson College

DON ISAAC ABRAVANEL

Also by B. Netanyahu

The Origins of the Inquisition in Fifteenth Century Spain
The Marranos of Spain
Toward the Inquisition: Essays on Jewish and Converso History in Late Medieval Spain

DON ISAAC ABRAVANEL
STATESMAN & PHILOSOPHER

Fifth Edition
Revised & Updated

B. NETANYAHU

CORNELL UNIVERSITY PRESS
ITHACA AND LONDON

Copyright © 1953, 1968, 1972 by
The Jewish Publication Society of America
Fifth edition, revised and updated, copyright © 1998 by Cornell University

All rights reserved. Except for brief quotations in a review, this book, or parts thereof, must not be reproduced in any form without permission in writing from the publisher. For information, address Cornell University Press, Sage House, 512 East State Street, Ithaca, New York 14850.

First edition, 1953, published by
The Jewish Publication Society of America
Second edition, 1968
Third edition, 1972
Fourth edition, paperback, 1982
Fifth edition, revised and updated, first published 1998
by Cornell University Press.
First printing, Cornell Paperbacks, 1998

Netanyahu, B. (Benzion), b. 1910
  Don Isaac Abravanel, Statesman and Philosopher / B. Netanyahu. —
5th ed., rev. and updated
    p. cm.
  Includes bibliographical references and index.
  ISBN 0-8014-3487-4 (cloth : alk. paper).
  ISBN 0-8014-8485-5 (pbk. : alk. paper)
  1. Abravanel, Isaac, 1437–1508. 2. Scholars—Biography. 3. Jewish statesmen—Spain—Biography. 4. Jewish statesmen—Italy—Biography.
5. Jewish philosophers—Biography. I. Title
BM755.A25N4   1988
296′.092—dc21
[B]   97-50254

Cornell University Press strives to use environmentally responsible suppliers and materials to the fullest extent possible in the publication of its books. Such materials include vegetable-based, low-VOC inks and acid-free papers that are recycled, totally chlorine-free, or partly composed of nonwood fibers.

Cloth printing   10 9 8 7 6 5 4 3 2 1

Paperback printing   10 9 8 7 6 5 4 3 2 1

To the memory of my father
RABBI NATHAN MILEIKOWSKY
(1879–1935)
*whose idealism, farsightedness,
and nobility of spirit
are still sources of inspiration*

CONTENTS

Preface ... ix

PART ONE
FINANCIER AND STATESMAN

I. PORTUGAL: HAPPY HAVEN ... 3
    Family, 3 — Childhood, 6
    Studies and Early Literary Efforts, 12
    In the Service of the King, 18 — Fall and Escape, 26

II. SPAIN: LAND OF PERSECUTION ... 33
    On the Portuguese Border, 33 — The Catholic Kings, 38
    Advancement at Court, 50 — The Great Crisis, 53

III. NAPLES: SCENE OF TROUBLE ... 61
    On Italy's Threshold, 61 — A Neapolitan Courtier, 62
    In Sicilian Exile, 67 — A Visit to Corfu, 71
    Monopoli: Shelter in the Storm, 74

IV. VENICE: THE LAST REFUGE ... 82
    New Rise to Prominence, 82
    The Final Efforts, 85 — Summary, 87

PART TWO
COMMENTATOR AND PHILOSOPHER

I. WORLD OUTLOOK ... 95
    Revelation, 95 — Creation, 103
    The Universe, 108 — Man, 112 — Man and Universe, 118
    Conclusions, 125

II. VIEW OF HISTORY   130
    The Principles, 130 — The Course, 135
    The Characteristics, 146

III. POLITICAL CONCEPTS   150
    Fundamental Problems, 150 — The Ideal Constitution, 158
    The Venetian Prototype, 166
    Monarchism, 173 — The Political Tradition, 180
    On the Divine Rights of Kings, 186
    Theocracy Is the Answer, 189

IV. MESSIANISM   195
    The Problem, 195 — The Method, 205
    The Date, 216 — The Revolution, 226
    Savonarola, 242 — Epilogue, 247

Appendices   261

Notes   265

Bibliography   327

Index   337

From the Preface to the First Edition

DON ISAAC ABRAVANEL is the outstanding historical figure among the Jews in the closing period of the Middle Ages. Statesman, diplomat, courtier and financier of international renown, he was, at the same time, an encyclopedic scholar, a philosophical thinker, a noted exegete and a brilliant writer. The combination of such diverse qualities so highly developed in a single man is a rare phenomenon at any time. It was no less rare among the Jews of the Middle Ages. In fact, in Abravanel there met and ended two long lines of tradition—the line of medieval Jewish statesmen and the line of medieval Jewish philosophers.

As a representative of these two great traditions, and as the last spokesman of the Jewish Middle Ages, Abravanel is of sufficient interest to merit a close study and examination. But Abravanel offers even more to the curiosity of the student of history. For he was also a mystic and apocalyptist of the highest stature and influence. As such, he threw a long shadow on centuries of Jewish history after him; and thus, while representing the closing phase of the medieval era, he also represents the opening phase of the era that followed.

Living at a time when the Jewish people was experiencing a fundamental transformation in the conditions of its life—spiritual, social and political alike—Abravanel offers in his works an explanation of the direction which that transformation had taken. The period that followed Abravanel's age was, for the general history of the world, the bridge between the Middle Ages and modern times. For the Jewish people, however, it appears to have been, not a bridge, but a gap. The three hundred years between the end of the Middle Ages and the French Revolution saw, as far as the Jewish people is concerned, not an emergence from the Middle Ages, but rather an intensification of their unfavorable aspects. They witnessed, moreover, a twist toward a development which was never apparent during the Middle Ages or any other epoch of Jewish history. For what characterized this period was a spiritual isolation which is not at all typical of Jewish life in the Diaspora, and what made it quite exceptional was a sustained messianic drive which was completely apocalyptic, completely divorced from politics or militarism, and which, unlike all earlier, purely mystical, messianic trends, was not limited to a small circle of dreamers and intellectuals but became a mass movement in the full sense of the word and affected the historical course of the Jewish people.

What was the cause of this dual phenomenon—this spiritual isolationism and mystical messianism—the like and extent of which we find in Jewish life at no other time? How could it be maintained at the very time when Europe was stirred to its very foundations by a succession of powerful revolutionary movements, religious and philosophical, and when a new rationalistic mode of thinking was gradually replacing the dogmatism and mysticism of the Middle Ages? What, indeed, was the cause, the underlying cause, for the fact that, at the very time the Jews banned Spinoza they accepted Shabbethai Zevi with general enthusiasm? Certainly this development was not the result of a single cause, but rather of a number of causes. It is equally clear that one of these causes, and not the least of them, was a particular ideology that gave impetus to this course, and that the influence of this ideology was fortified in large measure by the theories which had been expounded by Abravanel.

That Abravanel was the father of the messianic movements of the sixteenth and seventeenth centuries was already sensed and pointed out by a number of scholars, and it is this aspect of Abravanel's work that first aroused the interest of the present writer. But while working on this subject, it became clear to him that Abravanel's messianic views were closely interwoven with a complex set of ideas on politics and history which, in turn, formed an integral part of a well-constituted world outlook. The work—originally planned as a doctoral thesis for the Faculty of the Dropsie College—thus expanded to embrace Abravanel's worldview, and his historical, political and messianic conceptions. All of these themes form the subject of the second part of this volume. The first part, which deals with Abravanel's life and times, was written later, although—as the reader may well assume—the study of Abravanel's *curriculum vitae* and the conditions of his age were a constant point of reference for this writer from the beginning of his work.

This volume deals with times and views which may appear, not only remote and foreign, but also bizarre to a modern reader. But the times were of extraordinary importance, and, as for the views, the reader must be cautioned not to judge them by present-day standards and concepts. However fantastic Abravanel's views may appear to him, he must not fail to judge them by their historical impact. He must bear in mind that the man and his work constituted a first-rate historic force that helped direct the destinies of the Jewish people through that maze of complicated and tragic developments which led them from the Middle Ages to the present time.

Preface to the Fifth Edition

In the forty-five years since its publication, this book has been in constant demand by both lay and scholarly readers, and the new editions issued as a result have repeatedly enabled me to improve it. Thus, certainties replaced doubts, accuracies imprecisions, and missing links were provided where the sequence of events seemed questionable or indefinite. The current edition gave me another opportunity to continue this process of correction and amplification, so that the long time that has passed since the book's first appearance turned out to be to its advantage. Without exaggeration one may say that the present version rests on the largest amount of data ever employed in any discourse on its subject—data culled from many sources with much patience and great effort, after surmounting the obstacles commonly met with by inquirers into medieval affairs, and, in addition, a peculiar difficulty related to the nature and content of this work. A few brief remarks on this special difficulty seem to be called for on this occasion.

When I decided to write a biography of Abravanel, I intended to offer a fair account of his life and a proper exposition of his ideas. By his "life" I meant not only the particular events that affected his activities and personal fortunes but also the general historical developments that caused or influenced those events. Similarly, by his "ideas" I meant not only the theories that he espoused in his various writings but also the currents of thought in his age that shaped or steered his thinking. In brief, I sought to produce a portrait of Abravanel against the social and intellectual background of his time.

If the writing of such a comprehensive biography is a difficult task in almost all cases, it was especially difficult—I soon came to realize—in the case of Abravanel. No Jewish history was written in the Middle Ages, and no biography of any Jewish personage was left us from those tumultuous times. Consequently, when I began to gather data about Abravanel, I came upon the same kind of materials encountered by other modern researchers who sought to write biographies of medieval Jewish leaders. What I found were various pieces of information, fragmentary and touching isolated events in different places and limited periods. Disparate as they were, they could not provide a basis for an adequate account of Abravanel's life.

There remained only one more set of sources to resort to: the contemporary histories of the four states—Portugal, Spain, Naples, and Venice—in which Abravanel spent his life. And it was indeed only after delving into these histories, and finding data related to the above-mentioned fragments, that I could connect many of the latter to each other and to the general course of events. Later on, when I reread Abravanel's works with the broader knowledge I had acquired of his life, I could see how his experiences influenced his views and how these, in turn, were reflected in his actions. Then, after scrutinizing all the sources embracing both his deeds and thoughts, I could finally discern Abravanel's image as thinker and leader of his people.

It was this image that I presented in my book, which soon aroused interest in many quarters, changed the common view then held of Abravanel to one approaching my own conception, and inspired new inquiries into various aspects of Abravanel's life and thought. None of these favorable reactions, however, made me forget that a number of questions remained unresolved or clouded with doubt. Considering the state and nature of my sources, such an outcome seemed unavoidable. Nevertheless, I persisted in my quest for data that might fill the lacunae in my account, and, aided by some of the new inquiries referred to, I could supply missing items of undoubted importance.

When I approached the preparation of the present edition, however, I knew that the book still contained some assertions based on scanty or presumptive evidence; but I also knew that my own investigations, as well as those of others who dealt with Abravanel, have advanced to the point of settling satisfactorily most of the remaining uncertainties. And thus the results of these latest inquiries are likewise incorporated in this work. Perhaps further exploration may reveal new facts—but, of course, up to a limit. In this, as in other cases, we ought to bear in mind that the whole truth will always elude us and that we can attain no more than its close resemblance. I venture to hope that such a resemblance is offered in the present biography.

B. N.

September 15, 1997

PART ONE

FINANCIER & STATESMAN

CHAPTER ONE

PORTUGAL: HAPPY HAVEN

1. Family

DON ISAAC ABRAVANEL[1] was born in Lisbon, in the year 1437,[2] into a family which ranked high among the Jews of Portugal and, indeed, of the entire Iberian peninsula. The Abravanels were distinguished by their financial position as well as by their political achievements. Abravanel's father, Don Judah, was the financier of Prince Fernando, the son of Portugal's João I, and in all probability was similarly employed by other members of the royal family.[3] His grandfather, Don Samuel, had been a power in the courts of three successive Castilian kings, and in the days of the third of them, Enrique III, had reached the highest position in Castile's financial administration when he assumed the office of *contador mayor*.[4] Another Don Judah Abravanel, probably Isaac's great-grandfather, had been the treasurer of Fernando IV in Seville and, according to some indications, also Castile's *almoxarif mayor*.[5] From his ancestors, then, Don Isaac acquired his financial acumen, his skill in managing state finances and the diplomatic ability which goes with it.

To this tradition of wealth and power was added the fame of a long and noble lineage which, it may be assumed, contributed considerably to the family's prestige. The Abravanels themselves were both certain and proud of the nobility of their origin—so proud and certain, indeed, that they claimed descent from the Davidic dynasty and settlement in Spain in pre-Roman times. Although the family's genealogical tree does not go back farther than five generations before Don Isaac's time, there is evidence that the claim received credence, at least among some leading Jews, not only in Don Isaac's days, but also four centuries earlier.[6] Needless to say, the claim can be easily challenged; but the very fact that it could be maintained so long and so persistently seems to offer sufficient indication that the family not only had projected itself on the scene of history with important deeds and personalities of merit, but that it was also imbued with that sense of historic mission which we find so strongly expressed in Don Isaac's life and thought.

One more trait which is observable in the Abravanels is especially noteworthy. All of Abravanel's ancestors had been prominent Jewish leaders.[7] In view of their high social standing, and especially of their political connections, their position of eminence in Jewish life was almost a matter of course. The Abravanels, however, were unwilling to give themselves exclusively to leadership in Jewish affairs or to the field of state finances. For, besides material and political, they had strong moral and intellectual interests. Thus, one available record speaks of an Abravanel in the days of the "mighty and pious King Alfonso"—perhaps Joseph Abravanel, Don Isaac's great-great-grandfather, in the days of Alfonso X (the Learned)—who was admired as a "great sage" even by the most renowned clerics and whose wisdom and learning earned him an invitation to visit the royal court.[8] Again, Don Samuel, already mentioned, is described by one contemporary as a man who "loves learning, patronizes scholars, is concerned for their welfare and who, whenever he is relieved from the turbulence of the times, is possessed of a desire to delve into the works of the famous authors and philosophers."[9] In the lives of Isaac's ancestors, the intellectual bent was repressed or overshadowed by their public and financial interests. In his own life, however, as we shall see, both the spiritual and material tendencies, while clashing, came into full play. In any case, Abravanel inherited from his ancestors not only his financial aptitude and his inclination to leadership, but also that yearning for speculative thought which so deeply influenced his life.

The home-town of the Abravanels was Seville, and it is there that they lived after the reconquest as they had in Moslem and perhaps pre-Moslem times.[10] Seville, an old Andalusian capital, was Castile's only city of international importance. It was reconquered by the Christians in 1248, in the general southward sweep of Ferdinand III which wrested from the Moors other important centers, such as Cordova (1236), Murcia (1243), and Jaen (1246) and limited the Moslem holdings in Spain to the narrowest confines they had ever had. The capture of Seville was the crowning achievement of Spain's crusading effort for generations and it remained for almost two and a half centuries the terminus of Christian expansion. As a great commercial center in which Jews were powerful,[11] and as an advance outpost of Christendom in the historic struggle with the Moors, Seville had more than its share of friction, economic as well as religious, for the creation of a charged social atmosphere. Seville consequently became the breeding ground of the most virulent and relentless anti-Jewish agitation. It was Seville that gave the signal, in 1378, for a nation-wide campaign of persecution of the Jews. It was Seville that initiated the anti-Jewish massacres which swept the peninsula in 1391. And it was in Seville that the Inquisition opened its first tribunal in 1481.

To the bitter, warlike atmosphere of Seville—a hotbed of acrimonious religious disputations—must be attributed, at least in part, the zeal and skill in combating Christian dogma for which some of the Abravanels became famous. Don Samuel Abravanel, Don Isaac's grandfather, however, was not one of the latter. His defense of the Jews was not expressed in ingenious theological contests, but in repelling the arguments of their maligning enemies in the royal courts. So effective was Don Samuel in performing this task, and so often did he thwart anti-Jewish schemes, that the Jews of Spain considered him a "God-chosen leader" and virtually their "shield and shelter." One can therefore imagine their shock and consternation when they learned one day that their admired spokesman had converted to Christianity. The subject was too painful to be discussed in public, but for more than five centuries the Jews upheld the notion that Don Samuel's conversion occurred under coercion. The fact that it was voluntary was revealed only recently by modern Jewish scholarship.[12]

This of course raised the difficult question of what motivated the conversion. That a person of Don Samuel's background and upbringing became a believer in Christian tenets is, to say the least, hard to believe. To be sure, as a courtier he was known to have been lax in observing some or most of the Commandments;[13] but judging by our sources this may have reflected the attitude of a skeptic or a free thinker who doubted the validity of *all* religions.[13a] A man of such habits and bent of mind would not be led away by philosophical meditations from "rational Judaism" to "mystical Christianity." Nor is it likely that a leader of his stature would abandon his people for some temporal advantage. Yet if religious and utilitarian considerations are excluded, one is inclined to assume that Don Samuel's conversion resulted from a social crisis—i.e., one that led to an irreparable break between him and Castile's Jewish community.

Since the mystery surrounding this strange affair is not relieved, but rather thickened by the above conclusion, we shall here merely point out some facts concerning Don Samuel's life as convert. What we know is that he never "returned" to Judaism; that he devoted himself strictly to his social rise and the amassing of a great fortune; that he reached the highest station in the king's financial service; and that many of his offspring intermarried with Spain's nobles. Yet he must have been greatly perturbed by the split that his conversion had created in his family. At least two of his older sons, and the young Judah, who was to become Don Isaac's father, severed relations with him and moved to Portugal,[14] where their talents and inventiveness brought them wealth, reputation, and profitable connections with Portugal's princes. It was thanks to them that their family's name remained luminous in Jewish history.

The conversion of Don Samuel, and his failure to "return," left a deep impression on the consciousness of the Abravanels. Not by so much as a word does Don Isaac, in his copious works, mention the conversion of his grandfather. The matter must have been regarded by him as a blot on the bright annals of the family, a blot which he perhaps subconsciously sought to erase by his ardent devotion to his people and their faith. No other Jewish author in the Middle Ages dealt as extensively as Abravanel with the Marrano problem. But behind his complex attitude toward the Marranos, behind the harsh chastisement and deep compassion with which he repeatedly treats them in his writings, there may lie not only his considered reaction to the grave Marrano problem of his time, but also a reflection of his personal attitude towards the sad, and perhaps disreputable, experiences of the grandfather which he wanted to—but, alas, could not—forget.

2. *Childhood*

When the Abravanels settled in Portugal, the country was undergoing a process of rebirth. It was the period following the great battle of Aljubarrota (1385) in which Portuguese valor, winning a victory over Castile, helped to invigorate and solidify Portugal's nationalism. A milestone in the history of the Iberian peninsula, that battle accomplished much more than saving Portugal's independence at the time; its consequences were largely responsible for the fact that Portugal, in sharp contrast to Aragon, never really amalgamated with Castile. Geographically a direct extension of Castile, ethnically no different from, and linguistically closer to, Castile than Aragon, Portugal is an example of a nation born primarily out of politics. Unlike other states in Europe, its origin must be traced, in the first place, to the feudal scramble of the Middle Ages.

Until the battle of Aljubarrota Castile never gave up hope of reuniting with, or rather annexing, the realm of Portugal which she regarded as legitimately hers. As far as Castile was concerned, the independence of Portugal was merely a usurpation; for Portugal was originally a fief granted by the Leonese king, Alfonso VI, to his field-commander and son-in-law, Henry of Gascogne. The vassal, and especially his son, however, soon developed an itch for independence. In 1143 the Portuguese monarchy was officially born, and with it the Portuguese nation.

National consciousness was stimulated by the wars, both defensive and aggressive, which the people of Portugal fought against the Moslems. The land granted by Alfonso to his son-in-law constituted approximately half of modern Portugal; the other half had to be torn by bitter strife from the hands of the Moors. In a series of wars which lasted for another century, Portuguese forces, unaided by Castile, carved out this new territory, extending their land southward along the Atlantic to the southern tip of the peninsula. Born of conquest and nurtured by the sword, Portugal was among the first states in Europe to develop a strong nationalistic feeling.

Its wars of expansion and its struggle for independence determined, in large measure, Portugal's attitude toward the Jews. So long as the country faced double danger, from the Moslems and from Castile, the Jewish minority was left unmolested. The economic conditions, moreover, were no less favorable for the Jews than the political. In the newly conquered districts and half-desolate towns, Jews, the traditional revivers of ruined cities in the Middle Ages, were welcome as colonizers and traders. In the second period of Portuguese history, however, beginning with the conquest of Algarve, the last region to be taken from the Moors

(1249), both political and economic conditions took, from the Jewish standpoint, a turn for the worse. The fourteenth century saw the rise of a considerable burgher class in Portugal and, along with it, of hostility to the Jews.[15] The outcome of the Castilian-Portuguese conflict further aggravated the Jewish situation. For the decisive victory over Castile (1385) focused general attention on internal issues and greatly intensified nationalistic feelings, both developments contributing materially to a growing friction with the Jews. Thus the third period, which began with the rule of João I, the hero of the battle of Aljubarrota, witnessed increasing demands by the Cortes for the abrogation of the privileges granted the Jews by the Crown and for the subjection of the Jews to the limitations imposed upon them in neighboring Castile.

But in Portugal, even more than in other countries, the Crown's claim to the Jews was uncontested,[16] and the Crown had other problems to consider besides popular antagonism to the Jews. Again as in other countries in the Middles Ages, the policy toward the Jews in Portugal could be read on the political barometer which registered the relations between the monarchy and the nobility.

João I was most friendly to the nobility. The support and cooperation of the great nobles won the Crown for him in 1385 when the old dynasty had become practically extinguished, and the patriotism and valor of the nobility enabled him to defeat the forces of Castile. He demonstrated his gratitude by a shower of gifts drawn primarily from the Crown lands. In consequence he lost almost the entire income from that source and became completely dependent for the expenses of his administration upon the income derived from customs and other revenues which were not affected by the alienation of his possessions. He was, therefore, interested in supporting the Jews, a strong commercial element in Portugal and one that belonged to the royal patrimony.

For the same reasons João I was not opposed to the influx of *conversos* from Castile, even at the expense of their return to Judaism.[17] Clerical opinion was of course horrified by this move, which made Portugal notorious among all Christian countries for giving shelter to escaped heretics; but Portugal was an old trouble spot for the Church; and João, despite his private orthodoxy, continued in the traditional policy of Portugal's kings who had repeatedly defeated ecclesiastical attempts to intervene in the processes of government. Under the impact of popular hostility to the Jews, João, nevertheless, was forced, from time to time, to yield to the Cortes and promulgate laws against the Jews, including one which made the wearing of the badge mandatory (1391) and another which rendered the Jews ineligible for office in the royal service (1404). These laws, however, were not enforced, as is clear from the complaints of the clergy against João in 1427.[18] The Abravanels therefore came to Portugal at a time when the social climate of the country was hostile to the Jews, but when the prevailing policy was still pro-Jewish and when opportunity for financial enterprise was not lacking. There is evidence that already at the beginning of the fifteenth century the Abravanels were active in Portugal's commerce,[19] and it may be readily assumed that Don Isaac's father, Don Judah—the son of Castile's *contador mayor*—had little difficulty in advancing to positions of financial and political prominence.

The policy pursued toward the Jews of Portugal at the time of Abravanel's birth, however, was such as to give every reason for serious concern regarding the future. Four years before Abravanel's birth, in 1433, João I died, leaving the throne to his eldest son, Duarte. The latter, having none of his father's consideration for the barons, radically changed his policy toward them. Looking with disfavor upon the alienation of the Crown lands, he sought ways and means of redeeming the royal patrimony. In his struggle with the nobility, he needed the support of the Cortes, in which the cities and the clergy were represented; hence his attention to their complaints against the Jews and his manifestly anti-Jewish policy.[20] The pestilence which struck the country during his reign and an unsuccessful war in Africa only helped stimulate intolerance toward the Jews. But these calamities also cut short the king's life. He died in 1438, a victim of the plague, with none of his undertakings truly successful and none of his policies carried to conclusion.

Don Isaac was born the year before Duarte's death, and the same year offers the first record concerning Don Judah's position in Portugal. That very year Duarte dispatched his ill-fated expedition to Tangier, whose conquest had been, since 1418, the first objective of Portugal's policy of expansion. Among the leaders of this expedition was the Infante Fernando, master of the Order of St. Benedict of Avis and one of João's five famous sons. Before he left on his fatal mission—he subsequently died in an enemy prison—Don Fernando had prepared a will in which he ordered the payment of a debt of 97,100 reis to Don Judah Abravanel.[21] Whether Don Judah was a treasurer of the Infante, as some biographers of Abravanel asserted, or was otherwise in his financial service, cannot be definitely ascertained. In any case, in the year of Isaac Abravanel's birth, Don Judah, his father, was in possession of great wealth and had direct relations with Portugal's royal house. As Don Isaac stated in one of his writings, he was "brought up from childhood in wealth and honor."[22]

Yet Don Isaac's childhood was not entirely free from the oppressive spirit of an anti-Jewish atmosphere. During the minority of Alfonso V, the regency devolved upon Don Pedro, Duarte's brother. The latter, a vigorous and astute ruler, shared the late king's view on the necessity of curtailing the expanded powers of the nobles and, realizing that for this purpose he needed the people's help, he could be no supporter of the Jews. Don Pedro, as regent, was not strong enough to carry his policy toward the nobility to its extreme and there was, therefore, no reason for him to extend Duarte's measures against the Jews. Yet the tendency of Don Pedro's policies is clearly seen in the *Ordinances of Alfonso V,* a codex compiled under the former's guidance, which incorporated most of the anti-Jewish laws issued in Portugal during the previous reigns. That many of these laws were not enforced can be safely assumed, but it is also certain that many other anti-Jewish laws passed by the Cortes during the reign of his predecessor were carried into effect. Don Isaac's childhood therefore was passed under a regime that, on the whole, respected Duarte's decrees against the Jews, the decrees which emphasized and deepened the gulf between the Jewish and non-Jewish populations. It is clear, above all, that under Pedro's rule there was no relief from the severe restrictions concerning the right of Jews to be outside the *Judarias.* And thus, every evening, as the bells of the churches tolled for prayer, the child would know that the *Judarias* must close, that stern punishments threatened Jews who happened to be outside them after sunset, and that no one, except some privileged few, of whom his father might have been one, was permitted to pass through the guarded gates.[23]

Yet, the populace was not satisfied with Pedro's rigorous, but restrained policy, and the rising hostility to the Jews throughout the country sought an outlet in violence. It was in the year 1449, when Don Isaac was twelve years old, that the first major outbreak against the Jews of Portugal occurred in Lisbon, his home town. A rioting mob, bent on pillage and murder, surged towards the three *Judarias* of the city, but finding them fortified and vigorously defended—a phenomenon which was not uncommon in the peninsula—retreated to organize for resumed aggression. The situation of the Jews was so precarious, however, and the whole city was in such an uproar that Alfonso V, then at Evora, was urged by the state secretary to return to the capital. He returned, but the tension, instead of decreasing, now assumed the form of an uprising against the king. The stern measures which Alfonso employed to suppress the rebellious movement in the city and the severe punishment he inflicted upon the offenders finally convinced the burghers of Lisbon that the king was determined to defend the Jews with all the force at his disposal.[24]

The attempt to wipe out the Jewish community of Lisbon took place at a time of political upheaval. That was the year which saw the climax of the conflict between Alfonso V and his uncle, Don Pedro. The instigator of that conflict was Alfonso, Count of Barcellos and João I's illegitimate son, who strove to replace his half-brother, Don Pedro, in political influence at Court. To this personal ambition there was added a political motive which, from a historical point of view, was of far greater import. While Don Pedro was an advocate of Duarte's policy which aimed at limiting the power of the nobility, the Count of Barcellos, upholding the feudal principle, was strongly opposed to such limitation. To appease his half-brother, Don Pedro bestowed upon him, in 1442, the title of Duke together with the lordship over Braganza. But Alfonso remained unappeased. Like other nobles, he looked with anxious eyes to the king's approaching majority. When, in 1447, Alfonso V married Pedro's daughter Elizabeth, Braganza's anxiety, as may well be imagined, turned to alarm. It now became his aim to destroy the regent before the latter succeeded in employing the king as an instrument for his anti-baronial policy. And his purpose was fully accomplished when, after undermining the king's confidence in Don Pedro, the latter was declared a traitor to the kingdom and killed in an encounter with the royal forces.

It was in the year 1449, the year of the anti-Jewish riots of Lisbon, that Don Pedro met his death on the battlefield. The event cast a long shadow over the future history of Portugal and had a decisive effect on the fate of the Jews in that country. For more than three decades after 1449 the House of Braganza was the most influential in the realm. When the conflict was thus resolved, young Abravanel could hardly imagine that his own rise and fall in Portugal were to be inextricably bound up with the rise and fall of the powerful Braganzas.

3. Studies and Early Literary Efforts

The reign of Alfonso is considered to have been a period of prosperity for the Jews of Portugal. This undoubtedly is largely true; yet it would be erroneous to maintain that a radical change in the Jewish position occurred with Alfonso's assumption of power. The laxity of the Crown in enforcing anti-Jewish measures had been noticeable from the very beginning; but this laxity was, before long, effectively protested by the Cortes. In 1451, in the Cortes at Santarem, laws were re-enacted to the effect that the Jews must wear the badge as decreed and must not live outside the *Judarias*.[25] Similar laws were issued from time to time within at least the next decade, and it was only in later years that Alfonso came to feel himself sufficiently strong, or sufficiently inclined, to ignore the Cortes on the Jewish question. Thus, as far as the Jews were concerned, Alfonso's long reign may be roughly divided into approximately two equal periods: the first—lasting until the middle of the sixties—in which Pedro's policy was still in force although its effectiveness was gradually waning; the second, lasting until Alfonso's death, in which the king openly pursued a determined and full-fledged pro-Jewish policy.

Despite the official support Alfonso gave, in the first period, to legislation which was hostile to the Jews, his real attitude could not remain for long unnoticed by the élite of the Jewish community of Portugal who, for both political and economic reasons, strove to develop friendly relations with the Court. The most prominent among this élite in those days was Don Judah Abravanel, Don Isaac's father. It is true that we have no records about his activity, but even from the scanty material available, it is clear that he was, at least in the sixties, the head of the Jewish community of Portugal and a man of great influence and widespread fame. As Don Judah was not professionally devoted to a scholarly or a rabbinical career, his leadership in the community must have been acquired through his social and political position, or more clearly, through his relations with the Court.[26] But connection with the Court could not have been really valuable if not supported by the Duke of Braganza, who commanded decisive influence with the king and was the chief power in the administration. It is therefore safe to assume that the exceptional friendliness which, as we shall see, in later years marked Don Isaac's relations with the princes of Braganza was a continuation of a family relationship initiated in the days of the first Duke of Braganza by his father, Don Judah.

As the son of a powerful Jewish courtier, Isaac was accustomed from childhood to visit the "palaces of kings"[27] and princes, and his education was accordingly directed to suit the social stratum in which the family lived as well as to prepare him for assuming in the future his father's duties and responsibilities. Those were days in which Renaissance culture was pouring strongly into Portugal, and among the staunchest protagonists of the new movement were members of the royal family. Don Pedro was a confirmed Renaissance man and so was the king, Alfonso V. The study of Latin and the Roman classics was thus part of Abravanel's education.[28] His familiarity with the works of the Roman historians and Roman political thinkers and moralists, a familiarity which is noticeable in his writings, was therefore a heritage from those days, and the effect which these, particularly Seneca and Cicero, left upon his intellectual development was deep and indelible. His knowledge of Latin, moreover, enabled him also to delve—when his trend of thinking digressed from the Renaissance —into the writings of the Christian medieval scholastics and the works of the Church Fathers.

The first half of the fifteenth century witnessed, not only an increased interest in the classics, but also a marked and important advance in Portugal's national literature. The intensified Portuguese national spirit sought expression in the national language and gave rise to refined forms of literature which became the subject of general admiration. The lyric poetry of Portugal came to be considered superb throughout the peninsula,[29] while the art of historical writing in that country achieved unique distinction. This was the age of Fernam Lopez, known as "the father of Portuguese history," whose historical works are commonly rated among the most artistic and inspiring chronicles of the Middle Ages. Abravanel must have been personally acquainted with Lopez who was the secretary of the Infante Fernando, with whom Don Judah had close relations,[30] and it is quite likely that he acquired from Lopez and his writings much of the interest he showed for history in his works. Like the rest of Portugal's upper class, Isaac sought and attained perfection in Portuguese and he must similarly have mastered Castilian. This conclusion may be drawn from the following two facts: he was a member of a family which migrated from Castile, and Castilian was a familiar tongue among Portuguese intellectual and baronial circles.[31] Since the Castilian literature of the time was represented primarily by chroniclers and historians,[32] it undoubtedly contributed to his historical knowledge and had a share in developing his historical views.

Latin, Portuguese and Castilian were thus the three European languages in which Isaac Abravanel was versed. It is doubtful, however, that he excelled in any of these more than he did in Hebrew. For, early in his life he manifested a command of Hebrew which, not only surprises in its vivacity and beauty, but also indicates a thorough knowledge of all the phases of Hebrew literature. It was in Hebrew, moreover, that he must have received his basic education in all the subjects which formed his complex curriculum. In full accord with the prevailing tradition among the medieval Jewish intelligentsia, this curriculum comprised not only the study of the masters of Jewish philosophy in the Middle Ages, but also of their Greek and Arab forerunners, especially Aristotle, Averroes and Avicenna,[33] and it also included the "natural sciences," that is, medicine and astrology. In his writings

Abravanel shows a knowledge of medical theories which were prevalent in his time, as well as a familiarity with the fundamentals of astrology, a study which was connected with medicine and then regarded in Portugal as indisputably a science. He was destined, however, to be neither a physician nor an astrologer. By nature he was a theoretician and a writer, and both his intellectual capacity and writing ability revealed themselves fully in his first philosophical work, which he must have written in his early twenties.

The essay was called *The Forms of the Elements*,[34] and its contents fully agree with its name. In it Abravanel sought to determine the forms or, rather, the essential qualities of the elements—fire, water, air and earth—of which, according to Aristotle, the sublunary world is composed. There is nothing in this work to indicate a religious outlook or even an interest in religious views. Here one finds stated as axiom Aristotle's dictum: "Nature does nothing without purpose!"[35] Nature! There is no mention of God at all. There is no citation from the Bible, or indeed from any Jewish religious source. Here was philosophy in its purely pagan form—philosophy based not on religious dogma, but on cold logic, deduction and observation.

In his youth, Abravanel must have cherished an ambition to delve into the study of philosophy and find answers to at least some of the puzzles which the great philosophers had left unsolved. These problems fascinated him, and the study of philosophy remained his greatest passion for a considerable time. But finally a reaction set in. The more he became absorbed in philosophy, the more he realized that the task was beyond him—indeed, that it was beyond human capacity. He observed the contradictions, the uncertainties and limitations which mark every philosophical theory and came to the conclusion that philosophy is largely a useless exercise in dialectics. He was, however, by nature possessed of a thirst for truth, a thirst which philosophy, while it could not quench, intensified; and like other disappointed rationalists, he turned to religion and to mysticism.

Nevertheless, to assume that his change of heart was entirely the result of intellectual disillusionment, would be an over-simplification. For mysticism is rarely the result of speculative processes alone. The flight from rationalism usually represents a search for a solution to some very pressing personal or collective problems which available means are unable to offer. This is why mysticism is the product of the monastery, or of oppressed and afflicted societies, rather than of favorable, satisfying circumstances.

There is little reason for assuming that Abravanel's mystical inclination originated in some personal disappointment or dissatisfaction. Our knowledge of Abravanel's intimate life is, to be sure, quite incomplete. Nevertheless, we do know that he was married in early manhood; that he became, probably toward the end of the 1450s, the father of his first son, Judah, and, within the next few years, also the father of one and possibly two daughters.[36] We know, further, from certain indications he left, that he greatly enjoyed the company of his family and that, from early manhood, he was deeply involved in business. A man happy in his family circle, possessed of a strong spirit of enterprise and, on top of this, wealthy and considerably appreciative of the material values of life,[37] as Abravanel was in those days, is hardly the type for mystical speculation. Yet there was a social element in Abravanel's diversion to mysticism, and this can readily be discovered.

Born to "wealth and honor" as he was, Isaac Abravanel was, nevertheless, the son of a fugitive family from Castile, whose childhood was passed in the days of Duarte and Don Pedro and who grew to maturity in the first period of Alfonso when the former's policy was still in effect.[38] Bitter family memories of the past and the hostility surrounding Jewish life in the present must have left a deep imprint upon his sensitive mind which sought to understand the "why" and "how" of the mystery of his people's suffering and existence. Also, under Spanish influence, Portugal in the 15th century was, in all likelihood, a breeding-ground for Jewish mysticism[39] and, as in the case of other Jewish mystics, the mystical thinking of Abravanel revolved about a search for a solution to the Jewish problem. Moreover, apart from the direct influence which these thinkers had upon Abravanel, his attack on philosophy must have been further encouraged by the Jewish antiphilosophical, though not mystical, literature which, since the catastrophe of 1391, was increasing in Spain in volume and aggressiveness. The works of some of the representatives of this literature, such as Alami and Ibn Musa,[40] appear to have been responsible at least in part for Abravanel's radical change of view.

The change is apparent in Abravanel's second work—*Crown of the Elders*. When he wrote this book, he had already developed the fundamentals of his world outlook. All the major themes of his later writings are to be found in this brief dissertation on the concept of God and the meaning of prophecy. It is in this work that Abravanel first expresses his admiration for the cabalists, the "bearers of truth," and his criticism of the philosophers who "walk in the darkness."[41] His attack on philosophy was primarily directed at the leaders in the field, Aristotle and Averroes, as well as at its other standard-bearers within and outside of Jewry. The only exception was Maimonides from whose influence Don Isaac could not free himself.[42] And although his deep admiration for Maimonides was not unmixed with harsh criticism, it was through his abiding interest in Maimonides that Abravanel remained attached to philosophy to the very end of his life. His main interest, however, lay in the prophets, the perfection of whose teachings he contrasted in the *Crown* with the obvious failings of the philosophers. To interpret the prophets, to reveal the depth and grandeur of their wisdom, became his great ambition.

His plan for a commentary on the Pentateuch had in fact antedated the writing of the *Crown*.[43] But the plan soon had to be abandoned. In the middle of the 1460s, when Abravanel wrote his *Crown*, Don Judah was still alive, though no longer in his prime, and Don Isaac gradually must have taken over the business responsibilities of his aging father.[44] The business undertakings of the Abravanels were vast and ramified. They comprised tax-farming, banking and large-scale imports from Flanders, and they called for constant vigilance and attention.[45] Speculative life thus gave way to a life of action, and Abravanel had to limit his literary plans to a commentary on Deuteronomy. Yet, even this work long remained unfinished and, in a letter he wrote in 1472, we find him pledging himself that, as soon as he would have some peace of mind and a chance to return to literary work, he would "not rest or sleep" until the work was completed and the assignment fulfilled.[46] But peace of mind was far off, for at the very time Abravanel made that pledge he was drawn deeper and deeper into the tangled web of finance and politics.

4. In the Service of the King

The second half of Alfonso's reign was a period of prosperity for the Jews of Portugal, and especially for Don Isaac. The family aptitude for finance and commerce was now fully manifested in him, bringing to the fore for the first time the strange dualism which was to characterize his life: the philosophical writer showing great business ability and amassing a fortune.[47] His financial enterprise must soon have led him to associate with his father's Christian friends, the courtiers of Alfonso V, while the expansion of his financial activity and the extension of his contacts with the nobility raised his prestige in the Jewish community. In 1472, the very year in which he voiced his desire for leisure to complete his commentary on Deuteronomy, he already occupied a position of leadership among the Jews of Portugal and acted as their political representative at Court.

By virtue both of his personality and inclination, and under the inspiring example of his father, Abravanel must have developed, early in life, a sense of responsibility for his brethren. The problems which beset the Jewish community of Portugal offered ample schooling for the task of leadership. Abravanel's letter of 1472 to Yehiel of Pisa, the head of a large Jewish-Italian banking house—the principal document providing an insight into his activities and attitudes in those days—already shows the characteristics of Abravanel the leader, as he was to appear in later days.

The problem which then presented itself for solution resulted from Alfonso's expedition to North Africa in 1471. During the capture of Arzilla, a fortress on the Atlantic, that town's Jewish community, numbering two hundred and fifty, fell into the hands of the conquerors and was distributed as slaves among the Portuguese grandees. The enslavement of war captives was a custom of the time; but it was also a time-honored custom among Jews to redeem their brethren from the debasement of slavery. The Jewish community of Portugal organized for action, and Don Isaac and another leader were appointed to head a twelve-man committee charged with the responsibility of freeing the enslaved.[48]

The very phenomenon of "so many" Jews subjected to the misery and degradation of slavery, their women facing the danger of molestation and their children a prey to hunger and depravity, shocked him deeply. The thought of members of his own people—the "people of God"—in a state of bondage was for him intolerably distressing, and he summoned all his energies for their rescue. For six full months, he informs us, he travelled throughout the country, visiting the places where the enslaved Jews were encamped and dealing with their masters who sometimes were harsh and extortionate in their demands. When the act of deliverance was finally accomplished, at the great expense of more than 10,000 gold doubloons, Abravanel sought to care for the rescued and provide for their rehabilitation in their new home.[49] His treatment of these North African Jews, with whom he could not even converse,[50] affords an example of Abravanel's devotion to his people, as well as a manifestation of his strong will, his thoroughness, and his sense of deep, almost personal responsibility for the welfare of those entrusted to his care. All these are qualities of true leadership. At the same time another problem arose which not only appealed to these qualities, but also taxed—and revealed—his diplomatic skill.

The nature of this problem is not known to us, but it must have been connected with serious developments which endangered the rights of the Jews of Portugal. In this, as in many other instances, the attack against the Jews probably came from the clergy, since it seemed important for the Jews of Portugal to obtain the favorable intervention of the Pope. To this end Abravanel employed his friendship with João Sezira, scholar and courtier of Alfonso V, whom the latter was sending to Rome to congratulate Pope Sixtus IV on his election to the Papacy. To this man, whom Abravanel describes as "a great and pure-hearted friend of the Jews" who "always uses his strong influence to protect and improve their position," the Jews of Portugal submitted a memorandum in which they stated their case and enumerated their requests. João Sezira pledged himself to Abravanel to plead the Jewish cause before Sixtus IV, but apparently on condition of absolute secrecy, so that the matter was not to become known even to the other envoy of Alfonso, the head of the delegation, Don Lope de Almeida.[51]

On this occasion Abravanel writes to his friend, Yehiel, the magnate of Pisa, asking him not only to show Sezira special courtesy and honor, but also to extend any help and guidance that he might require while in Italy. "You will greatly oblige me," he adds, "if while speaking to these men, João Sezira and Lope de Almeida, you state, in your tactful and convincing manner, that our lord the king [Alfonso V] is universally praised for the justice he manifests towards all the inhabitants of his country, and for his friendly attitude towards the Jews. Also add that such a government promotes the country's welfare, enables it to expand and increases its prestige abroad. It is important that you say all this in order to impress these two envoys with the fact that we Jews have everywhere people of great influence who are well informed on all developments affecting their people's welfare."[52]

In 1472, when Abravanel wrote this letter which indicates his excellent connections with Alfonso's favorites, he himself, it seems, was not yet established in the position of a courtier. In describing Alfonso V to Yehiel, he does not mention direct relations with the king, an omission hardly conceivable if such relations had existed. The question as to when Abravanel acquired a definite position in Alfonso V's Court cannot be answered with certainty. There are good reasons, however, to believe that his rise to such a position took place between 1472 and 1475.[53] It was perhaps shortly after he had written his letter to Yehiel that he entered Alfonso's circle of favorites, and from then on both his friendship with the king and his influence in the Court made steady progress.

Alfonso was a man of strong will, moral fervor, intellectual interests and friendly disposition. Despite the criticisms levelled against him as king by some modern historians, his capacities as a ruler were not inconsiderable. According to Don Isaac, he was "just and righteous, vigorous and heroic, ardently seeking his people's welfare, learned and wise in the councils of leadership."[54]

The pattern that Alfonso V followed in his domestic policy was the same as that of his grandfather, João I. He completely abandoned, as unworkable or undesirable, the policies of his uncle and his father against the nobility, and, like João, had no scruples about securing the loyalty of the great barons by enriching them at the expense of the royal patrimony. Finally, when confronted with the financial problems which were the direct consequence of this policy, he solved them quite successfully, again like his grandfather, by developing the commercial resources of the country and by giving greater freedom to the Jews.

To his friendly policy toward the nobility and his special interest in developing trade must be added, as a feature of his reign, his expansionist policy beyond the seas. Inspired like his predecessors—João, Duarte and Pedro—by the theories of his uncle, Henry the Navigator, he strongly supported the exploratory efforts which were directed to the discovery of a new way to India and which had already netted Portugal important assets. In 1445 the Portuguese sailors, pushing southward along the African coast, discovered Guinea from which Portugal drew, not only considerable quantities of gold, but also—what was important for Portugal's agriculture—a large number of Negro slaves. The growing maritime enterprises of Portugal, as well as the protection of her expanding slave trade, made it necessary for her to possess bases on the strategic northwestern African seaboard. Alfonso consequently determined to resume the attempts, made with little success by his ancestors, to conquer Tangier and its surrounding outposts. In 1471, after dispatching to North Africa three large military expeditions, he finally saw his purpose accomplished, but at enormous cost. The expense of these expeditions was shouldered primarily by the Crown. Hence further need for money and another reason for a tolerant policy toward the Jews.

The same reason appeared even more valid during the ensuing Portuguese war with Castile (1475–1479). It was a war that drained all the resources of the Crown, and both during and after it Alfonso must have been greatly assisted by money and ingenuity provided by Jews. Nevertheless, it would be wrong to assume that Alfonso's friendliness towards the Jews was a result merely of his domestic and foreign policies. The interests of the Crown constituted, it may be assumed, the primary consideration in determining his attitude. But behind it, and this should not be ignored, was Alfonso's unusual, deep-rooted tolerance in matters of religion.

Two records testify clearly to this attitude of the king. They are contained in a contemporary chronicle and may have been considerably embellished by the chronicler, but they truthfully reflect Alfonso's stand on the religious controversies of his time.[55] Like other medieval kings in the Peninsula, he was intrigued by the problem the Jews presented, and listened with interest to disputations on religion between Jews and Christians. It was to satisfy his intellectual curiosity, rather than to lead the Jews to conversion, that he sometimes addressed to the Jews pointed questions concerning the validity of their principles; and, though rarely pleased with the answers he received, he nevertheless understood that matters of faith could not be compressed into logical formulae. Once, during a disputation between a Christian and a Jew, he is reported to have expressed his opinion that neither side could logically prove the veracity of its position. He is further reported to have stated on that occasion that the "Jews are destined to receive divine reward, since their religious motives are pure." And when this remark irked the Christian disputant, who asserted that the Jews did not speak thus of Christians, the king answered that the Christians were far less tolerant toward Jews, adding that the attitude of both camps did not surprise him, since "religion is rooted in man's fantasy."[56] In other words, it is imagination and emotion, rather than sober logic, which determines one's attitude toward other religions.

In the Middle Ages such broad-mindedness and tolerance were certainly rare, and Alfonso was in this, as in other respects, an unusual man. Particularly distinguished for his truthfulness, he offered the exceptional example of a king who ordered his official chronicler *not* to write the history of his reign while he was still in power.[57]

Such a king, whose basic policy was pro-Jewish and whose convictions were free of religious bias, would not shrink from having Jews among his courtiers. And, indeed, Don Isaac was not the only Jew in the Court; influential also were the two Yaḥya brothers: Gedaliah, who was Alfonso's physician, and Joseph, who was a counsellor of high rank.[58] Abravanel must have appealed to Alfonso especially, not only because of his various abilities, but also because of his intellectual honesty and vast erudition. For Alfonso was, besides, a patron of letters, a collector of books and a man of learning and keen intellect. All these elements were undoubtedly conducive to the development of that intimacy between Alfonso and Abravanel that led the latter to feel for the king, not only admiration, but also affection.[59]

Yet there was still another factor which helped secure Abravanel's position and contributed to the rise of his influence in the Court: this was his relations with the princes of Braganza.

In 1461 the first Duke of Braganza died, bequeathing his title and position to his son Ferdinand. The character of this prince is reflected in the fact that he refused to have a share in, and even openly opposed, the intrigues of his father against Don Pedro.[60] As Alfonso himself had come, in 1454, to recognize his error in judging the late regent, this fact was not held against Ferdinand, but on the contrary spoke in his favor. The influence which the duke exercised at Court surpassed even that of his father, and it was with the sons of this man—and also undoubtedly with him— that Abravanel struck up a deep friendship.

The first indication of this friendship is to be found in a letter of Abravanel's written to the Count of Faro, one of the duke's four sons, on the occasion of the death of the latter's father-in-law, the Count of Odemira.[61] Between the deceased and the surviving counts there had existed a deep affection, and it is interesting to note that the count, in his grief, wrote to Abravanel and expressed to him his feelings even before he received Abravanel's letter of condolence. This could hardly have happened if their relations had not been exceptionally intimate. From Abravanel's answer it is again clear that he was aware of the details of the relationship between the princes with which only a very close friend could have been acquainted.[62] The letter was written early in the seventies,[63] that is, before Abravanel became established as a courtier, and it would not be far-fetched to assume that it was to the princes of the House of Braganza that Abravanel owed his position in the Court.

The Braganzas were the wealthiest nobles in the Peninsula and their possessions in land were enormous. We do not know what services Abravanel rendered in the management of their tremendous fiefs, but he must have fulfilled some vital tasks for we know he was compensated in abundant measure. He himself became the owner of vast estates, some of which came to him, in all likelihood, as gifts from his grateful and magnanimous friends. It appears that, even while in the king's service, Abravanel continued to be in some form a functionary of the princes of Braganza.[64]

Of all the princes of this House, however, it was Ferdinand

II, the eldest son of the duke, with whom Abravanel developed the strongest friendship. So intimate indeed were the relations between them that it was universally considered inconceivable that Ferdinand would embark on any important activity without consulting Abravanel.[65] The assumption of the dukedom by Ferdinand II in April 1478—upon the death of his father, Ferdinand I— must have marked a rise in Abravanel's position, for never were the Braganzas so influential at Court as during the reign of this prince.[66] It was also in those years (1478–1481)—the last years of Alfonso V—that Abravanel reached his highest stage of prestige and power in Portugal.

These years, it must be remembered, came in the wake of the war with Castile, a war that plunged the country into a dangerous crisis, political as well as economic. We have no information on Abravanel's position during the crucial period of the Portuguese-Castilian conflict, save for what we can gather by deduction. In his writings Abravanel criticizes wars of aggression as unwise and unprofitable. Such wars, he maintains, rather than resulting in gain, are likely to bring misfortune upon the aggressor even if, at the outset, he appears by far stronger than the nation he attacks.[67] This, indeed, seems to have been Portugal's condition on the eve of the war, and Abravanel's criticism may well reflect, not merely his post-factum views on the Portuguese unprovoked onslaught on Castile, but also his attitude toward the conflict at the time when the onslaught was being planned. Abravanel's position at that stage may be further deduced from that of his patron, the Duke of Braganza (Ferdinand I), who opposed Alfonso's planned conquest of Castile as a dangerous adventure that could not end in success.[68] By taking the same stand, it should not be assumed that Abravanel incurred the king's disfavor. Despite the difference of opinion on the war issue that developed between the king and the Braganzas, the latter stood by him throughout the conflict; and when, upon realizing the extent of his failure, the king abdicated in favor of his son, the Braganzas dissuaded him from this act of despair and insisted that he resume the tasks of government. The correctness of their position at the outset of the war, coupled with their loyalty during its prosecution, strengthened even further the Braganza influence upon the king, and it also enhanced, we may safely assume, the influence of Abravanel, their chief adviser.

In fact, the king's confidence in and respect for Abravanel grew to such proportions that the latter became his most trusted councillor—and not in financial matters alone. Abravanel, impressed with his own far-reaching influence, had the feeling as though, like Daniel of old, he were "walking within the Palace of the Kings of Babylon."[69]

For Abravanel, moreover, these were not years of political prominence only; they were also years of great happiness and wealth. The immensity of his wealth may be gauged from the fact that in a loan of 12,000,000 reals, given to the Crown after the war with Castile (1480) by a group of Christians and Jews, Abravanel's share was more than a tenth; and Abravanel himself, in discussing his fortune, proudly states that it by far exceeded all the possessions of his ancestors.[70] He must have derived happiness also from his family, which now included three sons, Judah, Joseph (b. 1470) and Samuel (b. 1473),[71] all of whom were distinguished for their brilliance and two of whom were destined to attain lasting fame. Above all, the country now again enjoyed peace and, while Abravanel must have been largely occupied with the serious economic problems that beset Portugal in those days, he was able to concentrate, at least to some extent, on literary and scholarly work. It was in those days that he broadened his inquiry into the Bible and laid the basis for his commentaries on the Former Prophets which he was to write a few years later. It was also then that he must have begun his *Vision of God*, a work dealing with various aspects of prophecy in which he took a position opposed to Maimonides.[72] Most likely, it was also in those days that he delivered a series of lectures on Maimonides, and also wrote parts of his commentary on the *Guide*.[73] It was, furthermore, then that Abravanel rose to the position of undisputed leadership in the Jewish community of Portugal, and his home became the center of intellectual discussions as well as the source of all major decisions concerning the community's affairs.[74]

These were the happiest years in Abravanel's life, and in time to come he was to remember them with longing. But his happiness was short-lived. On August 18, 1481, Alfonso V, the protector of the Jews and Abravanel's great friend and benefactor, died unexpectedly at the age of forty-nine, a victim of the plague which so often visited his country. The shattering effect of his death on Abravanel is reflected years later in the latter's writings. But his sincere grief must have been accompanied by grave worries, if not for his own position, at least for the future of the Jews in Portugal.[75] These worries were not unfounded. Alfonso's death marked the end of an era for Portuguese Jewry and presaged a change in Abravanel's position.

5. Fall and Escape

João II, Alfonso's successor, though only twenty-nine years old upon coming to power, had a fully developed personality and definite views on government. The chroniclers of his time praise him highly as a ruler, and already during his lifetime he was surnamed the "perfect prince," a title in which not only his courtiers concurred, but also, it seems, the mass of the people. Later and more detached historians also agreed with this view. Abravanel's opinion, however, was quite different. According to him, João was not only far from perfection, but was one of the worst tyrants ever to ascend a throne. As Abravanel saw him, he was nothing but "greedy," "bloody," "deceitful" and "tyrannical."[76]

João II was, in any case, of quite a different nature from his father. Lacking the liberalism and good nature of Alfonso, he was severe, self-centered, cold and aloof toward friend and foe alike. He possessed a resolute will and exemplary courage, and from early youth distinguished himself in war. Yet no other monarch in Portugal more diligently pursued a policy of peace. For his major qualification was his ability to calculate, without being distracted by love of glory, how to secure with a minimum of danger a maximum of benefit for the Crown.

"The Crown," writes an authority on the period, "was the point to which he related everything, his appearance, dress, bearing and speech, as well as his thoughts, inclinations, plans and designs."[77] When he ascended the throne he was determined to achieve what in his opinion was the prerogative of royalty and what he believed the monarchy in his country sadly lacked: strength and independence.

Thus, carefully observing the policies and actions of the absolutist monarchs in the neighboring countries—of Henry VII in

England, Louis XI in France, and of Ferdinand and Isabella in Aragon and Castile—he resolved to follow their pattern and methods. His first and foremost aim, he realized, must be to break the power of the feudal lords. João II thus aspired to the same goal which Duarte and Don Pedro had sought to attain, but which had been completely nullified by his father. In fact, he now faced a more difficult situation than Duarte had been confronted with after the death of João I. For never had the nobility in Portugal been so entrenched and never had the royal patrimony been so impoverished as at the end of Alfonso's reign. So lavishly had Alfonso granted gifts to the nobility that João, in criticism of his father's generosity, is reported to have said: "All my father left me are the highways of Portugal."

Among those who had benefited especially from this generosity were the princes of the House of Braganza. When Alfonso V died, the Duke of Braganza was said to possess fifty towns and castles and about a third of the land of Portugal; and the great political and military power which he could muster by virtue of this wealth was enhanced by the positions of his three brothers. One of them, João, the Marquis of Montemor, was Constable of the Kingdom and, as such, in control of the royal army; another, Alvaro, the Count of Olivença, was Chancellor of the Kingdom; the third, Alfonso, the Count of Faro, was also active and influential as a courtier. João regarded these princes as usurpers of both royal wealth and power and as the greatest obstacle to his absolutist ambitions. Their destruction became his first objective.

To the reasons stemming from his general policy, there was added a strong personal element which made João especially anxious to reduce the power of the Braganzas. He seethed with deep personal animosity and an unquenchable desire for revenge. For he was the grandson of Don Pedro, the regent, who had fallen victim to the intrigues of Alfonso, the first duke and the founder of the House of Braganza. What is more, his mother, Pedro's daughter, had died, according to popular opinion, from poison administered by order of that duke. From childhood João harbored hostility for the Braganzas. He was only waiting for an opportunity.

The condition of the country after Alfonso's death was favorable to effecting the changes he contemplated. The country smarted from the wounds of defeat; the people were impoverished by the heavy taxes which the repeated wars of Alfonso had necessitated; and there was general clamor for reform. João II, appearing as the people's champion, was thus able to embark upon measures which aimed at destroying both the judicial and economic powers of the nobles. He subjected the entire administration of justice to the immediate authority of the Crown and compelled all the governors of cities and towns to swear allegiance directly to him. In addition, on December 15, 1481, he decreed that all holders of lands and estates formerly belonging to the Crown must produce for examination the documents on which they rested the claims to their possessions.

These measures, which implied a revolution in the entire feudal system, enraged and alarmed the nobility. The Duke of Braganza informed the king in unmistakable terms of the grievances of his order, only to be sternly rebuked for his audacity in criticizing a royal action. The Duke of Braganza had never before been spoken to in such language; yet his brother, the Marquis of Montemor, was even more deeply offended when, for some insignificant offense, the king ordered him into temporary exile. Thus tension mounted between the king and the princes of Braganza and both sides prepared cautiously for the final showdown.

The conflict between the king and the nobility soon was reflected in a disastrous manner in the life of Abravanel. It could already be gathered from his general policy and from his need to cater to the sentiments of the populace, that João II would take no pro-Jewish attitude; that, on the contrary, he would restrict the rights of the Jews and reduce their influence in the country. From some of the poems published in the *Cancioneiro* of the Portuguese poet Garcia de Resende, who from childhood was in João's service, we may gauge the strength of the anti-Jewish feeling that prevailed in João's Court.[78] A member of the powerful Yaḥya family, probably sensing the new political trend, left the country in those days.[79] But Abravanel stayed on and was to suffer, not only because of his Jewishness, but also—and primarily—for his close association with the House of Braganza.

In the atmosphere of conflict which was then developing, João's attitude toward him could not have been friendly, but he apparently continued in the king's service,[80] either at the request of the still influential duke, or because his services could not yet be dispensed with. Abravanel, however, must have labored in those days under constant anxiety. The attitude of the king was soon reflected in the open hostility of some of the new courtiers whom João II made his confidants and advisers.[81]

The plague which killed Alfonso V was still ravaging Portugal, and it was especially rampant in the cities. For three years, until it subsided, Abravanel was living with his family in the country, often moving, with the spread of the scourge, from one location to another.[82] This fact, too, may have contributed considerably toward weakening his ties with the Court, and when at last he was about to return to the capital, he found conditions radically changed. In his letter to his friend, Yehiel of Pisa, which he wrote on October 4, 1482,[83] on the occasion of the death of Yehiel's wife, we find the following words of despair which reflect his mood in those days:

"From the day that our City was laid in ruins, our Temple destroyed and our people exiled, we have known neither peace nor respite. The nations amongst whom we live do not stop taking council and devising means for assailing and harming us; and if we do enjoy peace for a brief moment, we are soon terrified by frightful news of savage persecution against the remnants of Israel coming from all the corners of the earth. What man subjected throughout life to the fear of enemies and the strain of distress, would grieve when his last hour arrives? It is all the more so with the noble sons of Zion who repeatedly witness how, with the rise of evil, their honor is besmirched and their name disgraced. How can they attach any value to their life of sorrow and not rejoice over the prospect of the grave? Weep not for the dying among Israel and do not bemoan them! Weep for those who are cast from one misfortune to another, and for whom God has blocked all avenues of relief. *For honor has departed from Israel, and I wish we were all dead and no more given to scorn and derision, to contempt and humiliation.*"[84]

Such words of bitter pessimism could have been written only by a man who personally experienced the condition he referred to. Abravanel was obviously deeply hurt. His honor was wounded, and it is not difficult to surmise what had transpired before that feeling of despondency took hold of him. He must have been treated discourteously by the king and perhaps also by some rivals in the Court, and he clearly discerned in the treatment accorded him, not only personal or political disfavor, but also the sinister marks of Jew-baiting. He felt a plot was being hatched against the Jews of Portugal and, as their leader, he no doubt realized that his downfall, if effected, might signal for them the beginning of the end. The future appeared bleak and fraught with disaster, void of any visible prospect of improvement. Nevertheless, mortified and offended to the core, he continued to cling to the hateful position, perhaps considering it a sacred duty to his brethren, perhaps still harboring a faint hope that an opportunity might arise that would give him an opening to gain the king's favor.

This opportunity, however, never came, for the political atmosphere became more and more charged with hatred and suspicion. Events moved swiftly and relentlessly to a climax since the discovery, some months before, by João of secret correspondence between the duke and Ferdinand, King of Aragon. From then on the duke was spied upon as a potential or actual traitor. That a conspiracy was brewing can hardly be doubted. At least one of the duke's brothers, the Marquis of Montemor, advocated armed rebellion against the king. It is not known, however, whether plans moved from the state of contemplation to that of resolution. In any case, these developments provided João II with an excuse for embarking on a drastic course of action. He decided on a purge which was to include all the discontented elements of the nobility, and first and foremost the princes of Braganza.

Although not a Portuguese noble, Abravanel was among the marked men. The king, it appears, came to suspect Abravanel as acting in the Court in the capacity of the duke's agent.[85] If the duke was indeed planning treason, as João II might have persuaded himself, it seemed obvious to him that Abravanel was involved; and even if he was not active in the conspiracy, his silence represented criminal complicity. Besides, Abravanel was a Jew and he was rich. His liquidation would meet with the approval of the Jew-haters, and his wealth could add significant assets to the possessions of the Crown.

Abravanel, of course, was aware of the deteriorating relations between the king and the duke. But it is most unlikely that he at any time believed in the seriousness of the intentions of any of the Braganzas to rebel against the king.[86] In any case, he never thought that his own loyalty would be suspected. His position on João's attitude toward the Braganzas, which he considered unduly harsh and iniquitous, was most probably an open secret; but he also knew that at all times he served the king most faithfully in whatever capacity he was requested to do so and in whatever way he thought proper.

Consequently, when, on May 30, 1483, a royal messenger came to his home and summoned him to appear before the king, Don Isaac unsuspectingly set out for the Court. Only the day before, on May 29, the Duke of Braganza had suddenly been arrested while conversing with the king in the royal cabinet. But the arrest having taken place in the fortress of Evora, the sensational news had not yet reached the capital. Abravanel must have left for Evora the following day (May 30th) in the morning, and, proceeding eastward, he arrived in the evening at Arrayolos,[87] where he and his companion stopped for the night. In this town, within a few hours' ride from Evora, knowledge of the arrest was already widespread. Arrayolos, furthermore, belonged to the duke, and Abravanel must have had acquaintances there. Thus, while at the inn, one of these approached him and imparted to him the shattering news. From this man, perhaps a member of the duke's household, who might have known in advance of Abravanel's arrival and was instructed to give him a timely warning, Abravanel learned, among other things, of the king's plan for a purge in which he, Abravanel, was included. His informant, it appears, urged him to flee the country.

Abravanel now had to make a difficult decision. He could hardly relish the idea of flight. It meant not only abandoning his family and possessions, but also strengthening João's suspicions. Would it not be more advisable to face the king, hear his charges, and then in his presence put up a strong defense in behalf of his life, honor and freedom? He soon realized, however, that such a defense would be hopeless. The king, he was convinced, was bent upon robbery and, to justify his planned large-scale confiscations, would go to any length, including death sentences for treason. Should Abravanel then offer him his property? But João, he knew, was not the type to take alms. Abravanel thought of his friend, the duke, who was humiliated, imprisoned, facing a trial for his life. If this could happen to the powerful Braganza, what chance would Abravanel stand?[88]

He arrived at the conclusion that escape was his only course; and he pondered over the route he should take. A distance of only sixteen leagues separated him from the Castilian border at its nearest point to the east, and a straight road led from Arrayolos to that point, and from there to the town of Badajoz on the Guadiana. But this road passed near Villa Viçosa, the residence of the Duke of Braganza. The place, he undoubtedly feared, was swarming with the king's agents, and it was also the route which they would expect him to have taken when the pursuit would begin in the morning. Instead of going eastward, he turned, therefore, to the south, and travelled throughout the day on Portuguese territory, suspecting that all the roads leading to Castile through the bridges of the Guadiana along the Portuguese–Castilian border might be guarded by the king's agents. When darkness fell he must have finally reached the river at a point where its passage was less likely to be watched over—perhaps not far from its western bend, where it is farthest from Castilian soil. There at last he may have turned east, proceeding, in all probability, in the direction of Barrancos. It was only in the middle of the second night[89]—the night of May 31— that he crossed the Portuguese border to Castile.

CHAPTER TWO

SPAIN: LAND OF PERSECUTION

1. *On the Portuguese Border*

ON CROSSING the Castilian border Abravanel continued eastward for an additional distance of eight or nine leagues until he arrived at the town of Segura de la Orden.[1] Segura belonged to the province of Badajoz, and, like Badajoz, had one of the largest Jewish communities of that region. Already sizeable in the middle of the 1470s, that community increased as a result of the influx of Jews who had been driven out of Seville (1483), so that by the time when Abravanel came there, it may have numbered some three hundred families.[2] Segura had also a castle and was administrative center for the Order of Santiago, to which it belonged. As such it seemed to offer sufficient protection to the fugitive from an outraged monarch. João, Abravanel knew, would not ordinarily trespass on the rights of his powerful neighbor, with whom he was resolved to live in peace. Still, there was no telling what he might do to capture an alleged rebel who was almost within his grasp. Abravanel, it seems, was hiding in Castile for some time after his escape; and from the one remark he left us on this point,[2a] it appears that it was not in Segura where he hid. Even so, he ultimately returned to Segura, and for a reason which can be readily understood.

The proximity of the town to the Portuguese border offered him obvious advantages. He still had many things to settle in Portugal. From Segura, it may be safely assumed, he dispatched warnings to his family, advising them to hasten their departure from Portugal and to take with them whatever property they could save. He must have succeeded in establishing—and maintaining—contact with his family, and perhaps also with some of his friends, for he soon received word that João II had confiscated all his possessions.³

Abravanel decided to write to the king. He dispatched a letter in which he pleaded his innocence and strongly protested the injustice done him. The letter had no effect upon the king as far as retrieving his property was concerned, but it was not altogether futile. João appears to have been weakened in his determination to bring Abravanel to account. Perhaps he began to doubt Abravanel's guilt. In any case, it is a fact that he permitted Abravanel's family—his wife and three sons—to leave the country. Had the king been fully convinced of Abravanel's complicity in the duke's acts of treason, he would not have hesitated to wreak vengeance upon him by inflicting severe punishment upon his family. For a king to avenge himself upon relatives of traitors was viewed as a normal act, and João, who was about to order the summary execution of the nobles who had opposed him, was capable of such a practice. Eight years later, as we shall see, he did not hesitate to take punitive measures against Abravanel's one-year-old grandson! But that was after his mind had been made up against Abravanel and after the latter had been officially condemned to death for treason.

The cause for this hardening in the king's attitude can be traced from both Abravanel's writings and the available royal documents relating to the affair. On at least one occasion Abravanel attributed the king's drastic action to enemies who sought his downfall. According to him, they coveted his great fortune and hoped to receive from the king, as gifts, part of his confiscated possessions.⁴ Such occurrences were not unusual. Since it was not uncommon for a king to pay debts of gratitude with the property of condemned men, those of the king's favorites who plotted a man's ruin often fell heir to his fortune. Whether any or all of Abravanel's property was actually thus disposed of, we do not know; João II was certainly not anxious to part with any property which fell into his hands. But he, too, was under obligations. The destruction of the old nobility brought to the fore a new group of friends and advisers, and they were hungry for gain.

Abravanel's flight from Portugal naturally strengthened the suspicion of his guilt, and it may be safely assumed that his enemies were not slow to make the most of this fact.⁵ At the same time, there was nobody at Court to support his pleas and claims of innocence. His Christian friends belonged to the old nobility which was now engaged in mortal conflict with the king; and in the reign of terror which João now let loose, hardly anyone would dare utter a word in defense of a man stigmatized as a traitor. Nor was intercession made on his behalf by any of his Jewish friends. Seized by the general panic, or perhaps persuaded to believe in his guilt, some of them, it appears, even helped João's agents in effecting the confiscation.[6]

His foes thus had a free hand to make their accusations stick. Gradually a case was built up incriminating him as an arch conspirator. Trumped up evidence was submitted to the effect that he participated in a secret meeting of the nobles, together with the Duke of Braganza and the Marquis of Montemor, at which time he offered expert opinion on the poor financial state of the realm and assured the conspirators that the king would be unable to raise, in the event of rebellion, more than six million reis. It was further charged that Abravanel, at that meeting, not only urged the rebels to start the uprising, but also undertook to pay the mercenaries whom they planned to bring from Castile. Months later the charges against him were expanded to include him in a second conspiracy against the king which was then being organized by the nobles. According to these charges, Don Isaac, while on Castilian soil, conferred with Alvaro, the deposed chancellor and the brother of the executed duke—who was the rebels' spokesman in Castile—and collaborated with him in furthering the conspiracy. As proof of Abravanel's association with the rebels, it was claimed that, when the leaders of the revolt, the Duke of Viseu and the Bishop of Evora, lacked funds to carry out the uprising, they ordered Abravanel to return secretly to Portugal and there to arrange to have his nephew and son-in-law, Don Joseph Abravanel, grant the rebels funds from the assets which Don Isaac still had there.[7] We know that Joseph Abravanel managed the estates of the Duke of Viseu and that he fled Portugal on the very day— August 23, 1484—his master was killed by the king in Setubal. Whether some activity of the nephew played into the hands of Abravanel's enemies and led to the intensification of the king's suspicion against him, we do not know. In any case, on May 30, 1485, and August 31, 1485—two years after Abravanel's escape and one year after the flight of Joseph—official death sentences were issued against Don Isaac and his nephew.[8]

Abravanel soon learned about the nature of the plot which was being engineered against him. He knew he was being "framed" and he also knew that he was powerless to thwart the plotters.[9] The unscrupulous tactics of his enemies aroused his indignation,[10] but his complete helplessness to interfere with their activities, and his evidently futile calls for justice, soon led him to resign any effort to re-establish his position in Portugal. That position, he realized, was lost, and he tried to accept the loss stoically. He could not, however, help pondering his strange and ironic fate. He had expected to reap honors from his political services, greater gain from his financial endeavors. Now his honor lay besmirched and his fortune was gone. Wherever there is punishment, there must be some crime; and searching for his sin, Abravanel came to the conclusion that while he had dealt fairly with others, he had dealt dishonestly with himself. It was his heated pursuit after temporal values, his neglect of the better side of his being, which had brought upon him divine wrath.[11] One should not betray one's mission in life!

His mind now turned more and more to the "spiritual and eternal," and, as Abravanel tells us, he delivered during that period a series of lectures on the Former Prophets. His presence became known in the border area, and before long he was surrounded by a group of admirers who urged him to put his comments in writing.[12] The lectures covered at least Joshua and Judges and must have extended over a period of two or three months, probably from August to October. Then Abravanel, seized by a creative urge of a strength and intensity he had never felt before, set about putting his ideas down on paper. He worked at a terrific pace and apparently with few interruptions. In half a month (October 11–October 26) he completed his commentary on Joshua; in less than a month (October 31–November 25) that on Judges; and then, in one hundred days (November 30, 1483–March 8, 1484) his commentary on both books of Samuel.[13] Altogether, within four and a half months—from October 11, 1483, to March 8, 1484—he produced four large volumes comprising about 400,000 words.

The quality of the work is no less surprising than its quantity.

While these commentaries set forth the results of his long and comprehensive studies of the Bible, they embody much more than the product of research. They represent also the conclusions he arrived at from his own observations in the political arena. Abravanel's neglect to complete at that time his commentary on Deuteronomy or on other parts of the Pentateuch, and his turning, instead, to the Former Prophets is significant. For in the writing of a commentary on the latter biblical books, which present a gallery of human leaders with faults and weaknesses, failures and successes, crimes, virtues and acts of heroism, Abravanel found a most suitable opportunity for incorporating his own observations and experiences in the fields of leadership and government. He was trying to fortify himself, as we have indicated, with a stoical attitude toward the misfortunes that befell him, but his mind remained agitated and sought expression for the stirring thoughts that crowded into it both in connection with his own fate and with the political events in Portugal. This is why these commentaries are so saturated with what one may call "living thoughts." It was the first and perhaps the only time that the main political part of the Bible was interpreted by a statesman.

But these were not casual, disconnected thoughts referring to specific phenomena or developments. There is a personal, human aspect to all these writings, but there is also an all-embracing idea. Abravanel sought to express in these commentaries an elaborate theory of history and politics, and his historical-political concept merges with his religious-philosophical outlook which, as we have seen, found expression in the *Crown,* but which here often assumed the character of an aggressive, crusading message. Abravanel's attacks against the rationalists sharpened and also broadened in scope. His assault was now directed primarily against the followers of and commentators on Maimonides—men like Narboni, Ibn Caspi and Albalag, whom he placed on the same level as Abner,[14] the notorious convert of the fourteenth century. In other words, he accused them of hypocrisy, intellectual perversion, and a deliberate intention to undermine and destroy the moral framework of their people's faith.

This illiberal attitude toward the rationalistic Jewish philosophers is, however, redeemed by a display of liberalism in a different direction. To substantiate his broad combination of views—

in religion, philosophy, history and politics—Abravanel in no way limited his sources to Jewish authorities of the anti-rationalist school. In fact, he did not even limit them to Jewish authorities exclusively. Seneca and Cicero and Thomas Aquinas, Augustine and Jerome and Nicholas de Lyra, and even the convert, Paul of Burgos, as well as a host of other scholars, Christian and pagan alike, were quoted or otherwise employed by him as contributors to the understanding of the Bible. With a broadmindedness and tolerance unprecedented in the history of biblical exegesis, he extracted the truth—or what appeared to him as truth—from wherever he found it. Hence the appeal which his commentaries held—despite the oneness and firmness of their central conception—for Christian as well as Jewish minds.

The writing of these commentaries in so short a time must have required Abravanel's total concentration; and Segura, the small border town, was a suitable place for such a work.[15] Yet the dualism of his nature manifested itself even at the height of his intellectual effort. For neither then, nor at any other time, did the political urge in his soul die; it clamored for relief; and thus, while the right hand of Abravanel was sedulously engaged in the "work of God," his left hand was spinning a new web for another political entanglement: slowly but systematically he was preparing the way for his assumption of office at the Spanish Court.[16]

2. *The "Catholic Kings"*

About the middle of March 1484, a messenger arrived at Segura de la Orden bringing Abravanel the good tidings that he was granted an audience with the King and Queen of Spain. By 1484, Ferdinand and Isabella were strongly established in their united kingdom. Their attitude was little short of autocratic and, being among the busiest monarchs of their time, they became difficult to approach. An audience with them, particularly for a fugitive who was backed by no political power, could be arranged only if they were led to believe that they might derive from it some benefit for the Crown. The identity of the person who led them to believe so cannot now be stated with certainty. But it is clear that somebody with great influence, somebody whom the sovereigns trusted, worked on Abravanel's behalf at Court.

One can readily surmise the main motives which prompted Ferdinand and Isabella to receive Abravanel. Spain was in its fourth year of war with the neighboring Moorish kingdom of Granada, and the sovereigns were having a hard time in obtaining the funds needed for its conduct. The financial problem became especially acute shortly after Abravanel's arrival in Spain. For in September 1483 the peace treaty with Granada, concluded only in the previous month, was violated by a Moorish foray into Castile, and from then on it became generally clear that the war with the Moors was to be resumed with full vigor and continued until Granada's total destruction. But the conquest of this kingdom was no easy task. The difficulty involved was highlighted by the heavy losses and the disastrous defeat which the Christian armies had suffered only a few months earlier in Axarquis (April 1483). Hopes for speedy victory having been dashed by that defeat, the outlook was now of a long, grim war; and Spain realized it had to gird itself for a great expenditure of blood and money. Of the two, money was by far the more precious and more difficult to get. When Ferdinand and Isabella had come to power, Aragon had just emerged from prolonged rebellion and upheaval, and Castile, after decades of anarchy and maladministration, had been among the poorest countries in Europe. Despite the severe measures taken by the new rulers to increase the financial resources of their realm, recuperation could not come overnight, especially when the burden of almost unremitting warfare—first with Portugal and later with Granada—pressed heavily on the impoverished lands. Consequently Ferdinand and Isabella often found themselves engaged in a desperate search for funds, and their mind was constantly occupied with the problem of how to find new sources of income and develop the available ones.

Abravanel's appearance in the Court was probably connected with this problem. He had been the chief financial counsellor, if not the treasurer, of Portugal. Furthermore, he had served in this capacity under a king often embroiled in military adventure. His experience in mobilizing funds for war, and perhaps also in supplying armies of invasion, was from the standpoint of Ferdinand

and Isabella an important and attractive qualification. The Spanish sovereigns had heard, in all likelihood also from the princes of Braganza, high praise of Abravanel's abilities, and particularly of his creativeness in the field of finance.[17] In addition, they could reasonably expect that Abravanel, once they enlisted him in their service, would exert all his efforts on their behalf. The Jews were noted for their devotion to the Crown, and Abravanel was on top of this a political fugitive, grateful for the haven the sovereigns offered him.

There can be little doubt that Abravanel who, as already indicated, must have initiated the negotiations for the audience, undertook to present to the Spanish sovereigns a plan for the alleviation of their financial difficulties. What the plan was, we do not know, but we do know that Abravanel's presentation made a strong and favorable impression on them. In any case, as a result of that first and all-important meeting between Abravanel and the Spanish rulers, he was for the next eight years in Spain's royal service.[18]

It was in Tarazona, the Aragonese town, that the audience of Abravanel with the sovereigns took place; and it was at a time when Ferdinand and Isabella were endeavoring to induce the Cortes of Aragon to agree to the extension of the Inquisition to their land.[19] Hesitating to yield their cherished liberties, the Cortes objected to the sovereign's plan, and the prolonged struggle between King Ferdinand and the Cortes of necessity became public knowledge. That a Jewish leader should have offered his services, particularly at such a time and place, to rulers who then were openly forging a most dangerous weapon to be employed against his brethren—brethren by origin, if no longer by religion—must appear extremely strange, and hardly explicable, to a present-day reader. What is more, it was the year 1484! Only eight years were to pass before the total expulsion of the Jews from Spain, and it was only a short time after their expulsion from Andalusia. The Crown's policy on the Jewish question—a policy directed toward the destruction of Spain's Jews—could, it seems, already be detected.

In view of these circumstances, the question arises: what drew Abravanel to the Spanish Court? What was his opinion of the Spanish rulers and their policy toward the Jews? And—most important of all—did he sense the approaching disaster? Before one can understand Abravanel's position in the Court and his life in Spain during that fateful period, these questions must be answered.

The tragedy that overtook Spanish Jewry in the last decade of the fifteenth century was, like similar tragedies in the Diaspora, the product of a number of factors. It was the consequence of a long process of Jew-baiting plus other developments which, although extrinsic to that process, gave it exceptional impetus and force.

The spearhead of the drive against the Jews in Spain, as against those of any other medieval country in the west, was the clergy; but its main force was derived from the burgher class who hated the Jew for economic and political as well as for religious reasons. For the burgher the Jew was not merely a non-Christian, but also and primarily a foreigner and a competitor who lived within his city, not by right, but by reliance on an outside force. That outside force was the king or the noble who had "planted" the Jew in the city out of selfish motives and, of course, against the city's will. The guardian of Spain's Jews in the later centuries of the Middle Ages—and this again was the case throughout the west—was the king rather than the noble.[20] And the downfall of the Jews of Spain came, as it did in many other countries, not through the rising strength of the burgher or, for that matter, of the clergy, but through a development in the monarchic policy itself which called for a total and often abrupt termination of the king's support of the Jew.

The stage for such a change was reached with the king's decision—whenever royal power seemed ready for it—to crush the power of the feudal lords. This task could not be accomplished without the king's alliance with the cities, and the indispensable condition for obtaining such an alliance was to meet the demands of the cities on the Jewish question. We have seen how the fortunes of the Jews in Portugal fluctuated with every change in the relations between the monarchy and the nobility. What happened in Portugal in the fifteenth century was typical of the general course of events in Europe. Thus, the Jews were banished from Britain by Edward I, who, while fighting the nobility, catered to the towns and was the first to call the Model Parliament in which the cities were represented. They were expelled from France by Philip the Fair, who summoned the first assembly which included the third estate, that is, the representatives of the burghers. They were driven from Spain by Ferdinand and Isabella, the kings who reduced the power of the nobility and formed a State Council composed mostly of commoners.

It was in the year of 1480—the year in which the Cortes at Toledo helped the kings break the powers of the feudal aristocracy—that the Spanish monarchy embarked upon a determined and unrelenting anti-Jewish course. In that year steps were initiated for the segregation of the Jews[21] and their elimination from Spanish life, and it was in that year that the Inquisition was established. The Inquisition, although directed not against Jews but rather against Jewish converts and their descendants, was nevertheless the most radical anti-Jewish measure taken at any time in the Middle Ages. It was furthermore the phenomenon most expressive of what was brewing in Spain at the time.

For what was then going on in Spain was a bitter and full-fledged racial war under the cover of religious agitation. The development was by no means exclusively Spanish. Race hatreds, it must be assumed, were a factor which operated against the Jews of the Middle Ages as it did in other periods of their history. The fact that the ruling theories of the Middle Ages are completely silent on the racial problem—a problem which is as old as man's ethnic division—is, of course, no proof to the contrary. The force of electricity also functioned in nature before modern science recognized its principles or learned to harness it for specific purposes.

Spain was the first land in Europe where the elemental force of racial antagonism was brought clearly to the surface. The explanation for the fact that the development took place in Spain lies in another outstanding occurrence for which Spain was a noted exception. Spain was the only country in the Middle Ages where Jews were converted to Christianity on a mass scale. Thus it was in Spain that the medieval theory that the Jews were persecuted solely for their religion was put to its severest test. It was therefore here that it first exploded.

The community of action between the Church and the burgher class, the chief anti-Jewish allies of the Middle Ages, has been repeatedly and strongly stressed. The conflicting aims of these forces, however, must be equally recognized. From the standpoint of the Church the anti-Jewish campaign had but one aim—conversion. To grant the Jew relief from all the disabilities that canon law decreed for him, the Church would be satisfied with nothing less; but it also demanded nothing more. The moment a Jew embraced Christianity, all discrimination against him was to end. But this was not the attitude of the burgher. The latter sought, not the Jew's conversion, but rather his annihilation or expulsion. For, as we have indicated, the fight of the burgher was directed primarily not against the Jewish religion, but against the Jew as a social, economic and political influence.[22]

These differences were clearly expressed in the events of 1391 and in the developments that followed them. It would not be too far-fetched to say that the mass conversion of the Jews in that year took the burgher by surprise. Following the time-honored precepts of the Church, the burgher—in the outbreaks of 1391—offered the Jew an alternative: "Death or Conversion." His secret hopes and expectations, however, were based on the Jew's religious stubbornness—a stubbornness for which he was famous in the Middle Ages—rather than on his religious surrender. When many Jews in Spain departed from this tradition, the burgher, dumbfounded by the outcome, could in no way object to it. Sanctified principles are not easily discarded, and what followed was inevitable: the discovery by the converts of the advantages of their new status; their rapid assimilation of the Christian way of life; and, finally, their phenomenal rise in all spheres of life, economic, political and even ecclesiastical.[23]

The Old Christians thus came to realize the fateful mistake they had made when they forced the Jews to embrace Christianity, thereby with their own hands opening for them the way to all the advantages and positions which they had so vehemently fought to deny them. Determined to rectify this error, the burgher now sought ways of subjecting the *conversos* to the same disabilities he demanded for the Jews. But what ways and means could be employed against a group so strongly entrenched in all positions of power and whom their Christianity gave immunity against persecution? A calculated answer to this knotty problem could not be easily found. In the meantime the burgher expressed his "natural" reaction to the *conversos,* or the Marranos, as he now derisively called them, in a new vitriolic campaign. From 1449 the Marranos were subjected to repeated waves of massacre, while the campaign against them assumed a cynical racial aspect hardly known before in the Middle Ages. The "reprehensible" features of the Marranos, their "sinister" character and their "polluting blood" now became favorite themes of the campaign and were stressed as proof that change of religion could not remedy the malady of the Jew. Indeed, the Spanish anti-Jewish literature of the second half of the fifteenth century and the German anti-Semitic literature of the first half of the twentieth century show a remarkable similarity.

As far as the burgher was concerned, this fundamental evil, the "criminal nature" of the Marranos, was a sufficient reason for persecuting and subjecting them to the same disabilities he demanded for the Jews. But this was not a reason that the Church could accept or that the State could seriously consider.[24] Since persecution in the Middle Ages could be initiated and justified by religious motives only, the Spanish clergy, facing an unparalleled dilemma, solved it in the only possible way. Gradually charges were built up, by a clergy which in sentiment was at one with the populace, about the religious hypocrisy of the Marranos, about their secret practices of Judaism, and about the danger they represented to the purity of the Christian faith. The ideological groundwork for the Inquisition—for the destruction of a group within the bosom of the Church—was thus carefully laid.[25]

The forces operating in an historical movement are seldom common knowledge among the generation involved. For both moral and practical reasons, people tend to substitute excuse for reality. In presenting the major motivations of the Inquisition, therefore, we should add that this is how we view them in retrospect. This, however, is not how they were viewed by Spain's people at the time. As far as the Jews of Spain were concerned, the motives which led to the establishment of the Inquisition *were* primarily religious. In other words, they succumbed to the official propaganda and, in keeping with the official presentation, considered the Marranos religious criminals. It is true that, according to the Jewish view, the essence of the crime committed by the Marranos was not in their alleged attachment to Judaism, but rather in their abandonment of it. Yet this did not change the approach fundamentally. The Inquisition charged the Marranos with religious insincerity, and this was a charge in which the Jews of Spain concurred.[26] They recalled that many of the forefathers of the *conversos* had changed their religion willingly, and they continued to consider the majority of their offspring as opportunistic deserters. In addition, some of the Marrano leaders were themselves arch-enemies of the Jews, and thus the punishment inflicted on the Marranos by the Inquisition was for many Jews not too shocking. In any case, it agreed with the lesson they sought to emphasize: religious insincerity and betrayal do not pay.[26a]

Yet there remains something else to be explained: did they not see in the persecution of the Marranos some danger for themselves? Common sense, it would appear, should have indicated to the Jews that, with such a fierce campaign being conducted against the Marranos in the name of their Jewishness, the Jews could not possibly escape involvement. But the Jews seem not to have sensed this. Their medieval religious outlook and reasoning, coupled with their negative attitude toward the Marranos, gave birth to a theory of the Inquisition which was as convenient as it was false. Furthermore, the Marranos, caught in the storm-center of persecution, seemed to have diverted toward themselves most of the enmity for the Jews. Instead of a social threat, they appeared as a social shield. We thus touch upon the most peculiar factor behind the mysterious Jewish optimism at the time: the Inquisition, instead of serving as a warning, contributed to a deceptive sense of peace.

The blindness manifested by the Jews in the Diaspora for developments laden with mortal danger is nothing short of proverbial. Its sources are a weakened political sensitivity and man's natural reluctance to draw radical conclusions which imply uprooting oneself from a comfortable spot. But whatever the cause, the phenomenon is there. Just as the Jews of Germany failed to foresee Hitler's rise to power at any time during the period preceding that rise, so the Jews of Spain failed to notice, even a few years before the expulsion, the mountainous wave which was approaching to overwhelm them.[27] We have seen that their erroneous conception of the Inquisition contributed to their misinterpretation of the events. We shall now see how another factor contributed significantly to the same result, namely, the shrewdness of the Spanish kings and particularly of Ferdinand of Aragon.

It was early in their career that the Spanish rulers, while grappling with the hard problems of their country, arrived at the conclusion that Christian Spain would never absorb the Jewish element. Although the decisive campaign against the Jews was embarked upon in 1480, the move must have been considered and planned years earlier, perhaps as early as 1474. It was in that very year that the cities of Spain witnessed scenes of bloody battle between Old Christians and Marranos, and it was impossible for the kings not to draw the conclusion that an all-out cooperation of the cities against the nobles must mean the sacrifice of the Jews. Actual steps in this direction, however, had of necessity to be delayed; and the chief consideration for the delay was no doubt the unconcluded war with Portugal. It was a war, it must be remembered, over the right to Castile's Crown which, at least formally, was claimed with equal justice by Spain's Isabella and Portugal's Alfonso V. A considerable part of the nobility of Castile was bitterly opposed to Isabella while, at the same time, many of the barons had intermarried with the Marranos. To launch a campaign against the nobility and the Marranos at a time when the war was not yet over, would mean to strengthen enormously the pro-Portuguese party. Hence the measures against both groups had to wait until the war's conclusion.

Unlike the campaign against the nobility, however, the attack upon the Jews—whether by religion or origin only—was undertaken by the Spanish sovereigns reluctantly. Regarding it as a mere concession to the middle class for supporting the policy of centralization, they considered it at best a necessary evil. This, however, was true only in the first phase. During the second phase things changed fundamentally. The Spanish sovereigns, and especially Ferdinand, came to see in the Jewish situation in Spain not only a problem, but also an opportunity. In other words, instead of merely yielding to the mass-hatred of the Jews, Ferdinand turned toward deliberate aggrandizement and zealous exploitation of that hatred. Behind this change was his realization of the advantages to be gained by the Crown from a systematic anti-Jewish policy: (i) the suppression, through the Inquisition, of the liberties of the Spaniards and, in consequence, the entrenchment of the absolutist regime,[28] and (ii) the exploitation, for the purposes of the Crown, of the vast fortunes of the Jews, and particularly of the Marranos. The second consideration might have been uppermost in his mind; and it is more than likely that it contributed to the fact that the establishment of the Inquisition took place in 1480, the year of the outbreak of the Granada war. Just as the expropriation of the German Jews in our time helped materially in building the German war machine, so the expropriation of the *conversos* was an important element in financing the war enterprises of the Spanish kings.[29]

All this, of course, was never stated in any public or open manner. Publicly there was but one motive for the anti-Jewish policy of the Spanish sovereigns: the interests of the Crown in Spain's religious purity and its desire to promote the honor of the Church. It is here that the greatest element of deception was introduced into Ferdinand's political game. To this very day it baffles many a scholar and historian, and, in consequence, opinion is still divided as to Ferdinand's true character. It would appear that Ferdinand was a master at political criminality, while, at the same time, playing the role of man of piety.

Having unusual regard for public opinion—unusual especially in his sphere and age—he also knew how to develop and exploit it, making full use of his keen sense of what to conceal from and what to reveal to the public. Thus, while it was he who pulled the wires of the Inquisition, dictated its course, chose its functionaries, encouraged its evildoers, and protected even its most revolting monsters, he preferred to appear publicly as merely bowing to its verdicts, or as merely carrying out the orders of the Pope whom he usually held in contempt.[30] The most ruthless of all the princes of his time, his main distinction lay in his ability to hide his ruthlessness under a mask of virtue. Not in vain does Machiavelli hold him up as the shrewdest of all princes and as the ideal of his *Prince*.[31]

Ferdinand's extreme political shrewdness was matched, moreover, by his mastery in diplomacy. As he fully controlled his words and his countenance,[32] it was difficult even for his closest associates to determine exactly where he stood. It was no less, and perhaps even more, difficult to guess his intentions for the future. For his plans were deeply laid, hatched in secrecy and revealed at the most unexpected moment with as little advance notice as possible. Consequently, Ferdinand fooled many in his time, but perhaps none so utterly as the Jews.

It has been indicated already that his policy against the Jews was launched together with his policy against the Marranos and that both policies had a common aim—the elimination of the Jewish element from Spain. Yet they differed in method and timing. It is more than probable that Ferdinand's plan for the total expulsion of the Jews was conceived already in 1483, when he ordered their expulsion from Andalusia. But in 1483 it was not in his interest to stamp himself, in the eyes of the Jews, as radically anti-Jewish. Then, and years thereafter, he was still badly in need of Jewish experience and ability, especially in the field of taxation. What is more, the expulsion of the Jews in those days would have increased considerably the power of Granada, where the exiled Jews would have gone. Ferdinand therefore employed a half-measure. By forcing the Jews out of Andalusia, he gained the enthusiastic support of the south which was the main bastion in the war against the Moors and where the feeling against the Jews ran highest. But seeking to diminish Jewish embitterment against the Crown, and to turn the banished Jews away from Granada, he left the rest of Spain open for their resettlement and, moreover, attributed the move to the Inquisition.

The Jews, for their part, failed to see in both the expulsion from Andalusia (1483) and the subsequent order of expulsion from Aragon (1486) any forecast of their approaching disaster.[32a] This was not only a result of Ferdinand's abilities at concealment and subterfuge,[32b] but also of the medieval Jews' historic experience and their general conception of their status. For centuries they had considered the Church as their persecutor, the king as their defender; and they had come to think of this twin phenomenon as an almost unchangeable order of things. That Ferdinand was under the pressure of the Inquisition, that he would follow the clergy up to a certain limit, seemed to them reasonable to believe. That he would seek to bring about their total ruin, and thus depart entirely from the traditional policy of Spain's kings toward the Jews, seemed to them most unlikely. Had Ferdinand shown personal hostility to the Jews in the Court or in his service, they would undoubtedly have been alarmed. But hatred and sadism played hardly any role in determining Ferdinand's attitude toward the Jews.[33] What motivated his policy against the Jews, and equally against the Marranos, was a cold, careful calculation of all the elements involved.

Another factor which tended to diminish the apprehension of Spain's Jews concerning their future was the fact that Jews occupied important positions in the farming and collection of the royal revenues, and that Marranos held some of the highest posts in various governmental departments and at Court. Such employment of Jews and Marranos was part of the strictly utilitarian policy which both Ferdinand and Isabella pursued. It enabled them to exploit needed talent, and at the same time to establish the necessary fiction of their unfailing justice and impartiality. Consequently many Jews believed, with apparently good logic, that the kings would not have "entrenched" Jews in their administration if they had contemplated their elimination. Any other conclusion from this state of affairs would not have made sense. In the crafty political game of Ferdinand, however, with its complicated double-dealings and long-range considerations, it made perfect sense.

Finally, what impressed the Jews more than anything else was the insistence of the Spanish kings on law and order. Law and order were indeed their passion; they would tolerate no mob rule or mass violence. If they adopted a policy against a group, it had to be enforced in the form, to the degree, and at the time that they considered appropriate. Any act of persecution, therefore, which they did not sanction, that is, which had not become law, the Spanish kings sternly opposed. And this strong insistence on the rule of law, coupled with the deceptive elements in their policy and the successful concealment of the plan for expulsion, contributed to the development of that strange sense of security which we find in those days among the Jews of Spain.

Abravanel shared the attitude of Spain's Jews.[34] In 1484, when he was summoned to the Court, he considered it an opportunity that he could not let pass. He was impressed with the friendliness displayed towards him by the rulers, but not by their fight to extend the Inquisition. The grave implication of that cardinal fact—that the days of the Jews of Spain were numbered—seems to have been indisputably clear. But Abravanel, like the rest of his Jewish contemporaries, did not read the signs of the times. That audience in Tarazona in the spring of 1484 was indeed a symbolic, ill-auguring beginning for his career as a courtier in Spain.

3. *Advancement at Court*

Having failed to realize the fundamentals of the situation, Abravanel, in entering the service of Ferdinand, undoubtedly believed that, with the growth of his influence, he might strengthen the position of Spain's Jews. Under the political system then prevailing in Spain, however, Jews could enter the royal service only in the financial field, and that meant primarily in the field of tax-farming. The way to higher, more powerful positions appeared, at least temporarily, closed.

The chief tax-farmer at the time was Abraham Senior, who was *Rab de le Corte* and, as such, the official head of the Jewish community in Castile. Senior's position in the Court was strong. In addition to the ability he revealed in tax-farming, he was a favorite of the queen, who well remembered the signal services he rendered her in critical times. Obviously, Abravanel could accept a position only secondary to that of Senior.[35]

Powerful enough to block Abravanel's way, Senior must have realized that he had nothing to fear from Abravanel's appointment. He must have felt that Abravanel was, like him, a "faithful observer of the laws of friendship."[36] And Senior may have welcomed Abravanel's cooperation also for other reasons. He was then seventy-two years old and beset with difficult problems. It was not easy to meet, under the strain of war, the increasing demands of Ferdinand and Isabella. He soon must have recognized Abravanel's great knowledge in matters relating to taxation and tax-farming, and he was undoubtedly strongly impressed with the personality of the famous courtier.

Abravanel thus assumed tax-farming responsibilities in Senior's elaborate system. That he was in a position to assume such responsibilities is another proof that he succeeded in transferring at least a small share of his fortune from Portugal. In August 1484, when his son-in-law, Joseph, fleeing João's wrath, arrived in Castile, he may have reinforced Abravanel's finances by loans or partnership. As the former treasurer of the Duke of Viseu, and as both Abravanel's son-in-law and nephew—the son of Don Isaac's brother, Samuel—Joseph was probably a man of great wealth.

The financier and the man of action were now fully re-awakened in Abravanel. Tax-farming was an exacting business and Abravanel was undoubtedly driving hard to rebuild his family's fortune. From Segura he moved to the heart of the country—perhaps directly to Alacalá de Henares, where the documents indicate his presence from June 1485 on.[37] From there, it seems, he could better direct and control his various tax-farming enterprises, and also cast his eyes on new financial projects which held the promise of expansion. Perhaps he was seeking not only greater fortune, but also greater independence. In any case, it is clear that he was not satisfied with remaining on the subordinate level at which he commenced in Spain. His financial ability soon proved itself, and he was forging ahead to distinction.

Thus on June 6, 1485, he signed an agreement with the powerful Cardinal Mendoza, in which he undertook to farm the latter's revenues in Siguenza, Guadalajara and other localities for a period of two years (1486–1487). It was a heavy undertaking no doubt, perhaps the heaviest he had hitherto shouldered in Spain, for Abravanel committed himself to pay the Cardinal (on specified dates in 1487–1488) sums totalling the huge amount of 6,400,000 maravedis.[38] Abravanel, it seems, carried out the agreement to the Cardinal's full satisfaction; for, as later documents suggest, he continued in the latter's service to the very end of his stay in Spain.[39] Moreover, it appears that it is to that deal which he struck with the Cardinal in 1485—or rather to its successful outcome—that we should attribute his subsequent far greater involvement in the affairs of the Mendoza House. For several years later—probably in 1490—Abravanel became the *contador mayor* of the Duke of the *Infantado*.[40]

Iñigo López de Mendoza, the second Duke of the *Infantado*, came to power upon the death of his father, Diego Hurtado de Mendoza, in 1487. Exercising authority over 800 places and 90,000 vassals who paid him tribute, his perennial income was one of the largest that any noble house in Spain could boast. But his income did not always match his expenses. For he was a lover of pomp and magnificence; his retinue resembled that of royalty; and the palace which he built for himself in Guadalajara was the most sumptuous of all the mansions of Spain's aristocracy at the time. He was also genuinely generous, it seems. And, faithful to the sovereigns and to his country, then at war, he also participated, with annually increasing forces, in the long and costly battle of Granada. As a result of all this, the Duke found himself repeatedly, despite his great resources, in search of funds; and when he appointed Abravanel his *contador mayor,* he no doubt hoped that the latter would relieve him of such concerns, perhaps—we may assume—by finding ways and means of increasing the revenues of his estates. Evidently Abravanel accepted the challenge. He moved to Guadalajara—the capital of the duchy—and received from its lord the financial keys of a kingdom within a kingdom.[41]

So seven years after his arrival in Spain, Abravanel was again in a position which was similar to the one he had in Portugal under Alfonso V. He was obviously following the same pattern of action when he engaged himself in the service of both king and duke; and the cycle of developments was repeating itself in more than one respect. Like the Braganzas in Portugal, the Mendozas in Castile held in their hands powers, economic and political, which made them uniquely influential in the realm; and this fact in itself was no doubt helpful to Abravanel in enhancing his status at the Royal Court. Indeed, that enhancement constantly remained his prime and ultimate objective. Therefore, while cultivating his relations with the Mendozas,[42] he sought closer ties with the King and Queen as well. He retained, and apparently increased, his holdings in the royal tax-farming system; and commanding large profits from his multiple enterprises, he could now make loans— comprising millions of maravedis—to the Queen and the war treasury of the state (from 1488 on).[43] He felt he was gaining in royal favor, appreciation and esteem.[44] By 1491 he became the Queen's personal financial representative.[45]

He may have been dreaming of higher attainments, of greater advancement at the Kings' court; yet by then, it seems, he could not have failed to realize the possible limits of his rise in Spain. Under Alfonso V, Abravanel was a power; he could have a say in all affairs of state. Under Ferdinand and Isabella, his activity and advice—and this applies to any other Jew—were strictly confined to the financial field. The only area where he could possibly touch upon the general policies of the Spanish state was the latter's position on the Jewish question. Abravanel, indeed, moved into this area. He must have represented Jewish interests before the Crown repeatedly and efficiently in the course of the years, for by 1492 he came to be regarded as the unofficial leader of Spain's Jews.[46]

Politics and finances thus again exhausted most of Abravanel's time and strength. His far-flung activities required extensive traveling, often from one end of the country to the other, and consequently his mind was rarely free to dwell on problems of a spiritual nature. To do so, as he tells us, he had to "steal time— either from the day, or from the night."[47] Nevertheless, he wrote on such "stolen time"—at the home of a friend (Abraham Çarfati) in Molina—his massive introduction to the third part of the *Guide*.[48] It is the only work which, beside his Commentaries, we know for certain that he composed in Spain.

His standing at Court, his material success, his leadership in the community, and, above all, the moral atmosphere of the Jewish scholarly circles[49] made the period of his life in Spain—difficult as this may be for us to comprehend—a happy and memorable one.[50] But the period was fast drawing to a close. From 1488 the Inquisition cast an increasingly ominous shadow over the Jews of Spain. The trials of Huesca (1489) and Laguardia (1491) which it organized, and in which Jews were sentenced to be burned at the stake, indicated some large-scale sinister design and signalled danger to the whole community.[51] Then, on January 2, 1492, Granada capitulated, and the Jewish leaders, it is likely, hoped that the end of the war would lead to a decrease in the fierce religious agitation. The following few months were, indeed, uneventful. A strange peace prevailed; but it was the calm before the storm. When the edict of expulsion was announced, it came like a thunderbolt out of the clear sky, tumbling, at last, the walls of illusions behind which the Jews of Spain had lived.

4. The Great Crisis

The edict of expulsion had been hatched in secrecy, was signed without giving the Jewish courtiers advance notice, and, unlike previous orders of expulsion, came from the sovereigns, and not from the Inquisition. From the standpoint of the Jews, these facts must have appeared as discouraging symptoms. Yet the Jewish courtiers were not alarmed. They still believed they could avert disaster,[52] and they hastened to request an audience with the king. The audience was granted.

The chief spokesman of the Jews—at least unofficially—was Abravanel. The other representatives were the aged Senior—then 80 years old—and his son-in-law Melamed. The latter was, since 1487, the chief farmer of taxes in Castile,[53] and apparently a man of great ability and considerable influence at Court.

The moment when Abravanel and his colleagues pleaded with the king for the life of their people was one of the most crucial in Jewish history. Yet we have little information as to what transpired in the royal cabinet at the time; the arguments employed on that occasion have not been transmitted to us. Nevertheless, we know that Abravanel's presentation was both eloquent and forceful. Many years later, and despite their failure to avert the expulsion, Abravanel's powerful words were still re-echoing in the reports, tales and legends of the exiles from Spain.[54]

Under the impact of this strong intervention, the first aim of the Jews was achieved: the matter was made subject to reconsideration and the publication of the edict was temporarily suspended.[55] Ferdinand was obviously impressed with what he heard. He probably wanted to think the matter over, and that was undoubtedly all he said, in his cautious and non-committal manner, to the representatives of the Jews. Abravanel and his friends, however, must have felt encouraged. The attitude of the king gave room for hope, and the suspension of the edict's publication provided them with time in which they could organize and bring to bear greater pressure upon the king.

Abravanel then appealed to his friends at Court, some of whom were among the "first in the kingdom," and determined representations were made by the latter in support of the Jewish plea. Among the chief courtiers were some of the great nobles—men like Cardinal Mendoza, the Marquis of Cadiz and the Duke of Medinaceli who were not imbued with fanaticism against the Jews. In view of the record of these men in the early history of the Inquisition, each of them might have been considered a potential advocate—and might have acted—in behalf of the Jews.[56]

It was perhaps from his reaction to their Christian friends that the Jews learned clearly where Ferdinand stood. To the courtiers who interceded in behalf of the Jews, Ferdinand communicated his firm resolve to go ahead with the expulsion order.[57] The situation clearly called for a second meeting with the king, and it was probably then that Senior and Abravanel decided to fortify their desperate pleas with a large offer of gold.[58]

According to Abravanel, the Jews offered the Crown the maximum sum they could possibly muster. It seems that Ferdinand again evinced interest,[59] and yet it must be assumed that he was again most careful not to commit himself in any manner. Perhaps he said that he appreciated the Jews' attitude, and perhaps he even asked what they meant by "maximum;" whereupon the Jewish representatives, prepared for the question, threw on the scales a huge sum, possibly 300,000 ducats.[60] The effect of such a figure must have been reflected in the attitude of the greedy king. The hopes of the Jews were again revived.

Just the same, it soon proved illusory. For when Abravanel and Senior saw the king the third time, perhaps to receive his final answer, it was clear that the offer had failed of its purpose. Again we know nothing of what was said at that meeting, but from subsequent developments we may conclude that Ferdinand—in order, perhaps, to end the unpleasant pressure which was concentrated against him—indicated that the expulsion was not a decision only of the King of Aragon, but also of the Queen of Castile. In despair, the Jews might have taken such a remark, not as an excuse, but as an explanation and as a hint for action in a new direction.[61]

Abravanel and Senior must have realized by now that they were up against an iron wall. They had one more chance, they thought, to bring about the revocation of the order—by changing the attitude of the queen. But what could they say to her? Entreaties, arguments, bribes were of no avail. Abravanel, it seems, decided at that juncture to take a different stand.

He now spoke to the queen—the haughty, fanatic and often ferocious Isabella—not like her financial agent, not even like a cautious, diplomatic courtier. He spoke to her now like a scion of the House of David and as a representative of an unconquered— and unconquerable—people. He spoke to her, moreover, like a prophet of old, in daring, castigating and threatening language. If

Isabella thought that, by measures like expulsion, the Jews could be brought to surrender or to extinction, she was greatly mistaken. He pointed out to her the eternity of the Jewish people, that they had outlived all who had attempted to destroy them, that it was beyond human capacity to destroy the Jewish people, and that those who tried to do so only invited upon themselves divine punishment and disaster.[62] Isabella, who had a mystic vein in her soul, could understand such an argument; but her reaction must have been along the same lines. She too invoked the name of God, but of course to prove the very opposite of Abravanel's conclusions.

"Do you believe," she said to the Jewish representatives, "that this comes upon you from us? *The Lord hath put this thing into the heart of the king.*" To Abravanel and Senior, who had come to believe that Isabella was chiefly responsible for the edict and that hers was the power that blocked its annulment, such a statement might have sounded hypocritical. Yet it was true. It indicated in definite terms that it was Ferdinand who had decided upon the expulsion and that it was he who was most determined to implement it. Would then the queen use her influence with the king to have the order withdrawn? No, she could not use her influence in this issue, even if she desired it. *"The king's heart,"* she said, *"is in the hands of the Lord, as the rivers of water. He turns it whithersoever He will."* This again was not an evasive phrase, adroitly concocted as an excuse for inaction, but one that bore the same testimony: it was the "king's heart" that insisted upon the plan, and it was God, not the queen, who could influence him in this matter.

All this was another example of Ferdinand's skillful diplomatic tactics and his ability to deceive and outwit the party with whom he negotiated. Heartless and ruthless as he was, he had a passion for appearing considerate and a talent for shifting onto others—including, as in this instance, his own consort—the blame for his cruelties. Isabella was undoubtedly in favor of the expulsion, but she was not the moving spirit behind it. If Abravanel placed major responsibility upon her, it was both because he misjudged Ferdinand and because Isabella was more open-minded and impulsive. Isabella, besides, left no room for illusions. When their audience with the queen ended, both Abravanel and Senior knew that the verdict against the Jews of Spain was sealed.[63]

It is obvious that no amount of pleading would have swayed Ferdinand from his decision. For he expected to reap a rich financial harvest from the expulsion of the Jews. The argument which has been advanced, that economic calculations could not have motivated Ferdinand in decreeing the expulsion, since he could easily see that Spain would suffer from the departure of so industrious an element as the Jews,[64] does not hold water. It may be argued just as easily that Ferdinand could foresee the destructive economic results which were implied in his political measures against the Marranos. The fact is that Ferdinand's economic policies were dictated not by long-range considerations, but by his closest political aims as well as pressing financial needs. Having come to the conclusion, as already indicated, that Spain could not absorb Jews or Marranos, he wanted to be the one to effect their liquidation, and with maximum *immediate* advantage.[65]

The immediate profits of the expulsion of the Jews were incomparably greater than any possible increase in the revenues which the Jews might have brought in decades. Their taxes in the years prior to the expulsion did not constitute an especially large income. In the year 1472, for instance, the taxes of the Jews of the whole of Castile amounted to 450,000 maravedis.[66] In comparison, some 7,000,000 maravedis were collected after the expulsion by the government from the moneys and sale of houses and valuables left behind by the Jews in Burgos alone![67] At the conclusion of the war, moreover, the rulers of Spain were placed in a grave financial situation; their treasury was empty, while the burden of the many debts and liabilities that accrued and multiplied during the war was pressing heavily upon them. The expulsion of the Jews presented to them a way of settling their financial difficulties, and Ferdinand made his calculations carefully. To stay the expulsion without obtaining from the Jews a considerable financial compensation would be, to his way of thinking, absurd. Yet, to obtain their money and revoke the order would be even less wise; for it would lay bare the tactics of the Spanish kings and convince everyone that their religion was for sale. They already had on their hands the problem of refuting the charge that the entire bloodletting of the Inquisition was merely a financial device. Still, this charge could be dodged: what was done in individual cases in the darkness which surrounded the Inquisition's procedures was a matter of conjecture. But whatever involved the expulsion had to be handled in broad daylight. The huge bribe suggested for the cancellation of the order would have to be collected from many people. Not for a single day would the deal remain secret. And the result: it would compromise the Inquisition beyond recovery and ruin the prestige of the sovereigns. Thus the balance of argument weighed heavily against the move; and Abravanel's pleas, coupled as they were by a large financial offer, could not possibly succeed.

The Jews of Spain had faith in their leaders, and confidently awaited the outcome of the negotiations. It was only when the edict was finally made public (April 29–May 1) that their patient expectations turned into panic.[68] The mass-hysteria that developed was conducive to conversion, and the Jewish leadership in Spain now faced the task of bolstering the spirit of their despair-ridden brethren—a task which was effectively performed—as well as the more grievous problem of swiftly finding suitable havens. The three months left until the day of expulsion were a frightfully short time for organizing such an exodus; and, except for the costly and hazardous sea-routes, no avenue appeared open. The opening to the expelled of a neighboring land on the peninsula seemed, therefore, to many a question of life and death, and the agreement reached soon after by a Spanish-Jewish delegation and João II, King of Portugal, regarding the admission of Spain's Jews to his country, was, despite its severe terms, at the moment considered a great and heartening achievement. Could Abravanel—knowing João as he did—have advocated this move which was soon to prove so fatal? We know nothing of the frantic, desperate consultations that the Jewish leaders in Spain held at the time, and we have no indication of the opinions they expressed in their fateful deliberations. As an expert on Portugal, Abravanel was, no doubt, asked to state his view on the migration to that country and, as the recognized leader of Spain's Jews, he must have been involved in whatever organized steps were then taken by the community.

The idea of turning to Portugal, however, could, in no event, apply to him personally; and, confronted with the problem of finding a refuge for his family and himself, it is interesting to note that he chose none of the courses which then appeared easier and safer. The fact that Abravanel did not go to Navarre seems to indicate that by then he saw no future for the Jews anywhere in the Peninsula. Nor did he go to near-by North Africa. His eyes turned eastward, to the countries across the sea—to Italy and, beyond it, as an alternative, to Turkey. It was there that he decided to go himself and undoubtedly urged others to go, and it was a decision which appears retrospectively as both wise and fortunate. For, harsh as was the fate of those who went in that direction, they fared on the whole incomparably better than those who took any of the other roads.

The family hastily prepared for departure. Funds were mobilized, debts were collected, among them a large debt from the Crown (1,500,000 maravedis) paid by Luis de Santangel.[69] Their major problem, however, was how to get these funds out of Spain. Since it was legally impossible to take out gold and jewelry, most of Abravanel's newly acquired fortune must again have been lost. But it seems he managed to save some of it, probably through the medium of bills of exchange; and he also succeeded in obtaining from Ferdinand a special permit for himself and his son-in-law to take out two thousand ducats each in gold and other valuables. In return, the Crown received from Abravanel the right to collect for itself debts totalling more than one million maravedis—only about two-thirds of the sum which Abravanel and his son-in-law were permitted to take with them.[70]

Obviously, it was a friendly gesture, an outstanding privilege granted Abravanel, apparently in recognition of his services to the Crown. Ferdinand was, to be sure, most reluctant to lose Don Isaac's services; and both he and Isabella made strenuous efforts to obtain the conversion of Abravanel, along with that of Senior and Melamed, the three leading Jews at Court and the chief forces in the financial administration.[71] Their conversion, the royal pair thought, would save their services for the Crown and would be regarded, in addition, as a great victory for the religious efforts of the Spanish kings.

Under pressure of Ferdinand and Isabella, Senior and Melamed yielded. They, and their sons, were baptized on June 15, in the church of Santa María de Guadalupe.[72] The sponsors of Senior were the king, the queen and Cardinal Mendoza, the "third king of Spain." It was perhaps hoped that Senior's conversion would induce Abravanel to follow suit. But when it became clear that Abravanel was adamant, a scheme appears to have been concocted at Court to steal his grandson, the son of Judah Abravanel, who was at that time only a year old, and convert him to Christianity. It was probably hoped that the conversion of the grandson would force his parents to follow suit and, in view of the great affection between Don Judah and Don Isaac, would lead the latter, too, to accept Christianity. The Abravanels, however, learned of the scheme in time, and, as they apparently were not yet prepared for departure, they sent the child, accompanied by his nurse, across the border to Portugal, from where they planned to bring him later to Italy.[73]

On the last day of July, so it seems, and apparently at the head of the group bound eastward, Don Isaac and his family boarded at Valencia[74] a vessel bound for Italy. It was the second time that his life was shattered; again he was uprooted from his home, his labor and fortune once more disappearing like a column of smoke. But the personal loss was now minimized in the enormity of the national tragedy. Here he was in the midst of the exiles leaving a land where their forefathers had lived for centuries upon centuries. Was the exile another episode in the long tragedy of Jewish wandering, or did it represent perhaps a move in a higher plan? There were many among the exiles who believed that the expulsion was actually the beginning of the Return, that the exodus from Spain might be comparable to that from Egypt.[75] Could this possibly be true?

When the shores of Spain disappeared in the distance, Abravanel must have pondered over the unknown objectives to which the hand of God was leading His people.

CHAPTER THREE

NAPLES: SCENE OF TROUBLE

1. On Italy's Threshold

THE LAND to which Don Isaac and his family, as well as many other exiles were heading, could hardly be considered, except for a few areas, as a haven for the Jewish exiles from Spain. Of the ten states of northern Italy, none of the five republics (Venice, Genoa, Florence, Lucca and Siena), nor any of the four duchies (Savoy, Milan, Modena and Ferrara), nor again the little Marquisate of Mantua was prepared to admit the Jewish exiles. The North Italian cities had been among the first to drive the Jews out of their limits and, throughout the centuries of the later Middle Ages, they persistently opposed the settlement of Jews. The Jewish communities in these cities were in consequence extremely small.[1] They consisted mostly of especially privileged Jews who were admitted for particular functions. They were traders with the East who, while crossing Italy, were tolerated to the extent that they brought profit to the city. They were physicians whose services were needed by the Christians. They were bankers who offered cheap credit to the poor and who were often invited to the cities— notably to Venice and Florence—for the specific purpose of providing such credits. In cities where republican rule was entrenched, like Venice and Genoa, restrictions upon the entry of Jews were severe.[2] In others, where a strong patrician family was in power— as was the case with the Medicis in Florence or the Dukes of Este in Ferrara—in other words, where the democratic elements were weakened—restrictions on Jewish settlement were slightly eased and the Jews settled in somewhat larger numbers. But no state in northern Italy, whether republican or oligarchic, would permit the influx of a large number of Jews, and least of all would they be inclined to allow the entry of an element like the exiles from Spain. Since the latter had left Spain without money, they could not be considered even as moneylenders. They could be regarded only as potential craftsmen and traders who would offer competition to the middle class. This, in brief, was the attitude of the cities towards the admission of the Jews of Spain.

The attitude of the papal states, comprising the center of Italy, was not much different. Instead of the opposition of the burgher class, there was here the opposition of the Church. In the second half of the fifteenth century the Roman popes were utilitarian rather than doctrinaire, but even so the admission of a large number of Jews would be little to their advantage. Considerable gifts of money in those days would do much to influence the decisions of the Papacy, but the exiles from Spain could offer little to attract the interest of the papal Court.

The only Italian realm where conditions differed was the kingdom of Naples. In this kingdom, which consisted of the southern half of Italy, general circumstances were similar to those in the monarchies in other parts of Europe prior to the development of the tendency toward absolutism. Here neither the burghers nor the Church, but the king—and the king alone—was the factor which determined the policy toward the Jews. It is true that the Neapolitan princes at the time—Ferrante, the king, and his son Alfonso—manifested a strong desire for centralization; and in the course of their struggle against the nobility, they used the same drastic measures employed by João in Portugal, that is, summary executions of the great barons. But unlike João, or indeed other absolutists, they failed to find a way, or understand the need for obtaining the support of the people for their plans. And thus, while they were opposed by the nobility, they were simultaneously hated by the people. Having developed the habit of ruling with an iron hand and of giving little heed to the wishes of the populace, the Neapolitan princes had no objection whatever to an increase of their Jewish subjects. On the contrary, they welcomed the idea. It meant the increase of a population loyal to the Crown, as well as a potential rise in the commercial development of the Neapolitan kingdom which, from a commercial point of view, was lagging behind the northern states.

2. *A Neapolitan Courtier*

On August 24, 1492, nine caravels carrying Jewish exiles from Spain arrived in the port of Naples.[3] The journey from Spain had been disastrous.⁴ The ship masters were ruthless, cruel and avaricious. The vessels were overcrowded and ill provisioned. Sanitary conditions were such as to invite disease, and the ships soon became plague-ridden. All these calamities combined to bring the exiles, after weeks of suffering, to the end of their resources. A Genoese historian who saw some of them, as their boat passed through his city's harbor, writes that "one might have taken them for spectres, so emaciated were they, so cadaverous in their aspect, and with eyes so sunken; they differed in nothing from the dead, except in the power of motion, which indeed they scarcely retained."⁵

The description is reminiscent of the Jews who survived the German concentration camps of World War II. The condition of the exiles, at least of many of them, was, in fact, similar.⁶ Already plague-ridden when they arrived in Genoa, they were not permitted entry into the city. They were allowed to stay on the mole, which was completely surrounded by sea and "was the only quarter vouchsafed to the wretched animals."⁷ This was the attitude of every other city into which they sought entry. It was with trembling hearts that this hapless human cargo surveyed the majestic Bay of Naples and the city on the rising slopes behind it. Would the Neapolitan government give them asylum?

Ferrante granted their request to land, and, on August 24, the first large group of exiles set foot on Italian soil, their hearts filled with boundless gratitude to the king of Naples, their saviour.⁸ Don Isaac and his family, however, were not among those who disembarked on that day.⁹ They were, as we have indicated, with the main body of exiles that left Spain on the last day of July; and, either because of the larger number of vessels, or for some other reasons, this group travelled more slowly and arrived in Naples at least a month later. The Abravanels must have made the same tour of the various western Italian seaports with the same distressing results. The length of the voyage must have increased the sufferings of many of their fellow-travellers, but the welcome they received in Naples by the king obliterated much of the sorrow they had experienced. Ferrante continued to be friendly, and to Abravanel he showed particular consideration. He offered him an invitation to the Court and even a position in his service. What did Abravanel think of the king and his son Alfonso, with whom

Ferrante shared the government? He called them "princes of mercy and righteousness,"[10] and in view of their attitude toward the Spanish exiles, this description is understandable.

The impression which we gain of these princes from other contemporaries is quite different. Thus, speaking of Alfonso, Ferrante's son, the French Ambassador, Philippe de Comines, says that "never was any prince more bloody, wicked, inhuman, lascivious, or gluttonous than he. Yet his father was more dangerous, because no man knew when he was angry or pleased; for he would betray men in the midst of his entertainments and caresses."[11] Actually Ferrante and his son Alfonso were no worse than the other despotic princes of the Renaissance age. They were ruthless and unscrupulous in their dealings with opponents; but they were also capable of repaying generously for loyal services. They were in any case no more ferocious than João II or Ferdinand the Catholic.

Abravanel must have assumed a position of importance in Ferrante's Court. Also, this position seems to have been connected with some great financial enterprise. Describing his situation in Naples in later years, Abravanel writes that his "wealth grew immensely" and that he became "as famous as the country's greatest magnates."[12] Indeed, two years after his arrival, we find Abravanel the most trusted courtier in the suite of the Neapolitan king. He seems to have had little or no difficulty in adjusting himself to the new Court. Ferrante I was the illegitimate son of Alfonso V, who was a member of the Aragonese royal house and uncle of Ferdinand of Spain. The system of government, the manners, the language were much the same as in Aragon. It was like serving in a Spanish Court, but it was a Court as in the good old days, before the Inquisition was established and when the royal policy was still pro-Jewish.

There was, however, need to be on guard. The clamor against the Jews in Naples was rising. The influx of the newcomers was considered by the populace as an infringement of their rights and interests for which they held the rulers responsible. Ferrante was under great pressure, and it was especially difficult to resist this pressure because of the ravages made by the plague which the exiles brought with them. "The disorder was so malignant and spread with such frightful celerity as to sweep off more than twenty thousand inhabitants of the city in the course of the year."[13]

Ferrante, however, remained firm. The Crown helped to combat the disease. Special camps were established for the afflicted; doctors were mobilized; and food was allotted by the Crown to the destitute whose number among the exiles was increasing.[14] It is reasonable to assume that Abravanel had a share in fortifying the king's attitude. In any case, he soon came to be recognized, not only by the colony of the exiles, but by the Jews of Naples as well, as their chief leader and spokesman at Court.[15]

His services at Court, however, seem not to have been as exhausting as they were in Portugal and Spain. Barely half a year after his arrival, Abravanel found it possible even to resume his writing, and towards the end of his first year in Naples he completed his commentary on the two books of Kings.[16] The period of the Kings was one which culminated in national disaster and exile. Within the framework of this commentary, he could, and did, incorporate his thoughts and feelings about the Spanish exile—the latest and most calamitous disaster the Jews had experienced in the Diaspora.[17] Indeed, the problem of the exile and the fate of his people occupied him greatly in those days. The cruelties which he and others had witnessed were bound to have a shattering effect upon the thinking of many an ardent believer. Is this world ruled by any moral principle? Is there reward for virtue, punishment for evil? Is there, indeed, a God in this world? And if God does govern the world, why does He not manifest His powers? These questions disturbed the minds of many, led faithful souls to despair and engendered a skepticism which threatened to breed cynicism and apostasy. To answer these questions, Abravanel wrote in Naples— soon after completing his commentary on Kings—a work entitled *Eternal Justice,* in which he sought to indicate the ways in which God demonstrates His justice in this world.[18] Another work he wrote at the time, which he titled *Principles of Faith,* was likewise aimed at combating disbelief. The old controversy over the principles of Judaism served as an excuse to doubt them all, and to check this tendency Abravanel thought it vital to uphold not only the belief in Providence, but all of Maimonides' "Thirteen Articles of Faith," as well as other concepts and directives incorporated in the divine Law. He completed the *Principles* on October 30, 1494.[19]

Naples was a great center of humanism. It was the seat of the Pontanian Academy which was famous throughout Italy. The academy's head, Giovanni Pontano, was also Chancellor of the Kingdom, and Abravanel may have had a personal relationship with him. The views of Pontano and Abravanel, however, were far apart. Pontano was a confirmed Aristotelian, while Abravanel, as we have seen, was opposed to Aristotle. Aristotelianism was also the prevailing philosophy among the Jewish intellectuals of Italy, foremost among whom was Judah Messer Leon, formerly a native of Naples, and the more famous Elijah del Medigo, who was fighting the new Platonic movement. Yet the neo-Platonist trend, which was strong in the north, especially in Florence, had its representatives in Naples, too. Especially inclined toward Platonism was the famous preacher Fra Egidio da Viterbo, who, like Pico della Mirandola, was also interested in cabalistic studies.[20] The extent to which Abravanel was influenced—if influenced at all—by any of the Neapolitan spiritual leaders, is perhaps impossible to determine. But it would not be too far-fetched to assume that his anti-Aristotelian position was encouraged by the Neo-Platonic movement in Italy, where Aristotelianism was sharply attacked, not so much from a religious, as from a philosophical point of view. The fact, furthermore, that his son, Judah, became a confirmed Neo-Platonist within the first years of their stay in Italy,[21] must have had a considerable effect on Abravanel, and it is perhaps to those days that we should attribute the beginning of his own positive attitude toward Plato. A few years later this attitude found expression in his philosophical work, *The Deeds of God.*[22]

In Naples, Abravanel found new happiness. The intellectual atmosphere and his renewed literary activity, together with his material and political successes, helped heal the wounds inflicted upon his soul by the exile from Spain. It was the second time he had built his home after it had been destroyed by political persecution. This time, he hoped, his home would stand. But then, as if to prove the ephemeral nature of human happiness, a heavy storm swiftly gathered and threatened to bring ruin and disaster upon the Neapolitan kingdom.

3. *In Sicilian Exile*

During the last decade of the fifteenth century, Italy, at the zenith of its Renaissance culture, was also at the height of political unrest. Divided into a dozen political entities, the Italian states were not based on uniform principle; they were monarchic, papal, feudal, and republican. To the bitter strife for power which raged within these states there was added an endless inter-state conflict. Politically, Italy was a house of cards. The whole structure was so delicately balanced that any serious trouble—from within or without—could easily upset it. And such trouble was brewing at the very time that the exiles from Spain settled in Naples.

Ferrante I had claims to Milan. According to him, control over Milan belonged to his grandson, who had already passed his minority but who was held in subjection by Ludovico Sforza, the real power in Milan and officially the regent. To offset these claims, Sforza incited France, to whose royal family Naples had belonged, to annex Naples to the French Crown.

The problem, then, which troubled the Neapolitan kingdom since the middle of 1493 was the danger of a French invasion. Charles VIII, the French monarch, was reported eager to conquer the kingdom. He knew that Naples could not muster a military force which would be a match for his army. The only factor which held him back was Ferdinand of Aragon. Naples was ruled by a branch of the Aragonese House and the official relations between Ferdinand and his kinsmen were marked by apparent understanding and cordiality. Yet it was no secret that Ferdinand, too, had designs on Naples. It was clear that France would not dare attack Naples if it received clear intimation from Ferdinand that he would resist such aggression. The efforts of both France and Naples were now bent upon securing Ferdinand's cooperation. A tense diplomatic battle ensued in which Ferdinand of Spain, while holding the best cards, played his game with utmost care and without revealing to either side his exact position and intentions. It may be assumed that at this juncture Don Isaac's opinions and advice, based as they were on his own acquaintance with Ferdinand, were considered by the Neapolitan rulers as worthy of special attention.

On January 25, 1494, Ferrante died, and in August of that

year Charles invaded Italy. When, a few months later, he reached Rome—and that last buffer state separating him from Naples had proved to be no shield for that kingdom—it was clear that the days of Naples were numbered. The hatred of both the nobility and the people toward the Neapolitan monarch, Alfonso, now manifested itself openly. Fearing insurrection and realizing his inability to organize resistance to the French, Alfonso, seized with panic, resolved to abdicate the throne and retire to Sicily. He was, however, so apprehensive that the rebellious populace of the capital might prevent him from implementing his plan that, according to Guicciardini, "he communicated his intention only to his mother-in-law, keeping it even from his brother and his son." The fact is, nevertheless, that besides his mother-in-law, he revealed his secret also to Don Isaac, who accompanied him to Sicily.[23]

It is very difficult to see any motive, other than sheer loyalty and friendship, for Abravanel's consent to accompany the king and leave his family, in confused times and in a land facing the invasion of the French who were known for their hostility to the Jews. Alfonso was in a state of mind which could arouse the compassion of a faithful courtier. Seeing Alfonso overwhelmed with fear, his kingdom facing ruin, his people rebellious, and hardly a friend left in whom to confide, Abravanel undoubtedly recalled how this monarch and his father had treated him and his brethren since their arrival in Naples. Despite all considerations to the contrary, he felt he could not abandon the king, even though he had abdicated, in his hour of greatest distress.[24]

On January 21, 1495, Abravanel, accompanying Alfonso, left Naples for Mazzara, a coastal town in southern Sicily which Alfonso had received the previous year as a gift from Ferdinand of Spain.[25] One month after Alfonso's departure—on February 22—Charles VIII entered Naples. The news of the occupation of the city, which must soon have reached Abravanel in Mazzara, was accompanied by reports on the pogrom which the Neapolitan population, assisted by the French, loosed against the Jews. The pogrom apparently almost destroyed the Neapolitan Jewish community. Although bloodshed appears to have been limited, many Jews were sold into slavery, while others were forced to embrace Christianity in order to escape a like fate. The Jewish quarters, of course, were thoroughly sacked and among the homes plundered was that of

Abravanel. "My entire enormous wealth was stolen," he writes, and much of his precious library as well as the manuscript of *Eternal Justice* were lost. The outrages of the French soldiery and the populace caused thousands of Jews to flee the city,[26] and, although Charles restored order, the emigration of the Jews continued. Among those who left Naples after the pogrom was Abravanel's son, Judah, who settled in Genoa as a physician.[27] Don Isaac, too, seems then to have decided to move the remainder of his family from Naples. His youngest son, Samuel, was studying in Saloniki, and Abravanel sent instructions to his family in Naples to prepare for departure there.[28]

In the meantime the political scene changed. On March 31, a Holy League was formed, consisting of the Pope, the Emperor, Spain, Venice and Milan, with the aim of ousting the French from Italy. Such a powerful combination, Abravanel might have thought, would restore the Neapolitans to their former position. It is most likely that he thereupon instructed his family to stay on in Naples for some time longer.

According to some contemporaries of Alfonso, his intention at the time of his abdication was to abandon forever any interest in politics and devote himself to the life of a hermit. The man who, as Comines said, "never kept Lent, nor so much as pretended to do it," now lived, according to the same source, "a most strict and austere life, serving God at all hours both of day and night," and "spending his time in prayers, fasting and alms."[29] This is further evidence that Comines was too extreme in his denunciation of the king's character. A man who was capable of such a transformation was not, as Comines intended to convey, a hardened, incorrigible criminal. Yet it would be wrong to assume that Alfonso spent all his time in fasting and prayer only. Despite his abdication, he was considered by the allies, and especially by Venice, as a king in exile, and hardly a move was taken by them without informing or consulting him.[30] Abravanel, therefore, was not completely cut off from political life, but, as we may readily assume, was fully informed of developments and was offering the king counsel on current problems. Perhaps he also succeeded in reviving Alfonso's interest in the throne.

On April 20, the king, accompanied by Abravanel, left Mazzara for Palermo. A Spanish fleet, headed by Admiral Requesens, was expected in Sicily, and plans for the invasion of Naples from the south were already under way. It is clear that Alfonso as well as his Jewish counsellor desired to be nearer the scene of action. In Palermo, where Alfonso was accepted with royal honors,[31] they stayed, therefore, only a short time, and proceeded to Messina which was the major base of the Spanish and Neapolitan invasion forces. In the second half of May, Ferrante II was already fighting in Calabria, and, on May 24, a Spanish expeditionary force arrived which was headed by Gonsalvo de Cordova who, in the course of the Italian wars, was destined to become famous as "the Great Captain." Gonsalvo, brother of Alfonso de Aguilar, was a familiar figure in the Court of the Spanish kings. His attitude toward the Jews was marked by that liberality which was typical of most of the nobles of Spain and especially characteristic of his famous brother.[32] Abravanel undoubtedly knew him from Spain, and although Gonsalvo stayed in Messina only two days,[33] it can be safely assumed that he met Abravanel, Alfonso's closest companion. It was perhaps this renewed acquaintance with the Spanish general that laid the foundation for the friendly relations which later developed between Gonsalvo and Abravanel's son, Judah.

The arrival of the Spanish expeditionary force, together with the events that had preceded it—the landing of the naval forces of Requesens, the first victories of Ferrante in Calabria, and the departure of Charles VIII from Naples (on May 20)—were hopeful signs for future developments. Most important of all, the attitude of the Neapolitans toward their former monarch changed in the extreme under the oppressive rule of the French, and "now," we are told, "the hateful name of Alfonso became agreeable to them, calling just severity that which they had been wont to note in him as cruelty, and interpreting as true sincerity of mind that which wrongfully they had been wont to consider pride and fierceness."[34] The abdicated king must soon have learned of this change of heart while still in Messina, and there is little doubt that his earlier vague hope of re-ascending the throne of Naples—a hope which, as we have indicated, might have been nurtured by Abravanel—now became an ardent wish.[35] Nevertheless, it was in those days that Alfonso, "despaired and discontented," left Messina and returned to Palermo where he entered the monastery of Monreal.[36] The reason for Alfonso's "despair" must be sought in the strained relations between him and his son. "These were times," writes Guicciardini, while discussing the morals of the political circles of that age, "in which the love of children for their parents was rare," and there is sufficient evidence to conclude that the attitude of Ferrante II toward his father did not represent one of those rare cases.[37] When the abdicated king and the ruling king met, the latter must have made it abundantly clear that he had no intention of yielding the throne.

If Abravanel had any hopes of again becoming a power in Naples under a renewed rule by Alfonso, such hopes must now have been shattered. And, when Alfonso resolved on escaping the world by assuming the monastic habit, Abravanel, the Jew, clearly could not follow him. Abravanel, then, remained in Messina,[38] although, as is obvious, for a brief time only. Messina, it must be remembered, was Spanish soil, and the presence of a Jew there was tolerated only so long as he was part of the king's suite. To stay there after the king's departure was undoubtedly difficult or, at least, most unpleasant. Abravanel, nevertheless, might have lingered on for a few additional days, perhaps considering passage to Reggio, in Calabria, which was then occupied by the Neapolitans, until he heard the news of the crushing defeat at Seminara which the combined forces of Ferrante and Gonsalvo suffered at the hands of the French. It seems that it was at that moment—with the end of the war appearing far off, its outcome uncertain, and his continued stay in Messina viewed with dislike by the authorities—that Abravanel decided to execute his plan, which he had harbored for a number of months, of leaving Italy and settling in Turkey. It was, therefore, we believe, in the second half of June that Abravanel left Messina.

4. A Visit to Corfu

The isle of Corfu was in those days an important way-station on a journey to Turkey. One needed only to cross the narrow straits separating Corfu from the mainland of Greece to be on Turkish territory. But Corfu was also a station for those who proceeded by sea to Constantinople or to the eastern parts of Greece. Corfu was under Venetian rule and, as in all Venetian possessions, the Jews of the island were free from the disabilities imposed on Jews in Venice proper, and their prosperous community could even absorb a considerable number of the exiles from Spain who passed through the island on their way to Turkey. Abravanel went to Corfu from Messina,[39] apparently with the intention of awaiting there the arrival of members of his family from Naples so that together they might proceed to Saloniki.

In Corfu Abravanel found a large group of exiles, including a number of Jewish notables, who had either come directly from Spain or escaped from Naples and other Italian cities which were occupied by the French. Among them was David ibn Yaḥya, the Lisbon preacher and the nephew of the Yaḥyas, Alfonso V's courtiers, who had been in Naples during the French pogrom and now was on his way to Turkey. Among them also was Eliezer Tanusi, scholar, physician and Abravanel's admirer, who was to rise to prominence in Turkey, as well as other men of learning.[40] To Abravanel, who for months had been cut off from Jewish society, the intellectual companionship of some of these men was undoubtedly a stimulus. At the same time, he was dismayed to note the great change that the misfortunes of exile had wrought in many an admired personality. As Abravanel put it, he had the feeling as if the "spirit of God" had departed from these people, and thus some he had considered "intellectual giants" appeared to him now as "broken pots of clay." In Corfu, furthermore, Abravanel noticed that sinister moral development which is typical of uprooted people, that total engrossment in material values, that abandonment of all interest in intellectual pursuits, that open or concealed contempt for everything spiritual, and that hunt after enjoyment and games and pleasures, which is the product of belief in the passing moment as well as of a desire to forget the past; he saw all this and he was deeply distressed. A year later, when writing his *Inheritance,* he gave expression to the grief he felt in Corfu over the spiritual deterioration of Spanish Jewry.[41] This was, to his mind, a greater misfortune than all the physical sufferings they had endured.

Once more relieved from service to kings, Abravanel resumed his literary activity. Having completed his commentaries on the Former Prophets, he turned to Isaiah, the first of the Latter

Prophets according to the traditional order of the Bible. The work was soon suspended, however, perhaps because the stirring events in Italy diverted his attention to historical problems. He may then have begun to write *The Days of the World,* a work in which he sought to give an account of the disasters that befell the Jewish people and to show the relationship between these disasters and the great upheavals in the history of mankind.[42] If such was the case, however, this work too was soon interrupted, this time the reason being an occurrence which was as joyful as it was unexpected. Abravanel found in Corfu a copy of the manuscript of his unfinished commentary on Deuteronomy which he had written decades earlier but had been lost in consequence of his flight from Portugal. In his great joy over the find,[43] he may have concentrated on the completion of that work first. But the task was not accomplished in Corfu; for in the meantime developments took place that must have changed Abravanel's plans and called for his return to Italy.

It seems that neither Abravanel nor any of his sons was anxious to migrate to a Moslem country. They were all steeped in European culture and accustomed to European ways of life. For them to settle in Turkey meant to separate themselves from a civilization in which they saw, not only faults, but also much beauty and genius. If an opening presented itself, therefore, for their continued stay in Italy, the plan of settling in the land of the Turks would readily be dropped. And such an opening actually appeared shortly after Abravanel's departure for Corfu.

When Abravanel left Messina, we have noted, the French still held Naples in their grip. Toward the end of June, however, Ferrante, despite the great defeat at Seminara, hastily recruited a new force and succeeded in landing before the gates of Naples. Assisted by the populace, who rose against the French, he soon established himself in the city. The French still maintained a position in Naples by their command of the city's fortress, but in October the French garrison surrendered and Ferrante could safely leave the city to prosecute the war in other zones.[44] Under these circumstances Abravanel's family in Naples—consisting of his wife, his son-in-law, Joseph, the latter's family, and perhaps also the family of Joseph, Abravanel's son[45]—decided to stay on in Naples and there await the end of hostilities which now seemed not too remote.

For Abravanel, however, to return to Naples at a time when French ships were cruising the seas along the shores of the Neapolitan kingdom was obviously a risky undertaking. He wished, nevertheless, to leave Corfu, now that the Turkish plan was abandoned, and settle somewhere in the Neapolitan area where he could maintain easier communication with his family and be nearer to them at the war's end. But where could Abravanel go? Calabria was still a theater of war. Most of Apulia was still occupied by the French. There was, it seemed to him, only one suitable place: Monopoli, and there he went.

5. Monopoli: Shelter in the Storm

The town of Monopoli, a seaport on the Adriatic, halfway between Brindisi and Bari, belonged to the kingdom of Naples. It was held, however, neither by the Neapolitans nor by the French; for, on June 29, a short time after Abravanel had left Messina for Corfu, the Venetian navy, under Antonio Grimani, captured Monopoli from the hands of the French.[46] The investment of this town by Venice, a member of the anti-French League, was a move in the direction of the allied war aims. Yet those who knew Venetian policies could not help suspecting that Venice also sought, under the cover of these war aims, to capture for herself certain positions on the strategically important south-western Adriatic, and that she was likely to defend these positions with all her might. The fact, in any case, that Abravanel left peaceful Corfu and went to Monopoli, which was in the war-zone and which, as it appeared, was likely to become a special objective for re-conquest by the French, indicates his faith in the power of the Republic whose strength and efficiency he no doubt felt in Corfu. In fact, when Abravanel left for Monopoli, this town was strongly held under Venetian administration, serving as an important naval fortress and a base of operations against the French.[47]

His departure for Monopoli took place, in all likelihood, in November or December 1495, shortly after he had received the news of the French capitulation in Naples. We have definite information of his presence in Monopoli, however, only from February 6, 1496, the day on which he completed his commentary on Deuteronomy.[48] It seems that soon after his arrival in Monopoli he resumed his literary activity; but his commentary on Deuteronomy is not at all typical of the rest of his writings there. The completion of this commentary must rather be considered a continuation of his previous literary effort. Soon thereafter, however, there began in his life a new period of creativity—a period inspired by new feelings, new motives, and a new set of ideas.

In Monopoli, Abravanel was relieved for the first time from the pressure of political and social duties; he was at long last free from the various distractions which until then had interfered with his literary plans. Here were those ideal conditions for speculation which he had sought so eagerly and so long. Yet in these externally peaceful surroundings he lacked what he needed most: peace of mind. A painful feeling of loneliness gripped him, the feeling that attacks strangers in foreign lands; and the tragedy of homelessness, of exile, of poverty—his financial resources being almost at their end—now dawned upon him with all its gruesomeness.[49]

He was then 58 years of age. He felt old, weak and abandoned. After a lifetime of enormous effort, he saw himself empty-handed. All he could call his own was his waning physical strength, deteriorating eyesight, and a heart confused, embittered and depressed with disappointment and failure.[50]

These pessimistic thoughts, however, were soon dwarfed by broader considerations. For his personal troubles, he clearly came to realize, were but an insignificant part of the great tragedy that had befallen his people. Filled with deep reverence for their power of endurance, he continued (or commenced) writing his *Days of the World,* in which he sought to present the manifestations of this power.[51] But work on this theme was soon suspended. The calamities of the present were too real, and Abravanel's thoughts turned upon the future rather than upon the past. How long could the Jews take such punishment, he asked himself, if the outlook for the future remained as bleak as the present? The problem of redemption became uppermost in his mind, and it was in his commentary on the Passover tales, which he called *Passover Sacrifice,* a work which deals with the first redemption of the Jews, that we first find him dealing in an elaborate manner with the problem of redemption.

He completed his *Passover Sacrifice* in April, and immediately began writing his *Inheritance of the Fathers*.[52] The *Inheritance*, a commentary on *Abot* (Ethics of the Fathers), was composed at the request of Samuel, his youngest son, who was still studying in Saloniki.[53] In it Abravanel expressed his great concern over the moral state of his people in general, and particularly over the rising materialistic tendencies which he noted among the survivors of the exile. As he saw it, the only real value the Jews still possessed, indeed the only asset which gave meaning to their suffering, was the moral heritage which they had guarded throughout the ages and which now was placed in jeopardy. Was it worthwhile to endure so many hardships, so many trials and tribulations for the sake of this heritage? His book aimed to provide an answer. And the answer is given through the presentation and interpretation of the teachings of Israel's sages. This, then, is the inheritance of the Fathers; behold how lofty, how inspiring it is! It is the essence of all truth, the meaning of all beauty, the sum-total of all virtue! And it is even more than all that: for it is the word of God as transmitted by inspired men! What can be more glorious than to guard such a heritage? What can be baser than to betray it? Yet that such betrayal was becoming widespread was a fact that could not be denied. The frightful thought passed Abravanel's mind that the day was approaching when interest in the divine teachings would completely disappear from Israel. "And what shall I do for you, my son?" Sorrowfully he utters the sacred oath: "If you forget the law of God, let my right hand forget its cunning!"[54]

The *Inheritance of the Fathers* was Abravanel's testimony to the worthwhileness of the suffering which the Jews endured; but it left unanswered the basic questions which kept troubling his mind. What was the reason for the suffering? Would there ever be an end to it? He heard these questions asked repeatedly since that tragic journey from Spain. Before his eyes passed all the tragedies he had witnessed or which had been brought to his knowledge. He saw the old dying on the roads, the young expiring of famine and plague, the mothers fainting with their children in their arms, the people taking their own lives.[55] And then his mind encompassed the horrors felt by those who remained in Spain and who apparently had left the fold. There must be a reason for all this suffering, and there must be an end.

His personal problems were now pushed far into the background. His mind was occupied more and more with that endless gallery of vivid, horrifying visions; his heart was filled with the agony of the martyrs;[56] and he found himself sinking deeper and deeper into a nightmarish state. The experience was overpowering. He felt as though he were "drinking poisonous wine" or taking in "venom of snakes." He felt as though his "essence was being poured out," his strength leaving him, and he heard his "soul sighing" from the depth of grief.[57] Weaker spirits might have cracked under the pressure of such emotions; but Abravanel shook off the visions of horror, and his mind began to look for a constructive way out.

He reflected over the events of his lifetime, the rise of Turkey, the growth of Ferdinand's power, the development of the Italian war. Was not the tragedy of his people part and parcel of the great earthquake which was shaking all nations? Here, in this town of Monopoli, in whose harbor was lying the great armada of Venice, and through which Venetian forces were marching to the battlefields, he was constantly reminded of the great war which was being waged in Apulia and in Central Italy—a war into which not only the whole of Italy was plunged but also France and Spain and Germany. Was the Spanish-Granadan war a mere episode? Was the French invasion an accident? Or were all these wars perhaps merely a prelude to a wider, indeed, a universal, revolution which held both the certainty of the greatest disaster and the promise of the brightest hope? Was not the hand of Providence behind these events and behind the harsh punishment they entailed for God's people?

On July 21, the war in Italy ended with a total victory for the allies. Ferrante II was reinstated as king of Naples; but Abravanel would not leave Monopoli. For he was engrossed, at that very time, in writing his *Wells of Salvation,* the first part of a messianic trilogy, in which he prophesied the future course of the world and suggested the year 1503 as the most likely date of the redemption.[58] It was only in January of the next year (1497) that the work was completed; and, after taking, as it appears, a short rest, Abravanel proceeded to make a thorough survey of the mystical parts of post-biblical literature as well as of all the biblical passages in which he found allusions to redemption.[59] The results of these studies, which aimed to substantiate the views and prophecies he expressed in the *Wells*, were comprised in two separate volumes—*The Salvations of His Anointed* and *The Announcer of Salvation*, which were intended to form the remaining parts of his comprehensive essay on redemption. With the completion of the *Announcer*, on February 26, 1498, the messianic trilogy was finished. It was the most original, most significant and most inspiring of Abravanel's works, and the greatest work that was ever composed on the messianic problem until his time.

His literary urge, however, was still far from spent. He now felt the need to strengthen and expand the theoretical foundations of the great miracle of redemption. Soon after completing his trilogy, therefore, he wrote his *New Heavens*, in which he sought to demonstrate from the order of the heavens the theory of Creation (*ex nihilo*) and to coordinate that theory with Maimonides' view.[60] Then he returned to his commentary on Isaiah which he had begun to write in Corfu, but which now, under the influence of his messianic views assumed an entirely new character.[61] On August 19, 1498, the commentary on Isaiah was completed;[62] then, on August 23, 1499, he completed his commentary on the Minor Prophets,[62a] and the end of this work seemed to mark an end to the tempestuous writing in which he had been engaged for almost four years.

In his commentary on Isaiah, as well as in each of the three parts of his messianic trilogy, Abravanel predicted a world conflict between Christendom and Turkey. As if to substantiate these predictions, shortly after the Isaiah commentary had been completed, war clouds appeared on the horizon, heralding the Turkish-Venetian war which broke out in June 1499. On July 28, the Turks emerged victorious in the great naval battle at Sapienza, which was soon followed by their seizure of Lepanto and the capture of most of the Morea. But the following year, the tide of battle turned when the Venetians, assisted by Spanish forces, defeated the Turks at Cephalonia. In Monopoli, the Venetian naval base, the impact of the war must have been strongly felt, and although we have no direct indication of Abravanel's reaction to the ebb and flow of battle, the period of the Turkish-Venetian conflict must have been for him one of great suspense; for we know that he was tensely awaiting the fulfillment of his prophecies.[63]

It is difficult to believe that all these years Abravanel remained detached from his family. Not before the end of the Turkish-Venetian war, however, do we find members of his family in Monopoli or its neighborhood. On February 6, 1501, Joseph, Abravanel's nephew, visited Gonsalvo de Cordova in Messina[64] (the latter having returned only the previous month from his campaign against the Turks), and it is most likely that this visit was connected with a visit to Abravanel. In the same year we find Joseph's brother, Jacob, staying and even doing business in Monopoli's neighboring port, Bari.[65] In the same year again, we find Judah Abravanel visiting his father in Barletta, also an Apulian seaport on the Adriatic and not very far from Monopoli. It is clear that the whole family, attracted by Abravanel, moved to the eastern part of the kingdom. Yet it was for a temporary stay only. For in Naples conditions were restored to normal and the ruling king, Federigo, the successor to Ferrante II, was friendly to the Jews and especially to the Abravanels.[66] The friendly disposition of the king no doubt served as an inducement also for Don Isaac to return to the city of Naples. And thus, on May 10, 1501, the king issued an order to the authorities of Barletta to assist the "esteemed" Don Isaac Abravanel, "whom we hold dear," as well as his son Judah and their families, in connection with their planned journey to the capital.[67] Such an order implied a royal invitation. But even as this invitation reached Barletta, and while the Abravanels must have been preparing for departure, another political storm was gathering which was soon again to bring havoc and ruin upon the unfortunate kingdom of Naples. The second French invasion was about to begin.

On June 1, 1501, the forces of Louis XII, Charles VIII's successor, crossed the Alps on their way to Naples in accordance with a secret French-Spanish treaty which stipulated the partition of Naples between these powers. On July 5, the Spanish forces, again headed by Gonsalvo de Cordova, began their invasion of Naples from the south and three days later, on July 8, the French crossed the Neapolitan border from the north. Judah, perhaps, ventured to go to Naples.[68] But Don Isaac, convinced of the coming of war and of the hopelessness of the Neapolitan situation, obviously refrained from making the trip. It is not likely, however, that he remained in Barletta which, according to the partition treaty, was to fall into Spanish hands. In all probability he returned to Monopoli which was still under Venetian rule, and indeed was to remain in Venetian hands until 1509.[69]

In about a month after the beginning of the invasion the Neapolitan kingdom collapsed. Peace was re-established. But Abravanel continued to stay in Monopoli. It was at that time that he wrote his *Deeds of God,* his most important and most artistic philosophical work. In the *Deeds of God* we find, as we have indicated, expressions of great admiration for Plato, and this development may be partly attributed, not only to Italy's intellectual environment, but also to Judah's particular influence at that very time. For when Judah visited his father in Barletta, he seems already to have composed the first part of his *Dialoghi d'Amore,* and stirred by the thoughts of this Neo-Platonic work, he no doubt discussed them with his father.[70] The *Dialoghi d'Amore* and the *Deeds of God* have, in fact, a number of fundamental ideas in common;[71] and yet they differ in the main thesis. While the aim of the *Dialoghi* is to explain the workings of the divine principle of love in the cosmos, the aim of the *Deeds* is to prove and expound the principle of divine power. As in *New Heavens* so in the *Deeds* Abravanel sought to support his theory on the possibility of a divine, miraculous redemption.

In July war broke out again—this time between Spain and France—for the possession of the entire territory of Naples. Barletta, where we found Don Isaac and his son shortly before the twin invasion, now served as the main fort of Gonsalvo's besieged forces. On April 28, 1503, however, the Great Captain emerged from the "old den," as Barletta came to be called, won his decisive victory in Cerignola, and finally, on May 14, victoriously entered Naples. We have seen that Abravanel's son-in-law, Joseph, had had dealings with Gonsalvo already in 1501; and Judah became, soon after the conquest, Gonsalvo's private physician.[72] Don Isaac, however, appears to have resolved not to return to Spanish territory. When, therefore, Joseph, his son, visited him in Monopoli shortly after the restoration of peace and invited him to proceed with him to Venice, where Joseph was engaged in the practice of medicine, Abravanel must have welcomed the invitation.[73]

The period of his stay in Monopoli had thus ended after seven and one half years. Abravanel had passed there one of the stormiest epochs in Italian and European politics as well as the most creative epoch in his life. That this had been possible was largely due to the particular location and condition of Monopoli. For Monopoli, although always in a theater of war, was also an island of peace. And thus Abravanel had been given there the opportunity of viewing events at close range, of being in direct touch with developments, and also of analyzing them peacefully and presenting his conclusions in writing. One usually likes places where one has been creative; and Abravanel, it appears, came to like Monopoli, or else he would not have stayed there that long. In any case, when he said farewell to the little fortress-town on the Adriatic, he did not experience the bitter taste of disappointment he had had at the conclusion of other phases of his life.

CHAPTER FOUR

VENICE: THE LAST REFUGE

1. New Rise to Prominence

ABRAVANEL'S arrival in Venice meant the end of his wanderings. Venice was going to be his last refuge, and it was, by a stroke of good fortune, a peaceful refuge as well.

In 1503, Venice was, by all external signs, at the zenith of her power. Barely half a year before Abravanel's arrival, on December 24, 1502, she concluded a peace treaty with Turkey by which she regained all of the possessions she had lost during the war of 1499–1500. Still controlling, despite the rise of Turkey, most of the strategic islands in the Mediterranean—including Cyprus, which she acquired in 1488—Venice was considered the major sea power. Her territorial expansion in Italy, moreover, was never as great as at that time. Comines, the French ambassador, described it as the "most triumphant city" he had ever seen.[1]

The splendor of Venice was great; yet its leaders knew full well that the Republic had been dealt some fatal blows. Her territorial expansion could not compensate for the losses suffered in her wars with the Turks; her treasury was exhausted, and her chances for replenishing her wealth had dwindled as a result of a new, menacing development. This was the discovery by Vasco da Gama, the Portuguese navigator and explorer, of the ocean route to India.[2]

The wealth of Venice derived from her monopoly of the eastern trade. This had been an inexhaustible source of income, enabling Venice repeatedly to stand vast financial loss. The Turkish expansion had hit her trading colonies in Greece, but her lifeline to the East had remained unsevered. For Venice thereupon strengthened her ties with Egypt, which commanded the sea route to India, and thus continued to import spices, although at a much higher cost.

The discovery of Vasco da Gama, however, threatened to stop this source of income. For now spices could be brought to

Europe by a direct ocean route and at a much lower price. The course of world commerce was about to take a turn which would bypass Venice altogether, and the Venetians, fully aware of the consequences, were frantically trying to avert disaster. First, they pointed out to the Egyptian sultan that if the Portuguese were permitted to trade with India, Egypt, like Venice, would be the loser, and they tried to induce Egypt to blockade the Indian coast against the Portuguese.[3] But Egypt was militarily unprepared for such action. Plans for building a Suez Canal, or of sending a Venetian fleet through the Straits of Gibraltar to the Indian Ocean were similarly abandoned as impractical. There was little left but to recognize the bitter fact: the sea route to India was open to Portugal. All that Venice could now attempt was to obtain from Portugal the kind of monopoly she had previously received from Egypt. But the chances for achieving this aim were slight: Venice did not control the routes from Portugal to Europe as she controlled those leading from the Eastern Mediterranean lands.[4]

It was at this critical stage for the Republic that Abravanel came to live in Venice. And shortly after his arrival he submitted to the *Consiglio dei Dieci,* the all-powerful Venetian Council of Ten, a plan for the regulation of the trade in spices which he believed could be accepted by both Venice and Portugal. Abravanel appeared in person before the *Dieci,* and here again his personality and presentation made a powerful impression. From an extant official summary of a meeting of the Council, at which Abravanel's proposal was discussed, it is clear that the prudent leaders of the Republic noticed the "good qualities and virtue of his person." They, furthermore, sensed his admiration for the Republic and his friendly disposition toward its leadership, and they were under the influence of the "serious and appropriate words" with which he had "ingratiated himself" to the Signoria. As for Abravanel's plan, they obviously considered it most advantageous for Venice, as the Council undertook not to "depart from these terms which seem reasonable and proper." They assured Abravanel that "if the matter truly comes out well, there will be nothing to stain the customary gratitude of our state."[5]

The gratitude which the Council promised to show was, however, not only for the plan, but also for its implementation. For Abravanel offered his services as mediator, and also proposed to send his nephew to Portugal for the purpose of conducting the negotiations.[6] The Council, having obviously considered Abravanel, a former minister of Portugal and now resident of Venice, a most suitable negotiator in this matter, approved of the proposal,[7] and consequently there can be little doubt that Abravanel's nephew was sent to Portugal to obtain an agreement from the king.[8]

That Abravanel, against whom a death sentence for treason had been issued in Portugal in 1485, could now offer his services for a purpose whose achievement depended on the good will of that state, must be attributed to the fact that the ruling king, Manuel, the successor to João II, was the brother of the same Duke of Viseu whom João had killed at his palace in Setubal. The attitude of Manuel to the alleged rebels is indicated by his invitation to the princes of Braganza to return to and stay in Portugal; and although he might have known that the accusations of conspiracy against the Abravanels were unfounded, he still might have considered them, in view of all they had suffered, victims of the same cause for which his brother had lost his life. Thus, far from harboring hostility for the Abravanels, he might have had a latent sympathy for them. Joseph Abravanel, as already noted, had been financial manager for the Duke of Viseu and it is a safe assumption that Joseph was the nephew whom Abravanel suggested as a messenger to Portugal.

The embarkation of Abravanel on a scheme which aimed at the solution of the Venetian-Portuguese economic conflict—a scheme which involved not alone the two greatest maritime powers of the time, but also the entire course of world commerce—shows the vastness of enterprise, breadth of conception and originality of planning which characterized Abravanel as a financier. In becoming a mediator between Venice and Portugal, Abravanel became an international factor of first rate importance. On Abravanel's mediation was now focused the attention not only of Portugal and Venice, but also of all the states and economic powers that had a direct interest in their outcome. Although the negotiations ended in failure, Portugal's reply having been negative,[9] the chiefs of the Republic continued to view Abravanel's efforts with the highest appreciation.[10] Evidently they recognized the force of the opposition and were certain that the negotiations failed, not because of Abravanel's conduct, but rather in spite of it. In fact, for the

Venetian rulers Abravanel remained an admirable figure to the end of his days.

2. The Final Efforts

The mediation between Venice and Portugal seems to be the only —and last—financial-diplomatic action in which Abravanel was engaged. Even while the negotiations were in progress, let alone after they had ended (1505), Abravanel devoted his entire free time to literary work. He was sixty-six years old when he arrived in Venice, and he was harassed by the thought that his literary aims were still far from fulfilled. Of the Latter Prophets, he had written commentaries only on Isaiah and the Minor Prophets, and of the Pentateuch only on Deuteronomy. Other literary projects he had begun working on were also awaiting completion. Thus, he wanted to rewrite his lost—and unfinished—*Vision of God*, which he hoped would serve as a "divine candle" for shedding light upon the mystery of prophecy.[11] He wanted to complete his *Eternal Justice*, which he had begun to write in Naples,[12] and his *Days of the World*, which he had started writing in Corfu (or Monopoli). And on top of all this, there was still the unfinished commentary on the *Guide*. He realized that the completion of these projects would require years of labor, and time was running out.

With his arrival in Venice, there began Abravanel's third period of literary activity, and it is well to note the difference between this period and the earlier one in Monopoli. The difference lies in the intensity of feeling and originality of ideas. In Monopoli, Abravanel had drawn very radical and extreme conclusions from his mystical world outlook. In Venice, he continued on the same path. But whereas the Monopoli period was one of "storm and stress," of revolutionary thinking in whatever Abravanel wrote, his works in Venice were characterized by a calmness and self-confidence which often are the evidence of a perfected system.

Three of Abravanel's works—*The Inheritance, Passover Sacrifice,* and the *Principles*—were published in Constantinople in 1505. These were the first of his works to be given to the press, and Judah Abravanel, who visited his father in Venice that year, wrote for each of them poetical dedications from which shine forth, not only his great love, but also his undiminished admiration for his father.¹³ The fact that Judah, whose philosophical system was in those days fully evolved, still considered his father his spiritual master, shows how deep was the father's influence on the development of the son's views. Indeed, their mutual admiration continued to the end of Don Isaac's days. In 1507, on the occasion of a second visit by Judah, Abravanel speaks of him as of the "choicest of all the philosophers in Italy in this generation."¹⁴

In 1505, Abravanel completed his commentaries on the Latter Prophets, in which he followed the principles laid down in his *Announcer,* and in which he also clarified or supplemented many points in his messianic scheme.¹⁵ Soon thereafter he began work on the first four books of the Pentateuch, incorporating there his final conclusions regarding the major historical, philosophical and political problems with which he had dealt in earlier works.¹⁶ The commentary on the Pentateuch may be considered, therefore, Abravanel's most authoritative presentation of his views, and it was not without good reason that he considered it the first and foremost of his works. As Abravanel put it: "I invested in it all my thought and all my knowledge."¹⁷

With the completion of this work, in 1506 or 1507, he completed the interpretation of the entire Bible, with the exception of the Hagiographa, of which he dealt only with Daniel. He seems to have had no desire to write a commentary on the Hagiographa, perhaps because he felt that he had said all he could say within the framework of a biblical commentary. He now hoped for the completion of his other cherished plans, and undoubtedly resumed work on them.¹⁸ But in March 1507, a diversion took place which occasioned, instead of the completion of old works, the writing of a new one. Saul ha-Kohen Ashkenazi, an author of philosophical works and a former disciple of the afore-mentioned Aristotelian thinker, Eliah del Medigo, addressed to him twelve philosophical queries, particularly with a view to ascertaining the position taken by Maimonides on the questions involved. Abravanel's answers to these queries constitute his sharpest and weightiest attack against the Averroist interpreters of Maimonides, and it is here that we find him at last relieved from the long and arduous internal struggle he had conducted with Maimonidean thought.

Abravanel's independence is especially noticeable in his clear analysis of the points of difference and agreement between him and Maimonides.[19] It is not unlikely that after completing this book, Abravanel returned to systematic work on his great commentary on the *Guide*.[20]

When he wrote his *Answers to Saul,* Abravanel was already seventy years old. He was at the height of his thinking capacity, but his physical strength was fast waning. In his letter to Saul, he complains of his weakness, his poor eyesight and his inability to write his works with his own hand.[21] He was also considerably distressed by the fact that his prophecies of redemption still remained unfulfilled, although there are clear indications that he kept his hopes alive. His literary work was his chief consolation, and he kept at it with tenacity and holy zeal, drawing heavily on his last reserves of strength. The end could, of course, not be far off. Exhausted, after a relentless literary effort which followed a turbulent political career, Abravanel died, at the age of seventy-one, in November 1508.[22] Since under the laws of Venice the burial of Jews was prohibited within the city, his body was taken for interment to Padua; but he was given the last honors by the leaders of the Republic, as well as by leaders of his own people.[23] It was an irregular ceremony, but most suitable in this case. For it symbolized, in a way, the dual course—the spiritual and political, the national and international—which Abravanel had followed throughout his eventful life.

3. Summary

The life of Don Isaac Abravanel as presented here is based on the conclusions we felt could be derived with a measure of certainty from the material available. The material, however, is often insufficient; and the biographer, who does not want to substitute imagination for fact, must keep within the bounds of recorded history. Yet the life of a man who served six kings, was associated with the most powerful personalities in Portugal and Spain, Naples and Venice, must necessarily have been far richer, more complex and more stimulating than this biography might suggest. Additional material from the archives of the states in which Abravanel lived may in time fill certain gaps in the picture here drawn. It is doubtful, however, whether the picture as a whole will change materially. The life of a diplomat or a king's counsellor—usually concealed from public scrutiny—is often half-lost to posterity. The life of such a man, and a Jew at that, in the Middle Ages, is especially apt to be obscured. Yet so great was Abravanel's influence upon his time that his image stands out clearly. Furthermore, from the material available we may draw certain general conclusions which may help sharpen its basic outlines.

Abravanel, as we have seen, employed his efforts in three major fields: the general diplomatic-financial, the Jewish communal-political, and the scholarly-spiritual. In each Abravanel attained great heights, and in each he manifested, not only different propensities, but also a different measure of ability and achievement.

It is clear that as a diplomat and financier, Abravanel was endowed with great ingenuity as well as with a magnetic, captivating personality. He would not otherwise have succeeded in rising so quickly, almost overnight, after each fall, and this while in the humiliating status of a fugitive or an exile in a foreign land. It was due to these outstanding qualities that he became not only the constant associate of kings, courtiers, magnates and state councillors, but also—which was unique in Jewish statesmanship in the Middle Ages—a figure of international stature. This fact in particular must be borne in mind. For that broad, international, world-embracing view which we find, as we shall see, in Abravanel's theories is largely the result of this fact.

For his people, Abravanel stood forth as the foremost leader, guide and spokesman.[24] His many-sided distinctions, his position in world politics, his vast and varied learning, his mastery of many subjects, particularly in matters Jewish, his devotion to his people's cause, and the great encouragement he offered them in his wonderful books on redemption—all these combined to create widespread and unlimited admiration for him. The Jews considered him the "great eagle" (in learning),[25] "as wise as Daniel" (in politics),[26] and a "man of God" (in morals and personality).[27] The very fact that he was held in such admiration was in itself a factor of historic importance. In times of tragedy and disaster like those in which his Jewish contemporaries lived, nothing so fortifies a people's morale as does a great leader whom they can revere and follow.

Considered from an historical standpoint, however, Abravanel's Jewish leadership did not merit such unreserved praise. There were probably few Jewish spokesmen in the Middle Ages who were as tactful, inspiring and eloquent as he. There were probably few who faced more difficult tasks and could register greater achievements. What Abravanel did for the Jews of Portugal, Spain or Naples can only be guessed at from the general information and the few details that have been preserved; but there is no doubt that his presence and activity in the leading circles of these states were powerful factors in favor of the Jews. That he was, indeed, as was said about him, "a fortress and a shield for his people," a "saviour of the oppressed from the hands of their enemies," and that he virtually "rescued Jews from the lions"[28] cannot be doubted. Yet, despite all these achievements, which undoubtedly contributed to make him popular and admired, there was a serious fault in Abravanel's leadership which cannot be overlooked.

It is doubtful whether Abravanel or any one else could have succeeded in changing anything substantial in the situation which confronted the Jews of Europe at the time. The historic current in which Jewry was swept was too strong to be resisted, and Abravanel therefore cannot be criticized for failing to arrest the raging tide. His responsibility, however, lay in his failure to sense the strength and direction of that tide and to issue a timely warning to his brethren when means of rescue were still possible. In other words, his fault lay with his policy. It was a policy which tried to resist the current, to save here and there those engulfed in its course, and stop the gaps through which it broke. Significantly he was described as one who "mends the breaches."[29] But the breaches could not be mended. And it is here where Abravanel's great error lay.

We have seen that this error of judgment was not peculiar to Abravanel, that it was shared at least by the majority of Spain's Jews, and we have tried to point out the causes which contributed to the development of that falsely optimistic view. But besides the general reasons which were common to his contemporaries, there was a personal reason which made Abravanel especially apt to make such an error. This was inherent in the third feature which was dominant in Abravanel's life—his devotion to abstract speculation.

As financier and diplomat in the general field of politics, Abravanel must have been a down-to-earth realist. Otherwise, he could not have gone very far with the shrewd and hard-boiled realist rulers, whose material interests he served with distinction. As a thinker, however, Abravanel was a mystic. Between these two opposite spheres of activity there was an area of contact, namely, his activity in Jewish leadership. As a Jewish leader, Abravanel was simultaneously realistic and mystical. Not only his general position on the Jewish question, but also his dealings with current problems were deeply influenced by his mystical views, and the influence of these views must have been especially great when he was detached from the management of state affairs. Such was the case in his last years in Venice, such was the case in Monopoli, and such had also been the case in Spain. A man whose mind was concentrated on the problem of deciphering the symbols of Ezekiel's Chariot, or of proving that Maimonides' concept of the angels was wrong and that of the anti-rationalistic school was right, a man who seized every opportunity to indulge in heavenly visions—such a man could not grasp the developments of his time with a cold and piercing realistic view. With all his experience in politics, his analytical mind, and his vast knowledge of human affairs, he saw the world through a veil.

That the veil was removed from time to time, and that Abravanel's genius as financier and diplomat then appeared in its full magnitude and effectiveness, must necessarily be assumed. Throughout this work we have attempted to point out the dualism manifested in Abravanel's life. And indeed, without assuming that such dualism existed, it is impossible to explain the achievements of the man in such varied and conflicting fields of action. The veil, however, was never completely removed when it came to the Jewish question. For the processes of his thinking on abstract questions were inseparably bound up with the Jewish problem, and when, in turn, he dealt with this problem, he must have been strongly affected by those processes. The influence of the world behind the veil, the world of visions and ideas, was always felt here to a greater or lesser extent, distracting his attention and blurring his view of the realistic conditions of the Jews in the world.

And yet, what Abravanel created behind that veil was his greatest achievement, the greatest even from the nationalistic point of view. For one wonders which would have been the greater contribution, issuing a warning to the Jews of Spain which might have rescued some of them from the calamities of the expulsion, or offering great hopes to the survivors of the disaster which was in any case bound to come. Abravanel lost the political battle for his people, and his struggle on their behalf in the Courts of kings and magnates was, as he said, "wasted effort." But Abravanel also fought for his people's soul, and in this struggle he won a considerable victory. For when the world in which the Jews lived was destroyed and everything around them crumbled in the tumult and shock of disaster, there emerged upon the ruins a substitute world, ghostly and fantastic, to be sure, but luminous and angelic and pregnant with hope—the world of inspiring visions and ideas, rising out of Abravanel's great heart.

It was the lasting influence of Abravanel's "world" that raised him to the high state of a first-rate factor in the history of the Jewish people. What were the elements, the principles, the dynamics of that world, which was at once so unreal and so effective? The following chapters will attempt to answer this question.

PART TWO

COMMENTATOR & PHILOSOPHER

CHAPTER ONE

WORLD OUTLOOK

1. *Revelation*

THE CENTRAL factor in the spiritual life of the Middle Ages was religion; the decisive spiritual factor in modern times has been science. Yet the hunger for scientific knowledge in the Middle Ages was always evident, just as the yearning for faith has never died in modern times. The difference is only that, while in modern times science and religion constitute two distinct approaches to problems of a universal nature, the best spiritual forces of the Middle Ages were involved in painful and futile efforts to coordinate these two irreconcilable viewpoints. Thus, the intellectual world of the Middle Ages was torn by the conflict between faith and reason.

Étienne Gilson, the discerning historian of medieval philosophy, divides all medieval thinkers into three "spiritual families," or categories, according to their position in this fundamental conflict.[1] Thus, one category consisted of those thinkers who declared for the primacy of Faith and, following St. Augustine's teachings, maintained that the only legitimate function of Reason was to try to understand what Revelation teaches us. A second category was represented by those who, while officially yielding to the primacy of Faith, actually subscribed to the primacy of Reason. Averroes, the foremost Moslem commentator on Aristotle, was the typical protagonist of this group, although he had many more followers in Christendom than in Islam. Between these two opposing spiritual families was another group which believed in harmony between Reason and Revelation. It postulated the existence of two sets of truth—one derived from Reason, the other from Revelation—but maintained that revealed truths, far from contradicting, complement truths arrived at by Reason, since they illuminate realms far beyond the borders of Reason's reach. The promulgators of this concept were the Thomists, the spiritual descendants of the foremost protagonist of the principle of harmony, Thomas Aquinas.

To be fully appreciated, this three-branched division of medieval intellectuals requires supplementation. What should be added is the element of time. To be sure, all types of medieval thinkers were found in practically all the centuries of the Middle Ages. But each of them characterized a special epoch when it appeared, if not exclusively, at least as the dominant force. The period of the primacy of Faith ended sometime in the second half of the 13th century, when the Thomistic idea of harmony between Faith and Reason gained decisive influence. The day of the harmonizers, however, rapidly declined, and, while their influence continued to be manifest for a long time, they steadily lost ground to the aggressive adherents of the primacy of Reason. We see, shortly after the time of Aquinas, mounting criticism directed against the very principle of coordination, and out of this criticism we see Reason emerging ever more victorious. Men like Roger Bacon, Duns Scotus and, particularly, Siger of Brabant were the heralds and precursors of the new age.[2] They destroyed the structure of scholasticism from within, at the very time when humanism attacked it from without. Thus we find Reason first yielding to Faith, then rising to a status of equality with Faith, then gradually attacking Faith and establishing itself in a dominant position.

Each of the foregoing spiritual families had its Jewish parallel.[3] Up to the time of Maimonides, the dominant group among the Jews, like the Augustine family in Christendom, stressed the subordination of Reason to Faith, of Philosophy to Revelation, and its philosophical speculation was confined to the limits permitted by religious tradition. The chief proponents of this position in Jewry, prior to the time of Maimonides, were Saadia and Halevi.[4] Maimonides stressed the value of philosophical investigation, elevated it almost to the status of Revelation and tried to coordinate the "two truths" in a manner similar to, although not identical with, that attempted later by Aquinas.[5] Among the Jews, the philosophical thinkers who followed Maimonides belonged mostly to the third spiritual family, the Averroists. Their leading representative was Gersonides.[6]

To what spiritual family did Abravanel belong? From the standpoint of the development of philosophical thought, Abravanel lived at a time when in Christendom scholasticism had already waned and the primacy of Reason had been definitely established by the insurgent spirit of the Renaissance. Among the Jews, the same tendency was evidenced by the fact that Albo, the most prominent thinker in the middle of the 15th century, reduced to three the number of Articles of Faith declared by Maimonides to be thirteen. Abravanel represents a reversal of this process, not its continuation. Not only are the thirteen Articles of Faith re-established, but Revelation is reinstated in its former position with its full and crushing impact.[7] Repudiating the supremacy of Reason and denying it a status even comparable to Faith, Abravanel goes back to the pre-Thomistic period in Christianity and the pre-Maimonidean period in Judaism. Although he was steeped in philosophical speculation, his hatred of "Greek philosophy" was as real as that of Halevi,[8] and while he frequently mentions Maimonides with reverence, his true teacher and mentor is not Maimonides, but Saadia.

Saadia's influence on Jewish theology in the Middle Ages was as far-reaching as St. Augustine's on Christianity. It was Saadia who posed the major problems that became the theme of all future philosophical thought in Judaism, and it was Saadia who outlined the general conclusions which were accepted theologically—although not always philosophically—by all medieval Jewish thinkers. Maimonides' thirteen Articles of Faith, for instance, are all present in Saadia's doctrine, although philosophically Maimonides arrived at them along different lines or gave them a new meaning. As for Abravanel, he agreed with Saadia not only from a theological point of view, but also, in large measure, from the standpoint of philosophy; and the chief reason for this conceptual affinity lies in the fact that the world views of both Abravanel and Saadia were based on the principle of the primacy of Faith.

To understand this world view, we must have a clear idea of what primacy of Faith implied. As we have stated, the defenders of this attitude viewed Reason as a medium for explaining Revelation. Revelation, however, was, for them, not only the final objective of Reason, but also Reason's guide. Man's thinking process, as they saw it, comprises the following three phases: the existing world presents the problems to our mind; Reason strives to analyze and solve them; Revelation presents the ultimate solutions. What then is the task of Reason? Its task is to solve the problems in harmony with the solutions indicated by Revelation. The whole thing may be compared to a book of arithmetical problems, to which a list of the answers is appended. We may feel absolutely certain that our reason has arrived at a correct solution; and yet we may be wrong. We therefore must compare our results with the truths disclosed by Revelation. If these truths convey something different, we must have erred and ought to resume the investigation. Should we feel that our reason is incapable of reaching a different conclusion, something must be wrong with our reason. We have only to rely on what Revelation teaches and we cannot go wrong.[9]

We should add, in further clarification of this view, that man's ability fully to grasp Revelation's profound truths was in any case considered most doubtful. Revelation offers the ultimate goal of Reason—a goal which, at best, can be approached, as in the squaring of the circle, but can never be attained.[10] Revelation presents to us the solutions of our problems, so that our reason, although unable to prove them, may sense their validity, if it operates in the right direction. The question, however, is: What *is* the right direction? Or, in other words: How can we be sure that the solutions indicated by Revelation are correct? It is in the certitude of these thinkers regarding the unquestionable veracity of Revelation that we find the primacy of Faith fully manifested. One must believe that these are the true solutions simply because one *must* have faith. This "must" is a practical possibility, since Faith, like Will, is subject to man's control. It is up to man to believe in something or not, just as it is up to him to do something or not. The implicit conclusion is that one may be commanded to believe what is true, just as one is ordered to do what is right.

This daring thought, first explicitly expressed by Irenaeus,[11] became dominant in Christianity, and later in Islam and Judaism as well. Saadia, who accepted it, stated quite openly that one who "in his thoughts" denies the existence of God should be punished even as one who commits a crime.[12] Maimonides, himself a fugitive from religious intolerance, did not hesitate to declare that one who denies any of the Articles of Faith is guilty of greater sin than one who commits all the crimes in the world, and that he should be "hated, rejected and destroyed."[13] Abravanel readily shared this opinion, namely, that a crime involving Faith is worse than a crime involving action and that chastisement for it should be correspondingly greater. According to him, the punishment for disbelief in

God should be "complete annihilation with fire and brimstone and raging heat."[14] Crescas and others maintained that commandments cannot apply to matters of faith and belief, but to actions which depend on freedom of choice.[15] Abravanel takes the position that "commandments do apply to matters of faith and it is exactly this which we were ordered by Revelation. When Moses said, 'these words, which I command thee this day, shall be in thine heart,' he commanded the points of faith in which Israel is bound to believe."[16]

Revelation then is not only the guide to our thinking and the objective of our reason, but also the dictator of our faith. It is the unimpeachable authority for settling all our inner conflicts. There remains, however, the fundamental problem: What *is* Revelation? More exactly, which are the sources that can be considered as the authoritative fountains of Revelation? In the scholastic rivalry for providing answers to these questions, the Jews were in a privileged position. The Christians repudiated the divine character of the holy writ of the Moslems; the Jews denied the divine source of both the Koran and the New Testament; but no one questioned the divine character of the sources of Revelation in which the Jews believed. In these writings, it was universally agreed, God had spoken to man. Since the Bible represents the direct word of God, "the hypothesis that it contains both important and unimportant things is heretical."[17] "Every word in it," said Maimonides, "contains wonders of wisdom for one whom God endowed with knowledge and understanding."[18] As a matter of fact, the prevalent opinion was that it contained not only "wonders of wisdom," but all the truths concerning all the problems which baffle the human mind. It is only through Revelation, through God's word to the Hebrew prophets, that man learned what he knew, and it is therefore on the foundations of revealed knowledge that all sciences rest. Since the Hebrew prophets were admittedly the first in whom Revelation was made manifest, all man's knowledge must of necessity be traced to them.

So universal was the acceptance of this concept that we find, not only Jews, but also Christians and Moslems vying with each other in emphasizing it. This was true of all the categories of thinkers, regardless of their position in the conflict between Faith and Reason. Among the Moslems, a conservative theologian like

Al-Ghazali was not alone in saying that "the Greeks stole their wisdom from Israel;" even a rationalist like Averroes stated that "there is no doubt that all sciences originated among the sons of Israel, the reason being the existence of prophecy among them which made their perfection in the sciences amazing."[19] Like Averroes, Roger Bacon, one of the most advanced thinkers of the later Middle Ages, maintained that the patriarchs and prophets had knowledge of all sciences, which God revealed to them directly, and it is from them that the ancient philosophers received it.[20] Bacon merely reasserted here a traditional Christian thought that goes back to the early Church Fathers. Thus, Justin Martyr repeatedly asserted that Plato had borrowed from Moses and the prophets.[21] Clement of Alexandria broadened this thesis by presenting Greek philosophy in its entirety as a plagiarism directly from the Hebrews, or indirectly through Chaldean and Egyptian sources. "The philosophy of the Hebrews," he said, "will be demonstrated beyond all contradiction to be the most ancient of all wisdom."[22] Influenced by Clement's vigorous and elaborate presentation on this point, Augustine, who carried the idea into the Middle Ages, made the sweeping assertion that all wisdom, including Greek philosophy, derived from the "prophetical doctrine" which "flowed from the fountain of Israel."[23] Halevi summarized the same theory, as it was accepted in the Middle Ages, in the following brief passage: "The roots and principles of all sciences were handed down from the Hebrews first to the Chaldeans, then to the Persians and Medians, then to the Greeks and finally to the Romans. On account of the length of this period, and the many disturbing circumstances, it was forgotten that they had originated with the Hebrews, and so they were ascribed to the Greeks and Romans."[24]

Abravanel's position fully corresponds to that of Halevi, whose theory he accepts and elaborates.[25] Revelation, as expressed in Holy Scripture, is for him a vital and fundamental source of man's knowledge, in fact, the only source possible. What man learns through his senses and by experience is at best but curtailed and partial knowledge. What he learns from Revelation is complete and wholly true.[26] His major premise was: "There is no other wisdom which is more comprehensive and more ancient [and hence, more exalted] than that embodied in our law."[27]

There seemed to be no question, then, that one must look to

Holy Writ as the source of all truth. But the question was how to understand or interpret Holy Writ. Here human reason, seemingly suppressed and relegated to secondary importance, began to manifest its strength. Instead of guiding and controlling Reason in accordance with what they found in Scripture, people began to interpret Scripture in accordance with the directives of Reason; and although it was never openly admitted, the reversal of the process was manifest in almost every biblical commentary which appeared in the Middle Ages.

That the Bible should not be taken literally, in fact, that it *cannot* be taken literally; that its words are symbols of and allusions to some higher meaning, some secret truths; that one has to decipher the Bible in order to understand it and, through it, what is happening around us, was one of the most prevalent notions throughout the medieval period. Once the concept was established that all truth lies in revealed truth, or at least must agree with revealed truth, the development of that other concept that the words of the Bible cannot be taken literally, and should be interpreted allegorically and symbolically—followed as a matter of course. The result was that with all their deep reverence for the Bible, its text was handled by most medieval commentators with but little respect. Since the words of Scripture were considered symbols and allusions, they might allude to anything, even to the very antithesis of their literal and apparent meanings. Maimonides almost cynically admitted that two opposing theories could be based on the same verse and that the text of the Bible need not offer any impediment to the process of Reason. Thus, as he confessed, he did not "reject the Eternity of the Universe simply because certain passages in Scripture confirmed the Creation," since he could "find" another "suitable interpretation" for these passages. "We should perhaps have had," he added, "an easier task in showing that the Scriptural passages referred to are in harmony with the theory of the Eternity of the Universe, *if we accepted the latter,* than we had in explaining the anthropomorphisms in the Bible when we rejected the idea that God is corporeal."[28] In brief, Holy Scripture was perverted into a mantle of authority to cloak current ideas.

The fact that medieval Jewish theology and Christian scholasticism based their views respectively on the early rabbinic authorities and the Church Fathers, all of whom treated the text in the most irregular and eccentric manner, gave this system the sanction of tradition. But the peculiar ease with which it was so used was due largely to the fact that the biblical text itself is full of irregularities, difficulties, ambiguous or little known words and phrases, sudden breaks and mysterious references to events long forgotten and records long lost. In other words, it was due to the fact that the Bible needed reconstruction, that in many places it resembled the site of archaeological ruins, and that it depended upon the judgment or the imagination of the archaeologist to decide what the function of each part was in the original structure. The men of the Middle Ages were poor in historical criticism but rich in speculative fantasy. When they considered the Bible, they gave their imagination the freest possible rein, and they used the ancient references, not to reconstruct the historical past, but to build their theoretical castles in the air.

The position of Abravanel on this question gives us a clue to his thought processes. As a philosophical thinker, he adopts the method of allegorical interpretation. As a faithful believer, he adheres to the literal meaning of the biblical text. He advocates this two-fold approach because of his dual form of reasoning, and also because of his training. Allegorical interpretation, it must be remembered, was especially practiced by the philosophical circles among the Jews who, since the days of Philo and the Church Fathers, endeavored to coordinate philosophy with Scripture. But parallel to allegorical interpretation, there persisted among the Jews a school of biblical interpretation which insisted on the plain meaning of the text. Abravanel, who was influenced by both tendencies, combined both methods of interpretation. "In the Law of Moses," he stressed, "the external reading is true and corresponds to its meaning," but at the same time we should strive to unravel "what is secretly implied in it."[29] What he emphasized even more strongly was that, before any allegorical interpretation is attempted, the literal meaning of the text must be established. God spoke to man in a language understandable to all men.[30] While the wiser and the more inspired could grasp the higher meaning, there could be no inconsistency between the literal and the symbolical. Since the Bible represents truth, it contains no contradictions. And just as this is true with regard to the "two meanings," so it is with regard to the Bible's different sections. Hence, to explain one part of the Bible correctly means to explain it in a way that would be in agreement with all other parts.

The fullest representation of Abravanel's system of thought is to be found in his commentaries on the Bible. And the impressiveness of the system stems from the fact that it was based, not on any one part of the Bible, as was the case with other medieval theories, but on the Bible as a whole. The gigantic task which Abravanel set for himself was to tie together all the parts of the Bible—and, with it, the entire literature of the later sages, "in whom the spirit of God spoke, and to whom the secrets of divine wisdom were revealed"[31]—into one cohesive system—a system based on Revelation.

2. *Creation*

The most striking and significant characteristic of Abravanel's world outlook is his emphatic insistence upon "creation out of nothing." He devoted two special books to this subject[32] and dealt with it repeatedly in all his works. To evaluate properly his position on this question, we should bear in mind the three basic theories regarding the creation of the world, that is, creation out of God, out of matter, and out of nothing. The theory of creation out of God, namely, that the universe is created out of God's own substance, that it emanated from Him "as light radiates from the sun" —the theory which received its first full expression in Plotinus' theory of emanations—really identifies God with the universe. It is a pantheistic theory which eliminates the whole problem of creation. The theory of creation out of matter, namely, that God gave form to matter, which prior to that was formless and lifeless, is the dualistic theory which received its first and perhaps most powerful expression in Plato. The theory of creation out of nothing was regarded as the theory of early Judaism.

Whether this was actually the case is of course a different question. John E. Boodin is undoubtedly right when he says that "the doctrine of creation out of nothing—*ex nihilo*—is nowhere expressly taught in Holy Scripture."[33] One may question, however, the grounds for his statement that the "biblical tradition is dualistic." What can be conscientiously said in this respect is that the Bible is rather vague on this point and that it may be interpreted in one way or the other with an equal measure of certainty or uncertainty. The truth of the matter is that creation out of nothing is a Christian rather than a Jewish doctrine. If we are to rely on Boodin, the early Church Fathers, who were strongly influenced by Judaism, were dualists, and it was Jerome's mistranslation of a certain verse in Maccabees that was responsible for Christianity's acceptance of the creation *ex nihilo* theory.[34] Long before Jerome, however, Origen vehemently fought the view that "God could not create anything when nothing existed" and branded "absurd" the notion that "matter is uncreated and co-eternal with God."[35] It is true that among the early Church Fathers, Justin Martyr and Clement of Alexandria interpreted the creation theory of Genesis as dualistic,[36] but they cannot be assumed to have spoken for all Christians of even that period. Irenaeus, who was a contemporary of both Justin and Clement, stated distinctly and without hesitation: "God created all things out of nothing and not from preexistent matter."[37] In any case, Jerome's presentation was not accidental, but a link in a chain of a conscious effort which, beginning with Irenaeus and continuing to Augustine, aimed at substantiating the theory of creation out of nothing.

The dualistic views of Clement of Alexandria and Justin Martyr should be attributed less to the vague and indefinite Jewish views on the subject than to the clear and definite views on this problem in Greek philosophy. As Clement says: "The philosophers, the Stoics and Plato, and Pythagoras, nay more Aristotle, the Peripatetic, suppose the existence of matter among the first principles."[38] The decline of Greek philosophical influence—which Justin and Clement were the first to undermine—marked the rise of the creation *ex nihilo* theory. At any rate, whatever the influence of Judaism on Christianity in the development of the theory of creation out of nothing among the later Church Fathers, the theory in its Christian formulation certainly influenced subsequent Judaism as well as Islam. We find it as the ruling concept in all the philosophical works, from Saadia to Maimonides, in which a systematic explanation of the universe is attempted. It is with Maimonides, however, that the concept receives its first setback, and the reasons for this setback are quite obvious. Although Maimonides decides in favor of creation out of nothing, his decision is far from conclusive. The very fact that he refuses to base his proof of God's existence on the theory of creation out of nothing was a strong indication that he must have had grave doubts about it. This position of Maimonides, no less than the ascendency of Aristotle's philosophy in which the eternity of the universe is a cardinal point, brought it about that the theory of creation out of nothing became a subject of bitter controversy, strongly contested by some of the best minds in the post-Maimonidean era.

The philosophical speculations which accompanied each of these doctrines are beyond the sphere of this discussion. What interests us primarily is the fact that the attitude one assumed toward the question of creation was the decisive factor in determining his world outlook. Theoretical proof was, in any event, of secondary importance in this case. Halevi, an ardent supporter of the creation *ex nihilo* theory, felt obliged to concede that the arguments in favor of creation or eternity are "balanced" and that this "obscure" question can be decided only by the "weight of prophetic tradition."[39] Abravanel goes even a step farther when he says that "one who looks into the world as it is and considers its natural law and order is more inclined to believe that the world is pre-existent rather than of recent origin."[40] Like Halevi, he maintains that the creation of the world out of nothing is a truth revealed by God's grace to His prophets, since "investigation by the means of human reason cannot arrive at this truth unless assisted by Revelation."[41] Abravanel evidently sensed the weakness of the rational basis of the theory. At the same time, however, he does not sound convincing when he argues that one must deduce it from Revelation. The biblical view on this point is, as we have indicated, far from clear, and both the advocates of creation and eternity could refer to the Bible for equal support. What motivated Abravanel's stand on this point was neither rational investigation nor the biblical position, but the consideration that any other doctrine jeopardized the whole concept of revealed truth.

According to the theory of creation out of nothing, God is not subject to nature to any extent. Nature is but the manifestation of God's will. Therefore, in reality, there is no such thing as natural law. What we call natural law constitutes, in fact, the decree of a potentate which can at any moment be abrogated at His will. If God wills it, the regular order of nature, or what we consider to be its regular order, changes in the twinkling of an eye, without any relation to what previously existed and without in the least depending on it. Miracles can thus be easily explained. On the other hand, the theory of creation out of matter not only challenges God's omnipotence by denying His ability to annihilate matter, or to create anything without matter, but it also limits God's work of creation to what can be done with matter. More exactly, the theory of the eternity of matter presupposes the theory of the eternity of the laws of nature, as well as the theory of creation by necessity. Consequently, miracles are impossible.[42]

Even Maimonides, since he could not or dared not explain away all the miracles, had to accept the theory of creation out of nothing. Gersonides and the rest of the rationalists, who promulgated the principle of eternity of matter, were even more persistent in explaining miracles allegorically, or as natural phenomena. But this conception of miracles was strongly opposed by Abravanel, and the nature of his objection is best illustrated by his position in the controversy regarding the miracle of the sun. The miracle of the sun in Gibeon consisted, according to Gersonides, not in the sun's stopping, which would have entailed a cosmic catastrophe, but in Joshua's success in achieving victory in the brief time left before the close of day.[43] In Abravanel's opinion, however, such an explanation is groundless. True, "according to the law of nature, the sphere of the sun can never rest; and if it did, the entire universe would be destroyed." But this is the essence of divine miracles, that they manifest the superiority of His Will over nature. "The nature of water is to flow downward. Nevertheless, when God willed it, it stood up like a wall."[44] Since miracles represent divine will and power, there is no such thing as an "impossible" miracle. Crescas, who denied the complete stoppage of the sun, but agreed nevertheless that it was slowed down,[45] committed therefore the same mistake as Gersonides. "The slowing down of the sun and its stoppage are equally impossible from the point of view of nature, but both are equally possible from the point of view of God." Why not better admit then that "the statement 'and the sun stood still' can in no way be explained as the slowing down of movement, but only as complete rest and complete stoppage of movement."[46]

The position of Abravanel was thus simple and direct. It was based on his triple axiom: the Bible is the word of God; the Bible represents truth; the Bible must be taken literally before it can be interpreted symbolically. According to the literal interpretation, all the recorded miracles took place, and these miracles *cannot* be explained by natural processes, as some of the rationalists attempted to do. This would be nothing but self-delusion which would ruin the entire credibility of the Bible and our faith in Revelation. If the Bible is to be believed, miracles must be believed as well, and they can be explained only by God's omnipotence, by His complete independence of nature and of matter. How can we establish the veracity of the Bible, which is threatened by the doubts placed in the miracle stories, and make it unchallengeable by the skeptics? Only by accepting creation *ex nihilo*, the greatest of all miracles.[47]

Abravanel stated quite explicitly that his insistence on creation *ex nihilo* was due to no consideration other than the desire to substantiate Revelation. "Only if we accept the belief in creation out of nothing can we recognize the existence of a creating God. If one denies the theory of creation out of nothing in preference to the belief in the eternity of matter . . . one cannot assume that God can lengthen even the wing of a fly, or shorten the leg of an ant."[48] If God's powers are thus limited, "there is no possibility of believing in the stories of Scripture, in the miracles and the reasons for the commandments."[49] Therefore, declares Abravanel, "if I had to lay down the principles of divine law, I would have laid down one principle only—the creation of the world out of nothing."[50]

In fact, creation out of nothing was for Abravanel not only the cornerstone of divine law, but the cornerstone of his entire world concept. It permeates Abravanel's cosmology as well as his historical and political philosophy. By making the entire existence of matter a product of God's will, he eliminates matter from the dominant position it holds in Aristotle's philosophy; and by insisting that matter was created out of nothing, he abolishes pantheism. Nevertheless, Abravanel's world view is not free from a pantheistic element, since his universe, as we shall see, does not consist of matter only. It consists of matter and spirit; and while matter was created out of nothing, the spirit originated from God as a source.[51]

3. *The Universe*

From the standpoint of its material structure, the universe of Abravanel is the universe of the Middle Ages. It is the universe of Aristotle and Ptolemy, of Dante and Thomas Aquinas, of Maimonides and Gersonides.[52] It is a finite universe, spherical and geocentric. In this universe, "the heavens surround the earth, half of them above it, half of them below it."[53] The terms above and below, however, are not to be taken as absolute. "If we say 'above,' it is only relative to our position, for what is 'above' in comparison to us is 'below' to someone on the other side of the globe." Furthermore, "what is now 'below' the earth will later be 'above' it as a result of the rotation."[54]

What rotates is not the earth, of course, since, in accordance with the Ptolemaic theory, the earth is immobile. The globe is surrounded by a series of spheres, enclosed one within the other, "like the skins of an onion,"[55] the outer sphere forming the circumference of the cosmic ball. The spheres carry the stars and the planets, the moon and the sun, and it is according to the particular luminaries they carry that the principal spheres were classified. The sphere nearest the earth is that of the moon. It, in turn, is surrounded respectively by the spheres of Mercury, Venus, Sun, Mars, Jupiter and Saturn. Around them is the eighth sphere with all the "fixed stars," ringed by the ninth sphere, which is starless.[56] We see all the stars as if they were in the same sphere because the spheres are transparent, their transparency being due to the special purity of the substance of which they are composed. This substance, ether, constitutes the fifth element, in addition to the four in the sublunar world whose quality lessens with their increasing distance from the heavens. Thus, encompassed by the etherial sphere of the moon are the respective orbs of the four sublunary elements—fire, air, water and earth. This is the natural order of the elements and this would be their actual order if the universe were at rest. Actually, however, only the immobile core of the globe is at rest. The spheres move, and by their movement they affect the order of the four elements which are thrown against one another and interpenetrate each other, the interpenetration being responsible for the various combinations of the elements and for the creation of the composite bodies on earth.[57]

To explain the complicated movements of the heavenly bodies, the cause of all change here below, there are the complicated theories of Aristotle and Ptolemy which Abravanel partly rejects and partly accepts. We shall touch upon some of the common and disputed points at a later stage of this discussion.[58] At present we note only his major premise, namely, that "God moves the outer sphere and, by this, all the other spheres move, just as the part moves together with the whole."[59] Thus, long before the machine age, the universe was conceived of as one gigantic machine, the wheels of which turn permanently and simultaneously, set in motion and cared for by the Machinist who created it.

We stress this similarity to a machine, because it may help us to understand Abravanel's concept of the world more clearly. Maimonides' concept of the cosmos is not of a machine, but of an organism. "This universe," he said, "is, as regards individuality, beyond all question a single being, like Said or Omar."[60] According to him, pure "forms"—or "separate intelligences"—exist *outside* the universe, but the universe as such is practically undivided, although theoretically it is composed of matter and form. The universe of Abravanel, on the other hand, is marked by duality. Parallel to the material world, described above, there exists, in his opinion, a purely spiritual world, built on a similar principle of hierarchy.[61] This spiritual world embraces Aristotle's separate intelligences, identified by Maimonides with the angels of the Bible;[62] but it does not consist of them only. According to Avicenna and his followers, the number of the intelligences, or the angels, is ten, nine of them corresponding to the nine principal spheres and the tenth—the Active Intellect—to the sublunary world.[63] According to Abravanel, their number is far greater. Do we not find in the Book of Job: "Can His hosts be counted?"[64] Is it not stated in the Book of Daniel: "Thousand thousands ministered unto Him and myriad myriads stood before Him?"[65] We may continue to regard the number as ten, suggests Abravanel, only in view of the fact that a thousand thousands are equal to ten hundred thousands and myriad myriads to ten thousand myriads.[66] Ten may thus be considered the basic, but by no means the absolute number.

The increase in the number of angels from ten to myriads, as well as the proof from the verse in Daniel, had already been suggested by Albo.[67] Nevertheless, Abravanel's view on the matter is not a mere reliance on authority. It is organically connected with his concept of the universe and of the task performed by the spiritual beings. He considers all angels to be what their Hebrew name indicates. They are *malakhim,* messengers on a divine mission, each having a special function to perform, either in the realm of nature or in the realm of man.[68] The departure from the Aristotelian concept becomes here most apparent. According to Aristotle, all changes in nature are explained by the movement of the spheres or by the combination of matter and form—form being the immanent potency for a thing to develop and act in a certain way. Abravanel, while accepting Aristotle's doctrine of form, evaluates its capacity as much more limited. The elements, plants and minerals may act and move by means of certain inherent powers, but these powers do not act on their own. They are in themselves controlled and directed by higher spiritual powers, that is, by the messengers of God. Every phenomenon of nature is a result of a spiritual force which acts at God's behest. What we consider causality is really the will of God implemented through a certain spiritual power, which we see as causality. Once the spiritual force is withdrawn, the effectiveness of nature disappears. "What destroys is not fire but the will of God, and the fire is His instrument. Our senses see that fire approaches a thing which burns, but they do not see the One who is responsible for the burning. If the fire did not touch Hananiah, Mishael and Azariah, if things did not act in accordance with their 'nature,' it was because the divine will, represented by an angel, was ordered to refrain from acting at that moment."[69] We can clearly see that Abravanel's angelology is constructed with the special view of explaining miracles, or, more exactly, of presenting miracles, not as eccentric, irregular phenomena, but rather as an integral part of the system which embraces the entire universe. In a way, as St. Augustine thought, everything is a miracle.[70] The phenomena of nature differ from miracles only in that they appear regularly, but they are miracles just the same, performed by divine agents.

This concept of the universe is clearly mystical. It sees beyond and within every material phenomenon some spiritual force which determines whatever happens, not by the law that operates within the universe, but by some outside will. Every development, therefore, does not depend on the so-called powers of nature, but on the powers behind nature. Thus, while the material world is a single, stupendous, organized structure, what we see are only the effects of a parallel spiritual organization which rules it. Because of the existence of this spiritual hierarchy, "the whole universe resembles an organized state, or an organized army, where there is a superior above a superior, and everything leads up to the highest of all, who is the general of the army."[71] The comparison of the universe to an army had already been made by Thomas Aquinas, who likewise conceived of the spiritual beings as forming an angelic hierarchy.[72] But it had quite a different, and a much more "realistic" implication in the theory of Abravanel. In his concept, God is actually the Lord of the hosts of heaven, of the myriads of angels and spirits who fill the universe and act at His command. He is the one Driver of the chariot of the universe, which is drawn by myriads of "horses of fire."

The forces appointed to the world of man are marshalled in a definite order and assigned specific tasks, just like the forces controlling the phenomena of nature. According to Abravanel, who here follows the cabalists, there are three classes of spiritual beings which influence the affairs of mankind. First and foremost are the separate intelligences which, indeed, dominate the heavenly bodies—and this is why they are placed in the neighborhood of the spheres!—but which also, unlike the Maimonidean thesis, exert direct control over human groups. The second division consists of intelligences called Angels of Service, or Angels of Mercy, who, while ordinarily residing above the spheres, act as agents of succor or salvation for the God-fearing. The third consists of spiritual beings whose habitation is in the sublunary world and whose task is to punish God's creatures for their sins. This is why they are called Angels of Destruction and Angels of Death, devils and demons and evil spirits.[73]

Maimonides included the belief in evil spirits and demons among the "great absurdities," which should be ridiculed by "intelligent people." He considered such a belief as one of the "lasting diseases of mankind," which seriously hamper the advance of the human intellect.[74] The determined battle which Maimonides conducted against this "disease" resulted, however, in no apparent success. Before Abravanel, we find Crescas, one of the best philosophical minds in medieval Jewry, discussing, in his *Light of God*, the existence of demons as unquestionable fact.[75] Albo, probably the least imaginative or mystically inclined of all medieval Jewish thinkers, held on to the "great absurdity."[76] The belief in demons was undoubtedly furthered by the teachings of Christian theology in which the devil and his satellites play an important role. In the theory of Abravanel, however, the function of the demons is quite different from that of the Christian concept. For Augustine or Thomas Aquinas the demons are fallen angels who rebelled against God and induced man to sin and evil.[77] For Abravanel, the demons are not rebellious angels, but act strictly at God's command, in the same way as the Angels of Mercy. The demons are not the originators of sin, but instruments of punishment for sin.[78] In Abravanel's opinion, sin, as we shall see, originates only with man.

4. *Man*

The medieval view of man and his powers represented a strange mixture of contempt and admiration. The prevalence of notions on the duality of flesh and spirit had a great deal to do with this view. "Man is a rational animal," was the way Seneca put it,[79] and all Medieval thinkers agreed. By virtue of his reasoning powers, man merits admiration. Because of the animal in him, however, he deserves contempt. Hence, if there were a compass for appraising man's nature, the moral needle would waver between these two extremes, changing its position for every individual according to the side of his nature which ruled his life and according to the extent of that rule. Since most men are dominated by their animal impulses, the medieval view of man could be well expressed in another aphorism of Seneca: "How contemptible a thing is man, unless he can raise himself above humanity."[80] In the language of the Middle Ages this meant: unless he became a saint.

This, however, was only one aspect of the attitude. The other aspect was even more fundamental and more typical of the Middle Ages. It was less a heritage of Greek-Roman philosophy than of Christian religious dogmatism, but it similarly resulted from two conflicting attitudes, deriving from two different evaluations of man: from the standpoint of nature and the standpoint of God. Compared to God man was utterly insignificant, wretched and miserable beyond limit. Within nature, he was the crown of creation, as Scripture clearly and decisively pointed out. So overwhelming, however, was the concept of God's pre-eminence that, if not for the doctrine of man's *potential elevation*, his status within nature would in itself be insufficient to engender any measure of respect for him. In keeping with this doctrine, man's greatness is truly *indicated* by his position in nature, but it does not *lie* in that position. It is embodied in his ability to rise above nature—indeed, to be "saved" from nature altogether—and to achieve eternal association with God. It was this inherent possibility of salvation, granted him by God but ultimately depending on man and his behavior, that caused man in the Middle Ages, with all the emphasis upon his reprehensible features, to be looked upon with mystical veneration.

Abravanel's conception of man is animated by this mixed attitude and the views motivating it, but is particularly adapted to his conception of the universe. Abravanel, as we have noted, conceived of the universe as consisting of two distinct worlds: the world of spirit and the world of matter. Man's special position, according to him, is that he stands between the two worlds and also provides a link between them. While all other beings are either matter or spirit, man—and man only—is both matter and spirit.[81] Patterned after the model of the universe, man is truly the microcosmos, as some ancient and medieval thinkers thought, except that he symbolizes, besides the visible cosmos, the invisible as well.[82] Man represents these two systems, because he is an outstanding creature that unites within itself all the aspects of God's powers of creation. Consequently, "man is the most perfect of all forms," which implies, according to the Aristotelian thesis, that he is the *final cause*. Translated into religious terminology, it means: "the purpose of all creation."[83]

This concept of man is not that of Maimonides. According to the latter, man is far from being the "most perfect form," nor is he the only being composed of matter and spirit. Relying on Aristotle, Maimonides declared that the spheres and stars possess rational souls and that they are, in body as well as in spirit, incomparably more perfect than man.[84] His arguments in support of this contention were based primarily on Aristotle's explanations of the movements of the heavenly bodies. To Abravanel, however, these arguments of Maimonides appeared fundamentally "empty and groundless and drawn out of the air."[85] As Abravanel puts it, "the heavenly bodies are not living and rational, but natural bodies whose movements are in accord with their material nature, and it is only because of their great distance from us that we cannot comprehend their real course."[86] One may assume that Abravanel is, at this point, closer than Maimonides to the modern conception of the universe. Such an assumption, however, would be wrong. An examination of Abravanel's motives for his position shows that, in essence, Maimonides was here, too, much nearer than Abravanel to the modern view.

The main motive for Abravanel's objection to the theory of living spheres and stars was his desire to establish firmly the anthropocentric view of the universe. Saadia, discussing the same problem, summarized this view in a few brief sentences: "Seeing the earth in the center of the heavens, and the spheres revolving around it on all sides, it is evident that the purpose of creation is on earth. Observing all its parts and considering that both earth and water are inanimate, and the animals devoid of reason, there remains only man to be considered as the purpose of creation. This is beyond doubt."[87] Maimonides fought, cautiously but determinedly, against this anthropocentric conception, which was predominant in the Middle Ages. He attacked it not only by emphasizing the insignificance of the earth, in size and structure, in comparison to the immensity and excellence of the stars and spheres, but also by attributing life to the spherical bodies and by stressing the inferiority of both man's body and soul to the body and soul of the spheres and stars.[88] Abravanel returns to the position of Saadia.[89] By denying life to the heavenly bodies, he is able to claim that their nature is not higher than that of man, but, on the contrary, man is of a higher nature than the heavens. "The fact that the heavenly bodies are great in size, while man is small, is no proof of their importance, as Maimonides thought. The tiny mosquito is more important than all the lofty trees of the Lebanon because it is alive and sensitive. Similarly, the fact that the heavens endure while man passes is no proof of their superiority, for the heavenly bodies are not everlasting, while the rational soul of man is truly eternal."[90]

The idea that the heavens are not living and rational, which seems radical and daring for the Middle Ages, was not an innovation by Abravanel. The contrary had already been questioned by Alghazali[91] and totally rejected by Thomas Aquinas,[92] although the latter was, on the whole, a staunch follower of Aristotle. To prove that man is superior to the heavens by insisting that the latter are but a mass of dead matter was, however, only part of the undertaking to demonstrate that man was the "most perfect of all forms," and hence the aim of creation. The other part, which was much more difficult, was to prove man's superiority over the pure spirits, that is, the angels, or the separate intelligences. Are they not superior to man? Are they not closer than man to God? Should we not assume therefore that they, and not man, were God's major purpose in creating the world? Abravanel's answer to these questions was definitely negative. If man is on a lower level than the angels, it is only in his present state, but not potentially. Ultimately he may be as near to God as the angels or as far from Him as the most spiritless creature, depending on man's choice of good or evil. But the very capacity for such choice testifies that God endowed man with the supreme, divine quality which the angels lack: the power of free will.[93]

We have seen that Abravanel's concept of the angels is not that of free agents, but of messengers of God, constantly on a divine mission, carrying out God's instructions and appointed for specific actions. This was also the position of Albo, who stated clearly that "man has freedom of choice which the angels have not."[94] This power of free will in which man resembles God performs a special function in man in accordance with the very nature and composition of his soul. Man's soul is not one unit, as Saadia or Maimonides thought.[95] It is a combination of two distinct souls—the animal soul and the angelic soul—a combination which places man in the scale of beings between the angelic and the animal.[96] The animal soul, possessing the four basic faculties—the nutritive, sensitive, imaginative and appetitive—is merely a "quality" of the body's constitution which vanishes with the body's destruction.[97] The angelic element is represented by the rational soul and it is by this soul that man becomes human. "The rational soul is not only of a higher nature than the animal soul; it differs from it both in kind and essence."[98] It is not a power or a capacity for rational thinking, a potency which can or cannot be actualized, as Maimonides thought; it is a distinct spiritual substance which has independent existence.[99] It was there before the body's creation, and it survives the body's death. It is immortal, because all that is spiritual is immortal; because, like other pure spirits, it was not created out of nothing, but hewn out of the "throne of God," of eternal and divine substance.[100] It is clear that by rejecting the position of Aristotle and his medieval commentators in favor of Plato's doctrine of the soul, Abravanel is better able to advance his theory of man's superiority and, with it, his anthropocentric conception.

We know, then, that "man is the purpose of the world's creation."[101] But what is the purpose of man? Abravanel's answer is again typical of the Middle Ages. It is basically the answer of St. Bonaventura and St. Thomas and a host of other mystics and scholastics. The final goal of man is to cleave to God through complete concentration of man's thought on God's essence.[102] This end, which embodies the supreme happiness of man, can be attained fully not in this world, but in the world beyond, when the soul is completely freed from sensual perceptions and detractive material influences.[103] In this world, man can achieve but a partial understanding of the "ways of God," and even this can be attained only by the exceptionally wise and holy and with the aid of divine inspiration.[104] Among the prophets, Abravanel maintained, only Moses grasped fully the essence of God.[105]

Consequently, all man can do in this world is to "prepare" his soul for that endless, sublime and other-worldly beatitude; and this "preparation" implies one thing: the establishment of the sovereignty of man's spirit over matter. If man gives free rein to the material side of his being, if he indulges in bodily pleasures and passions, the contaminating influence of such indulgence renders his soul unfit for association with the divine and thus vitiates the whole purpose of his creation. To forestall such an eventuality man must practice strict obedience to God's command—which, in the last analysis, is what man's "preparation" consists of. God's command aims at helping man keep his soul from undue attachment to matter; but, since God endowed man with the power of free will, this command carries with it advice, not compulsion. Hence, man's fate is in his own hands. Torn between his two souls and his two diametrically opposed temptations—the heavenly and the earthly—man must decide for himself which course to follow.

The problem of man's course of action is thus completely transferred by Abravanel from an intellectual to a moral plane. What determines the fate of man's soul is not, as Maimonides thought, the measure of its acquired wisdom (what wisdom can we acquire here, in any event?), but its behavior in executing God's Law.[106] It is the just, and not the wise, who inherit the Kingdom of Heaven; and it is the wicked, not the ignorant, who are doomed. Doomed they are, however, not to death—since the soul is immortal—but to something worse than death: eternal suffering and damnation.[107] Nevertheless, a sinful soul is not necessarily a lost soul. It can be purified by repentance.[108] This is the chance which God gives man in this life. But this is not the only chance. Because of His goodness and unlimited consideration for His creatures, God offers a possibility of rehabilitation even to souls which leave the body contaminated and full of sin, that is, without repentance. They are given the opportunity to purify themselves and get rid of the material sin which clings to them by being returned to another body where they can repent and achieve this aim.[109] Abravanel then believes in the transmigration of souls. He supports his position by pointing to the fact that this belief was shared by Pythagoras and Plato. His main inspiration, however, was derived from the Jewish mystics, the cabalists, in whose system transmigration of souls constitutes an important element.[110]

Transmigration can recur again and again, if the soul fails to purify itself, but the process does not go on endlessly. On the day of Resurrection, which is also the Day of Judgment, the soul's fate is finally to be determined.[111] We should now ask, however, what is meant by Resurrection, and how it will affect man's body and soul. Since, according to Abravanel, the soul is immortal, it does not stand in need of resurrection. Consequently, Resurrection means revival of the body and its reunion with the soul. But this leads to another question: why the revival of the body altogether? Saadia and Nahmanides at least thought that the body's revival is a privilege of the just, and hence, only the just would be resurrected.[112] But Abravanel objects to this view and maintains that Resurrection will embrace the wicked as well as the just. His reasoning is that the "evil-doers, who did not receive their proper punishment during their lifetime, will be resurrected to receive that punishment," for punishment must be, as was the act of crime, "in body as well as in soul."[113]

Resurrection, then, according to this concept, balances the scale of justice in this world.[114] It implies an admission that the world prior to resurrection is *not* conducted in accordance with pure justice—an admission that could be made even by the most faithful on the strength of the concept of man's life as a preparation for the world to come. What is more, that world is not merely the scene of the *final* performance of divine judgment, but where *major and overwhelming* punishment and reward are rendered for what is due;[115] for the ultimate verdict may be eternal bliss, or, conversely, eternal damnation, and these mean to man incomparably more than the suffering or happiness that may be his earthly lot. In brief, since what happens in this life is of such minor significance in comparison with what awaits man's soul in the future, the problem of justice in this world loses much of its point.

5. Man and the Universe

It is because of this predominant view of the future life and future justice that astrology could be introduced into the moral scheme of things of man in the Middle Ages. If man's material life is merely a testing-ground for his behavior toward the Creator, why should not this testing-ground be represented in the conditions placed by the heavenly bodies? For, while in some respects these conditions appeared arbitrary and unfair, in other respects they offered to large groups of men equal chances of behavior under equal circumstances. Morally, it was certainly not an attractive theory; but in lesser conflict with medieval principles than it has been usually thought to be.

To Abravanel astrology was in full harmony with his conception of the universe, his anthropocentric theory, as well as with the principle of predetermination in which, as we shall see, he firmly believed. Conceiving of the universe as of a hierarchic system, operating, on the whole, according to a discernible pattern, astrology was for him primarily the art of distinguishing the threads of which this pattern was woven. Consequently, it was not the element of blind fate that astrology signified for him, but rather the idea of a divine order to which all creation must necessarily yield. To be sure, this order embraces phenomena which are or which appear unusual in the extreme, but astrology is concerned merely with the *ordinary,* with whatever has fixity of signs and symptoms, while the *extraordinary* is beyond its scope. It was for him, as we have seen, axiomatic that the great universal currents stream downward, but the assumption that the heavens dictate man's fate in no way indicated to him man's inferiority. It rather confirmed man's exceptional value, since it is at him, and through the media of the heavens, that the main flow of influences is aimed. Moreover, Abravanel's conception of astrology agreed with his general idea of the universe in one other important respect: it was mechanistic and animistic at the same time.

Thus, in opposition to Maimonides, who repudiated astrology as a fraudulent science,[116] Abravanel accepts the theory that man's course of life, his good or bad fortune, can be predicted by the position of the heavenly bodies. As already indicated, the heavenly bodies influence the lower world by moving the four elements and causing their combinations. The character of any combination therefore depends upon the position of the heavenly bodies at the moment that combination is effected.[117] Since man, too, represents a combination of elements, and the four faculties of his "animal soul" are an aspect of that combination, the position of the constellations at the time of a man's birth affects his character and course of action. An astrologer can foretell, therefore, whether a man will be dynamic or phlegmatic (which is identical with rich or poor), or whether his life will be long or short. He cannot, however, predict whether a man will be just or wicked.[118] Relying on Aristotle,[119] Abravanel maintains that the constellations do not affect freedom of choice—a limitation which was designed to save morality in the framework of this deterministic concept. From a moral viewpoint, however, the result is obviously appalling. Man may be good or bad, sinful or righteous; his fate in life depends not on his moral behavior but on the position of the heavenly bodies. Providence, it would seem, has no place in this scheme.

Nevertheless, Abravanel cannot give up Providence altogether. "One who has faith in God," he says, "can be saved from the harm decreed for him by the constellations. The prayers of a just man can move Providence to intervention on his behalf."[120] Do they? The trouble is that, as experience teaches us, prayers very often fail to avail the virtuous. But Abravanel has an answer to that, too. "If we see a righteous man suffer, it is because his righteousness did not reach the degree which would warrant the cancellation of the effect of the constellations."[121] In any case, to cancel this effect means to change the order of nature, which belongs to the sphere of miracles, and this, of course, is exceptional. The ordinary course of events is that written in the stars, and the natural effect of the stars applies to all men, regardless of what class or people they belong to. "Just as the fire heats and the water cools both Jew and Gentile, so does the effect of the stars apply equally to both."[122]

The heavenly bodies determine not only the fortunes of individuals, but also dictate the fortunes of groups. "Every nation and every city has a particular star which influences or controls its course in life."[123] The effect of these "national" stars is stronger than the effect of the constellations upon individuals. Therefore, "if a city is hit by plague or famine, those who are there will die even if their individual decree from the heavens indicated longevity."[124]

While the stars exercise this influence upon nations and cities, they themselves are controlled by the separate intelligences. They are the "heavenly princes" mentioned by the sages, the messengers of God, appointed by Him to protect and guide, punish and reward all human collectivities.[125] Since the decisions of these "heavenly princes" are indicated in the position of the constellations, astrology is used by the nations who wish to learn their decrees. But, when we refer to the nations, we must exclude Israel, for, unlike any other human collectivity, Israel has no "heavenly prince." Its ruler is God Himself.[126] Israel, as a people, being under divine guidance, and not under the control of the constellations, it has nothing to learn from the heavenly princes, but from God, its master. Not the astrologer but the prophet, therefore, can foretell Israel's future.[127]

Prophecy, then, is God's medium of communication with Israel. What distinguishes it from astrology, however, is not only its source and the realm of its application, but also the very nature of its contents. "To know the future and to take proper action at the proper time, in accordance with this knowledge, are the things most desired by man,"[128] says Abravanel, and only prophecy can adequately supply this most vital and most desired information. While the forecasts of the astrologers are often erroneous and inadequate, the predictions of the prophet are always precise and true.[129] Furthermore, the information imparted to the prophet is not limited to unfolding the mysteries of the future. It also unveils the mysteries of creation, the constitution of the universe and the essence of God. It reveals to man his own nature and destiny as well as his correct course of action. In brief, it encompasses the entire scope of human interest and knowledge.[130] Consequently, the question of establishing the authenticity of a prophet is of primary importance.

It is difficult to find a single one among the better known Jewish thinkers in the Middle Ages who failed to discuss this question. In an age when people who claimed to speak in God's name were a recurring phenomenon, the question evidently had practical implications. Testing the prophet was a matter of vital importance which might avert serious trouble. Maimonides, who warned his contemporaries against false prophets, was significantly meticulous in his "test" of the prophet. Influenced by his rationalistic conception of prophecy, he limited the proof of prophecy to the materialization of favorable predictions. Unfavorable predictions were discounted by Maimonides on the grounds that their realization might be offset by the people's repentance.[131] Ostensibly, it was an argument to protect the prophet. In reality, it was intended to protect the people. Under the conditions of the Diaspora, it was quite easy for a clever man to foresee some sinister development. Gersonides, who adopted an even stricter rationalistic attitude, agreed with Maimonides that the proof of prophecy was in the materialization of a favorable prediction, but, as a believer in astrology, he took the further caution of adding that the prediction should be one that could be learned only from a divine source, and not from the constellations.[132] In other words, the prophet should not predict what the astrologer can see, but something unknowable by the latter. Crescas, who represented a much less rationalistic trend, facilitated the test of the prophet by broadening the basis for the demonstration of his authenticity. According to him, the proof of prophecy lies in the fulfillment of any prediction, regardless whether it is favorable or not, for God would not inspire an unfavorable prediction if the proof of prophecy depended on it.[133] Abravanel, while accepting Crescas' argument, sees in the fulfillment of predictions only a partial proof of prophecy. Once again he returns to the position of Saadia:[134] the real proof of prophecy lies in the prophet's ability to perform miracles.[135]

This conditioning of the prophet's recognition upon the manifestation of supernatural powers was not a result of a mere desire to combat the danger of false prophecy. It was rather a result of Abravanel's view that the entire phenomenon of prophecy belongs to the sphere of the miraculous and of his stern belief that prophets are or should be able to change the order of nature. He thought that the prophet, by virtue of his communion with God, not only expresses the word of God, but also becomes a man of God, part of the Divine and possessing Divine powers. Also for this reason he rejected the theory of both Maimonides and Gersonides regarding the form of God's communication with the prophet. According to the latter, God informs the prophet, not directly, but indirectly, through the Active Intellect and by means of dreams and visions.[136] Abravanel, while agreeing that prophetic messages are sometimes transmitted through these media, insists nevertheless that God communicates with the prophet also directly.[137] In St. Augustine, who held a similar view, we find the beautiful and stirring thought that God speaks to the prophet's mind.[138] According to Abravanel, God speaks, not only to the prophet's mind, but also to the prophet's ear. God speaks to the prophet as man to man, although not with His own voice, since God is incorporeal, but with a voice created in a miraculous way.[139] Indeed, it is this very form of communication which marks the highest degree of prophetic achievement. It is distinguished by its clarity as well as by its directness from the other forms of divine message which involve symbolic indications.

Abravanel, as we have seen, agrees that dreams were among the media through which God—or more exactly, the Active Intellect, God's messenger—informed the prophets of God's decisions. These prophetic dreams should in no way be confused with the "senseless dreams caused by the imaginative faculty."[140] Nor should they be misconstrued as dreams occasioned under the influence of the heavenly bodies. The latter can be experienced by every individual and their genesis can be explained by ordinary developments. Freed during sleep from the impositions of the senses, and from the thoughts provoked by the various perceptions, the sublime soul becomes capable of absorbing the forms embodied in the celestial substances. "What transpires is similar to the transfer of an image from one mirror to another when the partition between them is removed."[141] Dreams occasioned by the heavenly bodies contain information of things that *may* happen in the future, since they reflect the prearrangement of the constellations for individuals and for nations. There is no assurance, however, that these things *will* happen. Just as the astrologer and the prophet differ, among other things, in the accuracy of their predictions, so do the "astrological" and the "prophetic" dreams differ in the exactitude of their indications. A dream divinely inspired is true in *all* its parts and man is informed by it of what will come to pass "in all the details and the right time."[142]

Prophecy, astrology and dreams, whether inspired by the heavenly bodies or by a divine source, are not the only means of learning the future. Besides these "legitimate" means there is an "illegitimate" way which, however, is no less effective. This is afforded by the science of necromancy, invoked by Saul when he consulted the dead Samuel. "Gersonides," writes Abravanel, "maintained that the appearance of Samuel from the world beyond was a product of Saul's imagination, while Maimonides said that it was a magician's trick."[143] In Abravanel's opinion, both scholars were wrong. "They had no understanding of the science of necromancy, and denied its validity only because they could not prove it."[144] The "science of necromancy," according to Abravanel, is based on actual employment of demons, and its principles can be readily understood. As executors of God's orders, the demons possess knowledge of events scheduled to take place,[145] and as demons they have a special power to appear in the bodily frame of dead humans.[146] Abravanel, we should add, actually believed in the ability of the demons to "resurrect" dead bodies, even though for a limited time and purpose, and he objected to the view, held among others by Aquinas, that the devil only "impersonated" Samuel when the latter appeared before the eyes of Saul.[147]

Another science which makes use of demons, although in a different way from necromancy, is magic. Maimonides, who repudiated the belief in demons, maintained that magic, as the alleged act of demons, is a deceitful use of man's imagination, for "demons are imaginary things that exist nowhere except in man's mind."[148] But Abravanel, disregarding Maimonides' view, follows here Albertus Magnus and Thomas Aquinas, both of whom regarded magic as a manifestation of man's ability to employ a demon.[149] Thus, claims Abravanel, the Egyptian magicians, who knew the "science of the demons,"[150] performed their wonders with demonic powers. The fact that they could bring up the frogs, but could not remove them, is a confirmation rather than a denial of magic as a genuine art, since the power of the devils is only to hurt and harm, but not to save and help. The Law's prohibition of witchcraft, despite its ability to achieve real results, was due to the fact that the angels of destruction were created to be God's instruments of punishment, and the effect of these harmful beings should be felt only at God's will. Those who are engaged in magic prepare the lower bodies to accept the effect of these destructive influences in opposition to the order desired by God.[151]

Abravanel's demonology seems to contradict his entire conception of the world of spirits. As we have seen, he conceived of all the intelligences as messengers of God, whether they were angels of mercy or of destruction. As such, they were appointed to carry out God's orders and were even denied freedom of will. How then can one assume that man can divert God's messengers from their mission? It can be assumed only if one conceives of man as Abravanel obviously did. For man, according to Abravanel, is not only higher than the angels in that he possesses free will; he also can control the angels and subject them to his will. Just as the prophet can with his will subordinate nature, which in the last analysis means the spiritual forces behind the phenomena of nature, so the magician has the power of bringing under his spell one species of these spiritual forces. Man can accomplish all this because he is endowed with a divine element, a spark of the mysterious, divine powers which do not know the impossible. Abravanel's demonology should thus be viewed as an extension of his extreme emphasis upon miracles and creation out of nothing. How, indeed, could one doubt the feasibility of magic? After all, the Greatest Magician performed the most supreme act of magic long ago, when He created the world out of nothing.

6. Conclusions

In the foregoing pages, we have attempted to describe Abravanel's world outlook. Briefly summarized, it is an outlook based on the primacy of Faith, on Revelation and on Divine Will. It conceives of that Will as the source of two worlds, spiritual and material, the first of which stands directly under divine rule and the latter under the control of the spiritual. Both worlds were created for man, who is free from this complete subordination since his creator endowed him with the power of free will. Man, however, can exercise his freedom of will to his advantage or disadvantage, depending on whether he acts in accordance with the purpose for which he was created. This purpose is eternal speculation on the divine essence, which can be fully achieved by one's immortal soul only in the world beyond. In this world the task of man is to effect a mental preparation which consists primarily in guarding his soul from the contaminating influences of matter. Only a soul which emerges pure from the communion with matter enjoys the bliss of communion with God. The soul which falls for the temptations of matter—which falling is the essence of all sin—is doomed to everlasting suffering. To prevent this terrible outcome, God gave man guiding directives incorporated in the divine Law, granted sinful souls many opportunities for purification through repentance and transmigration, and gave man ample warning as well as information of future developments through prophecy, dreams and astrology.

The pertinent question now is to what extent this was the

world outlook of his age. In his emphasis upon the primacy of Faith, Abravanel, as indicated, was going counter to the general current, and this itself must have determined to a great extent his entire position toward his time. His anthropocentric conception of the universe, on the other hand, was still the recognized and prevailing conception—although it, too, was considerably undermined and marked for oblivion in his own generation. At the very time when Abravanel composed his biblical commentaries and philosophical works, preparations were being carefully made for a deadly attack against that universe by Copernicus. The theory of Copernicus, however, although completed in 1500, was not made public until 1543—a few decades after Abravanel's death. But long before this, in the first half of the fifteenth century, Nicholas of Cusa had declared that the earth was not the center of the universe, that it could not be at rest and that it moves as do the other stars in the heavens.[152] Perhaps Abravanel had no opportunity to get acquainted with this theory, and, if he had, it is difficult to assume, considering the other parts of his world view, that he would have readily accepted it. In any case, in Abravanel's writings, we find not a trace of the doubts raised in the fifteenth century regarding the validity of the anthropocentric view.

More far-reaching than the difference concerning man's position in the universe was the difference concerning the intrinsic value of man's life. Abravanel's moral platform was that of the Middle Ages. But in the fifteenth century, the ascetic ideals of the Middle Ages were dying; instead of preparing himself for admission to heaven, man was attempting to prepare himself to achieve greater accomplishments in this world. The ideal man of the Middle Ages is the "religious man" of Halevi, the man who "never acts, speaks or thinks without believing that he is observed" by a Higher Power, who is "afraid and timid, at times ashamed at his doings," but, on the other hand, whose "soul exults" whenever he shows "some attention to the Lord in enduring hardships in obedience to God."[153] This was not the man of the Renaissance, who was adventurous, enterprising, lustful, and who looked for his inspiration to the ancient pagan heroes. Machiavelli, in his famous reprobation of Christianity, expressed, in a striking manner, the sharp contrast between the ideals of man in the Renaissance and the Middle Ages: "The ancient religion beatified only men of mundane glory, such as generals of armies and founders of republics; ours glorifies contemplative rather than active men. For us the supreme good lies in humility and submission and in the contempt of the world, whereas for them it lay in greatness of spirit, in strength of limb and in everything that makes men bold. Ours teaches men to be strong in enduring rather than in doing; and thus the world has become the prey of scoundrels who have found men willing, in order to gain Heaven, to endure injuries rather than to avenge them."[154] In the fifteenth century, man's outlook became much more secular and materialistic, and the world beyond was constantly reduced to the position of an unimportant shadow. Even men like Luther, Zwingli and Calvin stressed to a considerably lesser degree the other-worldly conceptions of the Middle Ages. To Erasmus religion was a system of morals rather than a system of beliefs.[155]

Yet this secular, materialistic and this-worldly tendency was only one of the features of the fifteenth century. For, side by side with this return to the material world from which the Middle Ages had detached man to a marked degree, there was a growing tendency to spiritualism. It was after all in this age of heresy that Thomas à Kempis wrote his *Imitatio Christi* which is exclusively dedicated to preparing man for the world to come, and Savonarola preached that "we live only to learn how to die."[156] The Middle Ages were still powerful even at the height of Renaissance materialism, and in addition to the enormous amount of true knowledge which was unearthed and revealed in that period, it also witnessed an especially vigorous revival of the "dead spirits" of the Middle Ages and antiquity. "Magic," says Henry S. Lucas, "flourished mightily in the fifteenth century." "Even learned theologians and philosophers believed in the existence of evil spirits and in the ability of witches to employ them for nefarious purposes."[157] The second half of the fifteenth century was especially affected in this respect. So numerous were the practices of witchcraft that in 1484 Innocent VIII had to issue his sharply-worded bull to check them.

The belief in miracles was almost universal. And so was the belief in the supernatural forces operating within the realm of nature. A man with a modern outlook, like Machiavelli, thought "the air we breathe to be full of spirits, which in compassion for mortals forewarned them by sinister omens of the evils about to come to pass." And Francesco Guicciardini, the historian of Italy, went so far as to say, "Aerial spirits exist which hold familiar converse with men, for I have had practical experience of this, in cases that make it appear most certain."[158]

Pico della Mirandola's *Disputationes adversus astrologiam*, which appeared in 1495, constituted a shattering attack on astrology. But it marked only the checking of the rising tide of the belief in astrology in the fifteenth century. In 1472, Regiomontanus published a manuscript of Manilius, the ancient Roman astrologer, which quickly became a best-seller; and soon thereafter, all the old Arab masters of astrology were republished. In Poland a permanent chair for astrology was established at the university of Cracow in 1460, and Paracelsus still studied astrology at the Basle university.[159] Marsillio Ficino, the great translator of Plato and head of the Florentine Academy, quite seriously ascribed his "habitual melancholy to the influence of Saturn."[160] That Abravanel embraced astrology may be further explained by the fact that the belief in it was very prevalent among Jews, and that authorities like Abraham ibn Ezra, Bar-Hiyya and even Gersonides recognized it as a true science. Halevi evidently discredited astrology, since he defined it as a "doubtful" study of nature,[161] but he did not dare to discard it completely. Maimonides was the only Jewish, and indeed medieval, authority who fought astrology fiercely and unqualifiedly, thus preceding by three centuries the attack of Pico della Mirandola.[162]

Nevertheless, while we find most of the elements of Abravanel's world view widely accepted in his generation, it must be emphasized that they did *not* form the world outlook of his age. Indeed, what characterized the close of the Middle Ages was the lack of a world outlook. It was a time in which people believed in everything, and yet believed in nothing. It was a period of scepticism, during which "the old truth ceased to be truth and the new truth had not yet become truth." It was an age in which the conflicting concepts of the Middle Ages and the Renaissance simultaneously influenced and confused man's mind. In brief, it was a time marked by its duality—by its double set of truths. Abravanel was free of this duality. He accepted only one set of truths—the medieval. Taken as a whole, therefore, his position represents a revolt against the spirit of the Renaissance, and an attempt at the rehabilitation of the spirit of the Middle Ages.

CHAPTER TWO

VIEW OF HISTORY

1. *The Principles*

ABRAVANEL'S conception of history is closely connected with his conception of the universe. It is, in fact, the identical concept viewed from a different angle. We have seen that he considered the cosmos as permeated throughout with divine Will; we shall now examine his view on the working of that Will. Thus far we have seen the various parts of the cosmic machine and described their functions; we shall now see them in operation.

The fact that Abravanel rejected the Aristotelian theory of nature and the theory of the eternity of the world, radically affected his view of history. According to the theory which conceives of nature as subject to immutable laws, ever manifesting themselves in the same way, the course of history is at once infinite and limited to certain patterns. It is the history of a tree from its embryonic form in the seed, through its highest state of development, to its decay and decomposition—the same process repeating itself endlessly. So it is in the world of irrational nature; and so it is in the world of man. Man's forms of life and society are determined by his nature. They grow, develop and die like a tree; then grow again from the seeds inherent in the nature of man. This theory of nature views history as repetitious and evolutionist. In contrast, the theory of the world as the scene of the operation of an ever-active, all powerful and free Will, subject to no law but possessing complete freedom of action and capable of abrogating and overriding, at any time, the normal processes of nature, considers history as the most important field of observation for understanding the character of the divine Will. It sees history as full of unexpected, dramatic and revolutionary changes, the reasons for which cannot be adduced from the ordinary phenomena of nature, but rather from the extraordinary phenomena and forced changes of nature in which that Will conspicuously manifests itself. In a word, it is from the observation of history rather than from nature that we can learn whether the divine Will is arbitrary, or whether it acts in accordance with a plan.

That God does not act by accident or by chance was a principle accepted by all medieval philosophers, and it was a basic belief with Abravanel. They had to conceive of history as planned, for without a plan, not only would history become meaningless, but the entire concept of God would be destroyed. The fundamental aspect of this concept was the eternity of His nature and His immutability. Since His essence is unalterable, His Will, which is part of that essence, must also remain unaltered. Those who saw in history the manifestation of God's Will were thus confronted with the following problem: God's Will is unchangeable, but the world, which is ruled by God, is subject to constant change. There was one way to eliminate this contradiction. It implied the introduction of a certain design in the course of the world's history that ties together, by its uniformity and immutability, the shifting phenomena of the world.[1]

Thus, in the view of Abravanel, God directs the world according to a certain plan and this plan embraces all of history. Hence, just as it is impossible to know one part of the structure of the universe without knowing its entire composition and the interrelations of all its parts, so it is impossible to understand properly one period of history without comprehending its planned course from beginning to end. To know history means, therefore, to know not only the past but also the future, to know the entire process of historic development from the first stages to the last.[2]

We speak of the "last" stages of history because it was one of Abravanel's major premises that the world has a definite span of life. Just as he opposes the doctrine of eternity as far as the beginning of the universe is concerned so he opposes the doctrine of eternity as far as the end of the universe is concerned. Here, too, Abravanel departs from Maimonides, who believed the world was destined to exist forever,[3] and takes up the line of Jewish thought of the pre-Maimonidean period. His position is that the universe has been endowed by its Creator with the power to endure a limited time, at the end of which it must cease to exist.[4] This was exactly the position of Saadia, who wrote: "The heavens and the earth are compound and limited bodies. Therefore, their power must also be limited. Because their power is limited, it is necessarily transient. Since their power is transient, we must assume that the world as a whole is transient and will return to nothingness as it was before."[5] To Abravanel, as to Saadia, then, even as the universe is finite in space, so history is finite in time.[6]

The theory that the universe is perishable is of early date in the record of human thought. It is the theory of Empedocles as well as of Plato, to both of whom Abravanel refers for support.[7] There was, however, a major difference between his conception and that of the Greek philosophers. According to the latter, the universe is destructible insofar as it represents a combination of elements; the elements themselves being indestructible. The position of Abravanel, as well as of Saadia, is closer to that of Irenaeus and Augustine, in whose system of thought the destruction of the world occupies a central position. Since the latter believed in creation out of nothing, they could easily disregard the theory of the world's disintegration into basic elements. Their concept of the world's end, however, envisioned the world as emerging "purified" and "renovated" out of the great fire of destruction, but in no way reduced to nothing.[8] In medieval Jewry, outside of Saadia, the chief proponents of the return-to-nothing view were Bar-Hiyya and Nahmanides, and it is to them that Abravanel refers most often for support of his contention regarding the world's end.[9] His major concern, however, is to "prove" his assumption by the words of the prophets and the "tradition of the holy sages."[10] Thus, Abravanel finds the idea of the destruction of the world expressed in Psalm 102 in the following verses (13. 25–7):

> Thou whose years endure throughout all generations,
> Of old Thou didst lay the foundations of the earth;
> And the heavens are the work of Thy hands.
> They shall perish, but Thou shalt endure;
> Yea, all of them shall wax old like a garment;
> As a vesture shalt Thou change them and they shall pass away.[11]

Origen, who was the first among the Church Fathers to insist on the destructibility of the world, already referred to the same Psalm to prove his thesis.[12] Abravanel might have been directly influenced by Origen, but, in any case, he does not stop where Origen did. The mere knowledge that the world is headed for destruction does not satisfy him. He also wants to know *when* it will be destroyed. To determine this most significant of all dates, Abravanel follows the same line of thinking which was perhaps first suggested by Irenaeus.[13] From the records of Scripture we know the world's age. From the same records it is possible to deduce its total span of life. This "span" is indicated in the scriptural story of creation, and the very questions raised by that story embody the solution of our problem. God could have created the world in one instant. Why then did He take six days?[14] God is omnipotent and indefatigable. What then is the meaning of the seventh day of rest? The answer is that the days of creation were six, to indicate that the world would last six thousand years, since —as we can learn from another allusion in the Bible—the day of God consists of a thousand years.[15] The seventh day of rest was to indicate that in the seventh millennium God would stop moving this universe; consequently it would be obliterated.

We now come to the third phase of Abravanel's theory of history. According to it, the six days of creation do not testify merely to the length of the world's existence. They also testify— if one can comprehend the testimony—to the course of its existence from beginning to end. What was created in each of the six days represents not only the actual process of creation, but also alludes to what was to transpire in each of the six millennia of the world's life.[16] As in the case of the general theory regarding the destructibility of the world, we find the theory regarding the symbolic import of the six days of creation elaborated upon in the writings of Bar-Hiyya and Nahmanides, both of whom, as has been conclusively proved, were influenced by Isidore of Seville.[17] Whether Abravanel made use of the Christian source is difficult to ascertain; but it is certain that he was inspired by Bar-Hiyya and Nahmanides and, while differing from them with regard to the interpretations of the biblical allusions in some details, he accepts their general historical outline.[18] We shall later deal more extensively with Abravanel's thought on this point.[19] For the present we shall limit ourselves to emphasizing his threefold conception of history as (a) finite, (b) embraced within a definite period of time, and (c) planned in advance.

To complete our exposition of Abravanel's view on the general course of history, two additional points must be considered.

When he speaks of the world's span of life as lasting six thousand years, he refers only to the sublunary world. The upper world, according to Abravanel, will be destroyed after forty-nine thousand years, that is, after seven sabbatical millennia.[20] In support of this contention Abravanel mentions the view held by some medieval astronomers that each of the seven planets "rules" the world for seven thousand years, thus making a total of forty-nine millennia whose end will coincide with the end of the world.[21] The same view was mentioned by Bar-Hiyya only to be rejected by him.[22] The fact that Abravanel accepted it, however, should be attributed not to the indefinite influence of a non-prevalent astronomical theory, but rather to the influence of the cabalists who embraced that theory and claimed to have found allusions to it in the Bible. Believing that the cabala actually represented the secret teachings of the ancient Sages,[23] Abravanel could not reject the view regarding the prolonged existence of the heavens. It is difficult nevertheless to assume that he failed to notice that it stood in contradiction to his anthropocentric conception of the universe. What sense is there—the question presents itself— in the existence of the lifeless celestial bodies, when humanity for which they were created exists no longer? We cannot be far wrong if we assume that Abravanel had this question in mind when he said in obvious bewilderment: "Why God in His divine wisdom ordered that the sublunary world should exist six thousand years while the heavenly circle should last forty-nine thousand years, is one of those mysteries which God concealed from us."[24]

The other, and final, major point in the historical concept of Abravanel was his contention that the entire course of history was not a phenomenon which occurred only once, but one which repeated itself indefinitely.[25] According to Abravanel, Isaiah's prophecy, about the "new heavens and the new earth which I will make,"[26] indicates that after the destruction of the sublunary and celestial worlds, God will create a new universe.[27] The statement in Ecclesiastes, "That which hath been is that which shall be,"[28] indicates that the worlds that God will create in the future will follow the same pattern as those He created in the past.[29] Both the idea of the repetitious course of history as well as the references to the above biblical verses, are again to be found in the writings of Origen.[30] Like Origen, then, and for that matter, like the Stoics and Plato, Abravanel believed in the cycle theory, with the difference that, according to him, there was a fixed interval between each cycle in which the material world was completely nonexistent.[31] Thus, God created and destroyed worlds an infinite number of times, and He will go on creating and destroying them ad infinitum. Since the course of each world, and the interval between the worlds, are always the same, there is no change in the Will of God.[32]

2. *The Course*

Like Augustine, Maimonides and Thomas Aquinas, Abravanel believed that "God created the world because of His goodness, and for no other reason."[33] This is basically the view of Plato, which was embraced also by Saadia, both of whom were greatly admired by Abravanel.[34] One who proceeds on such an assumption must try to explain God's historical plan as the manifestation of this goodness; and this is exactly what Abravanel was trying to accomplish. Accordingly, he saw the world which emerged from creation—as Plato did—as "the best of all possible worlds," and man, its final cause, as perfect both in spirit and body when he first appeared in this world.[35] Spiritually his reason was of the highest order—so high indeed that the first man was declared to be made in the image of God[36]—and bodily he was at the apex of physical creation. "His temperament was so balanced, his composition so strong, his organs so excellently constructed and so perfectly fitted to each other, that, if he had only conducted himself as God ordered him, he would have existed indefinitely and escaped death."[37] The same view was held by Augustine.[38] The latter in particular comes to mind because Abravanel's conception of human history, especially in its early stages, coincides very closely with that of Augustine, whose philosophy of history influenced medieval thought more deeply than that of any other thinker before or after him.[39]

Returning to Abravanel's views, despite man's eminence at creation, it was God's plan that man should rise even higher. God created man in His rational image so that he would continually make an effort to elevate his soul by increasing both his knowledge of the Creator and his understanding of His deeds, until he became similar to Him in wisdom. "For the perfection of the image is in great similarity to the form."[40] The surroundings in which God placed man were most ideal for this purpose. The Garden of Eden was in the most delightful spot on earth, "right on the Equator, where the climate was well balanced,"[41] thus eliminating the possibility of death because of weather changes. "To save man from old age and subsequent death, God gave him the Tree of Life, whose fruit was so suited to man's natural composition that, by eating it, the tissues and humors which were newly formed were equal to those which melted away."[42] All things necessary for man's life were prepared for him by God, that is, they existed in nature.[43] There was no need for any artificial effort to obtain them, and man's mind was free from any worry over their acquisition. He could fully concentrate upon the elevation of his soul through constant contemplation of God and His works, and fulfill the purpose for which he was created.[44] As St. Augustine put it, man was planted by God "in a Paradise at once physical and spiritual."[45]

Like Augustine and most medieval theologians, Abravanel says that "in the beginning God created one man."[46] Out of the rib of this single man God created the woman. Abravanel's view of woman—intellectually and morally—is extremely low. It is a typical medieval view inspired partly by Aristotle, partly by oriental ideas, and largely by the teachings of Christian theology. Thus, the statement that man was created in God's image refers to man only, not to woman, his counterpart, for only man can comprehend the secrets of divine wisdom and therefore man alone was the aim of creation.[47] Woman was created for the propagation of mankind and also—which seems quite unnecessary under the conditions of primordial nature!—to care for the material necessities of man and enable him to concentrate more freely on the achievement of his rational perfection.[48]

The break in the happiness and felicity of man came about as a result of sin. In other words, sin was responsible for the first appearance of evil in a world permeated with God's goodness. The great question is: what is sin, and how did it come about? According to Augustine, sin originated not with man, but with the fallen angel, the devil, who used the serpent as his instrument for inducing man to sin,[49] and, basically, this was also the opinion of Saadia, who said that it was the devil who appeared to man in the form of a snake.[50] Abravanel, parting here with Augustine and Saadia, rejects this opinion categorically. As we have stated, the devil, according to Abravanel, is not a fallen angel who acts on his own, but an agent of God sent to inflict punishment. To assume that the devil induced man to sin would be equivalent to saying that God induced man to sin. For the same reason, we should not believe that the snake actually talked, which would constitute a miracle, that is, a divine or an angelic act. "It was only the imagination of the woman which made her think that the snake spoke to her. When she saw the snake climbing the tree and eating from its fruit, it was as if she heard it say: "You will not die."[51]

Thus, the origin of sin was not outside of man, but in man himself. It resulted from man's freedom of will. God, because of His goodness, endowed man with this highest of all capacities, which enabled him to rise to a divine position.[52] But man abused this extraordinary privilege, granted him by his Creator, by choosing the wrong course of action. Man's evil inclination was thus the origin of sin,[53] and sin, according to Abravanel as well as Augustine, consists of questioning God's order with the intent to misinterpret and deviate from it.[54] In his explanation of the purpose of God's order, however, Abravanel differs with Augustine. According to the latter, the Tree of Knowledge, from which man ate contrary to God's instruction, did not in itself constitute any evil, "for in that spot of singular felicity God could not have created and planted an evil thing."[55] God's order not to eat from the fruit of the Tree of Knowledge was, therefore, merely a test of obedience, and consequently man's crime was sheer disobedience to God.[56] In opposition to this view, Abravanel maintains that it was not a test of obedience that was placed before man. It was an order of divine wisdom regarding man's proper behavior, perfectly suited to man's nature, so that by transgressing it, man was bound to fall into trouble.[57]

The difference in conceptions of the nature of sin led to a difference of opinions on the initial urge to sin. According to Augustine, the source of man's sin was pride in his perfection, which led him to believe himself on a par with God.[58] According to Abravanel, the source of sin was lust, or, more precisely, man's dissatisfaction with the natural things God had prepared for him and his development of a passion for the abnormal and unnatural.[59] This dissatisfaction arose in man when he yielded to his evil inclination after the material, when he indulged in sexual passion, stimulated by the fruit of the Tree of Knowledge.[60]

Sin brought in its wake punishment; and the punishment for man's sin was twofold. It was the natural result of sin, on the one hand, and God's retributive justice, aimed at man's moral improvement, on the other. Both punishments implied death.[61] By deserting the path ordered by God, in which man could maintain himself by nature in the most perfect manner, man disturbed the balance of his body and was made subject to corruption. Augustine strikingly expressed the same idea when he said: "It was not the corruptible flesh that made the soul sinful, but the sinful soul that made the flesh corruptible."[62] The corruption of the flesh then resulted in man's death, which constituted the implementation of God's decree, Who, in addition, punished man with expulsion from the Garden of Eden and with diminution of the earth's fertility. Man no longer deserved that wonderful yield of the earth which brought him those marvellous life-giving fruits. Instead of the peace of mind he had experienced before he sinned, man was condemned to permanent worry and trouble. Instead of the leisure which he had enjoyed, man was now condemned to hard labor. Nature, in its perfect state, did not satisfy him because of his sinful inclination. Nature would not satisfy him now because of its impoverishment by the curse put upon it. For a perfect man, God created a perfect earth. For a man in the state of sin, the earth's perfection was reduced.[63]

Nevertheless, man, after his fall, was still in an extremely happy state. He no longer inhabited the Garden of Eden, but the earth was still a wonderful place to live in. Despite his fall, the first man and his immediate offspring were still on a high moral and physical level. This is why the first generations of men lived to such an advanced age. Maimonides maintained that the scriptural statements about the extraordinary longevity of men in those days applied only to the individuals named, while the rest of the people did not live beyond the ordinary span of life.[64] Abravanel disagrees with this view. Accepting Nahmanides' opinion that the first man—the direct creation of God—was such a perfect physical specimen that, although death was decreed upon him, longevity was still in his nature, he maintains that the powers of the first man were more or less common to the first generations. But, adds Abravanel, it is not because of their physical powers alone that men lived long in those days, but also because of their mode of living. Neither the first man nor any of his generation would approach a woman before he was sixty or seventy years old. The food they ate was only to satisfy their natural needs. They would not eat meat or drink wine—a custom which began only in the days of Noah—but were satisfied with herbs and vegetables and water. Vegetables are the simplest of foods, and, "as the medical books tell us, the simpler the foods, the more they are conducive to longevity." Therefore, although man was condemned to ultimate death, he was still able, according to his nature, to live a long time, owing to the perfection of his body and his general conduct.[65]

Because of their extraordinary beauty and strength and longevity, the men of the first generations were called the sons of God.[66] It is wrong to assume that the sons of God mentioned in Genesis 6.2, who took the daughters of men as wives, were angels. Since separate intelligences would not acquire the nature of material bodies, the sons of God were necessarily human beings.[67] But from this exalted position of Sons of God, man was gradually falling, and the reason for his fall was again woman, the symbol and object of man's lust. Because of his indulgence in material passions, there was a steady increase in man's deviation from the order of nature, his corruption progressed swiftly, and the people of the generation of the deluge were already engaged in robbery and all sorts of crime.[68] The deadly moral disease affected practically the whole of humanity, and "once wickedness becomes universal, it cannot be remedied."[69] Thus, man brought upon himself the great punishment of annihilation through the deluge. God decided to wipe out mankind, save for one just man.

The tendency of the first man toward the material and the unnatural, that is, toward deviation from his life's purpose as well as from God's order, was manifested in various degrees in Adam's three sons—Cain, Abel and Seth—who originated the three courses of man's life, the animal, the political and the rational.[70] Cain symbolized animal life, that is, life devoted to passions and to the artificial arts aimed to satisfy these passions. Attached to matter, to earth, he became a tiller of the soil; and, interested in artificial production, he built a city called Enoch, meaning "education," in which he taught his sons the different crafts and luxurious arts, including music and the forging of metals.[71] Abel represented man's ambition for leadership and honors. He is the father of the class of kings, rulers and counsellors, who conduct the people's affairs for the people's sake or for glory.[72] The type of life represented by this class is of a higher nature than the first, but is inferior to the third, symbolized by Seth. Seth initiated the class of men who understand that the real purpose of man's life is the worship of God and the attainment of knowledge; who reject material possessions and honors which are transitory, and devote themselves to the perfection of the immortal soul, which is of eternal value.[73] However, not even the sons of Seth were free from the inclination to matter, and they, too, fell under the spell of the sons of Cain who seduced all the people of the world to pursue the artificial crafts and indecent passions, involving them in crime and evil for which the deluge was brought upon them.[74]

The deluge was a catastrophe not only for man, but for all nature. Just as the first sin of man brought the first curse upon the earth and decreased the abundance and value of its produce, so, and even to a greater extent, did the deluge bring in its wake destruction whose effect was felt far beyond the bounds of mankind. Indeed, every change in the position of man brings in its wake a change in the position of nature, for nature in itself has no meaning and no purpose unless it serves man. Thus, as a result of the deluge, the weather became humid and the earth overmoist; the plants became weak and lacking in nutritive power; and postdiluvian man, looking for a substitute, began to eat meat and drink wine, which merely served to shorten his span of life.[75] God, however, permitted meat and wine to Noah and his sons, because man's soul was already hopelessly corrupted by the inclination toward the unnatural.[76]

Man escaped complete extinction by the deluge, but he could not escape his nature. The three sons of Noah, like the three sons of Adam, represent the three basic divisions in man's life—animal, political and rational.[77] Ham typifies the animal side; Japheth the political side; and Shem the rational side. The basic inequalities in mankind, and the basic tendencies, become again manifest, although now in a far more inferior man. For the nature of man after the deluge was of much baser quality than the nature of the man who emerged from creation. It was a nature weakened by both passions and punishments, corrupted by the pursuit of the artificial, which had already assumed the form of a second nature. The concessions to man's unnatural appetites, granted by God to Noah and his sons, did not satisfy man's evil inclination. The tendency toward passion, toward the luxurious and the artificial, broke out again like some morbid disease, striking first Ham and his progeny and spreading swiftly throughout the human race. It was Nimrod, of Hamite descent, who established the first city after the deluge, thus following in Cain's footsteps. And this tendency to urban life, which represents the artificial, in contrast to life in the field, which symbolizes the natural, was developed to the extreme in the generation of the Tower of Babel.[78]

The crime of the generation of the Tower of Babel represents the third fall of mankind, and the punishment which followed represents the third stage into which man deteriorated. The fall of Adam was followed by the expulsion from the Garden of Eden. The fall of the sons of God was followed by the deluge, and the fall of the generation of the Tower of Babel was followed by the dispersion and fragmentation of humanity and by the introduction of artificial differences into the status of man in society. Until the generation of the Tower of Babel, mankind was one big family. The development of material civilization introduced schisms into this family and turned man against man. Mankind was divided into nations, states and classes, and the origin of all this division was the confusion of languages.[79]

Abravanel's theory on the development of languages begins with Halevi's assumption that until the age of the generation of the Tower of Babel all men spoke Hebrew, which had been taught them by God.[80] "God spoke to man in that language and made him hear it through His created voice."[81] It goes without saying that Hebrew, the divine language, is the most perfect of all languages and the most suitable for assigning names to all things.[82] Why then did most people neglect the use of Hebrew? And how did they substitute other languages for it? Abravanel offers the following explanation: "So long as people would use the same natural things, they would give them the same names. But when they began to change their natural habits and to invent new and artificial things for their use, they had to create new terms and verbs for all those inventions and usages."[83] As a result, the builders of the Tower of Babel, who "chose artificial methods in their abominable desires to a greater degree than any of their predecessors," brought about the confusion of languages. Failing to reach agreement on the linguistic terms for the artificial things they had invented, "each family would give the objects a different name and, by the mixture of the newly-accepted terms with the original language, numerous new and mixed languages were created."[84]

The division of mankind into peoples and national groups, however, was not based only on the division of languages. Once the social unity of mankind was destroyed, its moral, intellectual and physical inequality became increasingly manifest. The corruption of man's original nature was thus responsible for certain splits in his makeup and for the development of that inequality in the human race. The differences between Shem, Ham and Japheth were more strongly evidenced in the post-diluvian period than in the ante-diluvian times, and these differences became even more conspicuous with the separation of mankind into peoples and states. Consequently, "all the nations that derived their origin from Ham —Kush and Egypt, Put and Canaan—are until this very day ugly in appearance. Their skin is as black as the raven; they indulge in sexual promiscuity and all animal passions. They have no capacity for reasoning or for acquiring knowledge, and have none of the fine manners and bravery which characterize ability for political life."[85] By contrast, "the sons of Japheth, from whom the Greeks and the Romans derived, are distinguished in appearance, in fine manners, in bravery and political ability."[86] But the source of wisdom and knowledge must be attributed only to the nations who originated from Shem.[87]

The division of mankind into languages and nations represented, like all punishments, the very opposite of the crime's aim.

Prior to the generation of the Tower of Babel, the people of the earth were "one nation, naturally united by one language and one mode of life."[88] Dissatisfied with that state of affairs, they wanted to create a society which would be more closely united, a society based on specialization and mutual assistance necessitated by the complicated inventions. Instead of greater unity, however, they achieved less unity, as a result of their ensuing dispersion and division. Nevertheless, this calamity—again like all punishments!—represented a divine plan directed towards the good of mankind. The purpose of the division was to separate the better elements from the worse, and the purpose of separation was selection. Out of the generation of the deluge, God selected Noah for the continuation of the human race. Out of the dispersed elements of mankind, following the generation of the Tower of Babel, God selected Abraham to fulfill man's mission on earth. Noah had been of the source of Seth, in whose soul reason was the dominant element. Similarly, Abraham was of the source of Shem, who symbolized rational life. The nature of Shem, however, was also deeply affected by the corruption of the animal and political tendencies and it was therefore by the process of birth and rebirth, of the selection of the best specimens of his race, that his nature was gradually purified from the contaminating influences of the other elements. Following closely in the footsteps of Halevi,[89] Abravanel maintains that the genealogical process of selection, which continued for ten generations, was not completed even with Abraham, since of the latter's offspring only one son, Isaac, displayed the predominance of the rational soul; nor did selection end with Isaac, whose son Esau manifested the negative side of man. The process was completed only with Jacob, all of whose sons were perfect specimens through whom the purpose of the human race could be realized.[90]

From now on, the history of humanity branches off into two distinct courses: the history of Israel and the history of the nations. While the nations are given over to the control of the heavenly princes, Israel is guided by God Himself.[91] The initial direction of Israel's historic course was aimed towards the fulfillment of the divine plan of creating a perfect man who would cleave to God and act in accordance with His order. Therefore, the law of life which God gave Israel was similar to the law of life given to the first man. It was similar, but not identical, since man's nature was changed so greatly that the original law did not fit him any longer. Thus, Israel was allowed to eat meat, but forbidden to eat blood or even meat of animals which most contaminate man's nature.[92] Similarly, since Israel, like the rest of mankind, was inseparably attached to the artificial forms of life, God permitted them the use of the known crafts and inventions. However, during the entire time of Israel's sojourn in the wilderness, God provided their needs, not with artificial, but only with natural things—like manna and quail.[93]

Just as God gave Israel the best possible law of life, so He gave them His direct care and guidance. The care was manifested by the numerous miracles enacted on behalf of Israel, and the guidance by the instructions and admonitions of the prophets. In this respect also, Israel was in the privileged position of the first man. Especially was this the case during their stay in the wilderness, when miracles were performed most frequently, and God's guidance was manifested at every step.[94] Furthermore, just as God selected the Garden of Eden as the habitation of the first man, so He selected for Israel a land most suitable to man's life from both the material and spiritual viewpoints—a land exceptionally fertile, "more elevated than all other countries," and most fitting for the development of man's rational faculties, for the stimulation of prophecy and the comprehension of God's instructions.[95] In brief, God gave Israel the ideal Law, the ideal care and the ideal land for the attainment of the desired perfection.

For a brief period, following the giving of the Law, Israel was truly the People of God. The entire people, to a man, was holy and divine, eagerly following God's orders.[96] But sin soon manifested itself in Israel, and the ensuing history is filled with the long and arduous struggle between the godly and the sinful elements within it, the latter steadily gaining ascendance until the whole nation succumbed to sin. Then followed God's terrible punishment. Just as the first man was expelled from the Garden of Eden, so Israel was exiled from the Holy Land. Just as God's Providence forsook mankind when He divided it into peoples and nations, so God's Providence now abandoned Israel, the only group of men among whom it was still manifest. And just as humanity, during the generation of the Tower of Babel, was punished with global dispersion, so Israel's punishment was to be scattered to the four corners of the earth.

According to Abravanel, the period of the exile began with the destruction of the First Temple and has continued ever since. As we shall see more clearly later, he refused to recognize the Second Commonwealth as a period of redemption.[97] In fact, he insisted that that period introduced the calamity of exile which has deepened and broadened with the passage of time. Israel was subjected to ever-intensified punishment by the nations, from which it will survive only by God's grace.[98] When the period of punishment is over, Israel will be ready for final purification and its redemption will be at hand.

What is to happen from then on represents the last stretch of the road. It represents the great era of salvation which will open some time within the sixth millennium. For, by now, more than five millennia have already elapsed and history has run its course as designed by God and as indicated in the story of the six days of creation.[99] In this sixth millennium, with the beginning of the Messianic Age, a complete break is to take place in the course of human history. That break will be expressed first of all in man's mind, in his attitude toward the world and his conception of God. Just as the redemption of Israel from Egypt implanted the truth of God's rule in the hearts of Israel, so the redemption of Israel from the last exile will implant that truth in the hearts of all men.[100] And the effect of the last redemption will be much greater because it will be executed through more spectacular miracles, including the most startling and astounding of all—the Resurrection of the dead. These miracles will compel even the most sceptical and most impious to recognize God's authority and yield wholeheartedly to His order.[101]

On that day, when mankind will return to God, Providence will return to mankind, and with that mankind will be reborn.[102] A new kind of man, purified and forever freed from the inclination toward evil, or, in other words, a man unable to sin, will appear on the scene of history.[103] The moral danger to man having been eliminated, man's soul will be able to rise steadily in unceasing contemplation of the divine essence. When man's intellectual perfection attains its highest and final climax, the purpose of creation will have been accomplished. The earth's existence will come to an end, and the sublimated human souls will all return, pure and untarnished, together with the angels, to the source from whence they sprang, the "substance" of God.[104]

Our survey of Abravanel's view of history could be terminated at this point. But Abravanel makes some additional remarks regarding the post-historical state of affairs that may be helpful for the understanding of his historical concept. They deal with the following mystifying questions: "What happens after the separate intelligences and the pure souls return to their Source? What kind of existence do they have then? Are they wholly united with the essence of God so that they completely disappear in it, or does some sort of distinction and plurality still exist between the One who gathers the spirits and those that are gathered?" "This again," admits Abravanel, "is one of God's mysteries which human reason cannot unravel." Nevertheless, he attempts to unravel it. "Perhaps," he says, "there is no complete plurality and no complete unity, but mutual cleavage between the spiritual beings, and between all of them and the divine Source. Things which are attached to each other in such a way cannot be completely united, nor completely distinct."[105] Does it imply a change in God's form of existence? Does it mean that the unity and separatism of God are ended? Abravanel, fighting off such heretical notions, further clarifies or perhaps changes his position. "By returning to the Source, the spiritual beings do not become identified with the First Cause." "For," he concludes, "He will always be One, simple in essence and separate from the rest, even though the angels and the souls cleave to Him and unite with Him as the spark is united with the sun."[106]

3. *The Characteristics*

We can now summarize the general characteristics of Abravanel's view of history. What should be noted first is the similarity between his conception and that of the mystics. The course of history, according to the Aristotelian doctrine, is similar to a straight line, endless in both directions. The historical conception of Maimonides is, also, of a straight line which has no end, although it does have a beginning. The historical conception of Abravanel is, like that of Eckhart and other mystics, not rectilinear but circular:[107] everything comes from God and returns to God.

The other major characteristic in Abravanel's historical theory is that history in its entirety, with the exception of its last phase, represents a continual decline of mankind. From the extremely high position of the first man, man falls steadily to the lowest possible level, and the cataclysmic events in man's history mark only the degrees of this fall. As is the case with mankind as a whole, so it is with Israel. Israel, too, was in a state of perfection only at the beginning of its national existence, and a survey of Israel's life, from Abravanel's point of view, leads us down a spiritual stairway. From the bottom of the abyss to which history brings mankind, it cannot climb back. It is *raised* from it, not by its own power, but by the limitless power of God. As far as man's role in history is concerned, Abravanel's historical view is pessimistic. It considers man a failure, dismal and hopeless, which can be rectified only by God.

It is questionable, however, whether, on the basis of Abravanel's theory, we can speak of "man's historic role" in any real sense. As we have seen, the entire history of the human race is a history of sin, punishment and purification—by selection and by the process of trial and error. It is a history of the establishment of the divine Will in the finest of God's creatures—man—whom He endowed with free will. It is a process of making this free will act in a certain direction, opposed to the one toward which it is inclined, thus exemplifying the paradoxical statement of Rousseau that "man must be compelled to be free." In truth, however, in the actual historical development, human will is of little or no significance. Man is allowed to act freely only to the extent permitted him by God, and this extent is extremely restricted.

It is especially restricted because the course of human events is not merely controlled by God but also follows God's advance decisions. For everything is preordained. Everything is prearranged by God. Man therefore can occupy no position either in the evolution of history or in its revolutionary changes. What seems to be a revolution is but the tick of the clock, a sign that the time is up for a certain rule or regime. It is but a landmark on the long road of man's journey on this earth, an indication that he has arrived at a certain spot on his way toward the goal fixed for him by God.

That man's will is of no consequence in the historical course of events is further proved by Abravanel's major assumption that the entire course of history, besides being planned by God, is also foreseen by Him. Even man's deviation from the path of righteousness, even his sins, are fully foreseen. The medieval thinkers, who shared this attitude, attempted, of course, to coordinate God's foreknowledge and man's freedom of choice.[108] But logic could never be satisfied with any of the solutions. God's foreknowledge evidently prevents any logical possibility of freedom of choice, and this assumption so permeates Abravanel's historical philosophy,[109] that his view of history must be considered deterministic.

It has been suggested that the historical conception of Abravanel was that of the Renaissance.[110] Nothing, in our opinion, is farther from the truth. For the best summarized presentation of the historical conception of the Renaissance, we must again turn to Machiavelli. "It is not unknown to me," he wrote, "that many men believed, and still believe, that the affairs of this world are so governed by Fortune and God, that the wisdom of man is powerless to direct or stay them, and that it is useless therefore to give them too much thought, and that we should let chance rule them."[111] Machiavelli cannot accept such a fatalistic concept which denies man all possibility to determine his future and his position in the world. "Fortune," he insists, "shows her power where virtue has not prepared to resist her, and vents her fury where she knows that neither bulwarks nor barriers have been raised to contain her."[112] Machiavelli believes that these "bulwarks" and "barriers" can be provided by human will and courage. He rejects the pessimistic and deterministic view of history and substitutes for it an optimistic conception, signified by faith in man's power and his ability to control his destiny. In brief, the historical creed of the Renaissance is based not on God, but on man, while that of Abravanel is based not on man, but on God. The historical philosophy of Abravanel is, as far as its principles are concerned, not that of the Renaissance, but that of St. Augustine and Isidor of Seville, of Bar-Hiyya and Nahmanides, that is, of the Christian and Jewish Middle Ages.

CHAPTER THREE

POLITICAL CONCEPTS

1. Fundamental Problems

IN HIS WORLD outlook and view of history Abravanel laid the utmost stress on the over-all direction and control of God. In his discussions of politics, on the other hand, Abravanel stresses the role and responsibility of man. This change of emphasis is occasioned by a change of perspective, not of view. We have seen that in Abravanel's historical conception man is permitted freedom to a very small extent and that his moves, as far as they are a product of his own choice, are confined to an extremely narrow sphere. Abravanel's attention is now focused on this sphere and these moves, that is, on man's performance within his own society and within the realm of terrestrial life. For this reason the world to come, so prominently featured elsewhere by Abravanel, is rarely mentioned in his political discussions. Like the divine Will which turns the "wheel" of mankind, so the future world—its ultimate destination—is placed momentarily in the shadow, while the spotlight is turned upon the "wheel" itself. The field of observation is more limited, while that which is happening within it is greatly magnified. But the impression that all this tends to create is of a different spirit and approach, a more mundane and practical attitude toward man's personal and social problems.

This impression is further strengthened by the fact that some of Abravanel's basic political views reflect a striking political radicalism which seems to agree more with modern than with medieval conceptions. This is at least how some of his political theories appear at their face value. When, however, we inquire into the inner meaning and purpose of Abravanel's allegedly radical statements, and when we consider their intellectual background and the sources which inspired them, they assume a quite different aspect. We soon realize how utterly removed Abravanel was from modern conceptions in his political thinking no less than in his cosmic and historical views. Radical he was, but his radicalism did not point toward any modern political trend. Nor did it approach even the political concepts which are typical of the Renaissance. His radicalism points backward.

Our discussion of Abravanel's political theory will begin with a presentation of his views on some of the most fundamental political problems—and first, on what is perhaps the most challenging of them, namely, *the origin of the state and man's natural relation to it*. Two radically opposed conceptions prevailed on this question in the Middle Ages—that of Aristotle and that of the Church Fathers. According to Aristotle, statehood is inherent in man's nature; it is, moreover, the moving principle of that nature, its final end, and the greatest achievement of man who, consequently, must be defined as a social and political animal.[1] The Church Fathers conceived of man as by nature *not* a political animal, even though a social being, as hating the state's authority and restrictions; and they believed that the final end of man lies not in the collectivity, but in the individual, in his ability to achieve beatitude through the contemplation of God.[2] Considering the question from a different angle, Aristotle held the state indispensable for man's welfare, for only the many-sided, mutual cooperation, which is consolidated and perfected by the state, enables man to fulfill all his needs.[3] The position of the Church Fathers was that in the state of innocence, that is, before his nature was spoiled by extravagant desires, man did not require the cooperation which the state supplies. The state, they said, is not a product of man's original nature, but of a nature corrupted by sin. Nevertheless, they maintained, that while the state is a result of man's sinful passions, it is also a force which restrains these passions.[4] In other words, the state is essential for man as he *is*, not for man as he *was*, or for man as he *should be*.

The political theory of the Church Fathers was dominant until the thirteenth century, that is, until Aristotle's theory conquered, or reconquered the field. Comparing St. Augustine's attitude to government to that of Thomas Aquinas, we can see how the concept of government as opposed to man's nature was replaced by a concept of government as immanent in man's nature. For Augustine there could have been in the primitive state no dominion of man over man, but of man over beast, and therefore the "righteous men in primitive times were made shepherds of cattle rather than kings of men."[5] Thomas Aquinas, on the other hand, maintained that only "if man intended to live alone as many animals do, each man would be a king unto himself,"[6] and government would be unnecessary. This, however, is not what man's nature dictates. "Man," St. Thomas stressed from the outset, "is by nature a social and political animal."[7] He is political because he is social, for "if it is natural for man to live in the society of man, it is necessary that there exist among men some means by which the group may be governed."[8] We see that the theory of man's fall holds no place here. It is not inclination to sin and the pursuit of luxuries, but the problems arising from the natural and basic necessities of life, problems that no man can answer satisfactorily "by his own individual reason," which make it essential for man to live in a group and, consequently, to adopt the principle of government.[9] Therefore, the more self-sufficient a society is, the more perfect it is; and in contrast to Augustine, who tends to see in the household a complete social unit by nature, St. Thomas sees a "perfect community" only in the city and "still more in the province."[10]

Abravanel's acceptance of the principles of the Church Fathers can be easily explained by his philosophy of history. What is rather strange is that he seems to have accepted also the views of Aristotle. He affirms, on the one hand, that man in the original state required none of the services which his country offers him, and that the rise of the city, and the government involved in it, is a result of man's deviation from his original nature.[11] He asserts, on the other hand, like Thomas Aquinas, that man is *by nature* a political animal and that the mutual, many-sided cooperation represented by the state is essential for man's existence and well-being.[12] He obviously had somehow to eliminate the inconsistency between the two ideas. And here, too, he followed the path trod by the Church Fathers who had to overcome a similar difficulty—to remove the inconsistency between their theory of the state's origin and their practical, positive attitude toward existing state institutions.

The position of the Church Fathers was, as already stated, that while government is a result of the corruption of man's nature, it is beneficial for man in his perverted nature. Abravanel's formula is very similar, although by no means identical. After describing the building of the first city—and *city* in Abravanel's view corresponds to *state*—as an act of sin and departure from man's nature, he could not help raising the question why Moses gave his people a state constitution. Abravanel's answer is that the constitution was given because in the days of Moses, Israel—like the rest of mankind—was already hopelessly removed from man's original condition and because the habit of living in a political society and its symptomatic "passion for the artificial and luxurious" had already become "part of man's nature."[13] Having arrived at this point, Abravanel could meet and accept Aristotle's principle: man is a political animal by nature, but by this we mean his secondary, acquired nature, and not his nature in its primordial condition.

We shall now consider Abravanel's views on another basic political problem, namely, the problem of *the natural equality of man*. Here, too, there were two conflicting principles which influenced the political theories of the Middle Ages, the conflict being again between Aristotle and the Church Fathers. Aristotle's position on the question was that men are by nature unequal, divided into the categories of masters and slaves, and that it is in the interest of the inferior to be subject to the superior.[14] The position of the Church Fathers was that men are endowed with natural equality and are all equal before God.[15] In the original state of nature, they maintained, all men were actually equal to each other, which means that they were all free. How then did slavery appear? The answer was that slavery is a product of sin; but—as is the case with the state—it is also a remedy for sin. In other words, slavery, according to the Church Fathers, is an expression of God's will; hence their acceptance of the institution.[16]

It was the position of the Church Fathers, rather than that of Aristotle, that became dominant in medieval political thought as far as it concerned itself with the question. Both in its practical and theoretical implications, that position was more suited to the Middle Ages. For the Church was as opportunistic as it was dogmatic. It found it convenient to reconcile itself to the temporal power, that is, the state and its institutions, including slavery, and at the same time to stress its own spiritual and religious supremacy through theoretical sublimations.

When we consider Abravanel's position on this all-important point of the natural equality or inequality of man, we again find him accepting, at one and the same time, both Aristotle's view as well as that of the Church. As we have seen, the basic inequality of the human races is an important point in his historical concept and, therefore, in accordance with the Aristotelian thesis, he says that men are divided into superior and inferior groups, and that it is proper for the inferior to be subject to the superior.[17] On the other hand, he says that the imposition of slavery is a crime comparable to murder; that, in fact, it is the "worst kind of murder," since slavery is "living death;" and that men should be free since they are equal before God.[18] The two attitudes are coordinated by Abravanel's sharp division between Israel and the nations, and by his application of the principle of equality to Israel, and the principle of inequality to Israel's relationship with the nations, as well as to relationships within the nations themselves. In the People of God, as in the Church of Christ, all are equal, in spirit as in practice. Outside the limits of the People of God, however, the situation changes both theoretically and materially.[19] Just as Aristotle could say that the civilized Greeks were superior to all other barbarian nations, and therefore entitled to rule over them,[20] so Abravanel considers Israel superior to all other nations, and therefore entitled to be their master.[21] The principle of inequality, however, invades even the sphere of Israel itself, for here, too, Abravanel recognizes one element, the priests, as superior to the rest of the people, and he says, in full accord with the Aristotelian thesis, that it was proper for the people to be ruled by them.[22]

The other fundamental aspect which has to be considered is Abravanel's position on the question of *law*. The prevailing opinion in the Middle Ages was that inherited from the Church Fathers which, in turn, was based on Roman law with its threefold division of law into (a) natural law, (b) law of nations, and (c) civil law. Natural law was considered as consisting of the principles of conduct which men, by their nature, recognized as good or bad. It was believed to be a universal law, common to all men, or, as Cicero conceived of it, "written in men's hearts."[23] The law of nations was regarded as universal, but not as natural. It concerned itself with social institutions like slavery, which are not dictated by nature but accepted by convention. Civil law was held to be conventional, like the law of nations, but was neither natural nor universal. It embodied the laws peculiar to each state, adopted in accordance with changing circumstances and conditions.[24]

The Church Fathers accepted this division with the important addition that the law of nature is identical with the law of God, thus redividing law into two basic categories: divine and human. According to the Church Fathers, the law of nature, which is truly the divine law,[25] operated in human society in the state of man's innocence; the other kinds of law represented sharp departure from the law of nature, or the law of God.[26] Slavery is, of course, the most striking example. According to the law of nature, all men are free; but according to the law of nations, humanity is divided into slaves and masters. Property is another example. According to the law of nature, none of the earth's goods belonged to any one in particular,[27] but property is an institution recognized by civil law, as well as by the law of nations. Both slavery and property are then not natural but unnatural, and, by the same token, the entire conventional law is a result of man's departure from the law of nature, a product of man's sin. Yet, in itself, it is not a sin, for it is beneficial to man in his present state.[28]

That law is fundamentally divided into divine and human was a view held also by Maimonides, except that he applied the terms in quite a different sense. According to Maimonides, divine law is *not* the law of nature, nor could man ever attain it with his own mental faculties. Divine law was not written in man's heart, but on the Tablets in God's script. It is divine because God revealed it to man through His prophets, and because of its higher scope and purpose. Human law, according to Maimonides, takes into consideration only one aspect of man's needs, the material or the political, while it completely neglects the higher aspect of man, his interests as a rational being. It is only the divine law which satisfies all the requirements of man, the spiritual as well as the material.[29]

Maimonides started from the Aristotelian premise that man is by nature a social being, that he is moved by virtue of his nature to form communities. But, he pointed out, man is also the most individualistic creature, there being no such variation among any species of living creatures as exists in mankind. To adjust these two essential but conflicting elements in man's nature, namely, the great variety and the necessity for social life, laws and leaders are needed.[30] The function of the law is to counterbalance the natural diversity by the uniformity of legislation. The function of the leaders is to formulate and enforce the law. It was God, Maimonides went on to say, who endowed mankind with the capacity to produce legislators and rulers. Since this capacity is embodied in man's nature, all law is, in a certain sense, natural, while in other respects it is artificial and constitutes an art, since it aims at perfecting nature and at solving a problem which human nature by itself could not solve. The difference between divine and human law is merely a difference in the degree of the art, the one being superb and embracing all man's needs, the other faulty and partial.

While accepting the basic division and the terminology of the Church Fathers, this conception of law formulated by Maimonides represents a complete departure from the position of the Church Fathers and is obviously influenced by Aristotle. It accepts Aristotle's view that political society is created by man to meet essential natural problems. But it differs from the Aristotelian theory in its insistence that political society cannot meet satisfactorily *all* of man's natural requirements, particularly the spiritual, which are the most important. According to Aristotle, man, through the forces of his own nature, can achieve the most perfect standard of law,[31] while in the conception of Maimonides, man's nature, if left to itself, would produce only a partial and defective form of law; and it is because of the limitation of man's nature in this respect that Revelation is necessary. God, through Revelation, grants man an "addition" to his nature, which, in fact, raises man above nature itself.

We have presented here Maimonides' view of law, because, in our opinion, it is this view of Maimonides which Abravanel adopted. One may conclude from Abravanel's references to this question that he recognized the existence of three kinds of law, natural, conventional and divine.[32] But, since the natural law, in

Abravanel's opinion, is void of any content; since, according to him, even the laws of conduct accepted by Adam and Noah belonged, not to the sphere of the natural, but to that of divine or conventional law,[33] what could he possibly have meant when he referred to natural law? It seems reasonable therefore to assume that the three forms of law were viewed by him as corresponding to the three forms of life—animal, political and rational—and thus the divine law would govern rational life, the conventional law political life, and the natural law animal life. In other words, he must have considered the natural law—the law of animal life—as the "law of the jungle," and this explains why in his basic presentation of his view on law, he disregards natural law completely and recognizes only the other two laws, the conventional, or human, and the divine.[34] In defining the divine and human laws as differing in scope and quality—one as material and spiritual, the other as material only—Abravanel obviously accepts fully the Maimonidean conception of law. But even more emphatically than Maimonides, he stresses the other difference between the two laws, namely, that the divine law was given only to Israel, while the human law is the law of nations.[35]

We can now summarize briefly the basic principles of Abravanel's political doctrine as they emerged from the conflicting political theories which greatly influenced his thought. Discounting his views on primordial historic conditions when there was no need for political organization and considering only man in his "fallen" state with his transformed or secondary nature, the principles of Abravanel's political theory, in the last analysis, are:

(a) Man is by nature a social and political animal.

(b) Men are by nature unequal, and mankind is divided into two elements—a superior one consisting of Israel alone and an inferior which comprises the rest of humanity.

(c) The laws governing human societies are likewise divided into two categories—divine and human—applying respectively to the diverse camps of Israel and the nations.

Each of these principles, we should add, was strongly fixed in Abravanel's mind. Regarded by Abravanel as incontrovertible political axioms, they formed together the theoretical basis for every constitutional or governmental structure ever advocated by him.

2. *The Ideal Constitution*

The question of the ideal type of government and constitution is touched upon by Abravanel quite often, but is dealt with at length in three significant passages. These appear in his commentary on I Samuel 8.4; on Deuteronomy 16.18; and on Exodus 18.13. The commentary on I Samuel was written in 1483. That on Deuteronomy was partly written in the 1460s, but revised and completed many years later, in 1495. The commentary on Exodus was not written until ten more years had passed, that is, in 1505. Thus, the above-mentioned commentaries were composed over a period of more than three decades.

It is reasonable to assume that during such a long time—a time, moreover, replete with drastic political changes both in Spain and Italy, where those commentaries were written—Abravanel's constitutional views underwent changes. Political considerations of a practical nature are after all more liable to be influenced by circumstances than are views of a purely theoretical nature. And, indeed, certain changes did take place in Abravanel's views on the concrete problem of government; and his statements on this problem—if placed side by side—sometimes appear as a mass of inconsistencies. When, however, we consider these statements as expressive of his position at a definite time, the inconsistencies not only become comprehensible, but even help us to trace the development of his political ideas and their final amalgamation into a well defined system.

Of the three major statements on constitutional questions that appear in Abravanel's biblical commentaries, the one in his commentary on Deuteronomy must be regarded as the most comprehensive, most methodical and most basic exposition of his political views. In accordance with that presentation, the laws of Moses were directed to serve two kinds of government, a secular and a sacerdotal. The lowest rung in the ladder of the secular authority was formed by the Lower Court which existed in every town; above it was the Higher Court which represented the entire people; and above that, the King. Taken together, these three institutions—the Lower Court, the Higher Court and the King—constituted the secular, that is, the political, or, as Abravanel calls it, the "human" government.[36]

Parallel to the "human" government there was the "divine" government, which Abravanel terms also the "spiritual." It, too, consisted of three degrees of authority, according to their "holiness, spirituality and proximity to God."[37] The lowest rank in its order was held by the Levites; above them were the Priests; and above these were the Prophets. Each of these governments, we should point out at the outset, had its own set of laws relating to its own special tasks and its own specific functions.[38]

The similarity between this conception and the major political theory of medieval Christendom suggests itself very strongly. What we seem to have before us is the division between the "temporal" and "spiritual" powers,[39] with its advocacy of two independent legislations: one on ecclesiastical matters affecting the clergy and also the laymen as members of the Church, and another directed only to laymen as subjects of the state. The similarity, nevertheless, is conspicuously anachronistic, for at the time when Abravanel wrote his commentaries the concept of the "temporal" and "spiritual" powers had become almost outdated. Two centuries earlier, Pope Boniface VIII could demand Church control over the state. Toward the end of the fifteenth century, however, the popes were vainly trying to ward off state control over the Church. As far as political reality was concerned, it was a time in which the temporal power was the real arbiter of human affairs. And as far as political theory was concerned, the idea of dual authority, while it still lingered on as one of the many ideas inherited from the past, was hardly applied anywhere as a guiding principle in political philosophy. The concept had been crushed already during the 14th century by a series of theoretical blows administered to the Church —such as Marsilius of Padua's *Defensor Pacis* and John Wycliff's *De Officio Regis*. In addition, the revolt against the authority of the Church as such, or, more clearly, the repudiation of the right of the spiritual power to exercise dominion even in purely spiritual affairs, was assuming the form of that tidal wave which was soon to reach its height in the Reformation. Hence, the basic concept upon which Abravanel seems to have built his political theory was one which was already greatly undermined, if not utterly destroyed, by the political developments of his time.

We should be careful, therefore, not to determine Abravanel's views on the question of government merely on the basis of terminological similarities or some general characteristics. As we shall see, the terms "spiritual" and "temporal" powers were employed by Abravanel not in the same sense as they were understood by the advocates of the dual authority system. To understand what his real position was, we must, first of all, examine Abravanel's views on the various institutions of his governmental system.

This brings us back to the first degree in the political or "human" order, that is, the Lower Court. Its existence, structure and functions are deduced by Abravanel from the following verse in Deuteronomy: "Judges and officers shalt thou appoint unto thyself in all thy gates ... which the Lord thy God giveth thee ... throughout thy tribes."[40] With this brief statement as a base, Abravanel builds an elaborate system. "The Lower Court," he says, "was composed of two bodies, one consisting of three members which handled cases relating to property, robberies and bodily injuries, and one of twenty-three members which handled cases involving the death penalty. This legal order prevailed in every community of at least a hundred and twenty souls. In the smaller communities there was only the court of three; while in Jerusalem, the capital city, there were two courts, consisting of twenty-three members each."[41]

None of these details is explicit in the biblical text. But they are no product of Abravanel's imagination either. The information is derived from statements of the early sages[42] who, as Abravanel was convinced, besides being inspired interpreters of the written Law were also the bearers of the divine precepts which had been transmitted orally since the days of Moses. That the statements of the sages on the Lower Court reflected a situation existing during the Second Commonwealth, and not in the much earlier period with which the biblical text deals, is a thought that did not occur to Abravanel. The want of historical criticism, which was almost universal in the Middle Ages, may well account for this fact. But lack of proper historical acumen was hardly the only reason. What is involved here are two principles which dominated Jewish thinking for many centuries during and prior to medieval times: the intrinsic unity of the Bible and the subsequent traditional literature, and the eternity of the Mosaic Law. The latter principle especially was stressed by Jews in the Middle Ages in their effort to refute Christian and Moslem claims that the Mosaic Law had been invalidated with the advent of the new religions.[43] Abravanel, for whom it was axiomatic that the sages introduced no modifications in the Mosaic Law,[44] would not even have entertained the heretical idea that they had deviated from it in framing their legal institutions.

It is necessary to draw attention to this point, because the same logic considerably affected, not only Abravanel's concept of the Lower Court, but also other elements and phases of his political theory. Institutions and views, belonging to the Second Commonwealth, are repeatedly presented as of Mosaic origin and, hence, as setting the model for the ideal state. All this, however, belonged to the realm of theory. In reality, Abravanel's political model was fashioned—unconsciously rather than knowingly—not by the traditional literature, but by his own convictions. It is therefore only those elements of the biblical and post-biblical literature which agreed with his views that he embodied in his political theory, while other elements he explained away or simply rejected. Thus he discounted the opinion of an early authority that, besides the Lower Courts (which were municipal) and the Higher Court (which was national), there were courts for each tribe (that is, regional).[45] Abravanel's opposition to the concept of regional authority was in all likelihood motivated by political considerations originating in his own time. Nahmanides, who had lived two centuries earlier under quite different circumstances, had accepted the principle of the tribal court.[46] Abravanel, in whose time the kings of Spain were successfully subjecting the regional dominions to the ever growing control of their centralized government, saw no place for a tribal arrangement. He obviously appears here as an adherent of the national state policy, which was trying to eliminate the influence of the provinces, while recognizing the special rights of the municipalities as the basic units of which the state is composed.

The other question of major interest to Abravanel was: how were judges of the Lower Courts appointed, or, more correctly, how should they be appointed? Should they be designated by the people, or by the higher authorities of the state? The biblical position is not too clear on this point. But Abravanel decides in favor of the first alternative. To prove his contention he translates the phrase *"throughout* thy tribes" as if it read *"to* thy tribes." According to Abravanel, "in this reference to the tribes Moses wished to indicate that the appointment of judges should not be made by the king, but by the people." The verse should therefore be understood thus: "Judges and officers shalt thou appoint unto thyself in all thy gates. [This is a right] which the Lord thy God giveth thee, *to* thy tribes, [and not to the King].⁴⁷"

In this emphasis upon the right of the people to appoint judges and in the specific denial of such a right to kings a major medieval controversy is involved. The struggle over the right to appoint judges marked, in large measure, the course of the political struggle in the medieval countries of the west. It signified the success or failure of the kings to gain fuller control over the state. According to Jean Bodin, the sixteenth-century absolutist, one of the king's prerogatives is to appoint and change judges.⁴⁸ But in the Middle Ages this prerogative was generally challenged, and in some cases successfully denied. The medieval state of affairs, which obviously influenced Abravanel's thinking on this question, is reflected in Abravanel's own presentation.⁴⁹ And the fact that he stretched the biblical text far beyond its apparent implications in order to coordinate it with his view on the subject indicates all the more that he considered the question of the authority to appoint judges a matter of major importance. It is clear that on this issue he sides with the anti-monarchist party and, whatever the reasons for his stand, his "first degree" of human government is essentially democratic. We shall now see whether the same attitude extends to the "second degree."

According to Abravanel, the Higher Court, which consisted of seventy-one members, was identical with the Seventy Elders who, with Moses, "bore the burden of the people," and was also identical with the Synhedrion of later times. "The Chief of the Synhedrion was called the Judge, the Head, or the President. The most important among the Seventy was the vice-president, bearing the title Father of the Court and sitting next to the Chief, to his right. Their meeting place was the Chamber of Hewn Stone in the Temple, and they used to sit in a semi-circle so that the President and the Father of the Court could see them all."⁵⁰

All these details about the Higher Court could in no way be derived from the biblical text, and, as in the case of the Lower Court, were taken from sources reflecting an institution of the period of the Second Commonwealth.[51] To be sure, Abravanel presents the Synhedrion, not only as modeled after the pattern of Moses' Seventy Elders, but also as its direct continuation.[52] And from an historical point of view, the "proof" adduced by him in support of these contentions has little if any substance. We are concerned here, however, not with the historical validity of Abravanel's statements, but with his opinions regarding political institutions. And, as far as this is concerned, the very fact that he introduced the Synhedrion into the framework of the Mosaic government is irrefutable evidence that he considered it an institution essential for the ideal state. Indeed, so great was the importance Abravanel attached to the Synhedrion that, when he commenced his discussion of the section in Deuteronomy which, in his opinion, dealt with it, he said: "This section undoubtedly presents the foundation and the essence of our Law."[53]

The Synhedrion, according to Abravanel, was composed of the "wisest and most learned in every art and science," that is, the intellectual aristocracy of the people.[54] This intellectual leadership, however, did not represent a cross-section of the people, but emerged mainly from a certain class, namely, the Priests and Levites.[55] Abravanel offers two reasons to justify the arrangement: First, "as servants of the Lord, the Priests and Levites were imbued with a greater degree of God-fearing, and endowed with a greater measure of wisdom." Second, since the Priests and Levites were freed from material worries, they could devote themselves fully to the study of the Law."[56] In the Middle Ages, when the majority of the "most learned in every art and science" were within the ranks of the clergy, such an argument seemed well founded.

The extraordinary composition of the Synhedrion was not without relation to its functions and prerogatives. The function of the Higher Court was, not only to decide controversies in legal matters, but also to abrogate the law if in its judgment the case required such action. This prerogative of acting contrary to the law belonged, according to Jewish tradition, to the King. But Abravanel at this point differs with tradition. He finds some support for his view in a statement of one talmudic authority[57] and declares that *"there was nothing which the King was entitled to do that the Synhedrion was prohibited from doing."*[58]

The statement just quoted is a cardinal principle in Abravanel's political theory. According to it, the Synhedrion had the final voice not only in all judicial, but also in all political matters. It constituted not only the legislative but also the executive branch of government, and its authority, which was supreme in peace, was even further extended in war. In brief, the Synhedrion, in his eyes, was a body with the widest range of responsibilities. It is therefore all the more of interest to note his opinion of the procedure by which the members of this body should be appointed.

"From the biblical text," he says, "it is not clear whether the appointment of this court was in the hands of the tribes, that is, the people, as was the case with the judges of the Lower Courts, or whether it was the privilege of the King or the Prophet. *I believe that in times when there were kings, it was the king who appointed the Higher Court.* But when there was no King, the Chief Judge, after having consulted the entire body, would appoint members to fill vacancies caused by death, while in the case of the demise of the Chief Judge, the group would elect one of their own number as Head."[59]

Thus, by granting the King the right to appoint the Higher Court, Abravanel assumes a position which is the very opposite of that which he had taken regarding the Lower Court. Here again his attitude can be more properly evaluated if viewed against the political background of his time. In Spain, the country where the representative system first developed in the Middle Ages, we find the Cortes of Castile and Leon repeatedly insisting, from the middle of the fifteenth century, on the right of the people to elect their representatives to the Cortes. In 1441, they protested against interference by the king in the election of representatives, and demanded that this function be left to the cities as their exclusive right. In 1442 the Cortes of Valladolid not only renewed this demand emphatically, but also claimed for itself the right to decide a disputed election. In 1447, the Cortes of Valladolid, and, again, in 1462, the Cortes of Toledo, insisted on this very point.[60] And the tradition of insistence by the Cortes on the freedom of elections was carried over into the days of Ferdinand and Isabella.[61] What caused Abravanel to adopt a pro-monarchic position in the matter of the Higher Court, in contrast to the pro-democratic position which he took with regard to the Lower Court? Certainly it was not the biblical text which, as he admitted, is "not clear on this point." The fact that he decided—in complete opposition to the political tradition of his own time and without any compelling influence on the part of Jewish tradition—that the Synhedrion should *not* have a representative character, but the character of a body appointed by high authority, clearly indicates that he considered such a body to be essential for the ideal type of state.

We shall soon see the reasons for this position of Abravanel. At the moment, to complete our presentation of his conception of the Synhedrion, we shall consider his view regarding the Synhedrion's "Head." We note, first of all, that he identifies that official with the "Judge" of the biblical period. In his opinion, the judges of that period, like the presidents of the Synhedrion, were appointed for life by the Seventy Elders, or, in other words, by the entire body of the Higher Court.[62] Abravanel's theory is that the judges were appointed for life, so that "there was no time in the Period of the Judges that Israel was left without a judge."[63] It is difficult to ascertain from Abravanel's presentation what was the difference between the prerogatives of the Synhedrion's chief and those of the general body. In any case, the judges, in Abravanel's opinion, were not only responsible for the conduct of war, but for the execution of the law in time of peace. Furthermore, in pressing situations they were entitled to issue orders and mete out punishments, not in accordance with the law, but in accordance with what they considered imperative for the people's welfare and security.[64] Judges had to be feared and respected, and one who disobeyed them deserved the death penalty. In this, as well as in the performance of the tasks of government, their position was similar to that of kings.[65] Nevertheless, the judge was no king, nor did he constitute an independent institution. He was part of the Synhedrion, and represented the authority yielded to him by the Synhedrion.

Thus the first two institutions of Abravanel's state represent two different systems of government, namely, the democratic and the aristocratic. Obviously he favored neither a pure democracy nor a pure aristocracy, but rather a form of "mixed government" which was suggested by Aristotle[66] and advocated by Cicero. This mixed government, which Cicero calls "the wisest and most evenly balanced system,"[67] is presented by the latter as the constitution of the Roman Republic. It was composed, according to Cicero's description, of three elements: praetors, senate and consuls. In the praetors, who were "minor magistrates, guardians of the civil law,"[68] Abravanel could see a similarity to the Lower Courts; in the senate which was originally the Roman Council of Elders, he could see a close resemblance to the Synhedrion; while the position of the two consuls might suggest a similarity to that of the Chief Judge and the Father of the Court. The subjection of the praetors to the senate, like that of the Lower Courts to the Synhedrion, is indicated in Cicero's words: "They (the minor magistrates, the praetors) shall do whatever the senate shall decree."[69] The similarity was further evident in the fact that in the days of the Roman monarchy, the members of the senate were appointed by kings, while in the early Republic they were appointed by the consuls. Furthermore, the consuls were also called judges, as were, in Abravanel's opinion, the Chiefs in the biblical period; and their prerogatives were both judicial and military, again as were those of the judges in Israel. Cicero described the consuls as having "royal powers,"[70] and we saw that Abravanel insisted that the functions of the judge were those of the king. Finally, like the Roman consuls, who in times of civil dissension and war were subject to no authority, not even to the law—for then "the safety of their people is their highest law"[71]—so the judges in Israel, in times of serious trouble, had the right to exercise their own judgment even if this were in opposition to the law.

Apart from the traditional Jewish sources, therefore, it is in Cicero, and perhaps also in Polybius—another staunch advocate of the "mixed government" system[72]—that we should look for Abravanel's political inspiration.[73] Yet, Abravanel's political views were not shaped by these influences only. They were shaped also by the living examples of the various state-systems with which he came in contact. Most important of these examples were those afforded by the city-republics of Italy, and especially by the state of Venice.

3. *The Venetian Prototype*

Our exposition of Abravanel's views regarding the Lower and Higher Courts is based in the main, as already indicated, upon his commentary on Deuteronomy (16.18). In his commentary on Exodus, which was written in a later period, we find him advocating the establishment of political bodies whose functions seem to parallel those of the Lower and Higher Courts and yet differ from them in more than one respect. Therefore, before proceeding to discuss his theory on kingship, it is our intention to deal with Abravanel's views on politics as presented in his commentary on Exodus, and to see to what extent they involve a departure from his earlier position.

The discussion centers on the appointment by Moses of "rulers of thousands, rulers of hundreds, rulers of fifties, and rulers of tens." What were the functions and the authority of these rulers? According to Exodus, their function was judicial. According to Abravanel, their function was both judicial and military. One might assume that, in Abravanel's opinion, the rulers of Israel, like the praetors of Rome, were judges in peacetime and commanders in wartime. But such an assumption would be wrong. As Abravanel sees it, the rulers were legislators and statesmen (entitled to declare and conduct wars) rather than judges and field commanders. This concept regarding the nature of the rulers' function becomes clear from his views regarding the scope of their authority.

According to the plain meaning of the text, the scope of that authority seems clearly defined. Rulers of thousands, hundreds, etc., were evidently officers whose jurisdictions were limited to a certain number of people. It would also seem clear that their powers increased with the number of people under their respective jurisdictions and, consequently, that the highest authority in the Mosaic system devolved upon the "ruler of the thousand." Abravanel, however, offers an interpretation according to which the highest authority rested, not with the "ruler of the thousand," but with the "ruler of the ten." And it is within the framework of this interpretation that he advances another political system as representing the ideal government.

"In every large and powerful city-state," says Abravanel, "there are matters which must be decided only by a body of a thousand people specifically authorized to make such decisions. There are matters which must be settled by the consent or with the advice of a hundred people, and others with the sanction of forty or fifty people appointed for such purposes. There are still other matters which can be determined only by a group of ten people who have the final say over all problems relating to the state."

"And you should know," he adds, "that each and all of these governmental bodies are to be found today in the great city of Venice. They have the *Consiglio Majore* of more than a thousand people. They have another council called *Consiglio dei Pregadi* which consists of two hundred people. They have a council of forty called the *Quarantis,* and one more council of ten called the *Consiglio dei Dieci*. I have no doubt that this is the true meaning of the titles: rulers of thousands, of hundreds, of fifty and of ten. It implies public officers who belong to the Council of the Thousand, to the Council of the Hundred, and so on. The numbers thousand, hundred, etc., refer, then, not to the judged, but to the judges."[74]

Even the most critical historical observer sees in the past much of what he sees in his own time. In the Middle Ages people unhestitatingly translated the past in terms of current realities. Three centuries earlier, Abraham ibn Ezra, for instance, had quite a different interpretation for the same chapter in Exodus. According to him, the appointment of the rulers constituted an act of punishment for the people, since it implied a change from a happy situation, in which Moses alone was the people's master, to a situation of enslavement by many lords. From the titles of the rulers Ibn Ezra gathered that each of them was granted a fixed number of subjects who had no rights of their own whatsoever and were completely at the ruler's mercy.[75] Living at a time when feudalism was still strongly entrenched and the yearning for a central authoritative rule was deeply felt, Ibn Ezra saw in the officers appointed by Moses, the counts, the barons and the knights of the Middle Ages, differing from each other in the size of their estates and the number of people subservient to them, but all equally intent on subjugating the people. Hence, he concluded, the more numerous the princes, the worse it was for the land.[76] Abravanel was opposed to the feudal system no less than Ibn Ezra, but his substitute for feudalism was not necessarily a "government by one." Numerous princes, he maintained, are a calamity only where all of them are of equal rank, that is, where none of them is obligated to pay homage to the other. But where there is an acknowledged order in the rank of the officers, "a hierarchy leading up to a supreme head," the greater the number of officers, he insisted, the better the management of public affairs. Such a hierarchy, according to Abravanel, represents governmental authority and not enslavement, since the officers are public servants and officials and not the people's overlords.[77] In brief, Ibn Ezra saw in the Mosaic arrangement a prototype of the feudal system, while Abravanel, who lived in different times, saw in it a prototype of the Venetian system.

"The great city of Venice! The Princess among the States!" These expressions of praise for Venice, which appear in Abravanel's writings repeatedly,[78] reveal his admiration for the Venetian republic. This admiration for the Queen of the Adriatic was by no means peculiar to Abravanel. It was shared by many statesmen and political thinkers throughout the period of the Renaissance. It emanated, as we see it, not from theoretical speculations about the best forms of state constitution, but from the amazement engendered in the minds of many by Venice's position among the world powers. For centuries Venice had played a decisive role in determining the balance of power in Europe. It dominated most of the strategic points of the Mediterranean. It controlled the sea routes to the East. Its navy ruled the waves and it enjoyed unequalled military glory. Financially it was probably the richest state in Europe. It had amassed immeasurable fortunes; and the merchant of Venice was not only the wealthiest but also the best protected merchant in the world. Above all, if there was any force which checked the Turk—that most formidable and threatening foe of Christendom—it was again Venice. Constantinople, along with its great Empire, had fallen prey to the Turkish conquerors, but little Venice held them at bay. What was the secret of her strength, her influence, and her wealth? What was the mystery behind the remarkable expansion of that tiny state, situated as it was on a few barren rocks in a corner of the Adriatic? The medieval mind, trained in strict logical deduction, was naturally inclined to attribute this extraordinary success to an outstanding feature in the life of that city. And what could that outstanding feature be, if not its constitution, which was unparalleled in Europe—its "government without a king" and "without a hereditary ruler,"[79] which most closely resembled that of Rome and the ancient Greek republics.[80]

From 1503 on, Abravanel lived in Venice. His long-standing

admiration for the great city, together with the opportunity now afforded him for a closer study of its political institutions—an opportunity which was undoubtedly enhanced by the fact that he was financial adviser to the Venetian Senate—were responsible for a modification of his political theory and for the form it assumed in his commentary on Exodus which was written in Venice (1505). There are good grounds, however, for assuming that the process of that modification had begun many years before, soon after Abravanel's arrival in Italy (1493).[81] As we have indicated, it was the general impact of the political example offered by the city republics of Italy—not only of Venice, the foremost of these republics—that was responsible for initiating a significant change in Abravanel's political conceptions.

Abravanel, then, used the Venetian constitution as a model for his "human government." Nevertheless, he did not copy it exactly. His most important departure from the pattern of the Venetian constitution was his insistence upon the people's election of the Four Councils. For Venice, it should be remembered, was not a democracy in the modern sense of the word, and its institutions were not created in a democratic fashion. The core of the Venetian Republic—the Grand Council—did not represent the people of Venice, but constituted the body of the Venetian aristocracy which was the source of all authority in political questions. True, the Grand Council elected the other institutions, but no one elected the Grand Council.[82] Abravanel's favored procedure is quite different. "Jethro," he says, "told Moses to *choose* and *appoint* the rulers according to his own will and selection, but Moses *told the people that they themselves should elect their leaders.*"[83] It is significant that this interpretation by Abravanel is directly opposed to the very text which serves as the basis of his comment. For in Exodus, it is clearly stated that it was Moses, and not the people, who "chose able men out of all Israel and made them heads over the people."[84] The fact that Abravanel ignores this definite statement and turns for support to a rather ambiguous version in Deuteronomy,[85] shows that he attributed great significance to the act of election by the people themselves, and that the democratic attitude—already manifest in his discussion of the Lower Courts—now became more firmly rooted and established in his mind.

Thus we have before us a governmental system composed of four councils engaged in judicial and military matters, varying in authority, elected by the people and dealing with what Abravanel would consider secular-human affairs. Does it imply that this system represents a substitute for the other system of government which is described in his commentary on Deuteronomy? Did Abravanel reject the Court of Twenty-Three as well as the Higher Court of Seventy-One in favor of the arrangement outlined here?

A careful examination of Abravanel's references to the subject leads us to the conclusion that he did not reject either the institution of the Lower Court or of the Synhedrion;[86] nor did he change in any way their function, character, or composition. He simply added to these institutions the governmental bodies of the Venetian state, and he could do so by introducing one important change in his earlier view of the ideal government. What did that change consist of?

We have seen that Abravanel, in his earlier discussion disavowed the assumption that, besides the Lower Court in every town and the Higher Court in Jerusalem, there were special courts for every tribe.[87] It appeared to us that he took this position under the influence of the rise of the national states in Europe, and especially of the developments in this direction in Spain. It seems that the years he spent in Italy, a country divided and subdivided into independent provinces and cities, changed his view on this question. In any case, we find him now asserting that the Four Councils "existed in every tribe,"[88] or, in other words, advocating their establishment neither as urban, nor as national, but as tribal or regional institutions.

It can therefore be posited with certainty that we are confronted here with a combination of two systems. What remains questionable is Abravanel's opinion regarding the differences in authority between the Synhedrion and the Four Councils. This involves the more basic question whether or not the tribe or the region represented, in his view, a sovereign political unit which—if the example of Venice is to be further pressed—could decide even on acts of war. In other words, do we have here a state within a state or a unitary political organization?

The answer to this question is embodied in Abravanel's views on the Period of the Judges. In that period we find one or two tribes separately declaring wars and fighting independently of the other tribes. Thus the active political unit was the tribe or, if we use the terminology of the fifteenth century, the province or the city-state which controlled a certain province. The interrelations among the tribes of Israel, however, were quite different from those among the Italian city-states. In Israel, according to Abravanel, the tribes were united in a sort of federation, headed by the Seventy Elders and the judge.[89] That institution of the Seventy Elders—the Synhedrion—cared for the welfare of all the tribes. It was the Synhedrion that appointed the judge, the supreme judicial and military leader; and while, in times of trouble, the judge placed himself at the head of the particular tribe—or tribes —involved in war, he was not the judge of this or that tribe alone, but the Judge of Israel, of the people as a whole. Thus, while recognizing the independence of smaller territorial units and rejecting the doctrine of complete governmental centralization, Abravanel remained an adherent of the political concept of a nation, although he visualized the nation as composed of a federation of city-states or tribal regions.

We can now summarize Abravanel's conception of the ideal political constitution as it appears in its final stage of development:

    a) Lower Courts of three and twenty-three members handling individual legal cases in every city and town. These courts are elected by the people.

    b) Four Councils, numbering from a thousand to ten members, dealing with judicial, political and military matters which concern every tribe or regional unit. These, too, are elected by the people.

    c) The Synhedrion, or the Highest Court, whose members have the highest authority in all judicial, political and military matters affecting the entire nation. They represent the aristocracy and are not elected by the people.

This constitution, which embodies Abravanel's latest formulation of his political ideas, contains elements of all the various political theories and systems which influenced him, and yet it is a highly original creation. It is neither a replica of the constitution of Venice, nor of that of republican Rome, but it combines the major principles of both with the institutions of the Second Commonwealth and the tribal system of the Period of the Judges.

It has a strong democratic foundation in the municipal and regional representations, which is in accord with the prevailing medieval theory that "the community is the source of all authority";[90] it has an aristocratic element in the Synhedrion, in which the principle of man's inequality is manifest; and it has a royal element in the judge whose powers approximate those of the king and who is elected for life. It is a "mixed" government indeed, but not exactly of the kind advocated by Cicero. For it differs from it in essence, no less than in detail. It is built, not on the principle of concentration of power in the hands of the central government, but on the reverse principle of granting the maximum measure of freedom and independence to the regions, which nevertheless are united into one nation through a central federal institution and one head. The federalistic element is perhaps the most significant in Abravanel's theory of government.

4. *Monarchism*

The elaborate governmental system, presented thus far, encompasses only two degrees of Abravanel's human government. It does not touch upon what Abravanel calls the "third and highest degree," the king. Nevertheless, it seems to embrace all the faculties and functions of a political society, and its state pyramid, built on a broad foundation, "climaxes in a head," in the person of the Chief of the Synhedrion, the judge, whom Abravanel invests with royal power. The evident question, therefore, is: what is the king needed for? What are the functions which he can fufill that are not fulfilled by the other state institutions? Is there some vital element which the state still lacks and which only the king can supply? This is indeed the cardinal question which Abravanel poses at the beginning of his discussion of the subject: "Is a king essential for the state, or can it exist without him?"[91]

"The investigators of this problem," says Abravanel, "answer the question in the affirmative. They say that the position of the king in the political order is like that of the heart in the body, or that of God in the universe. They think so because they believe that kingship represents three things: unity, continuity and absolute power. I consider this opinion about the indispensability of a king as false. [As to the value of unity,][92] it is not at all impossible for a people to have many leaders conducting the state and its laws in unison and concurrence. [As to continuity,] I know of no reason why their leadership should not be temporary, changing from year to year, or at other intervals, and thus making their actions subject to control and, if need be, to the punishment of those who follow them in office. [As to the benefit of absolute power,] I do not see any reason why their power should not be limited and regulated according to established laws and customs. Common sense dictates that one man in the position of a monarch is more likely to do wrong than many people acting together.[93] For if any one of them is inclined to commit a crime, his colleagues will prevent him from doing so, knowing very well that all of them will be called to account after a short while and will be subject to the punishment meted out by their followers and to public disgrace."[94]

"But," continues Abravanel, "do we have to rely in this matter on theoretical arguments? We have already learned from the philosopher that 'experience is more authoritative than logic.' We have seen many countries governed by temporary rulers and judges, elected at brief intervals, acting in accordance with the limitations imposed upon them, and at the same time they control the people, conduct their wars and enjoy real authority during the time they are in office. If it happens that one of them commits a crime, he is punished properly by those who succeed him, so that no one might dare follow his example. Have you not heard of the great power of Rome, yes, wicked Rome, the frightening 'fourth beast,' whose government ruled supreme and controlled the whole earth when it was ruled by her faithful consuls, but was subdued and became a tributary when it had a Caesar for its master.[95] We have in our own days the state of Venice, the great princess among the nations, the glorious state of Florence, the powerful state of Genoa, as well as Lucca, Siena and Bologna, and many other states which have no kings, but a government of temporarily elected leaders. These are states whose affairs are conducted properly and justly, without complications and without opposition on the part of the people.[96] This is why they have the wisdom, knowledge and understanding of how to conquer foreign lands.[97] All this clearly shows that the existence of a king is not at all essential for a people."[98]

But Abravanel's attack on kingship is not limited to this. He proceeds to the second proposition, namely, to prove that the king is not only unessential, but also harmful and even "dangerous."[99] This he does by analyzing the practical side of the king's rule and by comparing his position, functions and prerogatives with those of the judge. The three major tasks of the king are: to lead his people in war; to have, as the highest officer in the state, the final say in matters of law; and to act in emergencies in accordance with the need of the particular situation, even against the directives of the law.[100] All these three tasks, as we have seen, are fulfilled also by the judge. It follows that the difference is not in the functions, but in the prerogatives. And as far as prerogatives are concerned, the king is far superior to the judge.

This superiority is expressed, according to Abravanel, in the following priorities which are the king's by right. The king can collect taxes from the people for his own needs, as well as for the requirements of any war he may wage. No one has the right to evade the tax, while stealing from the fund is punishable by death.[101] The property and the funds of the executed belong to the king;[102] so does the land which he himself conquers.[103] People are duty bound to pay greater homage to the king than to a judge. It is forbidden for anyone to sit on his throne, to ride his horse, to use his sceptre, to employ his utensils, to marry his widow.[104] Finally, the greatest difference between the king and the judge is that the king's rule is hereditary while the judge's is not. The throne belongs to the king and his offspring for all time.[105]

Are these all the king's prerogatives? Does not the law grant the king outright mastery over his subjects and actual ownership of their property? Samuel says: "This will be the *law* of the king who will reign over you. He will take your sons . . . to be his horsemen, and your daughters to be his cooks . . . he will take your fields and vineyards and oliveyards . . . and you yourselves will become his servants."[106] What did Samuel mean by all this? Did he mean to say that all this is what the king is entitled to do by law, or is it only a prediction of his behavior? In opposition to Maimonides,[107] Abravanel decides that the king was *not permitted* to do any of the things mentioned by Samuel. On the contrary, the divine Law emphatically stipulated that he should not make himself superior to his brethren, nor deviate from the commandments in any manner or degree.[108] Hence, the king has no jurisdiction over the fundamental liberties of his subjects. Not only is he prohibited from treating them as slaves, but he has no right to force them to work for him in his fields or even to prepare instruments of war for him. Furthermore, Abravanel rejects the opinion that the king is permitted to requisition the services of peasants and artisans even for remuneration. His attitude is that "peasants and artisans should be free from any service to the crown," and that "Samuel, holding this opinion, only indicated the extent of the king's injustice by predicting that he would take even peasants and artisans to do his work," and this, "undoubtedly without any remuneration."[109]

The expropriation of fields and vineyards by the king is, in Abravanel's opinion, even a greater injustice than forced labor. In fact, it is nothing but "extreme robbery and extortion."[110] It cannot be assumed to have been permitted by law. "If the king were entitled to take the property of any one of his people, why did not Ahab simply take the vineyard of Naboth the Jezreelite? Why did Jezebel have to go to the length of slanderously accusing him of cursing the king and then executing him in order to be able to appropriate it, if the king was entitled by law to take any field and vineyard he coveted?"[111] In brief, insofar as the property of his subjects is concerned, just as with regard to their personal freedom, the king has no rights whatever.

In Aristotle's *Politics* Abravanel read: "Monarchies are royal insofar as the monarch rules according to law over willing subjects; but they are tyrannical so long as he is despotic and rules according to his own fancy."[112] This distinction between kings and tyrants and the very definition of kingship—rule according to law over willing subjects—formed the basis of the most prevalent medieval political conceptions.[113] Nicholas of Cusa, in the fifteenth century, summarized the position of the Middle Ages on this question in the following brief sentence: "The prince must rule according to the law, and is supreme only with respect to matters which are not clearly defined by the law."[114] Thus the position Abravanel takes toward kingship is typical for the Middle Ages in two major aspects: in its insistence upon the supremacy of the established law and in its emphasis upon the limitations of the king's rights with regard to both his subjects and their property by the very dictates of that law.

Now, since the king's powers are limited by law and all his actions must be in accordance with the law, wherein lies the danger of kingship? Abravanel points out the source of danger clearly. It lies in the fundamental attributes of kingship—unity, continuity and absolute power[115]—which imply that the king's authority is undivided and that his decision—any decision—has the power of law. In other words, the danger is inherent in the fact that the king is subject to the law only theoretically, but is not under its control in reality. This is why the sages said: "The Kings of Israel shall not judge [individual cases], nor shall any one judge them."[116] The king is in a position to commit any illegal act without fearing interference from other state authorities. "The king can cancel the verdict of any judge, but no judge can cancel the verdict of a king."[117] It is true that these extraordinary powers were granted the king by the law only to serve the law, and not to violate it. But where is the guarantee that the king will not abuse these powers? The guarantee can lie only in the king himself, in his moral character and his readiness to fulfill his duties. Therefore, says Abravanel, "only he whose thoughts are pure, who shuns sin and who is modest in his manners deserves to be king."[118]

That the king should be a symbol of perfect morals is another feature of medieval political literature and, like other medieval political ideas, can be traced back to the Greek and Roman political writers. Moral excellence, according to Aristotle, must be among the characteristics of the true king.[119] Among the qualities which Cicero considers essential for a public officer are: "Temperance, complete subjection of all the passions, and moderation in all things."[120] Seneca lists the virtues which a prince must possess, making him appear as a moral superman.[121] Influenced by Aristotle, Cicero and Seneca, as well as by their medieval followers, Abravanel had the same conception of what the proper king should be. His ideal king is likewise a moral superman. Not only is he law-abiding, God-fearing and modest,[122] he is also dispassionate, just, gentle, peace-loving, forgiving[123] and, most important of all, always mindful of his people.[124] The last qualification carries the main proof of the king's integrity. For, says Abravanel, should a king be true to his duties, while ostensibly acting as the people's master, he should virtually be the people's slave.[125]

Into the hands of a man with such extraordinary moral qualities, with such overpowering devotion to the people and with ability to practice severe self-denial, the prerogatives of kingship can be entrusted. But such people are obviously rare. They are still rarer among those on the throne. Indeed, it is a tremendous temptation for a man to have the powers of a king and not use them, or to use them only in accordance with the law. Because of this, and because of the king's practical ability to make use of both the people's manpower and property according to his own will and understanding, special commandments were enacted to bolster the king's self-restraint, and to prevent him from extending his prerogatives beyond the limits necessary for the benefit of the state. That is why it was forbidden to the king—and not to the judge—to take many women, to acquire many horses, to accumulate great fortunes.[126] This is why the law forbids the king especially to follow his passions, his desires and his pride. That is the remedy which the law provides against the danger inherent in the king's prerogatives. Is it effective? The answer is again given by experience. "Look at the countries governed by kings and see the detestable behavior of these rulers, their arbitrary laws, and the violence with which they fill the land."[127] The law provides safeguards against kingship, but safeguards are of little avail against a government which is inherently wrong.

This negative conception of kingship embodies, however, a great problem. If kings represent a menace to the people's welfare, why did nations accept their rule? Or, as Abravanel puts it: "How can it be assumed that sensible people would choose a king or any leader and grant him the power to act at will and disregard the just laws and regulations?"[128] In answer, Abravanel offers two theories. According to the first theory, kingship was established contrary to the people's will. It was imposed upon them by force of arms, and very likely by foreign conquerors.[129] But "even then kings were not accepted without a solemn covenant to serve the people" in the managing of its affairs.[130] The other theory—and this one is expressed with reference to Israel only—is that kingship was established at the wish of the people who, having had no experience with kings, considered them to be the most appropriate leaders and believed that the advantages resulting from their services would outweigh the harm that might follow from their exclusive powers. Nevertheless, the expectation and the understanding was that the king would act strictly in accordance with the law. "Otherwise, the Israelites would not have asked the *prophet* to select a king for them, nor would the prophet have listened to their request."[131]

According to both theories, therefore, the first kings were not appointed by the people (in one case, they were appointed by the prophet; in the other, the kings appointed themselves), and according to both of them, this appointment had to be sanctioned or authorized by the people. What is more, according to both theories, the kings were recognized by the people with the understanding that they would act solely for the benefit of the people and strictly in accordance with the law. Kingship, then, is a result of a definite pact between the people and the kings, a product of a social contract of the kind expounded later by Rousseau. What Abravanel advocates here, however, is not a pre-dated modern political theory, but something which is representative of medieval thought. For, long before Rousseau, the idea of the covenant between king and people was forcefully expressed by medieval political thinkers like Thomas Aquinas and William Ockham.[132]

Since nations accepted the rule of kings only on the basis of a solemn covenant, kingship as it was exercised is, in Abravanel's view, a product of sheer and outright deceit—of good faith on the part of the people and bad faith on the part of the kings. For what happened to all those covenants? The kings recklessly violated and ignored them by making themselves "Lords and masters of the people, as if God had given them the land, its wealth and its inhabitants."[133] By entrusting their fortunes into the hands of kings, the peoples of the world had committed a fatal error, and the evil consequences of that error have been felt by mankind ever since. As Abravanel put it, the entire phenomenon of kingship, "of a single man rising and holding sway over his people and leading them [wherever he wants], as though they were asses," is a "malignant plague," which corrodes humanity. And he summarizes his conclusion in the following pointed manner: "This condition is not the same in all kingdoms. In some of them, like that of Aragon, the power of the king is limited. In others it is absolute. But better off are those lands which have not experienced either."[134]

5. *The Political Tradition*

This unconditional opposition to monarchy, both limited and absolute, is perhaps the most significant characteristic of Abravanel's political thinking. It stands in complete contradiction to the entire political tradition of the Middle Ages down to his own time. The statement that the king is like the heart in a body, or like God in the universe, was made by no less an authority than Thomas Aquinas,[135] and this, at the very height of the controversy between the temporal and spiritual powers. Before the time of Aquinas, we have an unbroken succession of statements by Church authorities going back to the early Church Fathers, all taking a position in favor of monarchism. St. Augustine, who opens the period of the Middle Ages, and whose influence on Abravanel is unquestionable, does not even consider the possibility of any regime other than monarchy.[136] Isidore of Seville, another central figure who incidentally is regarded highly by Abravanel,[137] hails good princes and denounces bad ones, but he cannot recommend any form of government other than monarchy.[138] John of Salisbury was perhaps the most radical critic of monarchy among Church authorities. Nevertheless, he called the prince "the envoy of God on earth," and could not suggest anything better than a monarchy limited by law.[139] The centuries which followed the age of Thomas Aquinas are marked by consistency in this respect. In fact, both the power and prestige of monarchy grew, despite the rise of the semi-republics in Italy and the semi-representative institutions in Spain and England. There were, of course, divisions of opinion regarding the origin of monarchy and its rightful measure of authority. Opinions ranged from those expressed by Dante, who declared that "Monarchy is necessary for the welfare of the world"[140] and urged the creation of a world state under an absolutist regime,[141] to that of Nicholas of Cusa in the fifteenth century, who ardently advocated the limitation of monarchy.[142] But it is difficult to find anyone among the renowned personages of the Middle Ages who would challenge the principle of monarchism itself.

Nor could the inspiration for this position of Abravanel have come from Jewish sources. Jewish political tradition was even more strongly pro-monarchic than was the Christian, and this promonarchic attitude dates back centuries prior to the Middle Ages. Ever since the loss of Jewish sovereignty, the national longings and aspirations for independence were tied up with hopes for the restoration of the monarchy. The reason for this was a two-fold one. First, the period of David's reign was represented in the historic consciousness of the people as the period of the greatest national glory and achievement. And secondly, throughout the long course of Jewish history, the people enjoyed full freedom and independence only under monarchic rule. The period of the Judges, despite its attractive liberties, was reflected in the people's mind as a grim and tragic era. It remained in the nation's memory as "times of trouble," replete with heroic exploits, but marked by inner disunity, by inability to maintain law and order in the country and by failure to protect it from the repeated invasions and tyrannical subjugations which followed each other almost continuously. It was the institution of the kingdom under Saul, and especially under David, that really established Jewish supremacy in Palestine and guarded Jewish independence for many generations even against tremendous odds. The four centuries of the Davidic dynasty therefore left an indelible impression upon the historic consciousness of the Jews. This impression, with its implied admiration for kingship, was strengthened by the occurrences during the Second Commonwealth, when, following centuries of subjection to foreign rulers, climaxed by the threatening Hellenistic assault, the salvation of the Jews and their emergence into independence were associated with the kingly reign of the Hasmoneans. Indeed, save for the Commonwealth of Simon and his son John Hyrcanus, the Jews, as an independent people and as masters of their own country, did not experience any other form of government except monarchy.

Under the influence of this record, the movements for liberation, whether political or messianic, which followed the fall of the Hasmonean dynasty and, especially, the destruction of the Second

Temple, always had before them the Davidic Golden Age as the inspiring goal for their sacrifices and endeavors. Soon kingship came to be considered, not only as the most desirable form of government, but also as the only one possible for the nation to accept without violating a most sacred religious precept. Primarily because of this messianic halo which surrounded the monarchy as the symbol of the nation's hopes, the initial establishment of the kingship in Israel came to be viewed as a command of God.[143]

The idea that monarchism as a principle of government should be classified as a religious dogma, was carried over into the Jewish Middle Ages as a sacred heritage from the past, and as such it remained dominant throughout the medieval period. If we consider Maimonides' position as representative, it is sufficient, to grasp his attitude toward monarchism, to read the first rule of his "Rules of Kings" wherein it is stated very definitely that the establishment of the kingdom was a command of God.[144] Saadia, Halevi, and Abraham ibn Ezra are only a few of the medieval Jewish authorities who supported monarchism prior to Maimonides,[145] while Nahmanides, Gersonides and Albo can be mentioned among the many in the later period.[146] The fact of the matter is that Abravanel had to combat this Jewish tradition from beginning to end in order to establish his own position, and to use all his intellectual ingenuity to prove, in opposition to Maimonides and the rest of the Jewish authorities, that the establishment of a monarchy was *not* a command of God.[147]

The pro-monarchist tendency in the Middle Ages was especially powerful because it did not rely on theoretical and religious speculation alone. It was rooted in reality as no other governmental system could be. To the Church, monarchism was, despite centuries-long friction and antagonism, its backbone and its mainstay, its faithful ally in eradicating heresy and the only form of government that could establish some order in the political chaos of the Middle Ages. To the Christian populace it was the only force which could check the arbitrary power of self-seeking barons. To patriotic elements in later centuries, it was the only political principle which could cement new national states out of the European feudal system. And as far as the Jewish view is concerned, the monarchy was the only power that could grant the Jews some measure of security and stability in an essentially lawless political order and a religious society deeply anti-Jewish.[148] What were the motives and reasons for this antithetic position of Abravanel, to which we find no similarity among any of the Jewish authorities who preceded him?

Fritz Baer attributes Abravanel's anti-monarchist position to his humanism. "The humanist," he says, "is also a sworn republican."[149] This, however, was not the case. In the previous chapters we have shown that Abravanel was no humanist and that, in fact, his world view was opposed to humanism rather than influenced by it. Here we should state, in addition, that his anti-monarchist position, especially in its unqualified and determined form, could in no way be attributed to humanism simply because the humanists were not "sworn republicans." It is difficult to say that humanists per se were republicans at all, despite the fact that many of them lived in the semi-republics of northern Italy, and some of them were inclined toward republicanism as a political concept. In truth, humanism represented a revolt against the spiritual order of Europe, and not against its secular order. It fought against the subordination of human thought, human feelings and human instincts to the monastic spirit of the Church and to its dogmatic approach to every philosophical and scientific question, but it did not fight against any specific political system in Europe, nor did it identify itself with any political principle. Humanism emerged in Italy during the clash between the empire and the Church; and if humanism had taken any sides in this quarrel, it would be natural to expect it to side with the temporal, or, more exactly, the absolute power. But humanism, as a movement, did not take sides in the quarrel. It did not occupy a frontal position on either side, but played the role of a disinterested party. It was therefore tolerant even of the Church, and thus we find it flourishing under the kings of Naples, under the Medici princes in Florence, under the semi-republican system of Venice, and even in the Papal Court. This was the strategic strength of the humanist movement. It was a purely spiritual, non-political movement; and while it paved the way for new political concepts, it did so indirectly, through the inner development of the new ideas which it advanced.

Let us examine, for instance, the political views of the most typical representative of humanism during Abravanel's time, Erasmus. What was his position on the problem? He wrote biting satires against the kings and princes. He exposed their corruption in handling state affairs and accused them of being responsible for every war and every calamity that befell the human race.[150] The most illustrious examples in the history of monarchism, like Julius Caesar or Alexander the Great, are for him nothing but "pestilential royal heroes," while kings in general are described by him, as by Abravanel, as "the curse, the plagues and the pestilence of human nature."[151] Yet Erasmus had no other political system to offer except a monarchy ruled by a wise and just king. His *Education of a Christian Prince* is the answer to the political problem presented by monarchy; and the problem, as Erasmus saw it, was how to educate and influence the prince in the proper way, but not how to depose him; for Erasmus did not consider any substitute for monarchism as a political order. Machiavelli certainly did consider substitutes;[152] but with all his Florentine background and strong democratic leanings, he evidently decided in favor of government by princes. His *Prince*, like Erasmus' *The Education of a Christian Prince*, also aims at the education of the potentate, although Machiavelli's ideal ruler can hardly pass for a Christian. Erasmus educated his prince from the point of view of the people's interests; Machiavelli, from the viewpoint of the prince's interests. The common feature of both is their acceptance of the principle of "government by one." Neither took a determined position against it, such as we find in Abravanel, since neither was a "sworn republican."

There remains one more source to be considered, a source whose influence was certainly enhanced by humanism and the Renaissance: the Greek and Roman political thinkers. That Abravanel read the classical literature is unquestionable, but it is questionable whether he could derive from it his conception of the ideal state. Could he have deduced it from Plato's *Republic*? Hardly, for Plato's state is not a democracy, but a monarchy whose affairs are conducted by the great brains of the philosopher-king and in which the people have little or no say at all.[153] Could he have acquired it from Aristotle? But it was Aristotle who declared that "there is by nature both a justice and an advantage . . . to kingly rule,"[154] and who by his definition of tyranny as the perversion of true monarchy strengthened the position of monarchy in principle.[155] Seneca, whose name appears in Abravanel's writings almost as frequently as the names of Plato and Aristotle, knows but one form of government: monarchism. And it was he who called the emperor "The Vicar of God,"[156] a title which was later used by all advocates and supporters of monarchism in the Middle Ages. For Plutarch, as for Seneca, monarchy was the symbol of God's glory on earth and the prince was the administrator of divine power for the good of his people.[157] Other classical writers maintained a similar position. Cicero seems to have been the only exception.

The similarity between the expression "malignant plague," which Abravanel uses with regard to kings, and "pestilent race," used by Cicero[158] to describe tyrants, is very striking. Also Abravanel's praise of the Roman Republic under the consuls and his direct attack against Caesar, although meant to describe all Roman emperors, suggests the influence of Cicero.[159] Like Aristotle, however, Cicero made a major distinction between kings and tyrants, and as far as monarchy itself is concerned, he considered it the best of the "unmixed" forms of government.[160] True, Cicero's *Republic*, in which this view is most forcefully expressed, was not available in the fifteenth century; nevertheless, it was sufficiently reflected in Cicero's *Laws*.[161]

Although Cicero's influence, therefore, might have inspired an anti-monarchist attitude, it appears to be too weak and indefinite to explain such a determined stand as that taken by Abravanel on this question. Nor can we find a satisfactory explanation in Abravanel's personal experience with monarchs. While it must be remembered that his first attack upon monarchism, that which we find in his commentary on I Samuel, was written after his escape from Portugal—where a death sentence was issued against him by João II—it can hardly be assumed that this incident would have completely erased the long period of glory and prosperity which he had enjoyed under the reign of Alfonso V.[162] We should also note that he incorporated his statement on kingship in I Samuel almost verbatim in his commentary on Deuteronomy, although, in the meantime, he had served Ferdinand I of Spain and Ferrante and Alfonso II of Naples. It is difficult to discern anywhere in Abravanel's writings any personal animosity toward Ferdinand, despite the latter's role in the expulsion of the Jews from Spain. On the contrary, from all the biographical notes which Abravanel left, one is led to believe that his association with Ferdinand was on the whole a happy one.[163] As for his service under the kings of Naples—the last of his personal experiences with kings and the one which immediately preceded the final writing of his commentary on Deuteronomy—we find him praising the kings of Naples in glowing terms.[164] The most one can say in this respect is that Abravanel came in touch with "good" and "bad" monarchs, kings and tyrants, but in most cases more friendly than unfriendly to him personally. Otherwise, after all, his services would not have lasted in Spain as long as they did, nor would he have followed the king of Naples into exile when the latter fled before the conquering Charles VIII. Thus, we still face the difficulty of explaining Abravanel's attitude towards monarchism. And the question becomes even more involved when one considers yet another striking aspect of Abravanel's theory of kingship.

6. *On the Divine Rights of Kings*

We have seen that Abravanel emphasized strongly the limitation on the king's rights in accordance with the law and the king's "covenant" with the people promising adherence to the law. What then should be the position of a people towards a king who acts contrary to the law? More clearly: have the people the right to depose a willful, arbitrary and law-breaking king? On the basis of Abravanel's position as outlined thus far, we would expect him to answer the question affirmatively. His answer, however, is unqualifiedly in the negative.

According to Abravanel, one may not raise a hand against his king. Even if the king is the most bloodthirsty tyrant, "even if he is a born criminal," the people have no right to rise against him. Rebellion against a king is one of the vilest crimes and the "rebels justly deserve the death penalty regardless whether the king is a villain or a righteous man."[165] If the people are dissatisfied with a king; if they suffer under his oppressive rule, all they can do is to pray to God that he shorten the king's reign. They themselves should do nothing about it. Why? "It is God who brought kings to power, and it is only He who can depose them."[166]

The theory that kings derive their authority from God seems to be in complete contradiction to the theory of the covenant in both of the forms in which Abravanel presented it. When we examine Abravanel's reasoning more closely, however, the contradiction is considerably weakened. As we have noticed, Abravanel pointed out that in Israel the people had to ask the prophet to appoint a king for them, and the implication of this fact, according to Abravanel, was two-fold. Whether kingship should be established or not was a matter for the people to decide; but once the people decided to have a king, his selection had to be made not by the people, but by the prophet, that is, by God.[167] Abravanel's conclusion, therefore, was that no man could attain the lofty position of a king without being ordained by God. This was his view also as far as the kings of the nations were concerned. He believed, as we have seen, that the latter acquired their kingdoms not by divine ordinance, but by force of arms. He obviously maintained, however, that the very fact of their success and attainment of power was an indication that God had selected them for kingship.[168] In other words, Abravanel's position was that, while kingship is based on an agreement between the people and the king, that agreement is only with regard to the mode of government, but not with regard to the king's right to govern. Fundamentally, this was the same concept which prevailed in the Middle Ages. As A. J. Carlyle puts it: "The normal medieval conception was that the community was the source of all political authority, which was derived ultimately from God, but immediately from the community."[169]

The political theorists in the Middle Ages who took a similar stand, however, solved the problem differently from Abravanel. Using Aristotle's distinction between kings and tyrants, they claimed that while the king was indeed a representative of God, the tyrant represented the devil. Thus John of Salisbury, in the wake of Cicero and Plutarch, sanctioned the assassination of public tyrants.[170] Ockham forcefully advocated the same measure.[171] Thomas Aquinas, while opposing direct action against kings by individuals, nevertheless declared that a tyrannical king can be removed by "public authority."[172] The following passage from Thomas Aquinas is typical of this line of thought:

If to provide itself with a king belongs to the right of any multitude, it is not unjust that the king, set up by that multitude, be destroyed or his power restricted, if he tyrannically abuses the royal power. It must not be thought that such a multitude is acting unfaithfully in deposing the tyrant, even though it had previously subjected itself to him in perpetuity, because he himself has deserved that the covenant with his subjects should not be kept, since, in ruling the multitude, he did not act faithfully as the office of a king demands.[173]

To coordinate his position regarding the inviolability of the king's rule more closely with his theory of the covenant, Abravanel claims that it was according to the covenant that the people accepted unconditional loyalty to the king and complete subjection to his judgment under all circumstances.[174] This notion of an agreement between the king and the people, by which absolute power was irrevocably transmitted to the former, was later expounded by Hobbes.[175] But Hobbes was an advocate of absolutism, which Abravanel was not. Just the same, the position which Abravanel takes on the question of rebellion is in full accord with the theory of absolutism, "divine right" and "non-resistance."

The Middle Ages knew of this theory but never accepted it as a guiding principle. Although it numbered among its advocates men like Gregory the Great, it had little support among Church authorities. In fact, the theory of divine right, or, more broadly, of absolutism, became dominant in Europe's political thinking only in the sixteenth and seventeenth centuries, but never belonged organically to the Middle Ages.[176] Thus, on the one hand, Abravanel takes a stand of complete and utter opposition to monarchism, a stand foreign to medieval theories, and, on the other hand, he supports the principle of "non-resistance," which was equally unpopular in the medieval period. In fact, he upholds at one and the same time two radical doctrines which would have been hailed respectively by Rousseau and Louis XVI!

Nevertheless, while none of the political principles of Abravanel was truly typical of the Middle Ages, they did exist in embryonic form in the medieval theories of government. The twin concept that the "community is the immediate source of all authority, while God is its ultimate source," was separated by Abravanel into two principles and both were carried by him to their extremes.

The times were favorable to such "separation"; for the intrinsic duality of the medieval political theories could become more noticeable at the close of the Middle Ages, that is, when the medieval theoretical complex began to fall apart. We have a similar phenomenon in the case of Machiavelli, who at the same time wrote two books on politics in one of which, *The Prince,* he advocated dictatorial rule, while in the other, *The Discourses,* he set forth a republican platform. Machiavelli, at least, did not attempt to coordinate these theories. Nor was he decided on either. While leaning heavily toward the prince, Machiavelli was still wavering between the two doctrines. Abravanel, however, did not waver at all. There can be no question as to what his preferred political system was. If there is anything beyond doubt, it is his determined opposition to monarchism as a principle of government.

Hence the dilemma: radical opposition to monarchism on the one hand, and determined support of the theory of divine right and absolutism on the other! How did Abravanel harmonize these two opposites? How did he coordinate them? How can we explain the fact that he supported simultaneously two diametrically opposed attitudes? This is the problem posed by Abravanel's political writings, a problem which was completely overlooked in the studies of Abravanel thus far published. Moreover, while Abravanel's democratic leanings were often noted and stressed,[177] his theory of divine right was all but ignored. But this principle represents the other half of his political theory on kingship, and unless due attention is paid to it, his entire political conception can in no way be properly understood.

7. *Theocracy Is the Answer*

The key to Abravanel's powerful attack on monarchism, as well as other important aspects of his political theory, lies, in our opinion, in a proper understanding of his complete plan of government, mentioned above, that is, in his conception of the dual government: the secular-human and the spiritual-divine.

One may grant the influence of the medieval concept of government, with its dual authority, the temporal and spiritual, on the structure and the terminology of Abravanel's political theory.

But behind these external similarities there operated an entirely different idea. The theory of temporal and spiritual powers—even at the height of the antagonism between the Empire and the Church—recognized two realms of government, distinguished from each other by their separate functions, by separate laws and by separate prerogatives. It was a theory which did not aim to replace one power by the other, but rather to define their respective rights and limits. The medieval theory of dual authority was the expression of an historical fact rather than the advocacy of a definite ideal. What Abravanel meant by "human" and "divine" governments was something different. It was St. Augustine's division between the City of God and the City of Man that inspired him, and this, in contrast to the prevalent medieval theory, was an expression not of fact, but of an ideal.

Augustine's City of God was not an established power, as was the Church of medieval times, but a utopia which was once achieved by man, then lost, and which should be the final goal of all humanity's efforts. The City of Man was not accepted by Augustine as a legitimate phenomenon, as the temporal power was accepted by the Church. The purpose of history, as he understood it, was constantly to minimize and narrow the limits of the City of Man and broaden those of the City of God. These two domains were antagonistic to each other and their conflict was beyond compromise. The full materialization of the one ideal meant the total ruin of the other, and the purpose of history was, indeed, completely to eliminate the City of Man and to establish the sole reign of the City of God.[178]

Similar to this idea of St. Augustine's was Abravanel's conception of the human and divine governments. Superficially, it may appear that he speaks of both governments as of a harmonious creation of the Mosaic constitution. He did not, however, see harmony between them, but antagonism and strife. In fact, he did not recognize the human government as legitimate; and his radical opposition to kingship was part of this attitude. From his negative exposition of kingship one may assume that the evil lay in the very form of the monarchic government, and this certainly was *part* of Abravanel's conception. What Abravanel, however, stresses emphatically and repeatedly is that the *real* evil consisted in this:

Israel, by appointing a king, rejected God, Israel's one and only King.[179]

Here, too, as in every other phase of his theory, we must bear in mind his basic differentiation between Israel and the nations, which dominates his entire political as well as historical conception. "Even if we admit," he says, "that kingship is beneficial to other nations,"—and, in fact, in moments of forgetfulness he admits it[180]—"Israel, whose King is God, Who fights their wars and establishes their laws, has no need of a king."[181] He denounces Israel's request for a king as a product of the inclination toward evil, if not as a full-fledged sin,[182] because in no other way could he reconcile his theory either with the statement in Deuteronomy, which clearly permits kingship, or with the later Jewish tradition, which was pro-monarchic. But, again, in moments of forgetfulness he outspokenly calls it a crime,[183] and could he have had his full say in this matter, he would have declared it the greatest crime ever committed by a nation. For what sin could be more grievous than the rejection of God for man, the appointment of a mortal ruler over a people privileged to have the direct guidance of God? This, then, was the real crime, and kingship with all its evil manifestations seems rather an insignificant side-issue in comparison with this grave transgression.

"The crime of Israel," as he puts it bluntly in one place, "was their rejection of the Divine Kingdom and the establishment of a human kingdom instead."[184] It is clear, then, that before kingship was established, Israel was under a Divine Kingdom and not under a dual government. The course of this single government was initiated and terminated, according to Abravanel, under the leadership of prophets, the heads of the divine government. It began under Moses and was terminated under Samuel. Accordingly, Moses had been not only a prophet, but "also the first king in Israel as well as the first High Priest."[185] Or, as he put it more emphatically in another place, Moses was at one and the same time the head of both the human and divine governments.[186]

This "unification" of the two governments under the leadership of the prophet, the head of the spiritual order, shows what Abravanel had in mind. The "unification" meant the abolition of the "human government," which is what Abravanel considered as a pre-condition for an ideal state of affairs. Indeed, if any division between "divine" and "human" has to be introduced in Abravanel's ideal government, it is that the higher institutions, the Synhedrion and its Head, should consist only of divine people (Levites, priests and prophets), while its lower institutions should be in the hands of laymen.[187] The government as a whole, however, must be seen as a single divine authority, just as the Divine Law is one, although it consists of two parts, a higher, spiritual divine section, and a lower, material and human one.

Thus, what Abravanel was really after was not a democracy, but a theocracy. He visualized it in the form it had once assumed in the past, in the days of Moses, in the period of the re-conquest, in the times of the judges who were inspired by a prophetic spirit and carried out God's orders. He considered that period of theocratic rule the nation's golden age, the era of its greatest happiness and glory; and he also considered it as the exclusive privilege of Israel, as a blessing which was granted by God to His chosen people and which would have lasted, but for their sins, to the end of days.[188]

Evidently, Abravanel had great difficulty in coordinating his theory with the historical facts related to the times of David and Solomon. He undoubtedly realized that a period of a united and dominant nation, as was that of David and Solomon, could hardly be considered a retreat in comparison with the Period of the Judges. Therefore, just as we saw him insist that Moses was also king, so we find him making strenuous attempts to prove—contrary to the strong position of Maimonides[189]—that David and Solomon were also prophets; in other words, heads of a divine government.[190]

It was only after the days of Solomon, under the rule of the sinful, "human" kings[191] and the growth of the moral decadence of the nation, that the City of God began its headlong retreat. Only when we keep this period in mind can Abravanel's concept of two governments be taken in the sense of the temporal and spiritual powers. Here, indeed, we see the two orders, headed by king and prophet respectively, facing each other—not in a friendly or cooperative manner, as his theory of the "human" and "divine" government might imply, but principally as foes and unreconciled opponents. Largely under the influence of this period, Abravanel incorporated the double government concept in the Mosaic constitution; but as far as his own political convictions are concerned, he rejected kingship and the human government which goes with it. The only system which he truly recognized was the divine. For his political ideal was not a republic, modeled upon the constitution of Rome or Venice, but a theocracy, the establishment of the City of God and the reign of His law among men.

In this respect, Abravanel was a revolutionary religious theoretician. The democratic features of his government must be viewed merely as part of his theocratic concept of government, since theocracy agrees to a great extent with democratic principles and practices. His opposition to monarchy was radical because nothing could symbolize more vividly for him the reign of man with his man-made law, with his tyranny and injustice, than the reign of a king. The monarch was for him the embodiment of anti-divine rule, of a regime in which people must pay obedience to man instead of paying obedience to God. This was the same revolutionary concept which was the moving spirit in the democratic drive of another man, who was likewise fired by the vision of a theocracy— a man who occupied at that very time a unique position in Christendom comparable to the one Abravanel occupied in Jewry. That man was Savonarola.

Like Savonarola, Abravanel envisioned the perfect human order as a theocracy in which God was King and in which His law ruled supreme. But, unlike Savonarola, he was not prepared to take any action toward the establishment of this theocracy. Savonarola preached disobedience to tyrants,[192] while Abravanel advocated humble obedience to them. Savonarola appears as a theocratic revolutionary, while Abravanel appears as a theocratic opportunist. The truth of the matter, however, is that nothing was further from Abravanel than opportunism. The key to the understanding of his dual political theory lies in his very conception of kingship as one of the aspects of man's fall, that is, as both a product of sin and a divine punishment therefor—and his passivity regarding tyrannical rule is part of that fundamental conception as well as of his deterministic view of history. The present regime, he thought, was ordained by God and it is beyond the power of man to improve on it. To attempt to destroy it would only constitute another violation of God's will, another crime against God's law, which might well result in greater punishment and misery. Man was given his opportunity in the past. All he can do now is to pray for a change, the change which Abravanel felt was bound to come.

CHAPTER FOUR

MESSIANISM

1. *The Problem*

FOR ONE whose general world view was spiritual-mystical, whose view of history was deterministic and whose political ideal was theocratic, Messianism represented a unifying principle for all the aspects of his doctrine. For that matter, Messianism was basic to both the Christianity and Judaism of the Middle Ages—a fact which dictated the entire course of medieval thought.

Messianism, whatever form it assumes, is in the last analysis an expression of a vision: an alluring dream of an ideal life. To understand the import of medieval Messianism, we must therefore consider the highest ideals of life as the Middle Ages viewed them. In other words, we must know what the medieval *summum bonum* was and wherein it differed from that of ancient times.

Despite some influences to the contrary, the Greek and Roman society thought of life as centered in this world; that man could attain supreme happiness by enjoying the blessings of life and nature. Success depended on one's own qualities, his strength and vigor and wisdom—as well as on luck. The idea of God as intervening in human affairs was reduced to the vanishing point in the pre-Christian era. God was the Emperor, and every man could attain the position of a human god if he had enough strength, enough courage, enough determination and enough luck.

The Christian philosophy destroyed this concept entirely by carrying to an extreme the old Jewish idea that the life of every individual—and history as a whole—was controlled and directed by God, and by laying special emphasis on the theory of the two worlds. Contrary to common opinion in previous centuries, this world was subordinated to the other. In pagan mythology, Hades was but a gloomy shadow of this bright, beautiful and pleasant world. In the Christian conception, this world was the shadow of the real world into which man entered after death. Death, in fact, was the beginning of life, of real life, marked by supreme happiness or terrible torture and pain. There was no middle course in the next world; there was no mixture of sorrow and joy, such as one experienced in this world. It was either one or the other, and both in extreme measure.

The fate of man in the world to come depended on his behavior here, but only *partly* so. For no man, even the most just, truly deserved the happiness of the other world, because even the most just was not truly just. It is only by God's grace that one is destined for that happiness. Yet, in order to deserve that grace one must do something to earn it. Before one enters the Kingdom of Heaven, one must be completely purified from sin. Since this is a super-human task, God Himself atoned for humanity's crimes with his blood on the cross. All that was required of man from then on was to recognize the rule of Christ and accept the instructions of his representatives on earth, the officers of the Church. By becoming a faithful member of the Church, a man's soul may be saved and assured the happiness of the world to come. Otherwise, man is doomed and will be subject to the supreme punishment on the Day of Judgment, when Christ will reappear.

Throughout the Middle Ages, the Church saw itself in the position of the City of God on earth, as a divine messenger charged with a sacred mission. The mission consisted not only of guiding the members of the Church to make their behavior conform to the divine commands, but also of saving the rest of humanity by converting it to the Church, that is, by endowing it with the basic prerequisite for salvation and membership in the Kingdom of Heaven. Those who proved too difficult to persuade must have hopelessly wicked natures, and their destruction by the Church could in no way be considered a crime, since the wicked souls were in any case doomed to everlasting punishment. On the contrary, it was considered a good deed, since it eliminated those who offered a dangerous example, an inducement to sin, and it served as a warning to the hesitant elements not to deviate from the "way of truth." Thus, the Church throughout the Middle Ages was in the position of a militant missionary force whose purpose it was to save more souls for the Kingdom of Heaven.

In the process of achieving this task, the Church met with a powerful competitor in the form of Islam, which appeared barely two centuries after Augustine wrote his *City of God*. Like a gigantic octopus, Islam spread its tentacles from Arabia and surrounded the Christian world on three sides. It confined Christianity to Europe, blocking its expansion to the South and to the East, and excluding from its sphere of influence practically the whole of Asia and Africa. Furthermore, it threatened Europe itself and repeatedly attacked the gates of Christendom. The wars between Christianity and Islam are perhaps the most crucial chapter in the history of the Middle Ages.

The world outlooks of Christianity and Islam, especially in their later medieval phases, were not as fundamentally different as they appeared to be.[1] While Islamic theology did not stress the negative aspects of man's mortal life as strongly as Christianity, it too viewed life in this world as inferior and insignificant in comparison with life in the world to come. "The purpose and design of this world," Ghazali, the foremost Moslem theologian, wrote, "is to afford an opportunity for the future," and the future means "the state after death."[2] Life in this world was, according to this conception, nothing but "one stage of eternity"[3]—a sort of vacillating, swinging bridge which may lead us to the gates of Heaven or of Hell. It all depends on the manner of our crossing, on the steps we take and the side of the bridge on which we lean more heavily. In Christianity the two sides—sin and virtue—are reflected in the conflict between flesh and spirit. In medieval Islam, although asceticism was rejected, it was recognized that, while virtue was of the spirit, sin was of the flesh, of matter. "This world," wrote Ghazali—meaning thereby the material world—"is delusive, enchanting and treacherous."[4] Consequently, to save oneself from the world's material temptations, one should indulge in the four spiritual delights: "delight in knowledge, delight in worship, delight in prayer and delight in communion with God."[5]

Thus, in its general attitude toward earthly life and in its emphasis upon the life beyond, the Moslem philosophy of life in the Middle Ages was similar to that of Christianity. The difference between Christianity and Islam lay in their views as to the *media* by which man could escape doom and achieve eternal happiness. When Mohammed admonished men against sin and warned them of the Last Judgment, he fulfilled his mission, according to Islam. The rest was up to man. According to Christianity, Jesus not only taught men the truth and warned them of the Day of Judgment, but actually saved them from the taint of mortal sin; and this salvation constituted a prerequisite for man's heavenly future. Christianity and Islam thus diverged widely with regard to the idea of salvation, or—if we consider this idea in its broader aspect—of Messianism as instrumental in attaining the supreme good. This very concept, however, constituted the meeting-point between Christianity and Judaism, and it is also here that they most sharply clashed.

The concept of a God who revealed Himself as the saviour—the Messiah—and opened for humanity the gates of the Kingdom of Heaven was basically opposed to the original concept of Jewish Messianism, which hoped for a human Messiah who would save his own people and thus, through the instrumentality of a rehabilitated Israel, establish the reign of God on earth. The aspects of Christian Messianism were certainly present in some embryonic form in the later phases of Jewish Messianism; but Christianity completely changed the emphasis and the character of the Jewish position. The Jewish Messiah has divine powers, but is in essence man. The Christian Messiah has human faculties, but is in essence God. In Jewish Messianism, universal happiness is part of the messianic ideal, but national happiness remains at its center as the core around which universal happiness is achieved. In Christian Messianism, universal happiness is stripped completely of any national aspect. What is more significant, in the Jewish concept the Days of the Messiah are preparatory for the world to come, but are themselves of no mean importance. They constitute an era of happiness in this world, material as well as spiritual. In the Christian concept, Messianism promises no relief in this world, but at best security in the world to come.[6] The Messianic Age is a preparatory period for the Day of Judgment and the world beyond, where superlative happiness can indeed be expected, but it involves no fundamental change in man's position in this life. In brief, the Christian concept of the Messiah was divine, universal, spiritual and other-worldly. The Jewish concept was in the main human, national, political and this-worldly.[7]

Out of this basic difference between the two messianic concepts, there emerged the central point of strife between the two religions in the Middle Ages. According to the Christian view, the Messiah has already appeared. Man was already living in the

Days of the Messiah. The Jewish view denied this and affirmed that the Messianic Era should be looked for in the future, not in the present or in the past. Since both religions derived the major part of the evidence for their beliefs from the Bible, it was around the interpretation of the biblical passages, which implied alleged messianic prophecies, that this strange, mystical and indeterminable controversy revolved.

To understand the true meaning of the conflict one must detach himself completely from the prevailing attitude towards such controversies in our own times and bear in mind the all important fact that the world of the Middle Ages was a profoundly religious world in which people lived and died by faith in religious dogma. Man's knowledge was extremely limited; his credulity was unlimited. In the Middle Ages it was easier to raise an army of fanatical fighters for a religious slogan than it is in our own days for any national purpose. Men were more willing to die in the Wars of the Lord than to fight for king and country, and political wars therefore could often be stimulated only by religious catchwords and battle cries. It was on the basis of his observation of warfare in the Middle Ages that Abravanel wrote that "most of the wars between nations are due to differences in religion."[8] But religious wars were conducted not on the battlefields alone. They were conducted in peacetime as well, and in almost all fields of public life and action. Indeed, the psychological and theological wars were as real, as acrimonious and as deadly as the physical, and the use of violence against unconvincible minorities was only one of their destructive aftermaths. Thus, from a religious standpoint, the Middle Ages were in a permanent state of war, and as far as Jews and Christians were concerned, Messianism, the most exasperating and explosive issue, was the chronic cause.

For the Christians, the doctrine of the Messiah was a theoretical doctrine. It was purely a matter of religious dogma, the theoretical basis of the Christian faith. For the Jews, Messianism, besides its spiritual import, was a belief of great practical moment; for it was the only means by which they could improve their lot and radically change their position among the nations. To give up Messianism would mean for them to give up all hope for a better future. The Christians pressed them on this point steadily because the admission of the messiahship of Jesus meant conversion to

Christianity. This is why the question was re-opened so often by the Christians. On the other hand, it was re-opened by the Jews because Messianism, representing a dream of supreme happiness, was a source of moral stamina, a kind of national exhilarant, which helped to relieve the severe strain of their condition and soften the rigor of their persecution. Hence there was not a single Jewish authority who failed to deal with the question.

The Christians, as indicated, interpreted the messianic prophecies of the Bible as referring to Jesus. Jewish interpretations were less uniform. There were many divisions of opinion among the Jews in the Middle Ages regarding the meaning of these messianic prophecies, and there were no fewer differences on the solution of the key problem—the date of the "end of days." In addition, as if to complicate matters, there were the mystical and intricate allusions of the early sages regarding the biblical messianic prophecies which baffled every reasonable approach and, to the extent to which they were comprehensible, often differed from one another. It is easy to understand, therefore, why the Christian propagandists, among whom Jewish converts occupied no mean position, made good use of these differences in their religious conflicts with the Jews.

This was especially the case in the later centuries of the Middle Ages, when the Christian attacks upon the Jewish messianic concept became extraordinarily severe. Doubts and inconsistencies were revealed in the Jewish position, which shook the faith of many a Jewish believer. Christianity began to win converts, not only by compulsion, but also by persuasion. The mass conversions of 1412 in Spain indicate to a considerable extent that the ideological position of Jewry had been undermined and become greatly weakened. The process of undermining went on steadily during the fifteenth century, the spearhead of the Christian ideological attack being based, throughout the period, on attempts to prove the falseness of the Jewish messianic belief. The fifteenth century was the poorest in Jewish messianic literature, and this was not due, as some have thought, to the lapses which regularly occur after messianic disillusionments. The unfulfilled messianic expectations during the middle of the fourteenth century were not sufficiently deep-rooted or widespread to leave a lasting impression, and by the end of the century they were practically forgotten. An increase in messianic hopes always follows periods of persecution; and if the massacres of 1391 and the succeeding anti-Jewish outbreaks did not produce any messianic literature, it was because the Jewish messianic concept was shaken by the Christian ideological attack. It was not by accident that both Crescas and Albo eliminated the messianic doctrine from the list of the basic principles of Judaism.[9]

Coupled with this theoretical attack of Christianity—whose effect should in no way be underestimated—was the economic, political and physical aggression which resulted in the destruction of Jewish communities in Europe and culminated in the expulsion of the Jews from Spain. This event seems to have had the most far-reaching psychological effect on the Jews. It made the desperate character of the Jewish situation strikingly clear. The main body of Jewry was eradicated, dispersed and practically destroyed. Jewry reached the lowest possible position. Religious conversion and physical annihilation had vastly reduced its numbers, so that it appeared to be on the verge of disappearance. Yet there was no sign of salvation. The "Chariot of the Redeemer" was not heard even from afar. Was not the whole thing a dream? Could it possibly be true that the Messiah would never come, that Christianity was right? Indeed, Christianity appeared to have won the case.

Living in the midst of the Spanish exile, Abravanel saw this conviction growing and spreading like a "veritable plague." He heard "young and old, their spirit broken, utter words of blasphemy against God and His Anointed."[10] He heard them repeat the pertinent question: "Why does not he, the son of Jesse, come to establish his kingdom?" "Does he not see the enormity of our suffering?" And he saw them reach the seemingly inescapable conclusion that "the Messiah is either dead, or impotent, or imprisoned," that "our hope is lost," and that "the sun of justice and healing will never rise."[11]

The mood of defeatism within the Jewish camp was further intensified by a wave of scepticism, criticism and heresy, which emanated from the camp of the New Christians. It can be taken for granted that many of these left the Jewish fold, not by compulsion, but by their own desire to "share the benefits enjoyed by other peoples," or at least to escape the "curse" of the Jewish tragedy.[12] Such elements naturally sought to defend their action by pointing to the "senselessness" of Jewish messianic hopes. Those Marranos, on the other hand, whose forebears had accepted Christianity and who were brought up as Christians in a Christian environment, were permanently exposed to the Christian ideological pressure without having the opportunity to develop counter-arguments.[13] The later case of Uriel Acosta was not an isolated one. His type must have been common throughout the history of the Marrano movement. Greatly weakened in their Jewish faith, the Marranos were a mouthpiece for Christian arguments which confused the minds of Jews with whom they came in contact. To these two groups, a third one should be added—that of the genuine converts, who conducted a zealous agitation for Christianity.[14] The attitude of all these New Christians, whom Abravanel calls the "Sinners of Israel,"[15] was particularly demoralizing at this stage. It was similar to the agitation of a fifth column for surrender at a moment of a general tendency towards defeatism.

Thus, three hundred years of concerted Christian theoretical and physical aggression, brought Jewish Messianism, and together with it the Jewish faith, to the verge of capitulation. The historic task accomplished by Abravanel in reviving Jewish self-confidence and national hopes can be correctly estimated only if we visualize this state of affairs. It was Abravanel who, with powers of imaginative thought perhaps incomparable in the entire messianic literature, restored Jewish faith in salvation, and thus not only demonstrated the worth-whileness of the Jewish struggle for survival in his own time, but also gave meaning and purpose to the entire historic course of the Jewish people.

The answer he offered to the grave religious and national problem which confronted the Jewish people at the time was directed both at the sceptical Jew and the critical Marrano. Its core was the prophetic warning of Ezekiel:

> "And that which comes into your minds shall not be at all . . .
> That you say . . . we will be as the heathen. . . .
> As I live, said the Lord . . .
> With a mighty hand, and with an outstretched arm,
> And with fury poured out,
> Will I be King over you."[16]

What the prophecy conveyed, according to Abravanel, was a grim message to the Jewish renegades and deserters. It implied that there is no escape from the fold of Israel and from the fate decreed upon it. Not only does conversion fail to save Jews from the "curse God placed upon His people," but even racial fusion will not save them from it. "Even if they will intermingle with the nations and intermarry with them, God, as the prophet said, will separate them from the nations and keep them distinct and apart."[17] Those who tried to escape the fate of Jewry by means of religious conversion, Abravanel maintains, have only placed themselves in a worse position than that of the loyal Jew. It is the apostates and unfaithful, that is, the "Marranos," who are singled out for punishment and persecution, and even generations of assimilated life do not alter this condition for their progeny. "It is the Sinners of Israel, whose forebears departed from our religion many years ago, against whom the nations level the most vicious libels, and whom they mercilessly burn alive by the hundreds and thousands."[18] Furthermore, "those who betrayed our religion" are subject to the curse of chronic fear, which accompanies Jewish life in exile, even to a greater measure than the faithful. "For although in their present state among the nations they have amassed wealth and attained high honors; although they constitute, already for many years, the magnates and nobles of the cities, they cannot rid themselves of the morbid feeling that their lives are constantly threatened. They know that the nations remain their implacable enemies and that this enmity, like a sword of Damocles, is relentlessly aiming at them."[19] Thus, the converts are bound to Israel's fate in the present, and they are also tied up with its destiny in the future. When the prophet, speaking of redemption, said: "And I will bring you *out* from the peoples,"[20] he referred to these Sinners of Israel, whom God will take out from the midst of the nations. The gathering of the exiles will include *"everyone* to whom the name of Jacob and Israel applies," that is, it will be according to origin, not according to religion.[21] But the "Sinners" should not think that they will enjoy redemption equally with the faithful. This is indicated in the words of the prophet: "And I will bring you into the wilderness of the peoples and there will judge you face to face."[22]

The argument was undoubtedly forceful and effective. It

pointed to the realities of Jewish life in the Diaspora, to the fruitlessness of all attempts to escape the "Jewish curse" through conversion and assimilation, and to the horrible persecutions to which the Marranos were subjected. It attacked the tendency toward conversion by showing that it failed to attain its purpose—peace and security—and that, on the contrary, it placed the convert at a double disadvantage in comparison with the faithful Jew: it put him in graver jeopardy at present and it robbed him of his chance for full happiness in the future, in the era of blessedness when salvation will come.

However forceful and impressive, this argument alone could not carry sufficient weight until and unless it could be proved that salvation was a reality and not a dream. Abravanel clearly understood this. Similarly, he realized that the deferment of the messianic hope to some distant future would fall short of the mark. Definite assurances of *speedy* salvation was the only thing that could stem the tide toward conversion, just as it was the only medium for reviving the broken Jewish spirit. Indeed, the burden of despair was so heavy that he felt immediate relief was needed to prevent a total collapse of the Jewish power of resistance.

As is very often the case with theorists of redemption especially aiming to stir the masses, Abravanel used the national tragedy which confronted him as an argument in his favor. The fact that Jewry was in the lowest possible state, he stressed, was not a cause for despair, but for rejoicing. Did not the prophets promise redemption to Israel only when it would reach the very depths of agony and woe?[23] The disastrous condition only indicated that salvation was near, so near that the people of his generation might witness it in their own lifetime. This, therefore, was not the moment to doubt the arrival of the Messiah, but to listen attentively for his "knocking at the door."[24] It is on the basis of this assured assumption regarding the proximity of the time of the Messiah, he maintained, that earnest attempts could be made to determine the exact date of his arrival.[25]

Abravanel realized full well that he presented the messianic case at the psychological moment.[26] But we should not make the mistake of considering all this an act of shrewd propaganda. The problem unquestionably confronted Abravanel not only in its national aspects, but also, as it did others, personally; and it was because of his unshakable faith, which served him as a guide, that he believed he had found the solution in the veiled words of God. He himself was undoubtedly convinced that the time of the Messiah had indeed arrived, and that this must be embodied in the allusions of Holy Writ. This conviction stirred him to undertake the enormously difficult task of checking and reinterpreting the entire biblical messianic literature, as well as the entire talmudic messianic literature, so as to combine them into one coherent system—a system which endowed vague and mystical allusions with scientific clarity and certainty. Furthermore, while co-ordinating the biblical statements with each other, and all of them with the talmudic statements, he conducted a systematic fight against Christian Messianism, its principles and its total concept.

2. *The Method*

To refute the Christian claims concerning the Messiah, Abravanel had to prove that the prophecies of redemption had never been fulfilled. If the prophecies were not fulfilled in the past, they must be fulfilled in the future. To doubt this is to suspect the veracity of the Bible, a thought which no faithful Christian, no more than any believing Jew, could afford to entertain. If the veracity of the Bible could be doubted, there could be no basis for the entire Christian interpretation either. Now, since the veracity of the Bible is above doubt, there can be no question but that the prophecies of redemption were real and true.

The problem was how to ascertain that these prophecies remained unfulfilled. Two major difficulties were involved in this undertaking. The Christians asserted that the prophecies regarding the Messiah referred to Jesus, while the prophecies of consolation regarding Israel referred to the period of the Second Commonwealth. The Jews thought that part of the messianic prophecies referred to the Second Commonwealth, but insisted that another part referred to the Messiah and the future Messianic Age. According to the Christian view, therefore, all the messianic prophecies had been fulfilled, while according to the Jewish view, some of them had been realized and others were not. The Jewish position was thus ambiguous and controversial, and therefore weaker than that of the Christians.

Abravanel took a stand which was as radical and consistent as that of Christianity, but at the same time diametrically opposed to it. He set out to prove that none of the prophecies of redemption was fulfilled and that none of them was related to the period of the Second Commonwealth. To this end he followed a line of reasoning which was both simple and unassailable. To determine whether or not the Second Commonwealth represented redemption, one had to know what redemption implied. His task, in other words, was to present the basic symptoms and essential conditions of redemption as indicated by the prophets and to compare them with the conditions of the Second Commonwealth. Once he succeeded in proving that the basic conditions of redemption had not been present in that period, the entire body of messianic prophecies must of necessity refer to some later date. Thus, Abravanel devoted the second book of his messianic trilogy, *The Announcer of Salvation,* to a discussion of the fundamental conditions of redemption and to a demonstration that none of these conditions had existed in the Second Commonwealth.

The method itself was not new. Throughout the latter part of the Middle Ages it was the established form of procedure with which the Jews defended their case. In all disputations between Jews and Christians, the crux of the Jewish argument consisted in this: in order to know whether the Messiah had already arrived or not, we must see whether the characteristics of the Messiah and the Messianic Age, presented in the Bible, were ever fulfilled in the past. In their persistent effort and constant need to disprove what the Christians pressed them to admit, namely, that the Messiah had already arrived and that he was none other than Jesus, the Jews developed a set of cogent arguments which the Christians could hardly answer. Thus, in the disputation in Tortosa, in 1413, the Jews demanded that the question of the messianic symptoms be discussed first. The Christians opposed this procedure.[27] This was evidently their weak point.

We can see how during the last centuries of the Middle Ages the lists of the qualifications, symptoms and conditions of the Messianic Age grew with the additional study of the subject. David Kimhi speaks of five such symptoms.[28] Lorki, in his letter to

Solomon the convert, enumerates ten symptoms.[29] Abravanel enlarged the list to twenty-two.[30] It is the fullest list ever compiled in the Middle Ages and it may well contain all the symptoms that were at any time presented by a Jewish authority. Abravanel's innovation, however, was not only in the inclusiveness of his proofs, but also, and especially, in the strategy with which he employed them. He directed the entire weight of his argument against the period of the Second Commonwealth.

Upon surveying all biblical passages which could have reference to redemption, Abravanel found, among its unquestionable characteristics, that redemption could come only after a long exile; that the Ten Tribes exiled to Assyria would return; that God's terrible vengeance would be wrought upon the nations who persecuted Israel; that those among the nations who would survive the punishment would accept the true faith; that the dead would be resurrected; that the future redemption would resemble in many ways the Egyptian exodus; that Providence would return to Israel to an extent even greater than was manifest on Mt. Sinai; that there would be a wide recurrence of prophecy, miracles and divine signs; and finally, that a King of the House of David, imbued with the spirit of God, would rule over Israel, and his word would be law even to the remotest islands of the world. These are some of the basic conditions which must be present at the time of redemption. It was not difficult to prove that none of them existed in the period of the Second Commonwealth. "During the Egyptian redemption," says Abravanel, "the whole of Israel was redeemed, not even one of them remained in Egypt. In the case of Babylon, not only did the Ten Tribes fail to come back, but even out of the tribes of Judah and Benjamin only a small minority returned to the land."[31] In the Egyptian redemption, moreover, Israel emerged from slavery into absolute freedom. During the Second Commonwealth, the Jews in Palestine were not free, but subjugated. They were first under the dominion of the Persians, later of the Greeks, and still later, of the Romans.[32] Even the Hasmonean period should not be considered as an age of real freedom and sovereignty, but as a passing episode of a revolt against an oppressive rule, a revolt which failed rather than succeeded in establishing Israel's independence.[33] Furthermore, the kings who reigned during the Hasmonean period were not of the House of David, and this conflicts with another condition which is essential to the time of redemption.[34] In addition, none of the signs of Providence was manifest in the period of the Second Temple. There was no ark, no oracles, no holy spirit, no oil for anointment, nor fire from heaven.[35] "Since this was the case, how can we say that the period of the Second Commonwealth represented real redemption?"[36]

But, if the period of the Second Commonwealth did not represent redemption, what did it represent? With daring and consistency Abravanel draws the inevitable conclusion. The period of the Second Commonwealth was but the beginning of the long and arduous exile that started with the destruction of the First Commonwealth.[37] Far from representing fulfillment of the redemption promises, it represented an act of divine grace, an opportunity that God offered Israel for repentance, a final test before bringing upon the Jews the full and crushing weight of the exile. Since repentance did not take place, the entire period of the Second Commonwealth must be considered as the first link in the long chain of events which forms the history of the Diaspora.[38]

By eliminating the period of the Second Commonwealth as the subject of the redemption prophecies, Abravanel struck a severe blow at the Jewish sceptics, renegades and apostates who maintained that no further redemption for Israel could be adduced from the Bible, since the prophecies of redemption referred to the Second Commonwealth and therefore were already fulfilled.[39] On the other hand, it struck an even greater blow at Christianity. Since the period of the Second Commonwealth did not constitute the Messianic Age, Jesus, who appeared in that period, could not be the Messiah. From a Jewish point of view it was an iron-clad argument. From the Christian standpoint, however, it was open to criticism. Christians after all might have readily agreed that the period of the Second Commonwealth did not represent redemption. They could claim, as they actually did, that Jesus appeared at the end of the period and Christianity was established after its termination. Therefore, to forestall this argument, Abravanel undertook to prove that, just as the Second Commonwealth did not represent redemption for Israel, so the era that followed it—the age of Christianity—did not represent redemption for mankind. This he accomplished in two ways: by submitting the Christian era to the test of the conditions indicated by the prophets as essential for redemption, and by attacking the biblical foundations upon which the Christian concept rested.

Among these biblical "foundations," or, more exactly, interpretations of certain passages of the Bible that allegedly alluded to the coming of Christ as well as to the era that followed His appearance, Christianity's presentation of the "Fifth Kingdom" passages formed the backbone of the Christian claims. The issue of the Fifth Kingdom was perhaps the most crucial in the messianic controversy of the Middle Ages and it is little wonder, therefore, that Abravanel devoted to it a large part of his *Wells of Salvation,* the first and foremost of his messianic works.

The idea, of course, must be traced back to the Book of Daniel, where we find a chain of apocalyptic dreams and interpretations regarding the Five Kingdoms which were to rule the world. The two outstanding dreams are those of the "image" and the "four beasts." The dream of the image was seen by Nebuchadnezzar, the mighty Babylonian king who destroyed Jerusalem.[40] The mysterious, monstrous creature of his vision is described as having a head of gold; a breast and arms of silver; a belly and thighs of brass; and legs of iron. Its feet, however, were partly of iron and partly of clay. Then a stone "cut out without hands" smote the image upon its iron-clay feet, bringing about its total destruction, while the stone itself "became a great mountain that filled the whole earth."[41] This dream was interpreted by Daniel as indicating the existence of four kingdoms which would rule over humanity until the "end of days." The head of gold was a symbol of the kingdom of Babylon. Three other kingdoms would follow in succession, symbolized by the silver, brass and iron, which constituted the other parts of the image, and the fourth kingdom would be a divided one, which is indicated by the composite structure of the feet. The stone which smote the image is a symbol of the fifth kingdom which would be set up by the God of heaven, and which would never be destroyed.[42]

The other dream was seen by Daniel himself.[43] It opens with the scene of a violent storm, with "four winds of heaven" that "broke forth upon the great sea," accompanied by the appearance of four great beasts which came up from the sea. The first was like a lion and had eagle's wings; the second looked like a bear holding three ribs "in its mouth between its teeth"; the third was a leopard, with four heads and four "wings of a fowl"; the fourth beast was "dreadful and terrible and exceedingly strong." It had great iron teeth and ten horns. In addition, "there came up among them another horn," a little one, in which there were "eyes like the eyes of a man, and a mouth speaking great things" and "before which three of the first horns were plucked up by the roots."[44] Suddenly the scene changes. The "Ancient of Days" appears to pass judgment on the four beasts. In the process of executing this judgment, the fourth beast is slain and its body is burned with fire, while the rest of the beasts are deprived of dominion and their lives are prolonged for a "season and a time."[45] Then came the final vision:

> There came with the clouds of heaven
> One like unto a son of man,
> And he came even to the Ancient of Days,
> And he was brought near before Him.
> And there was given him dominion,
> And glory, and a kingdom
> That all the peoples, nations, and languages
> Should serve him;
> His dominion is an everlasting dominion
> Which shall not pass away,
> And his kingdom that which shall not be destroyed.[46]

The interpretation of this dream by Daniel is similar to that of the previous one. The four beasts are an indication of the four kingdoms which were to rule the earth. "Diverse from all kingdoms" shall be the fourth, alluded to by the fourth beast. "It shall devour the whole earth, and shall tread it down, and break it in pieces."[47] As for the ten horns, they allude to ten kings that will arise out of this kingdom. The little horn was meant to indicate that "another shall arise after them," diverse from the former, and "he shall put down three Kings";[48] and "he shall speak words against the Most High, and shall wear out the saints of the Most High; and he shall think to change the seasons and the law; and they shall be given into his hand until a time and times and half a time."[49] Finally, the Ancient of Days will destroy his power, and will establish the Fifth and final Kingdom, the "Kingdom of the people of the Saints of the Most High."[50]

Now, what are the five kingdoms indicated by Daniel? It is

obvious that the interpretations are deliberately cryptic and enigmatic, and that they have to be deciphered no less than the symbols of the dream. There was no special difficulty, however, in establishing the identity of three out of the five kingdoms, because Babylon is mentioned in Daniel's interpretation, and elsewhere he mentions Persia and Greece.[51] On the basis of this it was a simple matter to adduce that the fourth kingdom was Rome, the kingdom of iron which devoured the whole earth. Thus far, both Jewish and Christian interpretations agreed.[52] The difference began with the interpretation of the Fifth Kingdom, that of the "people of the Saints of the Most High." According to the Christian interpretation, this expression referred to the establishment of Christendom and the rule of the "Son of Man." According to the Jewish interpretation, it referred to the coming of the Messiah and the establishment of the kingdom of Israel. Taken in its general outline, the Christian interpretation seemed more plausible, since Rome had been destroyed and Christendom was established upon its ruins. There remained, however, a number of difficulties such as the ten horns, which Daniel interpreted as ten kings, and then the additional little horn, which grew among them. To which ten kings of Rome could this description apply? And what is the little horn? What is the meaning of the feet of iron and clay? A number of explanations were offered for these symbols, all of which aimed to fit into the Christian scheme. According to the most prevalent Christian interpretation, the little horn alluded to the anti-Christ who would appear before the Day of Judgment, that is, before Christ's second advent, whose rule would last three and a half years ("time and times and half a time"), who would offend and persecute the followers of Jesus, and would later be destroyed with the reappearance of Jesus on the great Day of Judgment. According to this interpretation, then, the Fifth Kingdom would be established with the second advent of Christ. And thus, there remained an unbridged period between the destruction of the Roman Empire, and the appearance of the Fifth Kingdom.

Abravanel attacks the Christian conception by making full use of the difficulty in coordinating the description of the fourth beast with the Christian scheme. First he rejects in principle the contention that the Fifth Kingdom can allude to Christianity by showing that "this is against the very indications of text."[53] According to Abravanel, each kingdom is described as belonging to a distinct nation and a distinct land. But if the Fifth Kingdom is Christianity, it necessarily applies also to the Greeks and Romans, who accepted Christianity, and thus to the same nations designated by the previous kingdoms.[54] Also, Daniel's statement that the rule of the Fifth Kingdom "shall not be left to *another* people,"[55] shows that it was given to a special people, and therefore it could not allude to Christendom which comprises numerous peoples and nations. A people, Abravanel points out, is something different from a religion. The same people can have many religions, just as the same religion may encompass many peoples. In the same way, one kingdom can, in the course of time, accept various religions, as was the case with the kingdom of Greece, which first worshipped idols and later accepted the faith of Jesus. Hence, a religion cannot be called a kingdom any more than it can be called a people. Yet Scripture clearly speaks about a "Kingdom" that "shall not be left to another people."[56]

The Fifth Kingdom cannot allude to Christianity for still another reason. Daniel said: "And in the days of those Kings"—referring to the kings of the fourth kingdom—"shall the God of heaven set up a kingdom which shall never be destroyed; nor shall the kingdom be left to another people; it shall break in pieces and consume all the kingdoms, but it shall stand forever."[57] Obviously, the Fifth Kingdom must be built on the ruins of all the other kingdoms. It must be the sole ruler of the earth. But this is not the case with Christendom. Christianity did not destroy all the other nations and kingdoms, Babylon, Persia, Greece and Rome. Nor did it establish sole control over mankind. "Only the people of Europe adhere to Christianity, while the majority of the world believes, not in Jesus, but in Mohammed!"[58]

The idea that Jesus could not be the Messiah, since neither he nor his followers ever established their rule over the entire human race, did not originate with Abravanel. The argument goes back to the earliest Christian-Jewish disputations in the Middle Ages. Joseph Kimhi, in his *Book of the Covenant,* composed in the middle of the twelfth century, uses this argument as "decisive" proof against Jesus' messiahship. He builds it on the statement of Psalm 72.11, believed to have referred to the Messiah, which says: "All kings shall prostrate themselves before Him" and "all nations shall serve Him." "This," says Kimhi, "can in no way be explained as referring to Jesus. We know that 'all Kings' and 'all nations' did not serve him in his lifetime, while the Moslems and Jews do not believe in him and do not worship him to this very day."[59]

The same argument, built on the same Psalm although on a different verse, was presented in even stronger form by Nahmanides in his disputation with Pablo Christiani in Barcelona in 1263. Psalm 72.8 says about the Messiah that he will have "dominion from sea to sea, and from the River unto the ends of the earth." "Jesus had no dominion whatsoever," said Nahmanides. "On the contrary, he was persecuted by his enemies, hiding from them and ultimately falling into their hands without being able to free himself from them. After his death, the sect of his believers had no dominion of its own. It was Rome that ruled the whole world before and after it became Christianized, only that in the latter stage it lost many of its domains. Even in our own days, the believers in Mohammed, the sworn enemies of Christendom, have greater dominion than you, the Christians, have."[60]

Thus Abravanel used the same argument which had previously been employed by Jewish scholars to refute the Christian interpretation of Psalm 72 to reject the Christian explanation of the Fifth Kingdom passages in Daniel. The criticism seemed sound indeed. But criticism alone, Abravanel felt, would not do. The main problem was to reconstruct the words of the prophet so as to agree with a different explanation. And here lay the main difficulty. If Christendom is not the Fifth Kingdom, what is it? What place does it occupy in the historic scheme of things? Once it was agreed that Rome was alluded to by the fourth beast, what else could possibly have replaced the broken empire of Rome except the empire of Christ? If Christendom is not the Fifth Kingdom, history came to its end with the fall of Rome, and what followed was a meaningless and inexplicable abyss. In brief, there is an unbridged gap, a wide chasm between the fall of Rome and the establishment of the Fifth Kingdom—a gap which is not indicated at all in Daniel's prophecy.

The answer which Abravanel gives to these questions is again radical and consistent. According to him, there is no gap to be bridged and no chasm to be filled, simply because the "Fourth Kingdom" of Rome still continues to reign over men. Rome still reigns through the instrumentality of Christendom, allegedly the Fifth Kingdom but actually a variation of the Fourth. Christendom could not have replaced Rome, because it appeared when pagan Rome was a world empire and because, as all historians agree, that empire continued to hold sway for centuries as a non-Christian power.[61] By its subsequent acceptance of Christianity, Rome came to be identified with Christendom, but it is that very Roman rule which continues to manifest itself in the empire of Christ. Indeed, Rome, Christendom's center, is still the center of the Roman Empire, and this is why the greatest Christian princes are called the emperors, or kings, of Rome.[62] Christendom is just a phase in the history of Rome, and only on the basis of this assumption can the prophecy of Daniel be correctly interpreted.

The interpretation offered by Abravanel agreed most conveniently with his philosophical and historical views, and—from a medieval point of view—it also corresponded amazingly with Daniel's symbolic allusions. The "four winds of heaven" are the four heavenly princes which were appointed to rule in succession over the "great sea" of humanity.[63] The "four beasts" are the four world empires—Babylon, Persia, Greece and Rome—through which these heavenly princes exercised their rule over mankind. The ten horns are indeed the ten kings to whom Daniel refers: they are the ten emperors who ruled over Rome before the destruction of the Second Temple and before Christianity began to take root. These ten emperors were: Julius Caesar, Octavian, Tiberius, Gaius Caligula, Claudius, Nero, Galba, Otho, Vitellius, and Vespasian.[64] The little horn which grew among them is an allusion to the bishop of Rome who was very unimportant at the beginning, but who later became Pope and whose rule began to spread over the entire earth.[65] In the three kings put down by the "little horn" are indicated the three successive forms of government—Kingship, Republic and Empire—which were displaced by the Papacy.[66] When, centuries after Rome accepted Christianity, Islam appeared, it represented a revolt against the domineering authority of the Christian-Roman world "kingdom" and split it into two.[67] The feet of iron and clay symbolizes this division in the originally united Roman empire, the iron alluding to Christian Rome, and the clay alluding to Islam.[68]

The introduction of Islam into the framework of the Roman

Empire seems to be the weakest spot in Abravanel's symbolic interpretations.[69] Yet, from the standpoint of Jewish eschatology, it was perhaps the most important as well as the most original contribution. It was obvious that Abravanel could not ignore the phenomenon of Islam and that he had to give it a place in his scheme of human history. He rejected the opinion of Ibn Ezra that "the third beast described by Daniel as a leopard referred to both Greece and Rome, and that the fourth beast alluded to the Moslems,"[70] first, because he clearly realized that historically Islam—even more than Christendom—failed to replace the power of Rome; and second, because this would have destroyed his entire anti-Christian position. In order to be able to claim that Rome, under its Christian masters, was the Fourth Kingdom, he had to present Islam as an element of the Roman Empire, and as a rebellious and discordant one at that.

The presentation of Islam in this way was also helpful in solving another problem. We have seen that Christendom was rejected as the Fifth Kingdom because it did not rule the entire world. But, if Christian Rome was the direct continuation of imperial Rome, if it was the fourth beast indicated by Daniel, it had to have world dominion, according to the prophet's own clear statement and according to Abravanel's historical views. If Christianity did not possess world dominion, it is true that it could not be the Fifth Kingdom; but it is equally true that it could not be the fourth beast either. Abravanel was obviously seeking to eliminate the inconsistency. Hence his theory that Christianity at the beginning ruled over the whole world, but was later confronted with a powerful revolt which it ever *failed* to suppress but which it was always *attempting* to suppress. Thus he reconciled the ambivalent situation of Christian Rome's being both a world empire and at the same time unrecognized by all men. According to Abravanel, the lasting revolt against the world dominion of Rome was the empire's irremediable condition,[71] a chronic malady which was gnawing into its vitals and pointing to its ultimate doom.

To this deep cleavage between Christianity and Islam, Abravanel insisted, the prophet alluded in his symbol of iron-clay feet. The "explanation" of some of the Christian scholars that the feet of iron-clay alluded to the emperors and vicegerents in the closing period of the Roman Empire, does not make sense. If vicegerents weaken a kingdom to the extent that half of its foundation may be considered as "clay," it would be more proper, he argued, to see "clay" in the kingdom of Greece, which was divided, after Alexander's death, into four independent domains, or in the kingdom of Persia which was composed of Media and Persia. Nevertheless, each of these kingdoms is described by one kind of metal: silver or brass. The symbolic allusion to two distinct substances points to a much deeper division.[72] It shows that the empire was broken up into two basically conflicting elements—such as was effected by the spread of Islam. As Abravanel saw it, the conflict between Christianity and Islam was a conflict between East and West, a conflict between Babylon and Persia (identified by him with Turkey!),[73] on the one hand, and Greece and Rome, on the other.[74] Islam revived the dead powers of the East—which had been "swallowed up" by the powers of the West[75]—and inspired them to resume an uncompromising struggle for regaining world mastery and dominion. The allusion in the dream to the stone that struck the feet of the image, the only part of the image composed of two substances, was intended to indicate that the Fifth Kingdom, which was that of the King Messiah, would arise at no other time, but in the days of the Christians and the Moslems.[76] All this, like everything else in history, would of course be executed by divine power. Therefore, the "great mountain" from which the "stone" emerged was an allusion to God, while the stone itself symbolized His decree and influence. It foretold that the destruction of Rome, comprising both Christianity and Islam, would come to pass "neither by human hand, nor by human force."[77]

By establishing that the prophecies of redemption could not refer to the Second Commonwealth, and that the Fifth Kingdom did not refer to Christendom, but to Israel, Abravanel cleared the way for the revival of the conviction that the redemption of Israel was a certainty. The third great problem was to establish the time and place of the Messiah's appearance.

3. *The Date*

In his attempts to determine the date of the Messiah's arrival, Abravanel followed the pattern of his mystical predecessors, except that his mysticism was largely pervaded with rational speculation. The major premise upon which that speculation was based was that the prophets had foreseen the future of the world as it was revealed to them by God. Is it possible to assume that the crucial date itself was not revealed to them? Nothing lends color to such an assumption. Could they then have kept the secret to themselves? This, too, is not likely. Prophecy, by its very nature, is a medium of transmitting divine messages to the people, although the transmission is often effected by enigmatic signs and symbols. If the prophets, therefore, did not convey their knowledge of the "end" in a clear and explicit form, it was for an obvious reason. They were compelled to conceal the date from the people because the length of the dispersion and the severity of the suffering would have terrified and profoundly discouraged the people.[78] But the date is implicit in their parables and allusions, and one has but to dig deep enough to find it. It is true that some of the greatest Jewish minds in the past, like Saadia, Bar-Hiyya and Nahmanides, erroneously professed to have found it. But the fact that they erred is no proof that the enigma could not be solved. Abravanel therefore considered it quite logical to assume that in his day, which "must certainly be close to the coming of the Messiah," the secret could be more easily revealed. It was the will of God to conceal it from His people until the very "end."[79]

He believed he found the secret in Daniel. Viewing human history in retrospect, he felt he understood fully the visions of the prophet as alluding to all the climactic events in human history which were preconceived and pre-ordained by God. Everything seemed completely clarified through this prophetic revelation. The historic design of God became suddenly illuminated with a dazzling flood of light. The cataclysmic events of the future as well as of the past became visible, not only in general outline, but also in detail, when the mysteries of the Bible were unravelled by him, as he was sure was the case. It is this combination of certainty, clarity and regard for detail in Abravanel's arguments that made a profound impression upon his contemporaries and succeeding generations. Even today one is almost captivated by that power of faith, conviction and persuasion.

The crucial problem concerning the date of redemption was solved by Abravanel in such a way as to show that redemption was at hand. The puzzling indication in Daniel that redemption would come after "a time, and times and half a time"[80]—an indication which had greatly troubled all previous calculators of the end—is interpreted by Abravanel in a simple and understandable and therefore impressive manner. "Time" means the period of the First Commonwealth which lasted 410 years. "Times" means a duplication of this number, or 820 years, while "half a time" means half of it, that is, 205 years. The total, which amounts to 1435 years, is the length of time from the destruction of the Second Commonwealth until the appearance of the Messiah. Since the Second Commonwealth was destroyed, according to Jewish chronological tradition, in the year 68 C. E.[81] redemption must come about the year 1503.[82]

There is another figure mentioned in Daniel—"unto two thousand and three hundred evenings and mornings"[83]—which was similarly the basis for much messianic speculation. What is the meaning of this veiled statement? Does it contain an allusion to the date of redemption? Abravanel interprets the verse as referring to the time which would pass between the division of the kingdom of Israel and the advent of the redeemer. As we have noticed, the division of the kingdom was for Abravanel a crucial date in the history of Israel and the world. According to him it indicated the beginning of Israel's decline which led to the destruction and the exile. The "two thousand and three hundred evenings and mornings" he interprets as an allusion to this condition. "Since then," says Abravanel, "there began 'evening' for Israel. Peace and unity were no longer among them: there was a mixture of good and evil, symbolized by evening, the link between day and night. This time of evening will last until 'morning' comes. It will last until the time when the breach created by the division of the kingdom will be healed by the reunification of all Israel's tribes under the King Messiah." According to the Jewish chronological tradition, the division of the kingdom took place in the year 2964 A. M.[84]; add 2300 years and you again arrive at the year 1503.[85]

There is still another allusion in Daniel to the date of salvation. Daniel says "a thousand and two hundred and ninety days."[86] The word "days" is interpreted by Abravanel to mean 100 years, according to the numerical value of the Hebrew letters of the word

ימים (days). Together with the number 1290 it makes a total of 1390 years, which is the time between the destruction of the Second Temple and the fall of Constantinople.[87] The fall of Constantinople and the Eastern Roman Empire was believed by Abravanel to mark the beginning of the end for Christian Rome. The very end, linked with the Messianic Era, would come in the year 1503, exactly fifty years after the conquest of Constantinople by the Turks.[88] These last fifty years of Israel in dispersion parallel the first fifty years of the exile, namely, from the destruction of the First Temple to Cyrus' declaration of deliverance, and they represent, according to Abravanel, the most agonizing period in the history of the Jewish people. This is the period of the most ravaging persecutions and widespread expulsions, a period of "death, starvation and captivity."[89] Few will be those who will withstand the great trials and tribulations and survive to see the day of the Messiah's coming. This is why Daniel said: "Happy is he that waiteth and cometh to the thousand three hundred and five and thirty days."[90] The latter part of this statement constitutes Daniel's next and final indication of the end. The word "days" must again be understood according to its numerical value, and thus redemption will come 1435 years after the destruction of the Second Commonwealth or, in other words, in the year 1503, which is the same date indicated by the three previous allusions.[91]

It was the year 1496 when Abravanel wrote his *Wells of Salvation,* the first book of his messianic trilogy, in which he thus interpreted Daniel's messianic prophecies. Seven years later, according to his assurances, the Messiah was to appear. Any man who would make such a statement in our time would be considered a lunatic or a charlatan. The attitude toward such prognostications in the Middle Ages was quite different. It was much the same as our own attitude toward people who make political predictions. It was evaluated according to the weight of the argument and the person who presented it. The mere fact that messianic predictions involved a superhuman, miraculous element, was not considered sufficient reason to diminish their prospects for realization. People everywhere were inclined to believe in miracles and the line of demarcation in man's mind between the possible and the impossible was very thin. Messianic predictions, moreover, were based upon the words of the prophets, and their materialization was therefore considered likely to the extent that it seemed reasonable to accept the interpretation on which they relied.

Nevertheless, it was always an act of great daring, involving an assumption of heavy responsibility, to make definite statements regarding the end. Especially did it require daring and responsibility for Abravanel. As the spiritual head of the exile, as the undeclared exilarch of his time, he had to be doubly cautious. By promising redemption seven years from the time he wrote his book, he placed his entire reputation at stake. The promise of imminent salvation unquestionably had a life-giving effect upon the desperate and morally exhausted people. But the effect would of necessity be merely momentary if the promised date should arrive and prove meaningless. Bitter disillusionment and even greater despair would be the inevitable result. What could one gain by making false statements, if the immediate future would disclose their true import? When he made his sensational predictions, therefore, Abravanel must have been certain beyond a shadow of doubt about the date of the Messiah's coming.

If we can rely on Abravanel's own testimony, the effect of the *Wells of Salvation* was powerful.[92] One can nevertheless safely assume that voices of suspicion and criticism were not lacking. For, who could check on Abravanel's interpretation? Did not all previous predictions of the end, based on similar interpretations which seemed so reasonable in their time, fail to materialize? Abravanel felt that, just as the assurances of salvation had to be speedy, they had to be based on the most impressive proof. Predictions of the end based on Daniel alone would not overcome the sweeping wave of scepticism. Corroboration was needed—positive, definite and unquestionable corroboration for his interpretation of Daniel's prophecies, for his auguries that the appearance of the Messiah was at hand. "Therefore," says Abravanel, "after I had composed my *Wells of Salvation* in which these forecasts were made, I decided to concentrate on the sayings of our sages, to consult them concerning the opinions I expressed about the end, and thus determine whether they were correct and reasonable, or deceitful and senseless."[93] He looked for evidence in the words of the sages, "because the great sages of Israel commanded all the treasures of knowledge and they had correct judgment which never failed. They received all the truths from the prophets themselves, who were directly informed of God's secrets. And while the words of the sages are cloaked in mystic legends and parables and their wisdom wrapped in enigmatic stories, it is not impossible to uncover their true meaning. I therefore scrutinized every angle of their statements to find some evidence, approval or consent to the opinions regarding the end which I expressed—as the conclusion of my own reasoning and conjecture—in my earlier work on the subject."[94]

There was, however, an additional reason that prompted Abravanel to make a thorough investigation of all the messianic references of the sages. The Jews, in their ideological war with Christendom, drew upon the Bible. Against any argument that the Christians could bring from the Bible to prove the authenticity of Jesus, the Jews could bring a counter argument. Against any interpretation of any biblical passage which offered support to Christian claims, the Jews had a ready interpretation of their own. Since the prophets lived centuries before the time of Jesus, and Jewish scholars had for centuries interpreted the Bible without even bringing Christianity into consideration, it is easy to understand the strength of the Jewish position—at least from a rationalistic point of view. Jews in the Middle Ages were not principally rationalists, but they had traditional interpretations which seemed true and plausible—at least as plausible as those of the Christians. In addition, Jewish authorities on the Bible were engaged in checking, improving and strengthening the effectiveness of the Jewish arguments and in providing decisive and convincing answers to every question that their opponents might address to them. It should be realized that this was the Jews' most vital defense belt, their "last wall" which they could not afford to lose. As we have stated, once the Christians succeeded in proving that the Messiah had already arrived, Jewish hopes would have been completely shattered and the inevitable result would have been a mass conversion to Christianity.

Even their opponents had to admit the effectiveness of the Jewish defense. In their disputations with the Jews, the Christians had to withdraw, if not defeated, at least with the feeling that their point was not decisively proved. This led the Christians to search for new sources of authority in their polemics against the Jews. And, strange as it may seem, they concentrated on the Talmud. Unlike the Bible, which was holy to both Jews and Christians, the Talmud was sacred to Jews only, and it was considered wise to attack the Jews on purely Jewish ground. To force the Jews to abandon their heretical position, they believed, one must use their own instruments of faith. They must be shown that it was the Talmud and their admired sages themselves that predicted the arrival of Jesus; that some of these stubborn men had known the truth although they rebelled against it.

In this calculated line of aggression, Jewish converts served as the spearhead, and they were most dangerous from the Jewish standpoint both because of the bitterness of their attack and their intimate knowledge of Jewish literature. Indeed, the ablest among these converts could argue with the most learned rabbis as equals; they could even outmaneuver them by attacking barely defensible positions; and by repeatedly emphasizing the weak points in the Jewish arguments they were able to raise doubts in susceptible Jewish minds. This is why we see converts figuring so prominently in all historic Christian-Jewish disputations in the Middle Ages.

The basis for their argument was provided by some bizarre and elusive talmudic statements regarding the Messiah and the Messianic Age which seemed to offer support to the Christian claims. Thus we find in the Tortosa debate of 1413 that the Christians sought to turn the discussion to talmudic legends of their own choice, while the Jews attempted to avoid this. There was no unanimity of opinion among the Jews regarding the credibility of these legends. Nahmanides openly stated that they may be believed or not believed according to one's inclination. He compared the talmudic legends to the sermons of the bishops. The value of such sermons depends on their content. They may be used as interpretations, when the interpretation seems correct, or rejected, when it seems wrong.[95] This had been the opinion also of Yehiel of Paris, during the disputation of 1240.[96] Yet he and others emphatically claimed that the sages of the Talmud were holy people and that it was inconceivable that they would utter foolish or nonsensical words.[97] Nahmanides, discussing one of these legends, said wonderingly: "It is quite possible that it contains some hidden meaning;"[98] but the question remained open and undecided. This duality of the Jewish position laid bare its weakness. The Jews were reluctant to discuss the messianic issue on the basis of the talmudic legends. Yet they were forced to do so by the very danger of compromising the Talmud as a whole.

Because of the sceptical attitude of Jewish authorities toward the intrinsic value of the legendary part of the Talmud, they failed to develop adequate counter-arguments to the Christian contentions. Abravanel's position on the question of the talmudic legends differed from that of his predecessors. It was marked by the same radicalism and uniformity of approach which characterized his stand on the biblical prophecies. Just as he denied that there were two kinds of redemption prophecies, some messianic and some not, so he denied that there were two kinds of redemption legends, some pregnant with symbolic meaning, others void of it. He maintained, therefore, that all of these legends must be taken as symbolic allusions to the "end" and interpreted as of unquestionable credibility.[99] By interpreting them successfully so as to agree with the Jewish messianic views, Abravanel eliminated a vulnerable spot from the otherwise strong Jewish defense line.

It will be helpful for the understanding of Abravanel's mind—and indeed of the medieval mind—to examine at least a few of these interpretations. The most significant were undoubtedly those applied by Abravanel to two well-known talmudic statements of which Christians, especially Jewish converts, made formidable use in their campaign against the Jews. According to one of these statements the world was to last 6000 years, divided into three equal periods of 2000 years each: the era of confusion, the rule of the Law, the Messianic Age (the Days of the Messiah).[100] According to a second statement, the world was to last eighty-five jubilees (that is, 4250 years) in the last of which the Son of David was to come.[101]

On the basis of these statements Christians attempted to prove the messiahship of Jesus. Since the period beginning with the fifth millennium represents the beginning of the Days of the Messiah, it is obvious that the Messiah had already arrived and he could be none other than Jesus.[102] Also the statement that the Messiah will come in the eighty-fifth jubilee of the world's existence clearly refutes Jewish hopes, since that period was long past and the Jewish savior had not arrived. On the other hand, it conforms to the Christian concept inasmuch as that was the very time when Christianity established its dominion.[103]

Whatever measure of support the Christians could draw for their position from these statements, the passages certainly did not hold out any encouragement for the Jews. Unable to fit them into the framework of their messianic views, Jewish authorities tended to dismiss these statements as inconsequential guesses of some sages. Abravanel realized that in order to coordinate these messianic statements with the Jewish messianic views, a new principle had to be introduced into the very concept of the Messianic Era. Thus, according to him, there were three limits of time fixed for the arrival of the Messiah. The first is the time in which it was impossible for the Messiah to appear at all; the second, the time in which he could have arrived had the generation deserved it; and the third, the time in which he must come.[104]

The time during which the Messiah could not come terminated at the end of the eighty-fifth jubilee of the world's existence, which coincides with the end of the first four centuries following the destruction of the Second Temple.[105] This is indicated in God's statement to Abraham that his offspring shall live as strangers in foreign lands where they shall be enslaved and persecuted for four hundred years.[106] This is why Bar Kokhba, who lived within that period could not be the Messiah, as some of the sages distinctly pointed out.[107] That Jesus, who preceded Bar Kokhba, could not be the Messiah goes without saying.

The time which followed was the time in which the Messiah could have arrived. This is what the sages meant by their "Days of the Messiah." These were times in which people were Messiah-conscious, in which they sensed the great possibility, although they abused it. This is the time in which the disciples of Jesus raised his banner and spread his faith. This is the time in which Mohammed "prophesied," pretending to be a messenger of God and drawing after him countless people. And this is the time during which many false Messiahs appeared among the Jews. In brief, this is the time in which the Messiah could have come, but did not.[108]

The third limit of time indicates the final state, at which the Messiah is certain to come, regardless whether the people merit his arrival or not. That final date is indicated by the sages, as it is indicated by the prophets.[109]

Abravanel, indeed, deduced the "final date," not only from

Daniel, but also from the talmudic legends dealing with the Days of the Messiah as well as from the *Chapters of R. Eliezer*—a composition of the eighth century which was mistaken in the Middle Ages for an ancient tannaitic source. In the twenty-eighth chapter of that book there is an alleged statement of one of the sages that "the reign of the four kingdoms will last one day of the days of God." Thereupon the opinion of another sage is adduced to the effect that the reign will last "one day less two-thirds of an hour." Abravanel, like many others, thought that a "day of God" meant a thousand years.[110] This was based on the verse in Psalms: "For a thousand years in Thy sight are but as yesterday when it is past."[111] According to Abravanel, however, this referred only to the illuminated part of the day, while a full day of God, comprising a day and a night, consists of two thousand years.[112] The statement of the sage that the four kingdoms would last a day of God means that Israel's subjugation will last two millennia. Since Nebuchadnezzar destroyed Jerusalem in the year 3319 A.M., it follows that redemption should come in the year 5319 A.M. However, since according to the divergent opinion this "day" would be shortened by two-thirds of an hour, namely, by 56 years, the date of redemption is advanced to the year 5263 A.M., or 1503 C.E. which is the year Abravanel found indicated in the allusions of Daniel.[113]

Relying on another statement from the *Chapters*, Abravanel reaches a similar conclusion, although not identical with the previous one. In the eleventh chapter, which deals with the creation of Adam, it is stated that a soul was infused into Adam in the fourth hour of the sixth day. Adam is, as we have seen, an allusion to the Messiah, and the sixth day refers to the sixth millennium.[114] It follows that the Messiah will appear in the fourth hour of the sixth millennium. We already know that an "hour" means eighty-three years. Therefore, the fourth hour begins in the year 5250 A.M., or 1490 C.E., and terminates in the year 5333 A.M., or 1573 C.E. The Messiah may arrive any time within this hour. He may arrive some fourteen years after its beginning, that is, in the year 1503. He may arrive in the middle of the hour, in 1531. He cannot appear later than 1573. This is the final date Abravanel fixed for the advent of the Messiah.[115]

That the year 1531, the middle of the fourth hour of the

sixth day of God, is a very likely year for the arrival of the Messiah was stated, according to Abravanel, in the Talmud itself. There the story is told by one of the sages about a scroll written in Hebrew, in Assyrian letters, that was found in the archives of Rome, in which it was stated that 4291 years after the creation of the world the "end" would come. This definite indication is accompanied by another statement, that God will renew the world after seven thousand years, which is followed by a cryptic correction: "after five thousand."[116] Now, according to Abravanel, the correction refers not to the time of the world's destruction, but to the date of the Messiah's coming. It meant to point out that the correct date of the "end" is not 4291 A.M. but 5291 A.M. This is the year 1531.[117]

As Abravanel sees it, there is no contradiction between the dates 1503 and 1531. It is quite possible that the beginning of redemption will take place in 1503 and its completion in 1531, the date indicated, in his opinion, in the scroll.[118] Both dates, in any case, signify momentous and decisive phases in the unrollment of the messianic drama. Both point to the one and only conclusion, that the time of inevitable salvation—the time in which the Messiah *must* come—is already at hand. It was the fourth hour of the sixth millennium—the crucial and promising date—which mankind was about to enter, and one could begin counting the years, which are only minutes in the timetable of God.

4. *The Revolution*

The three most significant features which will mark the epoch of the messianic arrival are, in Abravanel's own words, "Revenge upon our enemies, the Redemption of Israel, and the Resurrection of the dead."[119] Revenge is the theme stressed most often in Abravanel's messianic writings. It is one of the fourteen major conditions which Abravanel visualizes as present in the Messianic Era, and it is presented by him as the first in order.[120] Indeed, there is no other subject in which Abravanel indulges so readily and which he discusses with greater zeal than the revenge upon Israel's enemies in the Messianic Age.

To understand the reason for this emphasis upon revenge,

we must consider for a moment the state of mind of the Spanish Jew of that period. It was a state of mind born of persecution as it impinged upon his particular mentality. One should not try to comprehend it by analogy with Jewish feelings in our own time. The campaign of extermination waged by Nazi Germany against Jewry in the decade of the 1940s was certainly more drastic and merciless than was the anti-Jewish campaign in Spain at any time. But the hatred which the Spanish persecution engendered in the Jewish soul was incomparably deeper and more overpowering than that instilled in Jewish hearts by modern atrocities. The temper of that age and its moral attitudes were obviously different from ours.

In exalting the idea of revenge, Abravanel coined a phrase: "Revenge becomes great souls!"[121] which epitomizes the psychological attitude of Spanish Jewry. The Spanish Jew was not only a highly civilized person, but also a person with a keen sense of pride. For centuries he had lived in Spain under conditions of semi-freedom and independence which, to be sure, he had to defend constantly, but which developed his self-consciousness and self-respect. The harrowing humiliations to which he was later subjected inflicted deep wounds upon that self-respect. Unlike the modern Jew, who strives to understand objectively the historic forces confronting him; who is indeed ultra-rationalistic; who often suppresses his emotions even in the face of the most shocking evils, the reactions of the Spanish Jew were by far more natural. At the close of the long era of persecution which culminated in the expulsion, his soul was tormented by a burning hate and a fervent desire for revenge which were only intensified by the consciousness of his impotence. Abravanel gave vent to his desire. Revenge was the most popular slogan around which he could rally the interest of the Jews in his messianic prognostications.

But revenge offered a solution also to another important problem. It was the only effective answer to the pessimists, the faint-hearted and unfaithful, who questioned the rule of God on earth. Even in our own sceptical times, people with a highly developed sense of justice could not, at least so long as World War II lasted, reconcile themselves to the thought that so much crime and evil-doing would remain unpunished. For a Spanish Jew such a thought was even more disturbing. It was moral torture of the highest degree. He longed to prove to himself and to others that God does govern the affairs of the world, and that God is on his side, on the side of the righteous who believe in Him and endure oppression and martyrdom for His sake. He wanted to be able to give the lie to the renegades and Christians who claimed that the sufferings of the Jews were deserved punishment for their refusal to walk in the "ways of truth."

The execution of retributive vengeance on the criminals, Israel's foes, would mean the manifestation of God's justice and the establishment of His truth. Revenge is therefore, according to Abravanel, the first act in the messianic drama, the starting point of all cataclysmic developments as well as the basis for redemption itself. For it is out of the punishment of the wicked nations that Israel's redemption will emerge. The entire process is described by Abravanel with the clarity and forcefulness of one who worked out a plan in his mind to the minutest detail. "I have thought a great deal about it," he writes in his *Wells of Salvation,* "and this is how I visualize it."[122]

Before the Fifth Kingdom could be established, the Fourth Kingdom, as we have seen, had to be destroyed, and the "stone" of destruction would strike, as Daniel indicated, at its "iron-clay feet." This means that the destruction of the Fourth Kingdom will stem from its inner division, or rather, from a terrific clash between its two components, Christianity and Islam. This clash, according to Abravanel, is indicated by the "wars of the monsters"—Gog and Armilus—predicted by the sages as part of the messianic upheaval.[123] As he foresees it, Rome will be the initiator of this war. Christendom will decide to wipe out the power of Islam and reconquer Jerusalem and the holy places.[124] The prophecy of Daniel regarding the battle between the King of the North and the King of the South, refers not only to the wars between the Seleucids and the Ptolemies in the period of the Second Commonwealth, but also to the war between the northern power of Christendom and the southern power of Islam.[125]

The course of the war, as forecast by Abravanel, was to begin with a vigorous Christian attack on Egypt—the Moslem power which rules over the Holy Land—and with an initial victory for the Christians.[126] Egypt will suffer terrible punishment, and Isaiah's prophecy of doom on Egypt, with its vivid descriptions of Egypt's devastation, refers to the time of the messianic wars. From

Egypt the Christians will proceed to Palestine. The statement in Jeremiah 4.16, "*Noẓrim* come from a distant land," is explained by Abravanel as referring to the people of Rome who will attack Jerusalem in the messianic times.[127] The Romans were called *Noẓrim* because the prophet by his holy spirit foresaw that the Romans would believe in the Nazarene. They will conquer Palestine and turn Jerusalem into the spiritual and political headquarters of Christendom, from which they will spread their power over their world empire.[128] That rule will last for nine months, as indicated by the sages. Then, unexpectedly, something will happen which will radically change the face of things. The Christians will be confronted with a terrific onslaught by the armies of the Ten Tribes.[129]

Abravanel, we have said, saw the return of the Ten Tribes as a basic feature of the Messianic Age and as proof that the Second Commonwealth did not represent redemption.[130] In fact, Abravanel stresses the theme of the Ten Tribes almost as strongly as he stresses the theme of revenge. That he was not the first to introduce the issue of the Ten Tribes into the messianic concept need hardly be stated. Long before Abravanel's times the legend was widely believed in the Middle Ages. From the days of its revival by Eldad ha-Dani, the Jewish traveler of the ninth century, it was a common spiritual possession among Jews and non-Jews.[131] Nevertheless, it is only in the writings of Abravanel that we find the legend of the Ten Tribes transformed from a phantom into a factor. Only in Abravanel's messianic scheme do we find them playing an active role in the history of Israel and the world. What was the reason for this prominence which Abravanel gave to the Ten Tribes?

The reason was twofold. Speculation about the Ten Tribes during the Middle Ages usually became rife after the return of travellers from some spectacular journey beyond the limits of Europe, and the time when Abravanel wrote these works coincided with the beginning of the Age of Discovery. The sailors of João II, returning from their voyages along the western coast of Africa, brought back stories about Jewish kingdoms beyond these seas; while the same monarch's search for the lands of Prester John stimulated fanciful tales and widespread rumors about a Jewish kingdom in the East whose armies fought with those of the legendary

Christian king in that part of the world.[131a] The result was that for Abravanel's contemporaries the subject of the Ten Tribes assumed the aspect of more definite reality than it had had in any previous age.

This, however, was merely the extrinsic reason for Abravanel's discussion of the Ten Tribes. The other and more weighty reason was organically connected with his views on the Jewish situation. Abravanel's entire messianic theory came, as we have emphasized, as a reprobatory answer to the pessimists and alarmists who claimed that the Jewish people had reached the end of its road. One of the arguments employed by the prophets of doom was the pitiful numerical weakness of Jewry in comparison with the great and mighty nations. When one bears in mind that since the beginning of the Crusades, and especially since the middle of the fourteenth century, Jewish communities in Europe had been bleeding incessantly, everywhere greatly diminishing in numbers and in many places completely obliterated, one can realize the effect of that argument after the expulsion of the Jews from Spain. For the Jews of the Middle Ages, Spain was the last stronghold, and the process of reducing this stronghold, which had lasted for almost two centuries, was connected with enormously heavy losses for Jewry. After the forced mass conversion in 1391, the Jewish community in Spain never recovered its strength, and the expulsion of 1492 seemed to have given Spanish Jewry, and together with it, world Jewry of the time, the *coup de grâce*. The feeling, already prevalent after 1391, that everything was lost, became now almost universal among Jews. And to combat this feeling of growing despair, which was largely inspired by the numerical insignificance of Jewry, Abravanel made use of the widespread belief in the Ten Tribes.

The very existence of the Ten Tribes refuted the contention that everything was lost. It provided an answer to the annoying problem of the physical weakness of Jewry which disturbed the minds of those who sought to understand the feasibility of Jewish redemption in a realistic manner. Already one hundred years earlier, after the disaster of 1391, we can see this legend having the same effect. "Is it possible," asks Joshua Lorki of the convert Paul of Burgos, "that your leaving the fold was the result of a belief that our people was doomed to disappear from the scene of history? You are certainly aware of the well-known fact, related and confirmed by world travelers, that the majority of our people live in the lands of Babylon and Yemen, where the exiles from Judea settled first, while the exiles from Samaria live in the lands of Persia and Media, and their numbers are as countless as 'the sands of the sea.' Therefore even if God decreed the annihilation of all Jews in the Christian countries, the people as a whole would still exist and consequently there is no reason for the weakening of our faith."[132] Here was the same psychological problem that Abravanel attempted to meet. True, he attacked it from another angle as well when he stressed the numerical insignificance of Jewry as *proof* that redemption was at hand; when he repeatedly presented the words of the prophet—"And I shall take you out one from a city and two from a family"[133]—as an allusion to the condition of Jewry on the eve of the Messiah's arrival.[134] Yet this was a mystical apocalyptic answer. It might have satisfied the select faithful, but not the mass of the people. There had to be a realistic and positive answer to the feeling of national helplessness which was eating away the vitals of the Jewish spirit. And this worldly, concrete and understandable answer was provided by the Ten Tribes.

The question, however, was much more involved than anything said thus far would indicate. Indeed, it touched upon the vulnerable psychology of Jewish life in exile no less than upon its physical inferiority. "The three great curses of the exile," says Abravanel in one place, "are lack of courage, lack of honor, and lack of government."[135] Only a man who had a deep insight into the Jewish tragedy in the dispersion could utter such a statement. It is questionable whether the "three curses" were felt so strongly by the average Jew as they were undoubtedly felt by Abravanel. But it can be safely assumed that all the healthy instincts of the people yearned for power as never before. They must have dreamt of courage to withstand their oppressors; they must have aspired to the strength which would enable them to give an honorable answer to the harrowing humiliations inflicted upon them; and they must have dreamed of the force of a government behind them to deal with their enemies on an equal footing. As a proud Jew, as a high-ranking statesman, as a Jewish nobleman who believed in his royal origin, Abravanel must have shared these natural longings to an extent even greater than the rest of the people, and he found the fulfillment of these desires in the mirage of the Ten Tribes.[136] It was a counter-measure against the inferiority, impotence and sense of frustration which were consuming the Jewish soul to the point of self-destruction.

Thus the Ten Tribes in Abravanel's messianology fulfilled a national psychological need. In his messianic wars, the Ten Tribes play a prominent part in the punishment and defeat of Christendom. But although they fight the Christians, they are not allies of the Moslems.[137] They act independently. They participate in the battle, not to redeem Israel—since redemption could not come through human effort[138]—but because the destruction of Israel's enemies should not take place without Israel's participation.[139] Thus, by representing Israel in the act of vengeance, they manifest before the nations, to the latter's amazement and dismay, that there exist Jewish courage, Jewish honor and Jewish power.

Nevertheless, Abravanel does not predict an immediate Jewish victory. The attack of the Ten Tribes, as he foresees it, will indeed shatter the position of the Christian warriors, but the latter will succeed in staving off defeat. In the ensuing life-and-death struggle the Jewish forces will even find themselves hard-pressed,[140] but they will firmly hold their ground and the battle, which will continue with undiminished fury, will remain undecided. By then, however, the Moslems will have recovered their strength. Their vast resources of manpower in the East will be mustered for the formation of new powerful armies that will throw their entire weight against the Christians in Palestine caught in the struggle with the Ten Tribes. There, around Jerusalem, the decisive battle between Christendom and Islam will take place.[141] And it will be the most gory battle history has ever seen. The frightful scenes of death depicted in the thirty-fourth chapter of Isaiah refer, according to Abravanel, to this cataclysmic conflict.[142] Besides the mass destruction of war, God will release from heaven torrents of fire, sulphur and brimstone, which will be directed especially against the Christian warriors.[143] Thus the latter, who in the first phase of the struggle will appear to be successful, will ultimately be crushed and annihilated.[144]

The Christian defeat in Palestine will mark the end of Christian supremacy in the world. But the war will still go on. After having played the role assigned to them by God and after having lost their king in battle, the Jewish armies will withdraw. The Moslems, however, will be left on the scene, and they will pursue the victory over the Christians on land by attacking the Christian sea power which will be concentrated near Egypt and Palestine.[145] Once again the Moslems will emerge victorious[146] and, after destroying most of the Christian fleet, will proceed to conquer Rhodes, the key stronghold of Christianity in the Mediterranean.[147] The subjugation of Rhodes will open to the Moslems the way for the conquest of Venice[148] as well as for the invasion of Italy itself. The battle of Rome—the last stage of the messianic wars—will finally commence.

His deep hatred for Christendom leads Abravanel to insist that the prophecies of doom which Isaiah, Jeremiah and Obadiah announced on Edom referred to Rome.[149] That Edom was a synonym of imperial Rome was the opinion of the early sages.[150] In the Middle Ages it was taken by the Jews to refer to Christendom and especially to the city which was the seat of the popes.[151] Similarly, the opinion stated in the Talmud that the Romans were the descendants of the Edumeans was quite popular among Jews during the Middle Ages and was accepted as true even by Nicholas de Lyra, the great Christian commentator on the Bible.[152] The Bishop of Burgos, however, the scholarly convert, ridiculed the identity of Edom-Rome and said that the sages of Israel, out of hatred for the Christians, invented this groundless interpretation. The arguments which he presented were so solid and convincing that even Abravanel had to admit, "after a great deal of thought," that "the enemy presents here a strong case."[153] But what "case" is too strong for a trained scholastic mind? In a lengthy historical dissertation on the migration of nations, which relies largely on *Josippon,* the medieval Hebrew version of Josephus, Abravanel offers "decisive proof" that the Romans were actually the descendants of the Edumeans.[154]

From an historical point of view, the argument was of course groundless. But what did it matter? What mattered was that it sounded plausible and that it was based on certain authorities. Historical criticism, as we have already indicated, was almost unknown in the Middle Ages and any statement in any history book was taken at its face value as long as it did not conflict with Holy Writ, or at least with some interpretation of Holy Writ. It was obviously important for Abravanel to prove that, just as the Christian nations will be subjected to greater punishment than the other "wicked nations," so will Rome, the capital of Christianity, be singled out for specific chastisement. Thus, according to Abravanel, it was Rome that Isaiah had in mind when he spoke of the "great slaughter in the land of Edom."[155] Moreover, while her people will be massacred by the fierce enemy, the entire city will be put to the torch. All the stately buildings, including the palaces of the pope and the cardinals, will become a shambles.[156] So great indeed will be the fire that will devastate Rome that, as Isaiah said, "its dust shall turn into brimstone" and "its streams shall be turned into pitch"—by streams meaning of course Rome's rivers, the Tiber and the Ticinus.[157] Rome, the "metropolis of tyrants," will be obliterated from the face of the earth, never to be rebuilt.[158] The "eternal city" will become the eternal dwelling place of wild dogs, satyrs and evil spirits, covered by a cloud of smoke that will always go up from its ruins as a sign of God's everlasting curse.[159]

The destruction of Rome was a vision nurtured by Abravanel's blazing hatred for Christendom, but it was also a vision based on real historical factors and on a rather realistic evaluation of the political and military developments of his time. Abravanel's definite statement that: "Rome will be defeated by the Persians, that is, the Turks, who also captured Constantinople"[160] offers a clue to a clear understanding of his messianic prognostications. As the leading statesman among the Jewish exiles from Spain, his predictions regarding the war between Christendom and Islam must have been accepted most seriously by Jews. But they might have been regarded respectfully by Christians as well. For it was a prognostication supported not only by the events, but also by the political opinions of the time.

We must bear in mind that since the fall of Constantinople in 1453, the struggle between Islam and Christendom was ever present in the minds of most European peoples. The fall of the capital of the Eastern Roman Empire was considered a bad omen for the future of Christendom. In the following decades the Turks were advancing steadily toward the heart of Europe and harvesting one victory after another for Islam. Spain was the only country where the Moslems were forced to retreat. Everywhere else they were advancing. Within two decades from the fall of Constantinople, the Turks spread their rule over the Black Sea and the Crimea (1475), and pressed into the Balkans and toward Italy. In 1480 they laid siege to the powerful fortress island of Rhodes. In 1484 they overran Moldavia. In 1486, Turkey and Egypt planned to attack Sicily and reinforce Granada, a plan whose materialization would have constituted a great danger to both Spain and Italy. In 1496, the Turks resumed their attacks on Hungary, Moldavia and Poland, penetrating as far as Kanczug. In 1497, they captured Lepanto, the last important Venetian post on the Gulf of Corinth. This was preceded by an even greater victory, when the Turks wrested from the Venetians the island of Cephalonia which was strongly fortified and considered impregnable.

The conquest of Cephalonia clearly revealed the menacing character of the Turkish position. In the prolonged war between Turkey and Christendom, sea-power was believed to be the decisive factor, and the chief aim of Turkish strategy was to reduce the naval fortresses of Spain and Venice which controlled the sea routes of the Mediterranean. Abravanel, as we have seen, clearly emphasized that the decisive battles between Christendom and Islam would be not only on the continent, but also at sea; and in the capture of Rhodes, which had been predicted by him, he saw a prelude to the fall of Rome. Before the naval bastions of Christendom were overrun, an invasion of Italy by land was only a remote possibility. Nevertheless, it could not be completely excluded. Practically all of the Balkans were in the hands of the Turks who controlled the entire east coast of the Adriatic reaching to the borders of Italy in the north. Even before the fall of Lepanto the Turks raided the mainland of Venice, devastating the land and enslaving the inhabitants.

Despite the imminent Turkish threat which created panic and worry throughout Italy, the invasion of the French under Charles VIII caused even deeper depression. Charles VIII knifed through Italy with unbelievable speed. The northern city-states of Milan and Florence yielded abjectly without resistance. He entered Rome like an arrogant conqueror. And he climaxed his victorious march by the conquest of Naples whose king was forced to flee. The fatal weakness of Italy became all too apparent. Torn from within into small states and having no real army to defend it, Italy seemed to be a ready prey for any conqueror. Would not this serve as an inducement, an invitation, to the powerful and ruthless Turks? Besides Italy's military weakness, the entire position of Christendom in that country seemed to many devout Christians discouraging and demoralizing in the extreme. The Christian powers were engaged in fighting each other and ravaging Italy, instead of defending it against the dangerous infidel who was already threatening its gates. Venice, with her gallant navy, was the one force which held the Turks back. But how long would the little island republic be able to resist the Turkish invasion? The future of Italy, and in fact of all Christendom, was placed under a question mark.

It was in those days of general alarm, of dark foreboding for Christendom and of a pervading sense of impending drastic change that Abravanel wrote his messianic trilogy. What strikes us as particularly strange, therefore, is that the answer he gave to the immediate Christian problem—an all-out Christian crusade against the Turks—was one which would have been welcome from the Christian standpoint of his time. Indeed, his prediction of such a crusade was no hallucination. Only one year after Abravanel made that prediction, Pope Alexander VI issued a general call for a crusade against the Turks. The appeal met with no response, but everywhere in Italy and Spain people talked of the crusade as inevitable. Christopher Columbus ordered his son, Diego, on February 26, 1498, to employ his wealth in such a crusade. Furthermore, there were at least two important powers which were vitally interested in a concerted Christian effort against the Moslems. These were the two Mediterranean powers, Spain and Venice, whose possessions were directly threatened by the Turkish plans of expansion. In 1500, barely two years after Abravanel wrote the last part of his messianic trilogy, the combined fleets of Spain and Venice, headed by Gonsalvo de Cordova, the Spanish general, reconquered Cephalonia, after a bitter war. This checked the Turks. What did Abravanel think of these events? In his eyes they may have marked the turn of the tide, the turn from a defensive to an offensive war.

It is noteworthy that Abravanel did not believe in the nearness of a Moslem invasion of Italy. It seems that, despite the Turkish expansion in the East, he had no high regard for the military power of the Moslems. It is significant that he conceived Christian Rome as made of "iron" and the Moslem powers as made of "clay." Evidently, he was tremendously impressed by the military prowess and ability of Spain and by her victories over the Moslems in Granada. He undoubtedly believed that the Christians were actually, as well as potentially, much stronger than the Moslems. Therefore, in his political analysis of the situation, he regarded a new Christian crusade as inevitable and believed that this crusade would result, at the beginning, in great Christian military victories which would establish the rule of Christendom over the East. If in the later stage of the messianic battle, he foresaw a new rise of the Moslem forces, coming from the heart of Asia and attacking the Christians in Palestine, it was a theory which again was based on some realistic estimates and on historic experiences provided by the earlier crusades. In any event, he believed that Christianity could be defeated, not on its own ground, in Italy or in Spain, but in the East, far from the source of its power, just as it had been defeated in the same way repeatedly in the past.

One thing was crystal-clear to him: the world was on the eve of a cataclysmic change. Two world forces were arrayed against each other, and a decisive clash between them was unavoidable. Does not the appalling catastrophe confronting mankind imply a revolutionary change in the position of Israel? Are not these the apocalyptic wars of which the prophets spoke and from which the salvation of Israel must eventuate? Is it an accident that this mortal conflict between the great sea and land powers of the world is taking place at a time when the fortunes of Israel are at their lowest ebb? Is not this exactly the divine plan—to destroy the mighty nations at the peak of their power and to save Israel from the depth of its misery? Had not the corruption of mankind, the avarice and bloodshed, reached the lowest possible grade which calls forth the Day of Judgment?

In the intensity of the vision which possessed him, Abravanel heard in the rumblings of the coming war the approaching thunder of Judgment Day. In fact, the entire three-act messianic drama is for Abravanel a three-stage process of instituting justice, while the Day of Judgment itself, technically speaking, is only the climax, the "grand finale." The first act, portraying the course of the great wars, concludes, as we have seen, with the destruction of the main villain. Rome receives due punishment for its crimes and is eliminated from the scene of history. But the first act concludes also with the rise of Islam to a position of supremacy never attained by it before. It would be far from just if the "wild man from the desert," the other great and villainous oppressor of Israel, would retain that position for long. In the second act of the messianic drama, therefore, history takes another sharp turn, and the Moslems, removed from their position of supremacy, are put in their proper place.

The second act of the messianic drama brings Israel to power, and this greatest and final revolutionary change in the political and spiritual hegemony over mankind is effected solely by the powers of the Messiah. According to Abravanel, the Messiah will appear in Rome, just before she draws her last breath of life,[161] and from the dying center of Christendom the new order for mankind will be declared. That new order will be established without hindrance and without disturbance, for in the presence of the Messiah's supernatural powers, all human powers will be unavailing.[162] Even the mightiest nations, realizing their helplessness, will yield submissively to the Messiah's command.[163] Just as the Moslems will surrender Palestine to the Messiah—and this will be Palestine in its broadest boundaries, even broader than in the days of David—so will Venice and Genoa place their fleets at his disposal for the repatriation of Jews from Europe.[164] The employment of these fleets by the Messiah, however, will be mainly for the purpose of poetic justice, to demonstrate the subservience of the nations to Israel, rather than to solve the problem of transportation. For in fact there will be no such problem. In answer to the Messiah's call, Jews will stream to Palestine from all the corners of the earth and from the most distant places, miraculously overcoming the obstacles of time and space![165] The exodus, in addition, will encompass every single Jew in the Diaspora; it will include the Ten Tribes as well as the exiles from Judea; it will embrace even those who left the fold of Judaism and intermarried among the nations. Furthermore, it will include not only the living Jews, but also all who died in the Diaspora in all the generations of the exile.[166]

For, at the very time the exiles gather, the miracle of Resurrection will take place. Just as redemption will grow out of the process of revenge, so Resurrection will climax the act of redemption. Resurrection, too, has, as we have seen, as one of its purposes, the establishment of God's justice on earth.[167] To accomplish this aim, Abravanel insists, God will revive not only the faithful, but also Israel's persecutors in all the generations to make them suffer the penalty for their crimes "in body as well as in soul." The motive behind all this is significant. "If only those among the nations who will live at the time of redemption will receive their due punishment, and the rest of our enemies who tormented and destroyed us and who died honorably will not get their due, justice will be gravely evaded."[168] We should not be surprised at this extreme and unabated animosity toward the dead. For one who witnessed the horrors and cruelties to which masses of innocent people were subjected, for one who lived through the Spanish Inquisition and expulsion, it was difficult to be reconciled to the thought that those responsible for the dastardly atrocities would spend their span of life unpunished and even "die honorably" as men of good deeds. Such a thought bred feelings of desperation; it shattered the concept of final and ultimate justice and painfully frustrated Abravanel's longings for revenge. He could not accept it.

With Resurrection and the Judgment that will follow it achieved, the messianic prelude will come to an end. The Days of the Messiah will begin. "The whole world will be under the kingdom of God. The rule of kings and earthly princes will be abolished."[169] There will be one "earthly prince" only, if this title can be applied to him. He will be the Messiah—God's true envoy on earth and the only human ruler that the nations will know. His task will be to judge and to execute justice and he will perform both these functions, again, by supernatural powers. Never will he fail to recognize a culprit, or to exercise full justice. "If a man will commit a capital crime, he will kill the wicked person by 'the breath of his lips,' that is, by prayer." More clearly, at the Messiah's request, "God's fire will come down from heaven and will consume that man, or the earth will open and swallow him."[170] In this way will the King Messiah administer his rule not only among individuals but also among nations.

That all nations will accept the "true and only faith" was for Abravanel, as we have seen, an inevitable result of the resurrection.

But the nations will have to manifest their loyalty to the true faith by concrete acts of devotion throughout the Messianic Era. All nations and all peoples will therefore come to Jerusalem to pay homage to Israel and its leader. To refrain from doing so would be in any case unwise. "Nations and states that will refuse to come to Jerusalem to manifest their subservience to the divine religion will be destroyed by God's blows." And they will come to the Holy City "not with pride and glory, but with humility and submission, with heads bowed." This will be the price the nations will have to pay for the many wrongs they perpetrated against Israel in exile.[171] And this will be in full accord not only with the principle of justice, but also with the principle of inequality between the nations and the Jews. Even in the Days of the Messiah the nations will, in their very nature, be morally and intellectually inferior to the Jews, and consequently they will also differ in their status as well as in their functions. As Abravanel sees it, one of the tasks of the nations will be "to herd the sheep and cattle of the Jews and to cultivate their fields and vineyards," or, in other words, to serve the Jews and supply their material needs. In this way, the "people of Israel will not have to occupy themselves with any of the menial labors and will be free to devote themselves solely to the worship of God by prayer and to the study of the divine Law."[172]

Nevertheless, it should by no means be assumed that the lot of the nations will be bad or their spiritual elevation insignificant. It is true that most men will have to work in order to supply their own needs and those of the people of God; but work will be easy and unexhausting, since it was Abravanel's view that nature would be restored in the Messianic Era to a condition which would approximate that of the "beginning of creation."[173] The effects of the miraculous change of nature will be felt especially in Palestine, where, according to Abravanel, even beasts of prey will be friendly and docile. The prophecy of Isaiah that the "wolf shall dwell with the sheep" will be effectuated only in the Holy Land.[174] Similarly, the phenomenal fertility of the land will be restored as in the days of old.[175] Not materially alone, however, but also spiritually, mankind will approach the state of man before he first sinned. There will be a general increase in the love of wisdom and righteousness and a general diminution of man's passions.[176] But just as the restoration of the original nature of things will be more fully manifested in the land of Palestine, so will the restoration of man's original nature be more complete in Israel.[177] It is obvious that Abravanel conceived of the Messianic Era as an age of education for mankind under Jewish guidance and inspiration.

As we have noted, the rule of Israel over the nations and the latter's obedience to the divine law will be assured through the Messiah and his divine powers. He will be in truth the King of the Nations—and this is why he is called the King Messiah. For Israel, however, he will not be a king, but a spiritual head, a moral leader, which is indicated by the prophet's saying "and my servant David will be their chief."[178] In Israel the Messiah will have no governmental functions, because there will be no need for a government in Israel. The entire people will follow God's law without governmental imposition or inducement. While fear of human authority will disappear in Israel, God-fearing will be common to the entire people. As a result, there will be no crime in Israel, and consequently there will be no need for the courts and the Synhedrion.[179] Israel will be imbued with a new spirit and a new heart—a heart in which reason will be in full control over passion and the inclination toward evil will completely disappear.[180] Indeed, "so great will be the holiness and piety of Israel in the Messianic Age that Jerusalem as a whole will be called the Throne of God. For it will resemble the highest sphere, which is moved by God without intermediary, by virtue of the holiness and the cleavage to God which will be manifested in the people."[181]

Thus in the Days of the Messiah, Israel will represent the materialized ideal of a People of God, of a Holy Nation. It will also represent the ideal man who will live solely by speculation on things divine and be free from any earthly interests and worries. All material needs will be provided for him by the lesser spiritual elements of mankind. It is clear that according to Abravanel's concept Israel will be to all other nations what the priestly caste was to Israel. The priests in Israel, too, were, according to him, holy men, engaged only in divine study, while their material needs were provided by the people. Israel will be for humanity the spiritual élite, the divine aristocracy, the moral spearhead of the theocratic rule to which all mankind will yield.

Thus, the messianic conception of Abravanel embodies his ideal of pure theocracy. This ideal represents part of what he considered the aim of history—man's moral and spiritual perfection—which is finally to be achieved in the Messianic Era. And that accomplishment depends upon and incorporates the main principle of his cosmology—God's complete mastery over nature—which is fully manifested in the messianic process. In other words, the messianic concept of Abravanel comprises all the aspects of his world outlook in its fullest and broadest sense. Consequently, it embodies drastic changes not only in the history of the Jewish people, but also in that of mankind as a whole, and it entails, in addition, cataclysmic changes in nature, especially manifested by the miracle of resurrection and by the absolute domination of the spirit over the flesh. In brief, this is the Messianism of the Jewish mystics and apocalyptists, and not of the realists and the rationalists. This is not the Messianism of Maimonides, who saw in it only national freedom and independence, or in other words, a normal historical development.[182] This is not a worldly Messianism, although it is not other-wordly; it is not a heavenly paradise, although it is not an earthly one either. It is the dream of man in wonderland. It is something humanity has never experienced and never will, in the ordinary course of events. Hence it is not historical but post-historical. It belongs to the End of Days.

5. Savonarola

We have seen that Abravanel's messianic doctrine, although based on his particular world outlook, was an outgrowth of the critical conditions under which the Jews of Spain found themselves toward the end of the fifteenth century, and that it meant to provide an answer to very real moral and national problems. Yet the answer which it offered was so wildly fantastic that one wonders how it could have been advocated by an unquestionably honest and superbly analytical mind like Abravanel's, not as a mere theory for a distant future, but as an immediate and concrete solution. Clearly, such advocacy would have been impossible unless Abravanel were firmly convinced that humanity was on the threshold of the last millennium, which meant, not only the final epoch in man's history, but also the end of the world as we know it. Yet the very existence of this conviction offers a problem that cannot be easily disposed of. It seems, therefore, appropriate to inquire whether, besides the contemporary psychological and political causes which provided the background for Abravanel's messianic visions, there was not some contemporary millennial current which could help explain the ardor in Abravanel's millennial theory and the relative speed with which it was accepted.

The concept of the millennium can be traced back to ancient Jewish sources,[183] but it was more fully developed by the early Church Fathers who connected it with the reappearance of Jesus and the establishment of his thousand-year-rule on earth. Justin Martyr was the first among the Fathers to stress the millennial hope as an integral part of the Christian faith, presenting it, incidentally, in a form nearly identical with the Jewish concept. The rebuilding of Jerusalem, the ingathering of the exiles, and even the appearance of the Jewish Messiah are considered by him as the antecedent phases to the advent of Christ and the final judgment.[184] Irenaeus, the bishop of Lyons, discusses the millennium quite elaborately. It is for him the terminal period in the 6000-year life-span of the world.[185] It is the Fifth Kingdom which follows the Fourth—the Roman—and its beginning will be marked by the resurrection of the faithful and their inheritance of the Promised Land.[186] In the second century, the millennial current was evidently strong in Christian thought. In the third century, its influence began to wane. Tertullian still spoke with conviction of the millennial age.[187] But Origen, as has been correctly pointed out, "never speaks of the millenium except to condemn it."[188] At the beginning of the fourth century, the kingdom of heaven on earth was abandoned in favor of the kingdom of heaven in heaven. Jerome ridiculed the millennial doctrine as a "Jewish fable" and "figment," and stressed his belief that there will be "nothing terrestrial" after the second advent of the Lord.[189] This belief came to represent the official position of Christendom on this question. In the council at Rome in 373, the "Jewish" millenary concept was openly denounced, and the condemnation was so effective that "the heresy, however loquacious before, was silenced then; and since that time has hardly been heard of."[190] Nevertheless, the idea lingered on, and in the writings of Augustine, we find it cautiously, but quite clearly expressed.[191]

Throughout the Middle Ages millennianism was a forbidden doctrine in Christianity, abandoned and dead to all intents and purposes. It was revived only in the later centuries of the Middle Ages and only by heretics, mystics and opponents of the Church among whom the Italian monk, Joachim of Flora, of the thirteenth century, was perhaps the most notable.[192] The rise of millenarianism became later typical of almost every revolutionary movement in Christianity. The millennial idea in any religious movement indicates a secret weakness in that movement, a lack of faith in its inner strength, and the resulting necessity to fall back on the predeterministic idea of the millennium. Millenarianism affords confidence where reality does not. It lends fanaticism to the weak, when fanaticism must be their main weapon. This is why millenarianism is strong in the early stages of a religious revolution, decays with its advance and disappears with the accomplishment of its aims.[193] We see the millennial idea dominant in Christianity in the first two centuries of the Christian era, when the new religion had to fight for its existence against overwhelming odds. We see it again in the Hussite movement when the small and poorly equipped Czech people undertook the seemingly impossible task of fighting and defeating the Holy Roman Empire. We see it, especially, in the early phase of the movement, in its most radical elements and most fanatical fighters, namely, the Taborites. In the opening period of the Reformation, we find the millennial idea propagated by the Anabaptists; in the beginning of the Cromwellian revolution, by the Fifth Monarchy men. We see millennial concepts spread in Jewry with every rise of a messianic tide. Messianism in Jewry had all the aspects of a religious and national revolution, but under the circumstances of the Diaspora it was an entirely impotent movement, lacking any realism or practical power. Hence its particular reliance on the millennial hope.

We have seen that Abravanel's entire historical view is built on determinism and the millenarian scheme. In this respect he was no pathfinder in Jewry. His calculations of the "end" on the basis of the millennial principle are similar to those of Gersonides and

Nahmanides, Bar-Hiyya and Saadia. It is certain that he was influenced by the messianic prognosticators in Jewry just as there is no doubt that he drew inspiration from the early Christian Fathers as well as from Augustine. Abravanel's sources of influence, however, were not only limited to the literature of previous generations. The fact that a certain literature influenced a certain man can be explained only if we bear in mind contemporary factors which made a certain type of literature appealing and influential.

The major cause which prompted Abravanel to concentrate on the millenarian scheme was, as we have seen, the urgent and vital need for salvation, originating in the great calamity that befell Jewry in his time. This was the contemporary Jewish factor which provided the suitable background for the idea. But there was also a contemporary Christian factor which pointed to the idea itself. The hundred odd years which had passed between 1420 and 1530 witnessed the rise of short but powerful chiliastic waves in Christendom, which swept over Europe with sufficient force to make their effect felt long after their disappearance. We have already mentioned the Taborites and the Anabaptists. The influence of the Taborites, to be sure, evaporated shortly before Abravanel's birth, while the Anabaptists appeared a little more than a decade after his death. But there was a link between these two movements, a force which revived the millenarian idea with peculiar strength and which manifested its influence in the very land and at the very time in which Abravanel composed his messianic writings.

It is strange that none of those who have written of Abravanel ever mentioned the ideological affinity between him and Savonarola. Yet this affinity is so striking that we must look here for one of the main influences that shaped Abravanel's messianic theory. One of the points strongly stressed by Savonarola in his "prophecies" was the approaching disaster to the Church.[194] This was the time when Christendom was in a state of great moral degeneration. This was the age of Alexander VI, the least respected spiritual father Christianity ever had. Sternly Savonarola accused the occupant of St. Peter's Throne of treason to the precepts of God. He called him anti-Christ, and official Rome—Babylon.[195] He predicted destruction and punishment for Italy and the Church, and his prophecies struck terror into many hearts not only in

Florence but also outside its borders. He saw the skies of Italy heavily clouded, and a hand holding a sword emerging from the clouds and pointing towards Rome.[196] It was the same sword which Abravanel saw when he interpreted Isaiah's verses: "For my sword in the heavens is drenched in blood . . . Behold, it descends upon Edom, upon the people of my hate, for judgment."[197]

That the world was nearing its end was another favorite theme of Savonarola who prophesied the coming of the "deluge," the destruction of most of mankind and the salvation of the faithful only. The end of the world which Savonarola predicted, however, did not mean the actual end of the cosmos, but the end of civilization as it was.[198] It meant the elimination of the existing rule of Christendom and the emergence from its ruins of a purified Church of Saints. There was little or no difference between the basic redemption concepts of Savonarola and Abravanel, except for the identity of those who would be redeemed. For Savonarola, it was the faithful Christian, for Abravanel the faithful Jew. This Church of Saints would establish the Kingdom of Heaven on earth, the real and true theocracy toward the materialization of which Savonarola was taking practical steps. We have already noticed the fact that both Savonarola and Abravanel were not republicans, but theocrats. We now have to add that for both theocracy was part of the messianic ideal.

The impact of Savonarola's campaign on Abravanel's messianic predictions can hardly be doubted. Savonarola's campaign began only a few years before Abravanel embarked upon the writing of his messianic works, and was carried on at the very time of Abravanel's stay in Italy. The prophecies of Savonarola were especially tied up with the invasion of Italy by Charles VIII, in whom people saw the coming of the "sword," and the realization of Savonarola's prophecies. Charles VIII conquered Naples at the time when Abravanel was at the court of Alfonso, the king of Naples, and Abravanel was even forced to flee as a result of the French victory. During the entire course of Charles' invasion, Italy was in a state of terrific tension. From across the peninsula came the voice of Savonarola, foreboding greater evil and misfortune and constantly increasing that tension. "Oh, Rome," Savonarola cried, "like an iron belt will your enemies surround you! Your destruction is approaching! Sword, fire and flames will be visited upon you and effect your complete and total destruction! When the plagues of the Lord will be in your gates, you will shiver and tremble in the anguish of your heart!"[199] In the light of the events, Savonarola's prophecies assumed a concrete, frightful aspect. The special role which Florence, under Savonarola's influence, played in the French invasion was an additional factor for making Savonarola's name a byword throughout Italy,[200] and vastly publicizing his predictions. It is impossible to assume that Abravanel, who was undoubtedly well informed on all the aspects of the French invasion, would not be aware of the prophet of Florence who morally paved the way for Charles VIII.

Abravanel's world outlook certainly prepared him for the acceptance of the mystical concepts of Savonarola. His theory of the world as destructible, his view of history as thoroughly controlled by God, his firm faith in miracles, all made him inclined to listen attentively to the prophecies of the Florentine friar who predicted the coming of the "deluge," of the "sword," the end of the world, the Day of Judgment and the establishment of the Kingdom of Heaven. The influence might have been very general; indeed, it must have been very general.[201] But all that Abravanel needed in those days was a stimulus of this kind. The very fact that, in the great center of Christendom, a powerful Christian voice was expressing the belief that the end of Christendom was at hand must have been in his eyes proof that the materialization of the apocalyptic vision was near.

6. Epilogue

The study of Abravanel's views yields a number of conclusions regarding the nature of his theories as well as their historic effect. In the preface to this work we touched upon some problems presented by the era which followed Abravanel's times. The conclusions offered here, we believe, may provide partial solutions to these problems.

What we observe, first of all, is the inner unity and consistency of Abravanel's views, the existence of which some writers have been inclined to deny. Contradictory statements do appear in his writings, but these constitute only minor curves in his thinking which little affect the main trend. Abravanel knew exactly what he was aiming at and persistently proceeded towards this aim, although theoretical obstacles met on the way could not always be successfully overcome.

The charge that Abravanel was lacking in originality[202] may hold for the elements of his theories; it does not hold for the combination of these elements. Abravanel's ideas, taken individually, are traceable, as we have seen, to earlier thinkers—the mainstays of the vast literature of many centuries which was available to the people of his generation. The Greek literature, the classical Roman literature, the literature of the Church Fathers, the scholastic literature of the Middle Ages, the ancient and medieval Jewish literature, all contributed "building material" for his theories. The plan for the building, however, was definitely his own.

We have seen that Abravanel's system of thought was not at all a typical expression of his time. His world outlook, his view of history, his political views were all in marked degree at variance with the prevailing views and attitudes of his age. More significantly, the core of his theories, based as they were on an antirationalistic conception, was opposed to that of the theories of the Renaissance, which were based on a materialistic viewpoint.

The materialistic culture of the Renaissance, which lies at the roots of modern civilization, represented a sharp departure from the civilization of the Middle Ages. Abravanel clearly discerned the meaning of the new trend and opposed it intensely. His repudiation of the materialistic forms of life, of the "pursuit of luxuries," of the "crafts and inventions," did not express some "abstract" theory, unrelated to any specific time, but the definite reaction of a medieval spiritualist to the new course of life and the new concepts of human values which were developing before his very eyes. At a later stage of history, when modern civilization was about to make another sharp turn towards the mechanistic and materialistic position of our time, another spiritualist, Jean Jacques Rousseau, expressed his aversion for the new course by similarly advocating the return to the "state of innocence" and the primitive, "natural" mode of life.

Just as Abravanel does not represent his age in the basic contents of his message, so does he not represent it in the form of his thinking. The form of thinking of the Renaissance was that of the Greek and Roman logicians, unrestricted in its search for truth and ever striving to lean on facts. Abravanel certainly spoke in the terms of the Renaissance period—in the terms of Plato and Aristotle, Cicero and Seneca. His language as a whole, however, was not that of the Renaissance, but of scholasticism. His reasoning, like that of all scholastics, was never free or factual in any real sense, but controlled and restricted by religious dogma.

By the end of the fifteenth century, and even earlier, scholastic reasoning had lost its appeal; and, had Abravanel fought for his views with this obsolete weapon alone, it is doubtful that he would have had any historic effect. But his scholastic thinking was imbued with mysticism, and this was a mysticism which embodied a vision for the future at a time when mankind, treading a new path, wondered what the future held for it.

In all this we find a great similarity between Abravanel and Savonarola. Abravanel was a unique phenomenon in Jewry, just as Savonarola was unique in Christendom. Both were relics of the medieval past in an era which was forsaking the past. The contents of their message, however, was not the rehabilitation of the past, but the renovation of mankind through the instrumentality of principles which had been only partly employed in the past and which they advocated in their pure and extreme form. This extremist approach, plus the apocalyptic element in their theories, made both Abravanel and Savonarola, despite all the antiquity they breathed, appear as "men of the future."

Both Savonarola and Abravanel opened new historical lines. Savonarola was the forerunner of the great movement of the Reformation which stirred Europe during the sixteenth and seventeenth centuries. Abravanel was the forerunner of the messianic movement which stirred and agitated Jewry during the same period. The contents of their messages were essentially the same—moral-apocalyptic. The outcome was not the same. The difference in the outcome resulted from the difference in their motives, in the tasks they set themselves, and, what is more, in the circumstances under which their influence was felt. In Christendom, the moral element was of real interest, while the apocalyptic element, although it could agitate the minds of many, could not strike deep roots. In Jewry, on the other hand, conditions were conducive to quite the reverse process.

Abravanel's hatred for the world of his time—a world of passion, crime and violence—was in essence that of Savonarola, except that his animosity was even deeper. Savonarola still believed in the possibility of the world's salvation through repentance; Abravanel did not. A witness of the Spanish Inquisition and expulsion, he despaired of the world's capacity for moral recuperation and anxiously awaited its inevitable doom. Like Sodom and Gomorrah, he thought, it was too rotten to be improved; it had to be destroyed. This was the only way to put an end to the growing vice of generations born in sin, as well as the only conceivable conclusion to the evil course they had taken. He was possessed of the conviction that mankind, and Christian civilization which permeated it, were headed for destruction in a fantastically bloody world war, and that only after that will man perceive the true meaning of life and morality. Only then will also Israel's salvation be effected. The most pessimistic vision of the wildest annihilation is accompanied here by the most optimistic dream of national and universal happiness.

"The Day of the Lord will come *soon!*" This was the warning of Savonarola and the promise of Abravanel. The close proximity of salvation, proclaimed by Abravanel, was in itself an important factor in providing the impetus for the new messianic movement which was soon to be on its way. Historical movements can indeed be created only by those who promise help in the near, not the distant future; who offer immediate solutions, not long range plans. Jesus, who declared that the Kingdom of God was *at hand,* and Mohammed, who warned of the *impending* Day of Judgment, offer some of the outstanding examples in the field of religion; Marx, who in 1847 stressed the imminence of the Socialist revolution, and Herzl, who in 1902 envisioned the Jewish State as established in 1922, illustrate the same rule in the field of politics. The fact that their prophecies failed to materialize did not kill the tremendous driving force engendered by the stirring expectations that they had provoked. The promise of imminent salvation is of course not the only element required, but it is a prerequisite for the launching of a new historical course. Simon Duran, who in the first half of the fifteenth century predicted the arrival of the Messiah in 1850, could not possibly have started a movement; nor could his contemporary in Christendom, Nicholas of Cusa, who forecast the world's end in 1734.

To Savonarola's cryptic "coming of the sword," Abravanel gave a clear and elaborate interpretation based on his broader view of international politics and conditions. Abravanel's apocalyptic vision, moreover, was not only broader, but also clearer. The most fantastic developments are described by him in vivid, colorful details; the strangest dreams appear true and realistic by a strict and orderly sequence of events; the most incredible theories are backed by moving arguments, coordinated by "historical data," corroborated by authorities, until they seem not only feasible, but unquestionable. In brief, Abravanel's enormous power of logical thinking was devoted to prove the most illogical of all things; his entire knowledge of man's nature, world affairs and world history was utilized to prove something which neither human nature nor world history have ever seemed to promise.

That these qualities proved helpful to Abravanel in launching the most potent messianic movement in Jewish history, can be taken as a matter of course. But it is remarkable that he exercised a profound and lasting influence on the Christian world as well. Indeed, between the ages of the Reformation and the Enlightenment, no Jewish writer enjoyed greater fame, or aroused such widespread interest and discussion, as did Abravanel. Theologians and Bible critics, orientalists and historians, bibliographers and encyclopedists, belonging to a variety of Christian camps, diligently studied Abravanel's writings, investigated his life, wrote in defense or in refutation of his theories, and, above all, translated a large part of his works into Latin.[203] Among the outstanding Christian admirers of Abravanel we find men of genius like Hugo Grotius, Richard Simon, Johann Buxtorf the younger, Pierre Bayle, and Adrian Reland.[204] Among his outstanding Christian opponents, who fought him, often vehemently, on theological issues, we find renowned religious leaders such as Calvin, Heinrich Alting, Johann Franz Buddeus, Johann Benedikt Carpzov II, and Pierre Daniel Huet,[205] not to mention a long list of lesser luminaries of Christian theology, like l'Empereur, Schnell, Hulsius, Varenius, and Theophilus Grossgebauer, the forerunner of Pietism.[206] In the vast literature that grew up about him there were not lacking strains of open hostility or acrimonious personal attacks, like those of Bartolocci, De Castro and Moreri,[207] but the crystallized attitude in Christendom towards Abravanel was one of the highest esteem, and it is clearly reflected in the Jewish history presentations of such notable Christian authors as Jacob Christian Basnage, De Boissy, and Count Beugnot.[208]

What was the reason for this extraordinary influence that Abravanel exercised upon the Christian world—an influence which, in the period referred to, was not equalled by any other Jewish writer or thinker, not even by Ibn Ezra and Maimonides? As in similar instances, so in this case, the reason must be sought not in a single cause, but rather in an array of diverse factors. Accordingly, his influence upon Christian scholarship must be seen against the background of the new turn then taken by European learning. It was tied up with the emphasis placed by the Reformation upon the Bible as the source of religious truth—an emphasis that quickened the interest in biblical studies, brought forth an entire school of Hebraists and fostered, side by side with the study of the Hebrew Bible, a growing interest in its Hebrew commentators. These, then, were the general conditions which facilitated Abravanel's entry into the Christian scholarly world. However, what particularly appealed to Christian scholars in Abravanel, what led them to prefer him to other Jewish commentators, was that unique combination of qualities, which they found in no other commentator but him. Thus, his lucid and colorful style was preferred to the schematic, sometimes illusive language which characterized the works of other Jewish commentators. His elaborate, manysided method of discussion, often broadening into fullfledged dissertations, was preferred, despite its extensiveness, to the terseness of his predecessors, who left many problems undiscussed. The audacity he often displays in refuting views of famed Jewish authorities, ancient and medieval, was equally a trait that appealed to Christians, no less than the objectivity with which he treats certain Christian biblical interpretations. In fact, the very frequency with which he discusses Christian views—a frequency not met with in Jewish biblical exegesis—was an important factor in Abravanel's favor; for, while a Christian reading Abravanel might be opposed to him almost throughout, he would yet find himself on the same ground. Above all, one must add that particular blend of historicism, mysticism, classicism and politicizing in which Abravanel's works are steeped, and which formed basic elements in West-European thinking in the period following his times.

These, however, were merely contributory causes to Abravanel's influence in the Christian world. The main cause, from a Christian standpoint, lay not in the positive aspects of Abravanel's writings, but rather in their negative ones. More plainly, his influence in Christendom was due to his attack upon Christianity as a whole and its messianic doctrine in particular, and this is why it was in the religious world, even more than in the world of learning, that Abravanel's figure loomed large. The fact that in the battle against him there participated some of the greatest theologians in Christendom, shows the extent to which his onslaught was felt. Similarly, the fact that for more than two centuries Christian thinkers struggled with Abravanel's arguments, shows the measure of their cogency and force. Obviously it was believed that Abravanel had struck dangerously at the very fundamentals of Christianity, and to repel this assault became the aim and the ambition of scores of Christian writers in a dozen lands.

Here again the strong interest in Abravanel was rooted in a spiritual development in Christendom: it was prompted by the reexamination of Christian dogma which was initiated by the Reformation. In the protracted religious strife which accompanied this process, and which soon split the camp of the Reformers themselves, the doctrine of Chiliasm, suppressed for many centuries, came significantly to the fore. It encouraged the growth of dissident sects, which were held a menace to both Protestantism and Catholicism, and it burst forth in repeated waves of enthusiasm during the sixteenth and the seventeenth centuries. It was no accident that some of the best known theologians who tried to refute Abravanel's messianic concept—a concept held to have been akin to Chiliasm—were most active in the struggle against the chiliastic trend, especially as it revealed itself in the movement of the Pietists. Similarly, it was no accident that Christian interest in Abravanel was strongest at the turn of the seventeenth century, when Pietism was at its very height. One may say categorically that for

Christendom in that era Abravanel was a source of inspiration in many ways, and the full measure of his ramified influence upon the conflicting currents of religious thought at the time still remains to be determined.

It is noteworthy that in Christendom Abravanel's influence reached its climax at the time when in Jewry it had already passed its zenith. Yet his impact upon his own people was undoubtedly stronger and more decisive by far. In Jewry, as in Christendom, his inspiration was felt in diverse and numerous directions. It activated new developments in philosophy, historical criticism, biblical exegesis, mysticism, as well as in the entire concept of Judaism, and it stamped the work of such masters in their respective fields as Judah Abravanel, Azariah de Rossi, Moses Alshech, Manasseh ben Israel, Joseph Solomon del Medigo,[209] and Samuel David Luzzatto. In such a vast and many-sided sphere of influence one naturally seeks a center of gravity. Thus, for Luzzatto, for instance, Abravanel was the man who broke Aristotle's hold upon Jewish thought; and in this he saw his essential greatness.[210] Yet the greatness of Abravanel was not really in this.

The main historic achievement of Abravanel—in Jewry as in Christendom—was linked with his exposition of the messianic theme. The time certainly was favorable, but it was Abravanel who sowed the seed in the fruitful soil. We find his ideas reverberating in all the messianic movements that stirred Jewry down to the end of the seventeenth century. Laemmlein, Molkho, Reubeni, Shabbethai Zevi—all repeat Abravanelian principles. The basic idea of the clash between Christianity and Islam is ever present, in open or concealed form. There is no doubt that the appearance of Reubeni was built on a plan to hasten the arrival of the Messiah by provoking a war between Christendom and Turkey. This was the entire sense of his political adventure.

The rise of the mystical current among the Jews in the period following Abravanel's must be likewise attributed, at least partly, to Abravanel's influence. Although Abravanel claimed that he was no cabalist,[211] his admitted acceptance of cabalistic methods and doctrines and his undisguised admiration for the "ancient" cabalistic masters[212] who, he believed, held the answers to all the baffling mysteries of the world, paved the way for the acceptance of the cabala as the principal "science" in the field of human knowledge. The very fact that Abravanel, a renowned philosophical scholar, a man of immense learning and, what is perhaps most important, a man whose general authority among Jews was of the highest, bowed before the depth and greatness of the cabala, removed from that science much of the scepticism regarding its genuineness and importance from which it suffered from the very beginning. Similarly, Abravanel's teaching that all the mysteries of knowledge are incorporated in the Divine Law including the most intriguing of all mysteries—the date of the "end"—were another inducement to study the cabala and another reason for abandoning all interest in foreign learning.

Abravanel's messianic doctrine reflects the tragedy of the Jewish messianic movements and, in large measure, the tragedy of the Jews in the Middle Ages. It was the tragedy of a people who built castles in the air, who breathed the atmosphere of dreams rather than reality. The most sinister aspect of the tragedy was that, while the soul of the people floated among the bright clouds of heaven, its body was dragged on the ground, torn and bleeding from a hundred wounds. The gulf between the ideal and the real was utterly unbridgeable. Reality and ideal constituted two distinct worlds, the first applying to the Jew as an individual, the other to his collective life. The strange dualism is strikingly represented in Abravanel's own career. A realistic statesman when other nations were concerned, he was completely swayed by imagination when his own people was involved. His insistence that the approaching exodus during redemption would encompass every single Jew in the Diaspora embodied his conviction that the time for Jewry in exile was over and that there was no possibility whatsoever for Jews to continue living among the nations. Nevertheless, he regarded as futile any attempt on the part of the people to effectuate the exodus and gain salvation by their own efforts. Sternly and repeatedly Abravanel warned that salvation would not come by human will and planning, but by divine power alone.[213]

One is tempted to ask what would have been the historic course of the Jewish people if at that moment of disaster—when the tragedy of Jewish homelessness, accentuated by the Spanish expulsion, became all too evident—a man of the stature of Abravanel had arisen and propagated a realistic course, a plan of regaining the Promised Land by settlement and colonization. One is inclined to believe that the plan, while it would have been criticized at the beginning, would have finally struck root and paved the way for future champions. Such advocacy might have changed the entire historic attitude of the Jews toward their national problem and kept their eyes fixed on earth, rather than upon heaven. But this was not the fate of the Jews. The political Jewish leader of the age was agitating against a realistic approach to the question. The man who was filled with deep yearning for redemption was warning against any action on its behalf. It was the most sensitive moment in Jewish history, one of those moments in a people's life when the national soul is forged and cast anew by the people's spiritual leaders. This was a time for turning Israel's historic direction away from the Diaspora and toward Palestine, if there were some measure of political realism in Jewish leadership of which Abravanel was the outstanding figure.

Only one generation after Abravanel's time there appeared a great Jewish statesman with a realistic approach to the Jewish problem and with a concrete plan for its solution. I refer to Don Joseph Nasi, the Duke of Naxos, and his plan for Jewish settlement in Palestine. He issued a call for Jews to begin energetic colonization in the Holy Land. But his call fell on deaf ears. The Jews of his time were accustomed to thinking of redemption in a supernatural way. They were infatuated with the predictions of Abravanel and the miraculous messianic powers which could effect their deliverance at one fell swoop. The long, arduous and prosaic process of settling in a semi-desolate land did not attract them. Abravanel's maxim that the Jews can and should do nothing for their salvation was their "practical" motto. In brief, it was the influence of Don Isaac Abravanel that destroyed the influence of Don Joseph Nasi.

But whatever opinion one may form of Abravanel's historical effect, it is clear that he unconsciously represented a historical dynamism which led the Jewish people out of a terrible impasse. The logic of history is the logic of facts, not of theories. It is the logic of the imaginative rather than the rational forces that moves mankind in its struggle for achievement and power, for security and peace. Abravanel represented this historic logic. He gave his generation the answer it expected to hear when it stood before the abyss of black despair. He gave it the only answer that stirs despairing men and gives new meaning to their lives and struggle:— *Quo vadis,* Israel? was the question of the time. And Abravanel answered: toward the era of greatest blessedness, toward the Kingdom of Heaven.

APPENDICES, NOTES & INDEX

ABBREVIATIONS USED IN THE NOTES

Baer = F. Baer, *Die Juden im christlichen Spanien.*
Enc. Jud. = *Encyclopaedia Judaica.*
Graetz = H. Graetz, *Geschichte der Juden* (4th edition).
HUCA = *Hebrew Union College Annual.*
JQR = *Jewish Quarterly Review.*
MGWJ = *Monatsschrift fuer Geschichte und Wissenschaft des Judentums.*
REJ = *Revue des études juives.*

APPENDICES

A. THE NAME "ABRAVANEL"

The name *Abravanel* represents a difficult problem with respect to both its pronunciation and origin. It is sometimes spelled *Abravaniel* (Baer, *Die Juden im christlichen Spanien*, II, 116), *Abrabanell* (*ibid.*, I, 393), *Abravanell* (in the death sentences of João II against Don Isaac and Joseph Abravanel; see *Archivo Histórico Portuguez*, II, 31–33, 346–348, and Carl Gebhardt, *Leone Ebreo*, Regesten, 39), *Bravanell* or *Bravanel* (*ibid.*, 36, 40), *Barabanel* (Gil Vicente, introduction to the *Auto da Lusitania*), *Abravanella* (Nicola Ferorelli, *Gli Ebrei nell'Italia meridionale dall'età Romana al secolo XVIII*, Torino, 1915, 89, on the basis of Canc. Arag., Com. 17, f. 94 t.), *Bravanello* (*ibid.*, quoting Canc. Arag., Com. 10, f. 217 t.), *Abramanel* (*ibid.*, 88, quoting R. Com. Summ., Com. 36, f. 97 t., and 89, on the basis of Canc. Arag., Com. 17, f. 94 t.) and *Abrahamanel* (in a document of the *Archivio di Stato* of Venice, published by D. Kaufmann in *Revue des études juives*, XXXVIII, 147). Various other spellings of the name in Latin transcription (*Abarbinel, Abarbenel, Abrabinael, Barbanella, Barbinellus, Ravanella*) are cited by J. Ch. Wolf, *Bibliotheca Hebraea*, I, 627–628, Pierre Bayle, *Dictionnaire historique et critique*, 5th ed., Amsterdam, 1734, p. 42, and Hartmann, *Abrabanele*, in Ersch u. Gruber, *Allgemeine Encyclopädie*, I, 150a. In most cases, however, the name is spelled *Abravanel*. So it appears in Portuguese documents (Gebhardt, *op. cit.*, Regesten, 39, 41–44 and Antonio Caetano de Sousa, *Provas da História Genealógica*, I, 507), in Garcia de Resende's *Cancioneiro Geral*, Coimbra, 1910, I, 62, almost always in the documents published by Baer (see Baer, *op. cit.*, II, index), and in this form it is found also in the Neapolitan State Archives (*Can. Arag.*, Com. 18, f. 142: according to Ferorelli, *op. cit.*, 89), in Marino Sanuto's *I Diarii*, III, col. 1439, in Zurita's *Historia del rey Don Hernando* (*Anales de Aragon*, V, 342a: Habrauanel); in Usque's *Consolaçam ás Tribulaçoens de Israel*, III, Dialogo §32; in Aboab's *Nomologia*, 302–303. The Hebrew spelling of the name as given in Abravanel's own writings, as used by members of his family, or as it appears in works of contemporaries of Don Isaac or his sons, is sometimes אברבניאל (*Questions and Answers to Saul ha-Kohen*, Venice, 1574, 21d, 26a, and Abravanel's Comm. on Zechariah 12. 6); אבראבאניל (*Shebet Yehudah*, first ed., Adrianopol, 1554, VII); אבראבניל (*Questions and Answers*, 20d; *Shebet Yehudah*, chap. L; documents published by Marx in *J.Q.R.*, 1908, 250); אבראניל (*Shebet Yehudah*, VII, LI); אבראבנל (Gebhardt, *op. cit.*, Regesten, 58); אבראבניליא (statement of Meir Arama, *Ha-Maggid*, II, No. 25, p. 99); בראבניל (Joseph ben Zaddiq's *Zekher Zaddiq*, in Ad. Neubauer's *Mediaeval Jewish Chronicles*, I, 98); אברבינאל (vocalized: *Abarbinel;* Elijah Levita, *Tishbi*, Isny, 1541, p. 5b); but the most common form is אברבנאל (introductions to *Crown of the Elders*, Comm. on the Former Prophets, Comm. on Deuteronomy, *Wells*, and *Inheritance*). So is the name spelled also by Joseph Chajun (Kayserling, *op. cit.*, 75; note 1), Menahem ben Zerah, *Zedah la-Derekh*, introd., and Zacuto, *Iuchassin*, ed. Fil., 224b.

In view of the heavy preponderance of the spelling *Abravanel* in Latin transcription, and in view of the various versions of the Hebrew spelling, which include that of אבראבאניל, preference must be given to this form (*Abravanel*). The spelling and pronunciation of the name as commonly adopted in later times (*Abarbanel*) seem therefore to represent a distortion of the form *Abravanel*. This, nevertheless, does not preclude the possibility that the latter form is a distortion of the former. The assertion of Graetz, VIII, 324, note 1, that the "Italian and German Jews changed the name to *Abarbanel*" does not agree with the facts: confusion regarding the spelling, pronunciation and meaning of the name existed already in Don Isaac's times. Judah Abravanel, Don Isaac's son, seems to have insisted on the form *Abarbanel* (see his poem on *The Inheritance*, verse 13, and on Comm. on the Latter Prophets, verse 18, both reprinted by Gebhardt, *op. cit.*, Gedichte, 18, 22). This is how Judah's family name is given by Maximiliano Lemos, probably on the basis of documentary evidence (*História da Medicina em Portugal*, Lisboa, 1899, I, 91) and by Amatus Lusitanus, who saw Judah's *De Coeli Harmonia* where the name might have appeared in this form (Cent. VII, cur. 98, ed. Veneza, 1566, p. 152). Thus we have also the spelling of Jacob *Abarbanel* from 1501 (Ferorelli, *op. cit.*, 89, note 8) and of Henrique Fernandez *Abarbanel* from 1512 (Joaquim de Carvalho, *Leão Hebreu, Filósofo*, Coimbra, 1918, 17).

The problem of the right spelling and pronunciation can be definitely determined only on the basis of an ethymological explanation of the name. In this direction, however, little or nothing has thus far been offered. Judah Abravanel (introductory poems to Don Isaac's Comm. on the Latter Prophets, verse 18, and to *The Inheritance of the Fathers*, verse 13) attributed to the name a meaning which agrees with the common form of its Hebrew spelling: "A Limb of a Son of God" or "A Son of a Son of God" (בר בן אל; אבר בן אל). Of the two explanations the second appears more plausible (one might assume that the opening "A" was added under Arabic influence), but it still remains unacceptable in view of the fact that the name בנאל or בניאל appears nowhere in the Bible (although we have the name בניה which has the same meaning). A different interpretation therefore will be suggested here.

Assuming that the endings of the name *Abravanel*, i.e., *el, ell*, or *iel*, are merely the suffixes commonly found in Spanish names and that they have nothing to do with the Hebrew אל (God), there remains the body of the name: *Abravan*. This may be but a distorted form of the Hebrew *Abraham*. The form *Abrahan* for *Abraham* is very common among Spanish Jews (see Baer, *op. cit.*, I, II, indices) and the name might have originally been *Abrahanel*. The *h* however is often omitted, creating the forms *Abraam* or *Abraan*, or changed into *f* or *ff*. Thus we have for Juhuda (Yehuda) = *Jufuda* and *Juffuda* (Baer, *op. cit.*, I, index, 1116b and 1117a), for Cohen = Cofen (*ibid.*, 1115b, 1109b, etc.), and also for *Abrahim* (Abraham) we have the forms *Abrafim* (*ibid.*, 1096b) and *Abraffim* (1098a). The development of the name might have therefore been this: *Abrahanel, Abrafanel, Abravanel, Abrabanel*, and finally, under the influence of the Hebrew spelling, *Abarbanel*.

The difficulty in accepting this interpretation seems to us to be this: since the name Abravanel seems to appear already in the eleventh century (see above, p. 3), the above theory involves the assumption that the change was made in pre-Moslem times. The name Abravanel, however, must have been of old origin (witness the uncertainty regarding its proper form, and hence its meaning, among members of the Abravanel family themselves), and perhaps in the correct reading of the name is embodied the answer to the question of the time in which the Abravanels first settled in Spain.

B. ABRAVANEL'S ATTITUDE TOWARD THE REVOLT AGAINST JOÃO II

The death sentences against Isaac and Joseph Abravanel were first published by Anselmo Braamcamp Freire in *Archivo Histórico Portuguez*, vol. II, pp. 31–33 and 346–348. Even before these documents were published a number of Christian writers, notably Bartolocci (*Bibl. magna rabbinica*, III, 874; and cf. *Acta Eruditorum*, Leipzig, Nov. 1686, 529), considered Abravanel guilty of the crime imputed to him and fully deserving of the penalty he suffered. Yet most scholars used to rely primarily on Abravanel's testimony in this matter. The publication of the death sentences seems to have changed this attitude. On the basis of these documents, Carvalho (*op. cit.*, 10–11, 14) and Gebhardt, who republished them in his *Leone Ebreo* (Regesten, 36–44), came to the conclusion that Abravanel participated in the conspiracy of the nobles against João II (*idem., op. cit.*, 8, and Regesten, 35). Carvalho went even so far as to say that Abravanel, "far from being a victim of his friendship for the Duke of Braganza, or a simple puppet of the latter's plans, was an active collaborator and diligent organizer" in the rebellion (*op. cit.*, p. 14). Neither Carvalho nor Gebhardt offer any explanation for their complete disregard of Abravanel's refutations of the charges leveled against him. Gebhardt's view, which is somewhat milder than that of Carvalho, is supported by F. Baer in his article on Abravanel in *Encyclopaedia Judaica*, I, 585a, in his Hebrew study on Abravanel ("Don Isaac Abravanel and his Attitude toward the Problems of History and State," in *Tarbiz*, 1937, 242) and in his *Toledot ha-Yehudim bi-Sefarad ha-Nozrit*, Tel-Aviv, 1945, 494–495. Baer says in one place, in support of his reliance on the king's verdict, that "the rebellion of the nobles was, after all, a fact" (*Tarbiz*, 1937, 242). This does not prove, however, that Abravanel's participation was a fact. On another occasion, Baer says that Abravanel's refutations are denied by his own statements in which he expressed his hatred for monarchism (*Toledot*, 495). Abravanel, however, while objecting to monarchism as a system, also expressed vehement opposition to rebellion against any monarch under any circumstances (see on this in detail above, pp. 186–8), and this opposition, furthermore, Abravanel expressed in his Commentaries on the Former Prophets which he wrote shortly after his escape from Portugal (see above, p. 36). According to the official version Abravanel was plotting rebellion against João not only while in Portugal but also after his escape, that is, at the very time he was writing those commentaries in which he stated his emphatic opposition to anti-monarchic plots; and if we accept the official version as truthful, we must conclude that Abravanel was a hypocrite of the first water. This is a conclusion, however, with which no one who is familiar with Abravanel's writings, and who recognizes his character from these writings, would be able to agree. Against the testimony of Abravanel stands only the testimony of João II as implied in his death sentence against Abravanel; and João II, who established his rule by means of a blood purge and who, toward the end of his reign, evinced his excessive cruelty by his inhuman attitude toward the Jewish children of Portugal, could not be such a lover of absolute justice as his chroniclers endeavored to describe him. In our opinion, it was easier for João to take a man's life than for Abravanel to write knowingly one word of falsehood in his commentary on the Holy Bible! Furthermore, we find that Abravanel's denials of the accusations of João II were restated by him twelve years after his escape from Portugal, when he no longer had any hope of returning to his native country, and it was echoed by his son Judah twenty years after the events in question, in 1503/4. Judah charged João with deceitful preparation of an indictment against his father as belonging to the rebels' group (see his *Complaint Against Fate*, verse 32, republished by Gebhardt, *op. cit.*, Gedichte, 3). Moreover, when Judah made that charge, João was already dead and the ruling monarch in Portugal at the time was a brother of one of the rebel leaders! There could not possibly be any other reason for these repeated denials but the righteous indignation of Abravanel and his son against the injustice done them by the king.

There remains only one question to be answered: Did Abravanel hold back information from the king, and thus implicate himself in the conspiracy indirectly? "I discussed this question of rebellion against a king," writes Abravanel in one place, "with some of the great nobles. They maintained that a revolt against a tyrannical king is justifiable. I am convinced it is not" (Comm. on I Sam. 24. 7 [f. 124, col. 3]). With whom did Abravanel hold that discussion? In all probability, the discussion referred to was held with the princes of Braganza; but from this it does not necessarily follow that Abravanel participated in secret councils of the nobles in which decisions of a conspiratorial nature were adopted. Abravanel undoubtedly attributed to the debate he had with the nobles on the question of rebellion theoretical value only. It is quite possible that such a debate was provoked by the princes of Braganza on purpose and, after establishing that Abravanel's attitude toward an anti-monarchic conspiracy of any kind was uncompromisingly negative, they were cautious not to reveal to him—with all their reliance upon his loyalty—their most vital and most dangerous secret. It is also possible, on the other hand, that their considerations of revolt did remain after all—and this has not yet been fully disproven—in the theoretical sphere. Abravanel, in any case, was certain, at least for months after his escape from Portugal, that the princes of Braganza had committed no criminal act.

NOTES TO PART ONE

CHAPTER ONE

1 See Appendix A.

2 According to Baruch Uzziel Hesqeto (Forti), introd. to *Wells of Salvation* (*Ma'aynei ha-Yeshu'ah*), Ferrara, 1551, 3a, Abravanel was born in the year 5197 (fall 1436–fall 1437) and died in the year 5268 (fall 1507–fall 1508), at the age of 71 (*ibid.*, 4a). Abravanel's death seems to have occurred either on November 25, 1508, or on January 13, 1509 (see C. Gebhardt, *Leone Ebreo*, 1929, Regesten, 55–57, and below, Chapter IV, note 22). If the second date is the correct one, Abravanel could not have been born in 1436, for in that case he would have been at his death 72, and not 71, years old; consequently he was born in 1437. If, however, Abravanel died on November 25, 1508, he could have been born between November 25 and December 31, 1436, and still die at the age of 71, except that then he would have been close to 72 at his death, a fact of which the biographer would probably have been aware and which, in that case, he would not have failed to mention. The greater likelihood therefore is that Abravanel was born in 1437.

3 Antonio Caetano de Sousa, *Provas da História Genealógica da Casa Real Portugueza*, Lisbon, 1739, I, 507; see below, Chapter II, p. 10, 13.

4 Ayala, *Crónica del Rey Don Enrique III*, a. I, c. vii, 363 (in *Crónicas de los Reyes de Castilla*, II, Madrid, 1780); F. Baer, *Die Juden im christlichen Spanien*, II, 246; see also below, p. 5.

5 Baer, II, 116.—In 1306, a certain Don Yhuda writes to James II, king of Aragon, as *almoxarif mayor* of Castile (Baer, I, 193). Baer (*ibid.*, II, 116) suggests that he might have been identical with Don Yuda Abravaniel, the treasurer of Fernando in Seville in 1310. The title ראש בני ישראל ("Head of the Sons of Israel") with which Abravanel describes his great-grandfather (Com. on Josh., introd.) would be even more proper for a man who was *almoxarif mayor* than for one who was merely the king's treasurer in Seville. The date of his activity (1310) does not exclude the possibility for Don Samuel, Abravanel's grandfather, to have been his son. Baer also suggests the identification of this Yuda Abravaniel with a certain Don Yehuda of Cordova who was in Sancho IV's financial service in 1293–1294 (*ibid.*, 89–90) and almoxarif of the queen (*ibid.*, 92; see also Baer, *Toledot ha-Yehudim bi-Sefarad ha-Noẓrit*, Tel-Aviv, 1945, pp. 95, 200). The fact, however, that Don Yehuda of Sancho's days appears to have been a resident of Cordova, and not of Seville, and the early date of his appearance in the royal service (1293), which makes it unlikely for him to have been the father of Don Samuel, Abravanel's grandfather, renders this identification less plausible than that of Fernando's treasurer in Seville with Fernando's *almoxarif mayor*.

·265·   (p. 3)

6 See on all this Don Isaac's Comm. on Josh., introd.; *Wells*, 9b; *Principles of Faith* (*Rosh Amanah*), introd:; *Inheritance of the Fathers* (*Naḥalat Abot*), introd.; Comm. on Zech., 12.7, and other places. See also Judah Abravanel, introductory poem to Don Isaac's Comm. on Latter Prophets, verse 19, and *Shebet Yehudah*, VII, p. 33 (ed. Baer-Shochet, Jerusalem, 5707).—On Abravanel's claim to Davidic descent, see the criticisms of Bartolocci, *Bibliotheca magna Rabbinica*, Rome, 1683, III, 886, and G. B. de Rossi, *Dizionario storico degli autori Ebrei e delle loro opere*, Parma, 1802; German translation: *Historisches Woerterbuch* etc., 1832, 2nd ed., p. 14. Cf. Abraham ben David of Toledo (*Sefer ha-Qabbalah*, ed. Neubauer, in *Med. Jew. Chron.* I, 67), according to whom there remained in Spain after 4914 (1154) no person known to be from the House of David.

7 Comm. on Josh., introd.

8 *Shebet Yehudah*, 29, 30, 33, 35. Although it is impossible to associate many passages referring to "Alfonso" in paragraphs vii and viii of *Shebet Yehudah* with the times of either Alfonso X or Alfonso XI, as Graetz (VIII, 17, note 3, and supplementary note 4^1, pp. 419–420) has sufficiently proven, it is also not necessary, as Graetz suggested, to attribute all the historic elements which those passages embody to the 15th century. Decrees prohibiting Jews to wear expensive clothes (*Shebet*, 32) had already been issued by Alfonso X (Baer, *op. cit.*, II, 56, 60, 69). The complaints over Jewish usury (*Shebet*, 31–32) and the assertion that, because of usury, the "Jews hold three quarters of the land of Spain" (*ibid.*, 31) are more typical of the 13th and 14th than of the 15th century. Orders limiting the rate of interest for Jews and abolishing part of the debts that Christians owed them (*ibid.*, 32) were issued respectively by Alfonso X (Baer, *op. cit.*, II, 56) and Alfonso XI (*ibid.*, 171). The king's order that the Jews must return to Christians lands which the former held under mortgage (*Shebet*, 32) is reminiscent of the petition of the Cortes at Valladolid (1293) which was sanctioned by Sancho IV (Baer, *op. cit.*, II, 94). There can be little doubt therefore that the author used elements from the periods of Alfonso X and XI, although he combined them with views and events of the 15th century. The reference to Abravanel, the "great sage," may well be among those elements, while some of the arguments the author employed in this connection were borrowed from Don Isaac's writings (See *Shebet*, ed. Baer-Shochet, notes to chap. VII; Fritz Baer, *Untersuchungen ueber Quellen und Komposition des Schebet Jehuda*, Berlin, 1923, 58; Jacob Guttmann, *Die religionsphilosophischen Lehren des Isaak Abravanel*, Breslau, 1916, 15 note 1).

9 Menahem ben Zerah, *Ẓēdah la-Derekh*, introd. (ed. Sabbioneta, 1567–8[?], p. 16b).

10 Comm. on Zech. 12. 6; Baer, II, 116; *Ẓēdah la-Derekh*, introd. (שמואל אברבנאל, מתושבי אישביליא) ; *Shebet Yehudah*, 29.¹

11 According to Crescas' "Letter to the Jews of Avignon" (published as addendum to *Shebet Yehudah*, ed. Wiener, 128), Seville had in 1391 from six to seven thousand Jewish households. Baer's objection to accepting Crescas as a reliable source in this instance (Baer, II, 233) is in accordance with his general theory on the small number of the Jews in Spain. This theory, however, fails to explain the large number of *conversos* as well as the considerable number of Jews in Spain toward the end of the 15th century even within the limits conceded by Baer (*ibid.*, 582). Graetz' position and reasoning on this problem (Graetz, VIII, supplementary note 10) still remains, to our mind, unshaken.

12 That the conversion of Samuel Abravanel took place not during the

persecution of 1391, as indicated by Zacuto, *Juchassin*, ed. Filipowski, 1857, p. 224b (which might suggest that he was a forced convert) but at least several years earlier, was pointed out by Baer (II, p. 246, note 2), on the basis of a document from the archives of Seville, dated September 1388, which was published by R. Carande (see his "Sevilla, fortaleza y mercado," in *Anuario de Historia del Derecho Español*, II, p. 386). The identity of Juan Sánchez [de Sevilla], who is mentioned in this document as the King's chief treasurer (*tesorero mayor*) for Andalusia, with Samuel Abravanel, who assumed the former name upon his conversion, may be gathered from Joseph Arévalo (*Zékhēr Zaddiq*, in A. Neubauer, *op. cit.*, I, 98), Zacuto (*loc. cit.* above), and Ayala (*Crónica de Enrique III de Castilla*, BAE, vol. 68, p. 168a). According to Ayala, Juan Sánchez was most experienced in gathering the royal taxes, as well as expert in "matters touching" the contaduría. This explains in part the hopes placed in Juan Sánchez as the future *Contador mayor* of Castile, and apparently also as farmer of the King's revenues, so much so that the Duke of Benavente, a key figure in the Regency of Enrique III, insisted on entrusting him with both tasks. The double appointment, however, involved a conflict of interest (the *Contador mayor* was to supervise all tax-farmers) and therefore was opposed by the Archbishop of Santiago, another high authority of the Regency. Nevertheless, the Duke had his way. Juan Sánchez was made *Contador mayor* (see Ayala, *ibid.*, p. 198b) and, most likely, a high-ranking tax-farmer, obtaining thereby the terms of appointment he had probably stipulated to the Duke.

On Don Samuel's reputation as a Jewish leader, see Menaḥem ben Zeraḥ, *Ẓēdah la-Derekh*, Ferrara, 1554, dedicatory poem. See also my article "The Conversion of Don Samuel Abravanel," in B. Netanyahu, *Toward the Inquisition*, 1997, pp. 100 and 237, nn. 8, 9.

13 Menaḥem ben Zeraḥ, *op. cit.*, p. 5a.

13a His avid reading of philosophical works (see above, p. 4) may offer support to this assumption.

14 According to Hesqeto (*loc. cit.*, 3a), Don Isaac's "forebears" were "impoverished" because of some *gĕzēra* (persecutory decree) and ultimately migrated to Portugal. The decree referred to was in all likelihood the law issued at the Cortes of Soria (1380) that forbade Jews to serve in the King's Court. Accordingly, Don Samuel must have resigned his office and lost, in the wake of this, most of his fortune, so that some time later, when converted to Christianity, those of his family who refused to convert must have had limited resources when they left him. For the intermarriage of his Christianized offspring with Spain's nobles, see Fernán Díaz de Toledo, "Instrucción . . . para el obispo de Cuenca," in Alonso de Cartagena, *Defensorium unitatis Christianae*, ed. M. Alonso, 1943, p. 352. For a detailed discussion of these occurrences and the whole problem of Don Samuel's conversion, his failure to "return," and his behavior as convert, see my above mentioned article on Don Samuel, *loc. cit.*, pp. 99-125 and 237-242.

15 Kayserling, *Geschichte der Juden in Portugal*, Leipzig, 1867, pp. 22-24.

16 *Ibid.*, 8.

17 Graetz, VIII, 65; Kayserling, *op. cit.*, 38-39.

18 *Ibid.*, 45, 52.

19 *Archivo Histórico Portuguez*, I, 445.

20 Kayserling, *op. cit.*, 47.

21 Sousa, *Provas*, I, 507.

22 *Passover Sacrifice*, introd.

23 Graetz, VIII, 326; Kayserling, *op. cit.*, 48, 50.
24 *Ibid.*, 63–64.
25 *Ibid.*, 64.
26 Don Isaac describes his father as follows: in *Crown*, introd., איש חי אברבנאל יהודה דון הנשיא פעלים רב ; in Comm. on Josh., introd., איש חי רב פעלים דון יהודה אברבנאל בישראל גדול שמו; in *Forms of the Elements*, introd., הנשיא; in *Inheritance and Principles*, introductions, שר ונדול בישראל; in *Questions and Answers to Saul ha-Cohen* (*Beur Sod ha-Moreh*, end) 26a, בישראל נדול שמו.—Evidence on Don Judah Abravanel's close relations with Alfonso V's court, and especially with the royal exchequer, exists from the years 1453, 1467 and 1471 (See *Archivo Histórico Portuguez*, III, 153; VI, 362–363, 437).
27 Comm. on Josh., introd.
28 In the second half of the 15th century even the writing of poems in Latin was common among Portuguese poets. See Frederick Bouterwek, *History of Spanish and Portuguese Literature*, London, 1823, II, 20.
29 *Letter of the Marquis of Santillana to Don Peter*, Oxford, 1927, 62.
30 A.F.G. Bell, *Portuguese Literature*, Oxford, 1922, 87.
31 On his knowledge of Portuguese Abravanel writes in his *Questions and Answers*, 7a (pagination 11): כי [ב.לשון חכמים'] ואנוכי לא ניסיתי ללכת באלה בלעני־שפה ובלשון אחרת . . . בהיותי על אדמתי [פורטוגאל] דברתי בלשוני ולא בקשתי לי כי אם מחלקת לשון נכריה ולשון ההפוכות מעם לועז.—To his mastering of Castilian, and perhaps also of Catalan and other Iberian languages, we should partly attribute his ability, in later days, to establish close relations with the monarchs of Spain and Naples. Thus, speaking on Abravanel's appearance before Ferdinand and Isabella (neither of whom knew Latin), Eliahu Kapsali, whose testimony is based on what he heard from Spanish exiles, says: אין כמוהו בארץ איש צח . . . בלשון עם ועם (Excerpts from נכנס בחצרי המלכים וטירוחם, יודע דבר בלשונות ומבין דבר בדעת צחות שפתם *D'Bei Eliahu*, ed. M. Lattes, Padova, 1569, 71). Similarly Saul ha-Cohen, a contemporary of Don Isaac, who knew of the latter not only from his writings but also from acquaintances (*Questions and Answers*, 2d), enumerates among Abravanel's distinctions: שומע לשונות הגויים ספוריהם ודעת צחות שפתם (*ibid.*, 2d).
32 "Historians," writes Bouterwek, *op. cit.*, I, 138, "were never held in such high estimation in modern Europe as they were at this time (the 15th century) in Castile."
33 Abravanel must have studied the works of the Greek and Arab philosophers in Hebrew translations, as he did not know Arabic. See his letter to Yehiel of Pisa, *Ozar Nechmad*, II [1857], 67, in which he describes the Jews of Arzila, Morocco, who spoke Arabic, as "people whose language one does not understand."
34 That this was Abravanel's first work is clear from the fact that it is referred to, without being mentioned by name, in *The Crown*, 79 (ואני הנה כתבתי בזה דרוש אחד). *The Crown*, however, was considered by Abravanel his first worthwhile literary creation (ראשית פרי האדמה אשר נתן לי ה'). See Letter to Yehiel of Pisa, *Ozar Nechmad*, II, 69.
35 *Forms of the Elements*, printed together with the *Crown*, p. 111.
36 From Judah's *Complaint Against Fate*, verse 35, we know that in the year 1483 he was in possession of a considerable fortune which he might have acquired either through his practice of medicine (see Lemos, *História da*

Medicina, I, p. 91), or by his business dealings on behalf of his father. In either case it seems unlikely that he was born later than in 1458/9.—From a letter of Abravanel to Yehiel of Pisa, written, it appears, in 1482, we learn that at that time he was the father not only of sons but also of daughters (see the second of two letters to Yehiel, published by David Kaufmann in *Revue des études juives*, xxvi [1893], p. 104, and by M. Grossberg as an addendum to Abraham ibn Ezra's *Sefer ha Azamim*, London, 1901, p. 40). It appears that at least two of his daughters were among his elder children. In 1483, one of these daughters was already married to Joseph Abravanel, Don Isaac's nephew (see Gebhardt, *op. cit.*, Regesten, 42). Another, who may have also married an Abravanel and remained in the country when the rest of the family fled (see below, pp. 32–4), was perhaps the mother of Enrique Fernandez Abarbanel—"a grandson of Don Isaac and a nephew of Don Judah"—who lived in Lisbon in 1512 (see *Archivo Histórico Portuguez*, VII, p. 478; cf. J. de Carvalho, *Leão Hebreu, Filósofo*, Coimbra, 1918, p. 17).

37 See his Comm. on Josh., introd.; *Passover Sacrifice*, introd.

38 Indicative of the condition of the Jews in Portugal at his time is the personal exemption from wearing the badge that Don Isaac received from Alfonso V (see Carvalho, *op. cit.*, p. 9).

39 Kayserling (*op. cit.*, 70) and Graetz (VIII, 222) identify the Portuguese Jewish physician, Joseph Sarco, with Joseph ibn Shraga, the cabalist of Argenta (see on him G. G. Scholem in *Kirjath Sepher*, II [1925/6], p. 273; VII [1930/1], pp. 149, 151–2; and cf. also Cassuto in *Enc. Jud.*, I, 1049). The identification, however, is not well founded.

40 On Hayyim ibn Musa's attack on the philosophers, see Graetz VIII, supplementary note 4[III], 424–425.

41 *Crown*, 82–83, 84.

42 In *Questions and Answers*, 7d, Abravanel summarizes the change which came over him as follows: את חטאי אני מזכיר היום. בימי חבלי ובחורותי רדפתי אחרי עיוני החכמות, טבעיות ואלהיות, ואחרי אשר באו ימי הרעה וזקנתי מהיות לאיש, דברתי אל לבי למה תתחכם בספרי היונים ובילדי נכרים למה תשומם. ויחדתי לעצמי עיון ספר המורה ופירוש כתבי הקודש. As can be clearly gathered from the *Crown*, the change took place at a much earlier date than that suggested by Abravanel.

43 *Crown*, 83–84; 9 (ובפירוש התורה אשר לי פירשתי הפסוק באופן אחר); 52–53 (פירוש התורה אשר אני עושה); 91 (ובפירוש משנה תורה פירשנו הפסוקים באופן אחר).

44 Speaking of his father, in the *Crown*, introd., Abravanel says, איש חי וכו' ס"פ [סופו טוב].—The fact that when he wrote the *Crown* he was already working on the ambitious scheme of interpreting the Pentateuch shows that the work was not written too early. Furthermore, he must have been already devoting himself for years to business affairs as he complained that he had been detached from spiritual labor for a long time (*ibid.*, 3).

45 See Braamcamp Freire, "Maria Brandoa," in *Archivo Histórico Portuguez*, VI, 362–363, 437. Baer, *Enc. Judaica*, I, 584, is mistaken in stating that the last visit of Don Isaac's father to Flanders for the purpose of importing cloth to Portugal took place in 1479. Don Judah was no longer among the living already in March 1472, as is evident from the use of ז"ל appended to his name at the end of Don Isaac's letter of that date to Yehiel of Pisa (*Ozar Nechmad*, II, p. 70). The latest known document in connection with

Don Judah's business dealings in Flanders is from February 19, 1471 (see the above quoted work of Braamcamp Freire, in *Arch. Hist. Port.,* VI, 437). Even then he must have been—as the son of Don Samuel who already in 1366 was a famous man—over seventy years old, and it is not likely that at this age he often engaged in extensive travelling. Don Isaac's statement in the *Crown,* introd., 3a (והייתי נע ונד בארץ, פעם בחוץ וכו'), may therefore allude also to his own trips abroad on behalf of the Abravanels' enterprises.

46 Letter to Yehiel of Pisa, *Ozar Nechmad,* II, 69.—In the introduction to this Comm. completed in February 1496 (see below, chap. III, note 48), Abravanel writes that he began working on it "twenty years" before (זה לי עשרים שנה), i.e., in 1476. Since we know from the above-quoted letter to Yehiel of Pisa that part of that Comm. had already been completed in 1472, and since the same Comm. is already mentioned in the *Crown* (pp. 52–53), the number "twenty" seems erroneous. The suggestion made by one biographer of Abravanel (*Ha-Meassef,* 1784, ed. Letteris, 1862, p. 33) that the words עשרים שנה זה לי mean not "twenty years ago" but "when I was twenty years old" may offer a correct explanation.

47 On Abravanel's wealth we have the following testimonies: a) Comm. on Josh., introd.: בכל אשר כנסתי לי... כסף וזהב וסגולות מלכים עובר לסוחר מכל; b) *Passover Sacrifice,* introd.: אשר היו לפני בארץ ההיא... שדות וכרמים ובתים מלאים כל טוב ובתוך עמי הוספתי על כל אשר היה לפני... עבדים ושפחות ובני ביתי אוכלי; c) In the death sentence of João II (Gebhardt *op. cit.,* Regesten, 37), Abravanel is described as "a very rich man, and a holder of many lands" (*homẽ mui rico, e muy afazemdado*).

48 Letter to Yehiel of Pisa, *Ozar Nechmad,* 67.

49 *Ibid.,* 65–68.

50 See above, note 33.

51 Letter to Yehiel, *loc. cit.,* 68–69.—Since Abravanel describes Sezira as a "doctor," some biographers of Abravanel asserted that Sezira taught Judah Abravanel medicine and astronomy. According to Carvalho (*op. cit.,* p. 12, note 2), these assertions, which he erroneously believes to have been based on Hebrew sources, are "not confirmed in the histories of Portuguese medicine, chronicles and collections of contemporary documents; nor do we find there the faintest reference to [João] Sezira."

52 Letter to Yehiel, *loc cit.,* 68–69.

53 The period of 1475–1479 was a period of war with Castile. Alfonso spent a great deal of time abroad, and he was irritated, down-hearted and despairing as a result of the military and diplomatic defeats he had suffered. This was not a time in which he was likely to strike up new friendships. Less than three years after the war's end, Alfonso died. To assume that Abravanel became a courtier in the last years of Alfonso's life is also difficult. From Abravanel's description of his relations with the king, we gain the impression that his services were of a longer duration. Thus Abravanel says of Alfonso: כל הימים אשר הוא חי על האדמה בהיכל מלכותא די בבל מהלך הוית (Comm. on Josh., introd.). Our conclusion therefore is that Abravanel entered the king's service between the time he wrote his letter to Yehiel and the outbreak of the Castilian-Portuguese war.

54 Comm. on Josh., introd.

55 *Shebet Yehudah,* 87–90, 141–144. I see no compelling reason for

assuming, as Baer-Shochet, *ibid.*, 193 and 219, do, that both records are a pure invention of the author of *Shebet Yehudah*. In the second of them a discussion is reported between the king and Don Joseph ibn Yahya, Alfonso's celebrated Jewish courtier, who in the account before us appears in a rather unfavorable light. Would the author of *Shebet Yehudah* dare fabricate without any foundation such a story about a prominent figure, who was known and admired by many of his contemporaries? If he had no written report before him, he must have based his account on some stories on this subject which were circulated among his contemporaries and which had a core of truth. In any event, the fact that the above-mentioned records were attached to Alfonso's name testifies to the reputation he had acquired with regard to his position on religious issues.

56 *Ibid.*, 90. The statement, of course, did not originate with Alfonso, as the author of *Shebet Yehudah* himself indicates, and is found also elsewhere in the same work (*ibid.*, p. 36).

57 A.F.G. Bell, *op. cit.*, 87.

58 Cf. Graetz, VIII, 326–327; Kayserling, *op. cit.*, 74. Joseph ibn Yahya was considered, after Abravanel's departure from Portugal, the head of Portuguese Jewry. See Joseph ibn Yahya (the courtier's grandson), *Torah Or*, introd.

59 Comm. on Josh., introd.

60 Dunham, *History of Spain and Portugal*, 72a.

61 The letter was first published in the *Magazin fuer die Wissenschaft des Judentums*, 1891, 133–145, with a German translation by Jeanette Schwerin-Abrabanel; and later by Joaquim de Carvalho in *Revista de Estudos Hebraicos*, I, Lisboa, 1928, 231–238.

62 *Magazin fuer die Wissenschaft des Judentums*, 1891, 140–141.

63 According to Carvalho, *Revista de Estudos Hebraicos*, I, the letter to the Count of Faro (which is not dated) was written in 1470 or 1471. Carvalho's opinion is based on Braamcamp Freire who, in his biography of the Count of Odemira, arrived at the conclusion that by May 6, 1471, the Count of Odemira was already dead. Braamcamp Freire's conclusion in turn is based on information he found in Caetano de Sousa.

64 In the death sentence issued against Abravanel in 1485, he is spoken of, not only as a friend, but also as a "great servant" (*muito gramde servidor*) of the princes of Braganza (see Gebhardt, *op. cit.*, Regesten, 37). From the same document we learn also that Abravanel was greatly benefited by those princes (*ibid.*, 40).

65 Comm. on Josh., introd.: ביען מימי קדם קדמתא ... היתה אהבתי עצומה את השרים האלה, נדמו למו עצתי. Cf. Gebhardt, *op. cit.*, Regesten, 40, where the "great friendship and association" between Abravanel and the princes is adduced as proof that the former participated in the conspiracy of the Braganzas against João II.

66 Schaefer, *Geschichte von Portugal*, II, 594.

67 See below, p. 311, note 123.

68 See Alonso de Palencia, *Crónica de Enrique IV* (trans. by D. A. Paz y Meliá), Madrid, 1904, III, 353.

69 Comm. on Josh., introd.; see also *Passover Sacrifice*, introd., 2a.— Writing on Abravanel, Ribeiro dos Santos, in his "Memoria da Litteratura Sagrada dos Judeos Portuguezes" (*Memórias de Litteratura Portugueza* of the Academia Real das Sciencias de Lisboa, II, Lisbon, 1792, p. 289), says: "There did not exist

any serious undertaking, especially military, in which the king did not ask for his (Abravanel's) opinion; in such undertakings he frequently employed him in important tasks and bestowed upon him many honors." The particular emphasis put here on Abravanel's influence in military affairs is perhaps unjustified and is, at least, unsupported by available documentary evidence. In any case, Abravanel's own words that he was "close to the king" and that the latter "based his decisions on my advice" imply that his counselorship was not limited to financial matters only.

70 *Archivo Histórico Portuguez*, IV, 432.—Comm. on Josh., introd.; *Passover Sacrifice*, introd., 2a.

71 In his biography of Abravanel, published in 1551 and written in 1551 or 1550, Hesqueto states that Joseph Abravanel was, at the time of the writing, eighty years old. See *Wells*, introd.—On the date of the birth of Don Isaac's son Samuel, see Carmoly, *Ozar Nechmad*, II, 60, and note 52.

72 That the writing of this work began in Portugal is evident from the fact that the *Vision of God* (מחזה שדי) is quoted in his Comm. on Josh., which was written shortly after his departure from Portugal. See Comm. on Josh. 1.5 (f. 6, col. 2); 5.13 (f. 12, col. 3); 10.12 (f. 22, col. 2). In his *Questions and Answers*, 8c (pagination: 12) Abravanel states that he began writing the book in Spain.

73 Joseph Jabez, *Or ha-Chajim*, Zolkiew, 1848, XII, 28b, states: ואחד מגדולי העיר הנזכרת גדול מרבן, ושמו נודע ונתפרסם באיים מרוב חכמתו וגדולתו, חכמה וגדולה במקום אחד וקרוב למלכות [למלכוח?], צעק תמיד בחיבוריו על אלה האנשים . . . גם אני למדתי קצת פרקים מפיו מ.המורה׳ אשר נתחכם בו מכל האדם אחרי שחובר. וראינו אנו והחכמים אשר שמענו מפיו כי ההפרש שבין הזהב והנחושת הוא ההפרש אשר בין פירושיו לשאר הפירושים אשר נעשו בו . . . ואחרי שהיה מפרש כוונת הרב באר היטב היה אומר: זו כוונת רבינו משה רבנו לא כוונת משה רבנו. Jabez does not mention Abravanel by name, but he proceeds to quote a passage from the writings of this "commentator on the *Guide*"—a passage which happens to be part of Abravanel's Commentary on Joshua (10. 12–13, Reply to Question 1). This, in addition to the general description (,"קרוב למלכות" "חכמה וגדולה במקום אחד"), and the title גדול מרבן, which may well be an allusion to אב׳רבנ׳אל, makes the identity of the commentator unquestionable (cf. Jacob Guttmann, *op. cit.*, p. 8, note 1).—Abravanel's Comm. on the *Guide* is mentioned in his Comm. on I Samuel, 20.40 (f. 120, col. 4) which, like his Comm. on Josh., was written in part shortly after he had left Portugal.

74 *Passover Sacrifice*, introd.; Comm. on Josh., introd.

75 *Ibid.:* ״ואני נהייתי ונחליתי . . . חבלים נפלו לי בחבלי . . . צרה כמבכירה עלי תשתפך נפשי . . . ואתמשל כעפר ואפר.״ — ״ונותרה בת־ציון כסוכה בכרם . . . סר צלם מעליהם. וירב בבת יהודה תאניה ואניה.״

76 In his Comm. on Josh., introd., Abravanel describes João as איש חמודות בז ולבוז שלל לשלול יקח בעליו נפש את .בצע בוצע) ("A greedy and avaricious person who would take a man's life to satisfy his ambition for robbery"); in his Comm. on II Samuel, end, he refers to João as to איש מרמה ועולה ("A deceitful and iniquitous person"); in *Passover Sacrifice*, introd., he calls him מלך עריץ ובוצע בצע ("A tyrannical and avaricious king").

77 Schaefer, *op. cit.*, II, 662.

78 Garcia de Resende, *Cancioneiro Geral*, 1910, I, pp. 62–63, 229. On João's policy toward the Jews see Kayserling, *op. cit.*, 85–86, 97–98, 111ff.

79 Cf. Graetz, VIII, 326.

80 See Gebhardt, *op. cit.,* Regesten, 37.
81 See below, p. 34.
82 See his two letters to Yehiel of Pisa, published by M. Grossberg as addendum to Abraham ibn Ezra's *Sefer ha-Azamim,* pp. 34, 36, 40–41.
83 The letter referred to bears the date of הושענא רבא שנת ה' אורי וישעי. In the extant manuscript (the British Museum, Add. 27129, f. 109), however, there are no dots over any of the letters of אורי וישעי to indicate which of them should be counted numerically. Nevertheless, the contents of this as well as of Abravanel's other letter to Yehiel which bears the partial date of פרשת נצבים (published by Grossberg, *op. cit.,* pp. 40–43) enables us to determine the year in which they were written. The fact that one of these letters is concerned with the death of Yehiel's wife (which excludes the possibility that the letters were written prior to March 1472; see *Ozar Nechmad,* II, p. 70) and the fact that both letters speak of a heavy plague which afflicted Portugal for three years (we know of such a plague in the years 1480–1482) lead us to the conclusion that the letters were written in the year ה׳ אׄוׄרׄיׄ וׄיׄשׄעׄיׄ, i.e., 1482, the second on October 4th and the first a few days earlier.
84 *Sefer ha-Azamim,* pp. 36–39.
85 Gebhardt, *op. cit.,* Regesten, 37.
86 In his Comm. on Josh., introd., Abravanel represents the whole conspiracy as the king's deliberate fabrication: ויתנכל אליהם לאמור: בני מות אתם כי קשרתם עלי כולכם לתת אותי ואת ארצי ביד סלכי ספרד. According to Abravanel, the princes of Braganza "did no evil" (לא פעלו עולה). This view, at least regarding the duke, is also supported by some modern historians (see *Historians' History of the World,* X, 470).
87 Gebhardt, *op. cit.,* Regesten, 38.
88 Comm. on Josh., introd.
89 *Ibid.*

CHAPTER TWO

1 In his Comm. on Josh., Introd., Abravanel describes Segura as *'ir qĕẓē gĕvula* [*shel Qastilia*] ("a town on the edge of the [Castilian] border"). F. Cantera, in his review of the present work, *Sefarad* (1970), p. 54 (and in greater detail: "Don 'Ishaq Brauanel'," in *Baron Jubilee Volume* [to be published]), however, identified the place correctly with Segura de Leon, which lies some twenty miles east of the Castilian border with Portugal (hence, by *'ir qĕẓē gĕvula* Abravanel must have meant simply "a frontier town"). Cf. the document (from 1474) published by Amador de los Rios, *Historia,* III, 601, and L. Suárez Fernández, *Documentos acerca de la Expulsión de los Judíos,* Valladolid, 1964, p. 81, where Segura de la Orden is listed between Cordova and Llerena.
2 See Suárez Fernández, *op. cit.,* pp. 256–257. Our estimate of the number of Segura's Jews is based on the amount of the war-tax they paid (at the rate of one gold castellano per family; see Baer, II, p. 385).
2a In his Comm. on Josh., Introduction.

3 Comm. on Josh., Introd. It may be assumed, however, that Abravanel's possessions were placed under distraint, and that actual confiscation took place only after Abravanel had been officially convicted.

4 Comm. on Josh., introd.: ואנשים בני בליעל אשר חשבו לדחות פעמי, לקחת כל אשר לי זממו, שננו לשונם כמו נחש, וידברו עלי רעה אשר לא דברתי ולא עלתה על לבבי. For a similar case in Portugal, involving the property of escaped Jewish leaders in the days of João I, see Kayserling, *op. cit.*, 33–36.

5 Abravanel's escape is presented, in the death sentence later issued against him, as corroborating evidence of his guilt. See Gebhardt, *op. cit.*, Regesten, 40.

6 Comm. on Deut., introd.: ויקח [המלך] את כל קניני עד תומם . . . ובזה ספו תמו מן בלהות כל ספרי. כי אחי ועמי וכל שכני סביבותי צרי. גם הם עלו ובאו בביתי ובבית מדרשי.

7 Gebhardt, *op. cit.*, Regesten, 38–39.

8 See the death sentence against Joseph Abravanel published by Gebhardt, Regesten, 42–43.   9 See Appendix B.

10 Abravanel calls them בני בליעל. See above, note 4.

11 Comm. on Josh., introd., 1 ab.

12 *Ibid.*, f. 1, col. 3; end of Comm. on Josh. and Judges. It seems improbable that Abravanel's group of listeners came from the small community of Segura. It is more likely that his lectures were held in Plasencia, the town where his son-in-law, Joseph, settled later. See Baer, II, 387 (note), 412, 416f.

13 The Comm. on Josh. was written during the period beginning the 10th and ending the 26th of Marḥeshvan, 5244 (see end of Comm. on Josh.), that on Judges in the period of 1–25 Kislev, 5244 (see end of Comm. on Judges), and that on Samuel during the period of 1 Tevet—13 Adar II, 5244 (see end of Comm. on II Sam.).

14 Comm. on Josh., 10.12.

15 Comm. on Kings, introd.

16 In his Comm. on Kings, *ibid.*, Abravanel writes cryptically: נקראתי אל חצר המלך ("I was called to the King's Court"), without saying a single word about the moves and motives which led to this invitation. Abravanel further says in this connection that the audience, and what resulted from it, interfered with his literary work and prevented him from writing his Commentary on Kings. Thus, the audience with the king must have taken place shortly after he had concluded his Comm. on II Samuel (see above, note 13).

17 It is furthermore most likely that the audience with the sovereigns was arranged for Abravanel by one of the princes of Braganza. That Abravanel was in contact with them while in Spain can hardly be doubted. The fact that such meetings took place seems to have been established by João's agents in Castile, and it might have served as the "kernel of truth" in the otherwise false accusation that Abravanel cooperated with the exiled princes in plotting a new conspiracy. Cf. above, p. 35.

18 Comm. on Kings, introd.

19 Cf. H. C. Lea, *History of the Inquisition of Spain,* 1906, I, 239.

20 On the relations between the medieval burgher and the Jew and the economic and political reasons for the former's anti-Jewish stand, see Ignaz Schipper, *Anfaenge des Kapitalismus bei den abendlaendischen Juden,* Wien &

Leipzig, 1907, 24, 27, 29-31; G. Caro, "Die Juden des Mittelalters in ihrer wirtschaftlichen Betaetigung," in *MGWJ*, 1904, pp. 586f., 600f. —On the Jews as *servi camerae* in Spain, see F. I. Baer, *Studien zur Geschichte der Juden im Koenigreich Aragonien*, Berlin, 1913, 11-16; idem, *Toledot ha-Yehudim bi-Sefarad ha-Nozrit*, 61f; Abraham Neuman, *The Jews in Spain*, Phila., 1943, I, pp. 6-16; idem, review of Baer's *Studien*, in *J.Q.R.* (N.S.), vol. VII, 253-59.

21 The signal for the new policy was the decree of the Cortes of Toledo (1480) which strictly prohibited the Jews to live outside the limits of the *Juderías* (See Baer, II, 346). Although laws aiming at the segregation of the Jews were enacted in Spain time and again, this time the law was enforced (*ibid.*, 347, notes to paragraph 335). Even from the case of the town of Trujillo, where enforcement of the measure was delayed, it is clear that there was no relaxation in the effort to carry the law into effect (*ibid.*, 359). See also Graetz, VIII, 295, note.

22 Alonso de Palencia, in his *Crónica de Enrique IV*, trans. by D. A. Paz y Melia, Madrid, 1904, III, 107-108, clearly states that the main reasons for the outbreaks against the *conversos* in 1473-4 were their extraordinary wealth and high social positions which aroused the envy and hatred of the Old Christians. The "Judaic ceremonies" of the conversos are presented by him as a secondary cause only, but even this presentation must be regarded with caution. The author wrote his book in the heyday of the Inquisition, and the alleged Judaizing "crime" of the *conversos* could not possibly be ignored by him.

23 On the positions occupied by the Marranos in Spain, see José Amador de los Ríos, *Historia Social, Política y Religiosa de los Judíos de España y Portugal*, III, Madrid, 1876, pp. 89-103; F. Márquez, "Conversos y cargos concejiles en el siglo XV," in *RABM*, LXIII (1957); B. Netanyahu, *The Origins of the Inquisition in Fifteenth Century Spain*, 1995, pp. 950-974.

24 The fact that Spanish churchmen, like Espina and Bernáldez, were spokesmen for the new racial theories only shows the extent to which popular animosity influenced clerical opinion in Spain. This, however, did not reflect the official policy of the Church.

25 Since the Spanish Inquisition was motivated, in our opinion, by ethnic, economic and political rather than religious reasons, it must be treated as a case apart in the history of the European Inquisition. It cannot be compared, for instance, to the Inquisition in Languedoc, which really grew out of religious warfare and aimed at destroying religious opponents—i.e., the Cathari and the Waldenses. For nothing of the kind happened in Spain. The Marranos did not constitute a religious sect. They were not conducting a campaign against the Church. They did not carry into Christendom a new aggressive dogma which might offer a threat to the Papacy as a system or to Catholicism as a faith. The overwhelming majority of the Marranos were undoubtedly detached from Judaism, save for some customs to which some of them may have clung out of habit rather than out of conviction. If, again, the intellectuals among the Marranos were Averroistically inclined, as has been claimed (Baer, *Toledot*, 531), and manifested laxity toward religion in general, they certainly could not be that religious as to adhere to Judaism in a clandestine manner and in the face of mortal danger. The Spanish Inquisition, in seeking to identify the whole Marrano group with a secret Jewish heresy, was therefore operating with a fiction, and it was driven to this operation by racial hatred and political considerations rather than by religious zeal. This is why in Languedoc the Inquisition was imposed by the Pope, while in Spain it was imposed, in reality, by the Crown.

26 See the critical statement about the Marranos in a document published by A. Marx, in *J.Q.R.* (o.s.), vol. xx (1908), 252.

26a For a detailed discussion of the attitude of Spain's Jews toward the Marranos during the time of the Inquisition, see my *Marranos of Spain*, N.Y., 1973², pp. 54–76, 135–215, 224–234.

27 That the Jews of Spain lived during the eighties without seeing any major threat to their existence, can be concluded from Abravanel's own writings. Thus he states in his Comm. on Deut., introd., אחרי כן עשר שנים (the ten years preceding the expulsion) וישכון ישראל בטח בכל ארצות ספרד המונים המונים. שלוים ושקטים עם שוקט ובוטח. אוכלים למעדנים. האמונים עלי תולע ואין מכלים. See also *Wells*, 6b–7a (שאנן ואין מחריד בשוכבו ובקומו). Similar evidence for this feeling of security may be found in Isaac Arama's statement about the horrible fate of the deserters of Judaism and the deniers of its principles (referring, no doubt, to the Marranos in the 1480's) as contrasted with the peace and tranquility enjoyed by the faithful Jews (see *'Aqeda*, V, p. 160a; to describe the latter's condition, Arama uses the identical expression which we find in Abravanel: שקטים ושלוים).—In their letter to the Jews of Rome and Lombardy, written in 1487, the Jews of Castile describe Ferdinand as a "just and righteous" king (see Baer, II, 385).

28 That the Inquisition was an instrument of political absolutism is also the view of Kayserling, *Christopher Columbus*, 26. Lea is opposed to it (*A History of the Inquisition of Spain*, I, 27–28), although his own presentation of the manner in which the Inquisition was introduced in Aragon shows that it was due to the Inquisition, and to the anti-Jewish sentiment it represented, that the Spanish sovereigns succeeded in annulling some of the most cherished liberties of the Aragonese (*ibid.*, 229–231).

29 "According to a memorial address to Charles V by the Licenciado Tristan de Leon in 1524, the enormous sum of 10,000,000 ducats was realized from the confiscations of condemned heretics during the period of the war" (see H. C. Lea, *A History of the Inquisition of Spain*, II, p. 367). Isabella's claim that she had "never touched a maravedi of confiscated property" and that she had "employed the money in educating and dowering the children of the condemned" is branded by U. R. Burke (*A History of Spain*, II, 107) as a "most deliberate and daring falsehood" (cf. G. A. Bergenroth, *Calendar of State Papers*, I, 37, 45–46). Baer (*Toledot*, 503) sees in the saving by Ferdinand of the lives of men like Alfonso de la Caballería and Luis de Santángel, who were prospective victims of the Inquisition, proof that the Spanish sovereigns did not use the Holy Office as an instrument for fiscal robbery. The fact, however, that only such outstanding men, whose services were most probably too vital to lose, were saved by the sovereigns' interference is rather proof to the contrary.

30 "Inquisitors were in the habit of sending him reports of the autos de fe celebrated by them, to which he [Ferdinand] would reply in terms of high satisfaction, urging them to increased zeal" (Lea, *op. cit.*, 189, 191–202).—Ferdinand's disrespect for the Popes may be illustrated by many recorded incidents. See on this Burke, *op. cit.*, II, 71, 78; Lea, *op. cit.*, I, 14; W. H. Prescott, *History of the Reign of Ferdinand and Isabella* (ed. American Publishers Corporation), II, 146; B. Netanyahu, *The Origins of the Inquisition*, pp. 1033–1034.

31 See *The Prince*, xxi. See also Guicciardini, *Storia d'Italia*, vi, 12 ("He [Ferdinand] covers almost all of his greed under the colors of an honest zeal for religion and of holy intentions for the common weal").

32 See Prescott, *op. cit.*, II, 338.

32a On the expulsion from Andalusia—i.e., from the archbishopric of Seville and the bishoprics of Cordova, Jaen and Cadiz—see especially F. Fita, "Nuevos datos para escribir la historia de los judíos españoles," in *Boletín de la Academia de la Historia*, XV (1889), pp. 323–328; Baer, II, pp. 348–349 (document No. 337) and 357–359 (doc. No. 344); and Luis Suárez Fernández, *Documentos acerca de la Expulsión de los Judíos*, Valladolid, 1964, pp. 35–36, 224–226 (doc. No. 69).—On the order of expulsion from part of Aragon, or more precisely, from the archbishopric of Saragossa and the bishopric of Santa María de Albarrazín, see Baer, I, pp. 912–913 (doc. No. 563). It is questionable, however, whether the latter order was actually carried out, fully or partly (see *ibid.*, p. 913, note).

32b The tactics of camouflage employed by Ferdinand in his treatment of the Jews of Spain are perhaps nowhere so strikingly displayed as in the issuance and execution of the expulsion orders referred to. While it was the Inquisition that was officially responsible for the expulsion of the Jews from Seville, Ferdinand—and Isabella, who supported his maneuvers—appeared as if they came to the rescue of the expelled when they offered them as havens (albeit for "a certain tribute") the nearby Corral de Xerex and the deserted old fortress of Seville (see Suárez Fernández, *op. cit.*, pp. 224–225 [doc. 157]). Then, when the Jews, ousted by the inquisitors(!) from these localities, too (*ibid.*, pp. 225, 361), demanded restitution for the investments they had made in reconstructing half-ruined houses, the Kings first assured them consideration of this claim (*ibid.*, pp. 225–226, doc. from July 1484) and finally, in March 1491, allowed them to sell or dispose of, in any other manner, "some houses" which they had built or repaired in the old fortress (*ibid.*, pp. 361–362). Moreover, since the Jews, who had been ordered (on January 1, 1483) to leave Seville within a month (see Baer, II, p. 343), could not manage, in that brief period, to sell their properties or collect their debts, the Kings (in September 1484) permitted the claimants to return to the city for the purpose of liquidating their possessions (again, in any manner they would see fit: vender o trocar o canbiar o enajenar e atribuar los dichos sus bienes e faser dellos como de cosa suya propia) and collecting outstanding debts (see Baer, II, pp. 357–358). Thus, the impression could be fostered among the Jews that it was the Inquisition that was the real villain, while the Kings were at heart, and *de facto*, their protectors. Indubitably, Ferdinand, who was jealous for his royal prerogatives, would not surrender even a particle of his powers to anyone, the Inquisition included, and the latter, having no jurisdiction over the Jews, *could take no such large-scale actions against them, unless specifically instructed by Ferdinand to do so.* Ferdinand's letter to the Inquisitors in Aragon, ordering them (es nuestra voluntat!) to expel the Jews from Saragossa and Albarrazín (see Baer, I, p. 913 [doc. 563]), in accordance with the instruction they had received from Torquemada, is one of the many decisive evidences that can be adduced to this effect.

33 That his feelings, however, were not averse to the punishments inflicted by the Inquisition appears clearly from the letter he wrote in September 1509 to the Inquisitor Juan Alonso de Navia, in which he speaks, after witnessing an Auto de Fé, of the "great pleasure it had given him as a means of advancing the honor and glory of God and the exaltation of the Holy Catholic faith" (Lea, *op. cit.*, I, 189).

34 See above note 27, and see also Abravanel's statement on his life in Spain in his introduction to *Passover Sacrifice*.

35 On Senior see Alonso de Palencia, *op. cit.*, III, 183–184; A. Bernaldez, *Historia de los reyes católicos*, 1869, 252; Kapsali, Excerpts from *D'Bei*

Eliahu, ed. M. Lattes, Padua, 1869, 6of.—On the position of the Jews in the financial administration of Ferdinand and Isabella, see Baer, *Toledot,* 492-495; Baer, II, 329, 347, 355, 358, 360, 363, 373.

36 Palencia, *op. cit.,* 183.

37 See F. Cantera, "Don 'Ishaq Braunel'," in *S. W. Baron, Jubilee Volume,* I, 1974, 244, where a document is cited from which it is apparent that by June 6, 1485, Abravanel was a resident (*vecino*) of Alcalá de Henares. Judging by this date and that of March 8, 1484, on which he no doubt still stayed in Segura (see above, p. 36), there is little likelihood that he resided in the interim anywhere except in Segura and Alcalá. There is no evidence, we may add, that, after leaving Segura, Abravanel settled (or, in fact, lived at *any* time) in Toledo, Madrid, or Seville, as claimed respectively by Graetz (viii, 330), Kayserling (*Biblioteca Española-Portugueza-Judaica,* p. 6), and Pflaum (*op. cit.,* 59). Regarding the latter's assertion, we should also point out that in June, 1483 (when Abravanel arrived in Spain)—and certainly in March, 1484—the Jews of Seville had already been expelled and resettlement of Jews in the city was prohibited (see above, note 32a; A. Marx, *loc. cit.,* 249; and Graetz, viii, 294, n.2). Abravanel resided in Alcalá de Henares also in 1488 (see Baer, II, p. 387, document from 1488).

38 See Cantera's article cited above, in which the stipulations of Abravanel's contract with the Cardinal (copy of which is found in the *Archivo Provincial de Toledo*) are presented in detail.

39 See *ibid.,* and Suárez Fernández, *op. cit.,* pp. 472-473.

40 See Cantera, *loc. cit.,* and see *id.,* "La judería de San Martín de Valdeiglesias," in *Sefarad,* XXIX (1969), p. 224, on the basis of a document dated Sept. 10, 1490 (cód. 9/832, Colección Salazar, in the Academia de la Historia, Madrid), in which Abravanel is described as the *contador* of the II Duke of the Infantado and his wife María de Luna. With the full title of *contador mayor* (del . . . duque del infantazgo) he appears in a court record of June 14, 1491 (preserved in the Archivo de la Real Chancillería de Valladolid), which was first quoted by N. Alonso Cortés, in *Boletin de la Real Academia Española,* xxix (1949), pp. 279-280. And cf. Cantera, *loc. cit.*

41 On the Mendozas generally, see F. Layna Serrano, *Historia de Guadalajara y sus Mendozas,* Madrid, 1942, and on Don Iñigo, in particular, see *ibid.,* II, pp. 216-219. See also C. Artega y Falguera, *La Casa del Infantado,* I, 1940, pp. 231-268. To Abravanel's residence in Guadalajara attests the document cited by Alonso Cortés (*loc. cit.,* p. 279); Baer, II, p. 388, note, doc. from 1491; and A. Marx, *Studies in Jewish History and Booklore,* New York, 1944, p. 89, note 6. On Abravanel's relations with Isaac Aboab, who was also a resident of Guadalajara, see *ibid.*; Joseph Caro, *Beth Joseph,* on Oraḥ Ḥayyim, 168; and Immanuel Aboab, *Nomologia,* 302.

42 See introd. to Comm. on Kings: "And God made me *find favor* . . . in the eyes of the princes who held first place in the kingdom," and especially the phrase "[the magnates] *who were fond of me* (*mĕahavay*) and who were seeing the king [regularly]" (*ibid.*), from which we may gather that his relations with the Mendozas, who were doubtless among the nobles referred to, developed to the point of close friendship. And see below, n. 56.

43 Baer, II, pp. 387-388, and Manuel Serrano Sanz, *Origenes de la dominación Española en America,* Madrid, 1918, p. 133. According to Amador de los Rios, *op. cit.,* III, p. 295, Isabella and Ferdinand placed in the hands of Abravanel and Senior the supply and administration of the royal armies which

were then fighting the Granadan War. Both performed their task efficiently. They also "employed their own vast fortunes for the provision of food and acquisition of arms, and induced other Jews to follow their example."

44 On his general relations with the King and Queen, see Comm. on Kings, introd.: "And the Lord *made them favorably disposed toward me* . . . and I was *close to them* for a long time and was engaged in their work for eight years; both riches and *honor* which men attain and live by, I acquired in their courts and castles." And see also introd. to *Passover Sacrifice:* "I have earned the *respect of kings* and the princes of the land." For the special consideration shown to Abravanel by the Kings on the eve of the Expulsion, see below, p. 59, and the sources cited in note 70.

45 Baer, II, pp. 387-388 (note).

46 *Passover Sacrifice,* introd.: "I was the head of all my people in Spain. They eagerly listened to what I would say and faithfully followed my instructions." Cf. Kapsali, *D'Bei Eliahu,* 70-71; A. Marx, *loc. cit.,* 250.

47 Comm. on the *Guide,* ed. Landau, Prague, 1831-1832, II, 53b.

48 *Ibid.*

49 *Wells,* Introd., 7a-7b; *Passover Sacrifice,* introd., and in other places. On the spiritual leaders of Jewry at the time of the expulsion, see *Excerpts from D'Bei Eliahu* (ed. Lattes), 55.

50 *Passover Sacrifice,* introd., 2a.

51 See Baer, II, 484, 509; Lea, *op. cit.,* I, 134f.

52 Marx, *loc. cit.,* 250.

53 See Baer, *Toledot,* 493. And cf. A. Bernaldez, *Historia de los Reyes Católicos,* I, 337, and Baer, II, 384. Kapsali (*D'Bei Eliahu,* Excerpts, ed. Lattes, p. 69) erroneously states that Melamed was Senior's brother-in-law. Melamed seems to have occupied also a position as secretary of the king (Marx, *loc. cit.,* 250).

54 *D'Bei Eliahu,* excerpts, ed. Lattes, 71: ביום ההוא ניתן רשות לדון יצחק אברבנאל לדבר ככל אשר זכות וסנינוריה על עמו. ושם עמד כארי בחכמה ובגבורה ובלישון מדברת גדולות לשון זהב. And see below, note 58.

55 Cf. Baer, *Toledot,* 553.

56 Comm. on Kings, introd.: קראתי למאהבי רואי פני המלך לבקש על עמי ורוזנים נוסדו יחד לדבר אל המלך בכל עוז להשיב ספרי האף והחמה ואת מחשבותיו אשר חשב על היהודים לאבדם. The assumption that Alfonso de la Caballeria participated in the delegation of the grandees (Baer, *Toledot,* 553) cannot be derived with any certainty from the source on which Baer relies (Baer, II, 459). Alfonso, who did not dare oppose the introduction of the Inquisition to Aragon and who was carefully watched by the Inquisition, seems to have been the last man to assume that strong stand which the nobles, according to Abravanel, took.

57 According to Abravanel, Comm. on Kings, introd., the king showed on that occasion particular stubbornness (וכמו פתן חרש יאטם אזנו לא ישוב מפני כל).

58 Abravanel had three meetings with the king concerning the expulsion edict (see Comm. on Kings, introd.). It is rather difficult to assume that a money-offer was made at the first meeting when the Jewish representatives, in all likelihood, presented a strong case against the expulsion on grounds of principle. Cf. above, note 54.

59 Comm. on Kings, introd. According to Marx, *loc. cit.,* 250, an agreement was even reached regarding the financial compensation the Jews were to make for the cancellation of the edict.

60 See Graetz, viii, 344–345, on the basis of Llorente, *Histoire Critique de l'Inquisition d'Espagne*, I, 260. Kayserling, *Geschichte der Juden in Portugal*, 100, note 2, discards Llorente's story as based on fabrications, but the essence of the story is substantiated by a document concerning the expulsion which was published by Marx (*loc. cit.*, 250). The figure mentioned by Llorente is 30,000, and not 300,000 as stated by Graetz. The latter figure, however, appears to be the more plausible one. Although large in itself, 30,000 ducats would be an insignificant sum as a means to repeal the expulsion order. In order to ransom the 450 Jews of Malaga, who were held in bondage after the conquest of that city by Ferdinand, the Jews of Spain had to pay 20,000 *doblas!* (See Bernaldez, *op. cit.*, I, 252). To cancel the expulsion order, which involved hundreds of thousands of Jews, an incomparably larger offer had to be considered. 300,000 ducats was certainly a *huge* sum; nevertheless, it was not beyond the means of the Jews of Spain. According to Abravanel, *Wells*, 8b, the possessions of Spain's Jews were worth more than 30,000,000 gold ducats, and 300,000 ducats would thus represent only one percent of that sum (the ducat was equal in value to the dobla.—On the value of Spanish coinage during the reign of Ferdinand and Isabella, see Diego Clemencín, *Elógio de la Réina Católica Doña Isabel*, Madrid, 1821, pp. 593–595, 598–599, and Lea, *op. cit.*, I, Appendix iii, p. 560).

61 That a representation was made to the queen separately appears clearly from Marx, *loc. cit.*, 250. On the contents of the conversation see the following note. Abravanel believed that the queen was responsible for the stiffening of the king's attitude: והמלכה עומדת על ימינו לשטנו. הטתו ברוב לקחה לעשות מעשהו החל ונמור (Comm. on Kings, introd.). Abravanel's view on the queen's role in the expulsion seems to have become the prevailing opinion among the Jews of Spain (See Kapsali, *D'Bei Eliahu*, Excerpts, ed. Lattes, 66).

62 This, I believe, is the core of truth in the story of Kapsali (*ibid.*, 71) about a harsh memorandum Abravanel sent to Isabella prior to his "escape" from Spain. According to Kapsali, Abravanel wrote as follows: שהשי״ת יקח נקמת היהודים ממנה ומבני ביתה, וכהנה רבות עמו, והזכיר לה כל אותם שהרעו לישראל ואחריתם עדי אובד.

63 See on all this Marx, *loc. cit.*, 250.

64 Baer, *Toledot*, 503, 557–558; Prescott, *op. cit.*, I, 353.

65 The promise given by the Spanish kings that Jews who would convert, and thus might remain in the country, would for ten years not be subjected to the investigations of the Inquisition (*D'Bei Eliahu*, 68)—a promise in which some writers see proof that the main motive of the expulsion was religious—rather testifies to the great fear of conversion which was universal among Spain's Jews at the time. Had the kings of Spain suggested to the Jews conversion without offering some immunity from the Inquisition, the offer would have been considered too obviously hypocritical. And Ferdinand, as we have indicated, constantly strove for his statements to have the semblance of sincerity. It cannot, indeed, be too strongly emphasized that without bearing in mind the particular respect that this shrewd monarch had for public opinion, the act of the expulsion, like other puzzling acts of his career, cannot be properly understood. Ferdinand undoubtedly also believed that only a small number of the Jews would convert, and that even these would be placed in a position in which he could, sooner or later, strip them legally of their possessions. In fact, prolonged and severe persecutions against the Jews who were tempted by this promise were begun before long by the Inquisition (See *Shalshelet ha-Qabbalah*, Venice, 1586, p. 115b).

(pp. 55–57)

66 Baer, II, 336. Taxes paid by the Jews during Ferdinand's reign increased to almost twentyfold by 1485 by the special war tribute imposed upon them. Shortly thereafter, however, this levy was reduced to almost half the amount indicated, evidently because of the difficulty to collect it (see Suárez Fernández, *op. cit.*, 55–56; Baer, II, 366–371, 385).

67 I. Schipper, who noted this fact and who, unlike Baer, thinks that the Inquisition *was* a "political and financial instrument," nevertheless maintains that "the expulsion was not a result of financial planning on the part of the kings of Spain, but rather of the pressure exercised upon the kings by the officials of the cities as well as of the ideological position of the Inquisitors" (*Toledot ha-Kalkalah ha-Yehudit*, Tel-Aviv, II, 5697, p. 301). That the pressure of the cities was the *main* cause of the policy pursued by the kings on the Jewish question cannot, of course, be doubted (see above, p. 46); and this is also fully confirmed by the added documentation, recently published, which was drawn from the archives of Simancas (see the summary of this evidence by Suárez Fernández, *op. cit.*, 31–36, 40–45). Nevertheless, it is only reasonable to assume that, once the kings decided on that policy, they sought to exact from it (as in the case of the Marranos) as much financial benefit as they could. To be sure, for reasons explained below (pp. 57–58), they wished to convince the general public that, as far as the expulsion was concerned, they had no material gain in mind, and accordingly they proclaimed in the expulsion edict that the Jews could sell their possessions freely. Soon thereafter, however, this right was nullified by a series of strict counter-instructions—at least, in all the realms of Ferdinand (Aragon, Catalonia and Valencia)—and Jewish property of vast proportions was sequestered and then taken over by the Crown (on the legal pretense used, and the Inquisition's cooperation, no doubt at Ferdinand's order, in these large-scale expropriations, see Serrano, *Orígenes*, pp. 55–61, 492–493; Zurita, *Anales*, Lib. I, cap. vi). We further see how, after the expulsion, legal excuses were devised to justify confiscation of all financial assets the Jews still owned in Spain (see Suárez Fernández, *op. cit.*, pp. 62–64, 479–481). The inconsistency apparent in the procedures followed, alternating between moderation and severity, was due, as I see it, to Ferdinand's desire to achieve, by a single measure, two conflicting aims. —All this may also be said in reference to Baron's remarks on my view concerning the motives for the expulsion. See *Social and Religious History of the Jews*, XI, pp. 403–404.

68 On the reaction of Spain's Jews to the expulsion see Abravanel, Comm. on Kings, introd.; *D'Bei Eliahu*, 69–70; Bernaldez, *op. cit.*, chapters 110, 111.

69 Serrano, *Orígenes*, 133.

70 Baer, II, 410, 411.

71 Kapsali (Excerpts, 73) speaks of the effort to convert Senior and Melamed and indicates that threats were involved.

72 See *Cronicón de Valladolid*, ed. by Pedro Sainz de Baranda, in *Colección de Documentos Inéditos para la Historia de España*, XIII, p. 195; Baer, II, p. 411, note to doc. 380.

73 See Judah Abravanel's poem *Complaint Against Fate*, reprinted in Gebhardt, *op. cit.*, Gedichte, 3, verses 24–25.—The child might have been sent to Abravanel's daughter in Portugal. See above, p. 268 f., note 36.

74 Baer, *Toledot*, 555, writes that the Abravanels left Spain in the beginning of July. Baer seems to have been led to this conclusion by the available evidence that Abravanel's nephew, Joseph, testified before the Inquisition in Valencia on July 3 and that the last available royal instructions to the authori-

ties in Valencia regarding the departure of the Abravanels are from July 5. This, however, does not prove that the Abravanels left Spain in the beginning of July. Joseph Abravanel might have moved to Valencia a month prior to their actual departure for a very valid reason: his continued stay in Plasencia was made impossible, or at least dangerous, by the growing enmity toward him and his family (see Baer, II, 416–419). In Valencia he probably awaited the arrival of Don Isaac whose departure from Spain might have been delayed, not only for personal, but also for commual considerations. From Abravanel's references to his departure from the country we gain the impression that he left Spain together with that body of exiles who chose to sail in the direction of Italy, and that this departure took place on the very day on which their permit to stay in Spain expired (Comm. on Kings, introd.: a—וילכו בלא כוח שלוש מאות אלף רגלי העם אשר אנכי בקרבו מנער ועד זקן טף ונשים ביום אחד מכל מדינות המלך b—. . . ונם אני אבחר דרכם, דרך אניה בלב ים, ואני בתוך הגולה באתי עם כל ביתי פה העיר נאפולי וכו'. . .). In view of these statements, it is also difficult to decide unreservedly, as Baer does, that the final date for the departure of the Jews from Spain was July 31, and not August 2 (the ninth of Ab), as Abravanel states (Comm. on Jeremiah, 2. 24, ed. 1641, f. 100, col. 3). It is difficult to believe that Abravanel would change such a fateful date in contradiction to the definite knowledge on this matter of the tens of thousands of survivors of the expulsion. It is also not unlikely that the departure began on July 31 and continued for three days (especially from the ports, where ships may have been detained for a number of reasons). According to Joseph ha-Kohen, who was born to a family of Spanish exiles in 1496, the Jews of Spain (evidently meaning by that the last group) left the country on the tenth of Ab (on a Friday) in sixteen large vessels from the shores of Cartagena (*Emek ha-Bakha,* ed. M. Letteris, Cracow, 1895, p. 100). This, incidentally, may have been the basis for the erroneous assertion of I. W. Etheridge, *Jerusalem and Tiberias,* London, 1856, p. 291, that Abravanel left Spain from Cartagena (cf. Gebhardt, *op. cit.,* 11, and Regesten, pp. 13–14).

75 See Baer, "Ha-tenu'ah ha-Meshiḥit bi-Tekufat ha-Gerush," in *Zion,* V, Jerusalem, 5693 (1933).

CHAPTER THREE

1 See Ignaz Schipper, *Anfaenge des Kapitalismus bei den abendlaendischen Juden,* 103.

2 On the agitation against Jews in the Italian cities in the last decades of the 15th century, see Graetz, VIII, 255–256; Cecil Roth, *The History of the Jews of Italy,* Philadelphia, 1946, pp. 153–176. For a summarized presentation of the condition of the Jews in Italy at the time, see Dubnow, V, sections 58–59.

3 Eliahu Kapsali, *D'Bei Eliahu,* passages selected by S. D. Luzzatto and published as addendum to M. Wiener's German translation of Joseph ha-Kohen's *'Emeq ha-Bakha,* Leipzig, 1858, 17, gives the date as the first of Elul, 5252— which is August 24, 1492. For the number of caravels see, Lea, *History of the Inquisition of Spain,* I, 141 (probably based on E. H. Lindo, *Hist. of the Jews in Spain and Portugal,* London, 1848, p. 291).

4 On the fate of the exiles see *Shebet Yehudah*, 122-4; Excerpts from *D'Bei Eliahu* in *'Emeq ha-Bakha*, 16-17; Excerpts from *D'Bei Eliahu*, ed. Lattes, 73-83; Abravanel's Comm. on Kings, introd.; *Wells*, introd., 8ab; Bernaldez, *Historia de los Reyes Católicos*, XII; B. Senarega, *Commentaria de rebus genuensibus*, in Muratori, *Rerum italicarum scriptores*, t. xxiv, col. 531; Abraham ben Solomon of Torrutiel (Ardutiel?), *Sefer ha-Qabbalah*, in Neubauer's *Med. Jew. Chron.*, I, pp. 111-114; Judah Ḥayat, introd. to his *Minḥat Yehudah* (Comm. on *Ma'arekhet ha-Elohut*, ed. 1779); *Shalshelet ha-Qabbalah*, ed. 1586, pp. 115b-116a.

5 Quoted from Senarega (see preceding note) according to the English translation of Prescott, *op. cit.*, I, 358.

6 Cf. the description in Luzzatto's Excerpts from *D'Bei Eliahu* (Wiener's ed. of *'Emeq ha-Bakha*, 17).

7 Prescott, *op. cit.*, I, 358.

8 See the praises of Ferdinand of Naples in Kapsali's *D'Bei Eliahu* (*'Emeq ha-Bakha*, ed. Wiener, 17, 19). These praises undoubtedly reflect not only the author's own opinion, but also that of the exiles from Spain whose stories he recorded (cf. Lattes' Excerpts, 38, and *'Emeq ha-Bakha*, ed. Wiener, 16).

9 According to Abravanel, Comm. on Kings, introd., they arrived in Naples in the year 5253 (גר״ג), which began on September 22, 1492. Heinz Pflaum, *Die Idee der Liebe*, Tuebingen, 1926, 61, note, refers to Hesqeto as the source of our information that Abravanel arrived in Naples in 5253. Hesqeto, however, only followed here Abravanel's statement in his introd. to Kings. In view of this definite statement by Abravanel, the assertion of B. Zimmels, *Leo Hebraeus*, Breslau, 1886, 23, that Abravanel reached Naples on August 24, 1492, must be rejected. Zimmels' assertion is an undue extension of Graetz, VIII, 357, who merely states, on the basis of *D'Bei Eliahu* (see above, note 3), that the first exiles to reach Naples arrived there on August 24. On the other hand, there is no compelling reason to postpone Abravanel's arrival to the year 1493 (as do G. B. de Rossi, *op. cit.*, 15; Wolf, *op. cit.*, 629; Jost, *op. cit.*, 105; and others), merely because most of the year 5253 falls within 1493.

10 Comm. on Kings, introd.; *Passover Sacrifice*, introd.; Hesqeto, *loc. cit.*, 3b; cf. Ferorelli, *op. cit.*, 87. That Naples was not the fixed destination of the exiles and that they had no previous arrangement with the Neapolitan rulers is evident from Kapsali, *D'Bei Eliahu*, Wiener's ed. of *'Emeq ha-Bakha*, 17.

11 *The Memoirs of Philip de Comines*, ed. Andrew R. Scoble, London, 1906, II, 151.

12 *Passover Sacrifice*, introd.

13 Prescott, *op. cit.*, I, 357-358; *D'Bei Eliahu* in *'Emeq ha-Bakha*, 18.

14 *D'Bei Eliahu*, ibid., 18-19.

15 *Passover Sacrifice*, introd.

16 Comm. on Kings, end.

17 *Ibid.*, f. 189, cols. 1-2.

18 *Questions and Answers*, 8c (according to the printed pagination: 12).

19 See *Rosh Amanah*, Constantinople, 1505, at the very end; and cf. M. M. Kellner's translation of Abravanel's *Principles of Faith*, 1986, p. 256, n. 34. That the proper translation of the title *Rosh Amanah* is "Principles of Faith" appears clear from Abravanel's own introduction to this work (end) and Don Judah's introductory poem, verse 6.

The *Principles* is mentioned in Abravanel's Comm. on Deut., 13.1, in *The Inheritance*, iv, 21, and in *The Salvations*, I, 3; IV, 4, all of which were composed or completed in 1496. The reference in the *Principles* to the *Announcer* (completed in February, 1498) was evidently made during a revision of the *Principles,* perhaps when it was prepared for publication. The fact, on the other hand, that the *Principles* is mentioned in Abravanel's Commentary on Deuteronomy, part of which was composed in Portugal, is of course no proof that it was written in Portugal and was probably due to a late interpolation. At least in 1472, when Abravanel sent a copy of his unfinished Commentary on Deuteronomy to Yehiel of Pisa, he states that, besides that incomplete commentary and the *Crown,* he had produced no literary works (*Ozar Nechmad,* II, 69).

20 See H. Pflaum, *op. cit.,* 74.

21 See Gebhardt, *op. cit.,* 12–16.

22 *Deeds,* VIII: 6 (55b). See below, p. 80.

23 Guicciardini, *Storia d'Italia,* Eng. trans. by Geffray Fenton, third ed., London, 1618, lib. I, p. 50; Hesqeto, *loc. cit.,* 3b.

24 In contrast to Abravanel's loyalty stood the treacherous attitude of Pontano. See in this connection the derogatory remarks about Pontano in Guicciardini, *op. cit.,* II, 70. See also Abravanel's criticism of the Neapolitans' betrayal of "their king," Comm. on Deut., introd.

25 Guicciardini, *op. cit.,* I, 50. Comines, *op. cit.,* 155. Kayserling, in his biographical article on Abravanel in *The Jewish Encyclopedia,* I, 127a, as well as in his *Biblioteca Española-Portugueza-Judaica,* p. 6b, makes a double mistake when he states that Abravanel "followed King Ferdinand to Messina." Ferdinand, Alfonso's son, left Naples only on the eve of the fall of the capital, that is, about a month after Abravanel's departure with Alfonso, and the latter went, as we have stated, not to Messina, but to Mazzara. The plan of Alfonso and Abravanel to go to Messina developed months later. See below, pp. 69–70. Kayserling's erroneous assumption that Abravanel followed Ferdinand might have originated in a misinterpretation of Kapsali (Excerpts, *D'Bei Eliahu,* in Wiener's ed. of *'Emeq ha-Bakha,* 19).

26 Abravanel's Comm. on Deut., introd.; *Passover Sacrifice,* introd.; cf. also Kapsali, *D'Bei Eliahu, 'Emeq ha-Bakha,* 19.

27 Hesqeto, *loc. cit.,* 3b.

28 Carmoly, *Ozar Nechmad,* II, 60. Explaining why he lacked a certain book, Abravanel writes to Saul ha-Kohen, in 1507: "For together with the rest of my books that were left after the upheaval and escaped the hands of robbers [during the French pogrom in Naples], I sent it to Saloniki, as I intended going there because of the pressure of war" (*Questions and Answers,* 18b).

29 Comines, *op. cit.,* II, 151, 156.

30 See Marino Sanuto, *La Spedizione di Carlo VIII in Italia,* Venezia, 1873, 310–311,·314, 322, 346, 348, 395, 415, 417, 636, 673.

31 *Ibid.,* 348.

32 Kapsali, in Wiener's ed. of *'Emeq ha-Bakha,* 21; Graetz, IX, 6.

33 Prescott, *op. cit.,* II, 43.

34 Guicciardini, *op. cit.,* II, 67.

35 *Ibid.,* 87.

36 Sanuto, *op. cit.,* 420.

37 Guicciardini, *op. cit.*, II, 87; V, 195.

38 Graetz, VIII (1890), 359, and IX, 5, states that Abravanel was with the king until the latter's death in June. Graetz wrote this on the basis of Hesqeto, *loc. cit.*, 3b, whose statement that Abravanel stayed with the king until the latter was "affected with the sickness of which he died" may not necessarily mean "until his death." Alfonso, in any case, died not in June, but on November 19, 1495 (see Giannone, *Civil History of the Kingdom of Naples* [Eng. trans. of *Istoria Civile del regno di Napoli*], London, 1731, II, 442; and cf. Guicciardini, *op. cit.*, II, 86, from which it is also clear that Alfonso died at about that time). Gebhardt, *op. cit.*, 18, states the correct date of Alfonso's death, but is wrong in assuming, on the basis of Hesqeto, *loc. cit.*, 3b, that Abravanel stayed with the king until after November 19. In the second half of July, after Ferrante II had established himself in Naples (July 7), Abravanel, it may be stated with certainty, was no longer in Sicily. Had he heard of Ferrante's victory while still in Messina, he would not have gone to Corfu, but somewhere on the Italian mainland. See below, p. 73.

39 Comm. on Isaiah, end; Comm. on Deut., introd.; *Questions and Answers*, 2d.

40 *Questions and Answers*, 2d. Saul ha-Kohen calls Tanusi: "A most learned scholar, an expert physician engaged by the King and the great nobility" (*bĕ-masa melekh vĕ-sarim*). On David ibn Yahya see Graetz, VIII, supplementary note 13 (pp. 482–483).

41 *Inheritance*, introd., 1d (without pagination): "They neglect eternal values and, like slaves, are interested in temporal matters only. They spend all their days either in diligent pursuit of money and comforts, or in the ways of the sinful, in the company of the lightheaded, where they indulge in slanderous gossip or in gaming with dice, laughing and jesting in their callousness, and God's deed—the gift of His law—they do not see even in their dreams." It is clear that the criticism of the Spanish exiles that we find in the *Inheritance* was written by Abravanel under the impact of what he saw in Corfu. His evaluation of the exiles' colony in Naples seems to have been quite different. See *Passover Sacrifice*, introd.

42 He conceived the plan of this work while still in Naples (see his Commentary on Kings, introd. f. 190, col. 2). Concerning its contents, see his remark in *Ma'aynei ha-Yeshu'ah (Tamar 3)*, Stettin, 1860, p. 9a. It would seem that this was one of the "works" for which he interrupted the writing of his commentary on Isaiah (see the end of this Commentary, Jerusalem, 1956, p. 296b).

43 Comm. on Deut., introd.

44 Marino Sanuto, *op. cit.*, 501; Guicc., *op. cit.*, II, 86.

45 I could not establish the source for the assertion of Graetz, ix, 7, that Joseph, whom Graetz erroneously calls Isaac II (*ibid.*), lived for some time in Reggio, Calabria.

46 On the capture by Venice of Monopoli and the neighboring town of Polignano, see Sanuto, *op. cit.*, 492–494; [Cardinal] Pietro Bembo, *Della Istoria Viniziana*, Venice, 1790, tomo primo, lib. iii, 107–108; Guicciardini, *op. cit.*, lib. ii, 85.

47 Sanuto, *op. cit.*, 543, 576, 650.

48 Comm. on Deut., end (20 Shevat 5256).

49 *Passover Sacrifice*, introd.: ריקם שלחני הזמן. כבודי מעלי הרחיק. חדלו קרובי ומיודעי, בני ביתי ואמהותי. אשתי ובני יצאוני והנם בארץ אחרת. ונשארתי אני לבדי, נר

באָרץ נכריה. יאחזוני ימי עוני. ותתעטף עלי נפשי. הלך אלך ובכה על נהרות. And see *ibid.*, 2b.

50 *Ibid.*: כי זקנתי מהיות לאיש, עזבני כוחי ואינני כתמול שלשום ואור עיני גם הם אין אתי, כי חשכו הרואות בארובות. מעטל וכעס אביט לבי סחרחר, רע ומר, ואנה אני בא.

51 See *Wells*, p. 21b.

52 *Passover Sacrifice*, end, eve of Passover, 5256; Guttmann, *op. cit.*, 19, erroneously fixes the date of completion of this work as 1497.—*Naḥalat Avot* (Commentary on Aboth) was completed on June 23, 1496 (11 Tamuz, 5256). See end of *Inheritance*.

53 *Inheritance*, introd., 1a (without pagination).

54 *Ibid.*, 1d (without pagination).

55 *Wells*, introd., 8a.

56 *Ibid.*, 8b; *Inheritance*, 2a (without pagination).

57 *Ibid.*

58 That the three messianic compositions of Abravanel, *Wells*, *Salvations*, and *Announcer*, formed three parts of one work was indicated by Abravanel in *Questions and Answers*, 8b (pagination: 12). Abravanel called it *Migdol Yeshuot* (*Tower of Salvations*, *ibid.*). The name "Messianic Trilogy" for this work, suggested by Simon Bernstein, *Shomĕrei ha-Ḥomot*, 1938, 15, is therefore a proper one. Jost (*Geschichte des Judenthums*, III, 107, n. 5), who likewise saw in the work a trilogy, erroneously incorporated in it also *New Heavens*.

59 That Abravanel worked after that on both his *Salvations* (which deals with post-biblical Jewish mysticism) and the *Announcer* (which deals with biblical messianic passages) simultaneously, can be deduced from the fact that between the completion of *Wells* (on 1 Tevet, 5257: see *Wells*, 139b) and of *Salvations* almost a whole year passed (*Salvations* was completed on 20 Tevet 5258—December 16, 1497: see *Salvations*, end), while between the completion of *Salvations* and of *Announcer* there was an interval of a little more than two months only (the *Announcer* was completed on 4 Adar II, 5258—February 26, 1498). Since the *Announcer* represents a summation of inquiries encompassing the entire Bible, it is difficult to believe that the whole work lasted merely about two months.

60 *New Heavens* (*Shamayim Ḥadashim*) is a commentary on the *Guide*, II, 19. In his general *Commentary on the Guide*, ed. Landau, Prag, 1831–1832, Abravanel does not deal with that chapter. *New Heavens* was completed on the 14th of Nisan 5258—April 7, 1498. See *New Heavens*, end.

61 Accordingly, the Introduction to Isaiah, which contains an exposition of the conclusions Abravanel arrived at in the *Announcer* regarding Isaiah's messianic prophecies, was probably written not in Corfu, but in Monopoli.

62 Comm. on Isaiah, end: 1 Elul 5258–August 19, 1498.

62a See Gregorio Ruiz, *Don Isaac Abravanel y su comentario al libro de Amos*, 1984, p. 246; citation from MS G-I-11 of the Escorial (17th of Elul, 259).

63 See below, p. 220 and 289, n. 15.

64 Sanuto, *I Diarii*, t. III, col. 1439 (see also col. 1474). Ferorelli (*op. cit.*, 88–89), unaware of the sojourn in Naples of Joseph, Abravanel's nephew, erroneously maintained that the Joseph Abravanel who visited Gonsalvo in 1501 and who in 1503–1505 was "involved with the royal treasury of Naples in the traffic of oil and salt" was Abravanel's son, the physician who, Ferorelli

surmised, "devoted himself out of preference to commerce." Following Ferorelli, Gebhardt, *op. cit.*, Regesten, 54, fell into the same error.

65 Ferorelli, *op. cit.*, 89. Finding in the royal archives of Naples that Jacob was the brother of Joseph Abravanel, and believing that the Joseph referred to was Abravanel's son (see above, preceding note), Ferorelli arrived at the wrong conclusion that Don Isaac "had four and not three sons" (*ibid.*). Cassuto (*Gli Ebrei a Firenze nell'età del rinascimento*, Florence, 1918, p. 89), who pointed out this error, was however, like Marx, wrong in assuming that Jacob was Don Isaac's brother (See Marx, in *HUCA*, I, 616, and Cassuto, *Encyclopaedia Judaica*, I, p. 586). Jacob was the brother of Joseph, Don Isaac's nephew, and prior to the expulsion from Spain, he lived, like the latter, in Plasencia (See Baer, II, pp. 416–417). On the privileges Jacob received from the royal Court in 1512 and 1520, see Ferorelli, *op. cit.*, 89–90.

66 In 1501, a relative of the Abravanels (Muser Cerfati from Spain— perhaps related to Abraham Carfati, see above, p. 52) obtains from the Court, out of regard for "our beloved Joseph Abravanel," royal orders to be well treated and favored in every matter (Ferorelli, *op. cit.*, 89).

67 Ferorelli, *op. cit.*, 88; the full document was first published by H. Pflaum, *op. cit.*, 147, and later by Gebhardt, *op. cit.*, Regesten, 20.

68 This is the conclusion arrived at by Gebhardt, *op. cit.*, 21, on the basis of Judah's poem *Complaint Against Fate*, verse 79: "And I left her [i.e., Judah's wife] and went to serve my king whom God made my benefactor." It is not impossible, however, that in "my king" (מלכי) Judah alluded not to Federigo, but to Gonsalvo. From *Complaint Against Fate*, verse 73, it is clear that Judah, while writing the poem, was in "palaces of kings." From verses 24 and 43 of the above-mentioned poem we learn the approximate date at which the *Complaint* was written. In verse 24 Judah states that his son was, when sent to Portugal (June or July, 1492), "about a year old," and in verse 43 he says that, at the time of the writing, he was twelve years old. Judah, therefore, wrote the *Complaint* in 1503/4, and since he indicates he was then in "palaces of kings," we may conclude that in 1503/4 he was already in the service of Gonsalvo. If we now assume that the poem was written not in 1503, but early in 1504, shortly after Gonsalvo had been appointed viceroy, the term "king" (verse 79) might have referred to Gonsalvo whom Judah, out of both poetical exaggeration and admiration, was likely to call not משנה למלך but מלך. (Judah's close relationship with Gonsalvo was correctly pointed out by Gebhardt, *op. cit.*, Regesten, 54.) The term "benefactor" (מיטיבי) seems also to be more applicable to Gonsalvo—who, as we know, *was* Judah's benefactor—than to Federigo in whose service Judah could not possibly be more than a very brief time (June-August, 1501). It is therefore not unlikely that Judah, like his father, cancelled his planned trip to Naples, that he stayed with his father until after the capitulation of Federigo (August 25, 1501), and that he then "left" his wife (probably with his parents, in Monopoli) and went into the service of Gonsalvo. This assumption is also supported by verse 80 in which Judah states that, after leaving his wife and while serving his "benefactor," he was wandering from place to place: וכן נדתי ולא נחתי ונעתי ואשכון בין אדום תוך עם להבי. As a private physician of Gonsalvo he *had* to move, in the years 1501–1503, with the army of the Great Captain, and thus he lived בין אדום תוך עם להבי. All this leads to the conclusion that the third of the *Dialogi d'Amore* was composed not in Naples, as Pflaum, *op. cit.*, 80–81, and Gebhardt, *op. cit.*, 22, suggested, but somewhere else, while Judah was in Gonsalvo's service. Army

life and philosophical creativity do not usually go well together, but the third dialogue, it must be noted, was composed in the year 5262 (fall 1501–fall 1502: see *Dialogi d'Amore*, III, 50b, ed. 1535), which was on the whole a peaceful interval in that turbulent period.

69 During the first French-Neapolitan war, Ferrante II delivered in pawn to Venice, for a loan of 15,000 ducats and as guarantee for paying Venice's war expenses, five towns, including Monopoli and Polignano which were occupied by Venice in the course of the war (Guicc., *op. cit.*, lib. III, 109). They remained in Venetian hands until 1509 (see Guicc., *op. cit.*, lib. VII, 296).

70 See Pflaum, *op. cit.*, 80–81; Gebhardt, *op. cit.*, 19.—That Don Isaac and his son used to discuss philosophical questions appears evident from *Questions and Answers*, 20c.

71 Thus, for instance, Abravanel's views on the creation, duration and regeneration of the world are found also in Judah's *Dialoghi d'Amore*. See Leone Ebreo, *The Philosophy of Love*, London, 1937, pp. 281, 288–289, 293, and cf. below, Part II, chap. II, §1. Close similarity of views between Don Isaac and his son is also evident in their concepts of the soul (Leone Ebreo, *op. cit.*, p. 204) and its union with God (*ibid.*, pp. 49, 51), as well as concerning the theory of the "circle of beings," which occupies a central position in Leone Ebreo's thought (*ibid.*, pp. 335, 449–450, and cf. below, pp. 115–6, 147, 295 n. 96).

72 *Questions and Answers*, 20d. This is also clear from Judah's *Complaint Against Fate*, verse 73. See above, note 106.

73 Hesqeto, *loc. cit.*, 4a. The year of Abravanel's departure from Monopoli is not mentioned by Hesqeto. The date given here is in accordance with De Rossi, *op. cit.*, p. 16.

CHAPTER FOUR and Summary

1 Comines, *Memoirs*, II, 170.

2 Even before Vasco da Gama's achievement, Venice saw the writing on the wall: when Bartholomeu Dias rounded the Cape of Good Hope, Priuli, the Venetian diarist, wrote that "all Venice was alarmed and amazed, and the wiser heads took it for the worst news" that ever reached the Republic. See Horatio F. Brown, *Studies in the History of Venice*, London, 1907, I, 353.

3 See John Yeats, *The Growth and Vicissitudes of Commerce*, New York, 1878, 103.

4 Horatio F. Brown, *Venice, an Historical Sketch of the Republic*, 2nd ed., London, 1895, 32.

5 See D. Kaufmann, "Don Isaac Abravanel et le commerce des épices avec Calicut," in *R.E.J.*, xxxviii, 145f, and particularly the document from the Venetian State Archives, *ibid.*, 147–148.

6 *Ibid.*

7 From the document published by Kaufmann it appears that the final answer to Abravanel was delayed "until the return of our triremes from Alexandria" (*ibid.*). Venice still feared to render the sultan of Egypt hostile to the

Republic by negotiating a deal with Portugal (see Brown, *Venice*, 325). That Abravanel's proposals were finally accepted is clear from Zurita, *Anales de Aragon*, V, 1670, 342a, who states that the Venetians "tried to come to an agreement with the king, Don Manuel, through the mediation of a Jew called Habrauanel."

8 Cf. Zurita, *op. cit.*, 342ab. Gebhardt, *op. cit.*, thinks that the visit of Abravanel's nephew in Portugal was employed by the family for engineering the escape of Don Judah's son, Isaac, who had been forcibly converted to Christianity together with the other Jewish children of the country (1497). This is not unlikely, although the departure of Isaac Abravanel, the grandson, from Portugal might have taken place, not before 1507, when permission was given for Marranos to leave Portugal. That Abravanel's grandson returned to Judaism after having settled in Turkey (against Graetz, viii, 359) was first suggested by Geiger (*Ozar Nechmad*, II, 224–225). Isaac Abravanel of Saloniki, who possessed a copy of Don Isaac's Commentary on the *Guide* in 1558 (see Comm. on the *Guide*, ed. Landau, introd., iii) might have been Judah's son. He is described by the copyist as הנבון הישיש השר דון יצחק אברבנאל. The term ישיש may perhaps be accounted for either by the appearance of the man who might have looked older than his age, or perhaps by the copyists tendency for exaggeration. In 1558, in any case, Don Isaac, if indeed he was Don Judah's son, was 67 years old.

9 See Zurita, *op. cit.*, 342f.   10 Hesqeto, *loc. cit.*, 4a.

11 *Questions and Answers*, 8c (pagination: 12); Abravanel decided to rewrite the book under the title of *Lahaqat Neviim* (Group of Prophets), *ibid.*

12 *Ibid.* The work was lost during the French pogrom in Naples (*Inheritance*, IV, p. 477a), but from Abravanel's Comm. on the *Guide*, 32a, it appears that he found it toward the end of his days. The work is not extant today. It is possible, however, that Abravanel finished it, and there is proof that he completed at least a large part of it. Chapter 79 of the first dissertation (שער) of this work is quoted by Isaac Lopez, in his *Kur Mazref ha-Emunot u-Mar'eh ha-Emet* (Metz, 1847, p. 19a), which was composed not later than the end of the 17th century.

13 *Questions and Answers*, 20d. Judah's poems were all republished by Gebhardt, *op. cit.*, Gedichte, 17–20.

14 *Questions and Answers*, 20d. Judah Abravanel, introductory poem to the *Inheritance*, verses 15, 17.

15 Of the dates of completion of the commentaries on the Latter Prophets only that on Jeremiah is known: the eve of Shavu'ot 5264 (Comm. on Latter Prophets, f. 152b). The Comm. on Ezekiel was completed toward the end of 1504 (Comm. on Ezekiel, 20.33: ואני בד' אצפה שנשלמו הארבעים ההם בשנת חמשת אלפים ורס"ה לבריאת העולם היא השנה הזאת. The year 5265 ran from the fall of 1504 to that of 1505. The above remark of Abravanel, expressing hope for the arrival of the Messiah in 5265, shows that the bulk of the year was still before him.)

16 Jacob Guttmann, *op. cit.*, 17, states that the Comm. on Genesis was composed in Naples. This, in our opinion, is an error. The last words in the Comm. on Genesis: "completed in the city of Naples . . . in the year 5282 (אפאר'.) were obviously written by the copyist (cf. Steinschneider, *Catalogus*, 1077), since in 5282 Abravanel was no longer among the living. The Comm. on Genesis was composed, in all likelihood, in the first half of 1505. The date of the completion of the Comm. on Exod. is known: Sept. 29, 1505 – 1 Marheshvan 5266.

17 *Questions and Answers*, 8b (pagin. 12).   18 *Ibid.*, 8c (pag. 12).

19 *Ibid.*, 7d (pagination: 11): לא שאאמין אני כל מה שכתב הרב בהחלט כי
את הטוב נקבל ואת הרע לא נקבל, אבל שדברי הרב עורדו הלבבות לבקש הטוב והישר וישמע
חכם ויוסף לקח... עלינו לשבח לרב המורה צדק על אשר הקים סוכת התורה הנופלת בשלושה
דרושים בפרט, שהם פנותיה ויסודותיה, והוא מלא ידו לה' בעד תורתו תורת אלהינו, כנגד
הפילוסופים ב ח י ד ו ש ה ע ו ל ם, ו ב י ד י ע ת ה א ל ו ב ה ש נ ח ת ו, כי עמד בפרץ למלטם
מיד צר... אמנם בשאר הדרושים אין ספק שיערער התורני עליהם.

20 In his *Secret of the Guide*, added to his *Answers to Saul ha-Kohen*, Abravanel writes that he intended to interpret every chapter of the *Guide* in detail. Joseph Solomon del Medigo, in a letter to Zerah ben Nathan, states that Abravanel actually composed a commentary on the entire *Guide* (והר״ר יצחק אברבנאל פירשו כולו) and that he, Del Medigo, had seen the manuscript (see Abraham Geiger, *Melo Chofnayim*, Hebrew part, p. 18).

21 *Questions and Answers*, 142a.

22 See Gebhardt, *op. cit.*, Regesten, 55–57. As Gebhardt showed with sufficient proof, Abravanel died either in November 1508 or in January 1509. In either case, he died not in the year 5268, as Hesqeto, *loc. cit.*, 4a, states, but in the year 5269. In view of Hesqeto's assertion, however, the first of the two dates suggested by Gebhardt should gain greater credence. Hesqeto obviously did not know the exact date of Abravanel's death. He must have heard nevertheless from a reliable source (perhaps from Abravanel's son, Samuel, with whom he was probably acquainted) that Don Isaac died in 1508, and this may account for his mistaken statement. Most of the year 1508 falls within the year 5268, and Hesqeto might have written what he wrote not with absolute certainty, but on the basis of an assumption which he considered more plausible. Graetz' conclusion (VIII, supplementary Note 5, p. 429) that Abravanel died in 1509, based on a statement of Judah Menz's son-in-law, Meir Katzenellenbogen, that "in the same year that our rabbi (Judah Menz) died, Padua, the city of his residence, was plundered," is not well founded. Katzenellenbogen undoubtedly had in mind not the Christian but the Jewish year (5269). Judah Menz's death and the capture of Padua both occurred in the same year according to the Jewish calendar, even if they took place in two different years according to the Christian calendar (the capture and plundering of Padua by the forces of the Emperor Maximilian I took place in July 1509).

23 Hesqeto, *loc. cit.*, 4a.

24 See Abravanel's own statements on his position in Jewry in the introductions to his commentaries on Joshua and Kings and to *Passover Sacrifice*. On the attitude of unbounded admiration which prevailed toward Abravanel, see also *Questions and Answers*, 2a–2b, 3b, and below, notes 25–7. Similarly testifying to this attitude is the dirge on Abravanel's death, first published by Halberstam in *Qovez 'al Yad*, XV (1899) and recently by P. Navè in *Romanica et Occidentalia*, Jerusalem, 1963, pp. 65–67. Although it is not excluded that this lament was penned by Judah, Don Isaac's son, as Navè suggests (*ibid.*, pp. 56–65), the evidence adduced (Carmoly's statement in *Revue Orientale*, I, 1841, p. 258) is not conclusive. It is doubtful that Carmoly had more information about the poem than offered by the caption copied by Halberstam.

25 *Beth Joseph*, Oraḥ Ḥayyim, 168; *Kesef Mishneh*, Hil. Berakhot, III, 8.

26 Kapsali, *D'Bei Eliahu*, 71.   27 *Questions and Answers*, 4b.

28 Judah's introductory poem to the Latter Prophets, verses 26–27.

29 *Ibid.*, verse 28.

NOTES TO PART TWO

CHAPTER ONE

1 Étienne Gilson, *Reason and Revelation in the Middle Ages*, New York, 1935, pp. 5, 15, 38, 70.

2 See Henry Osborn Taylor, *The Mediaeval Mind*, London, 1930, II, pp. 433, 522–529, 539, 554.

3 On the conflict between Faith and Reason in Jewish thought see Isaac Husik, *A History of Mediaeval Jewish Philosophy*, New York, 1916, pp. XIII–XVI, 28, 159, 330–331. A systematic exposition of the particular issues of this controversy in the post-Maimonidean era, but without an analysis of the philosophical principles involved, can be found in J. Sarachek, *Faith and Reason*, Williamsport, Pennsylvania, 1935. For an important study, illuminating some of the philosophical and religious intricacies of the problem in Judaism as well as Christianity and Islam, see Harry Austryn Wolfson, *The Double Faith Theory* etc., in *J.Q.R.* (New Series), 1942, pp. 213–264.

4 *Emunot ve-Deot*, introduction, section 6; *Kitab al-Khazari*, Eng. trans. by Hartwig Hirschfeld, London, 1916, I, 64–65; III, 7.

5 *The Guide for the Perplexed*, trans. by M. Friedlaender, 2nd. ed., London, 1904, introduction (p. 2); I, 50; II, 3. On the similarities and differences between Maimonides and Aquinas see Étienne Gilson, *The Philosophy of St. Thomas Aquinas*, Cambridge, 1929, pp. 48, 52, 66, 83, 168, 170; Jacob Guttmann, *Das Verhaeltniss des Thomas von Aquino zum Judenthum und zur Juedischen Literatur*, Goettingen, 1891, pp. 31–92; and C. and D. Singer, "The Jewish Factor in Medieval Thought," in *The Legacy of Israel*, Oxford, 1928, pp. 217–271.

6 See Husik, *op. cit.*, pp. 330–331.

7 Abravanel's *Principles of Faith (Rosh Amanah)* is primarily devoted to proving the validity of Maimonides' 13 Articles of Faith. Albo's *Sefer ha-'Iqqarim* (The Book of Principles) is denounced by him as *Sefer ha-'Oqĕrim* (The Book of the Uprooters). See *Salvations of His Anointed (Yeshu'ot Meshiho)*, Koenigsberg, 1861, p. 27b. In the closing chapter of his *Principles* (ed. Koenigsberg, 1861, p. 29a), however, Abravanel writes: "I believe that as far as the divine Law is concerned, it is improper to lay down principles or foundations in matters of faith, since we are obligated to believe in everything written in it and cannot place doubt even on the smallest detail." His conclusion is that "each sentence, word and letter of the Law is a principle and a root in itself" (*ibid.*, p. 30b). These cardinal statements of Abravanel fully agree with the rest of his concepts and therefore cannot be taken, as D. Neumark (*Toledot ha-'Iqqarim be-Yisrael*, I, Odessa, 5679, p. 79) suggested, as

mere lip service to orthodoxy, but rather, as S. D. Luzzatto (Jost's *Annalen*, 1840, p. 24b) understood, as expressing his innermost belief.

8 "The Law of Moses does not include philosophical theories, or logical investigations, or proofs involving high inquiries. For man's success is above Reason, and outside the sphere of Nature . . . therefore the poet said, '*I selected the way of Faith*,' adding 'and I hated theorizing' (*Crown*, 42)." Cf. *Salvations*, 73b, where "Greek philosophizing" is presented by Abravanel as opposed to the "ways of truth" manifested in Scripture and the "wisdom of the early sages in whom the spirit of God spoke." On the inferiority of knowledge acquired by Reason to that acquired by Revelation, Abravanel writes: "Investigation is proper for man as such in order to prepare his reason to emerge from a potential to an actual state, but that association with God which was manifest on Mt. Sinai, and especially prophecy, was not given to man as such, but to man as higher than man, as similar to the first separate intelligence or to the uppermost sphere" (*Crown*, 42).

9 The following citation from Abravanel (*ibid.*) implies the idea quite clearly: "Man's success depends on Faith and good deeds and the *understanding of the results of all inquiry as we are informed of them by the Mosaic Law, and not upon the knowledge of the proofs which lead to them.*"

10 For Abravanel's view on the insurmountable limitations of man's reason and the perfection of revealed truth, see his long dissertation on the subject in his Commentary on I Kings, 3. 12 (f. 206, col. 2—f. 211, col. 2). I am quoting Abravanel's commentaries on the Former Prophets according to the Leipzig edition of 1686.

11 Irenaeus, *Adv. Haer.*, IV, 37:5. The doctrine, as it appears in Irenaeus, is undoubtedly a development from Clement's notion that faith—"an ascent of our reasoning faculty"—is an act of man's free will. An analysis of Clement's original conception of faith, as well as his references to it, are to be found in Harry A. Wolfson, *loc. cit.*, pp. 223–225, 263.

12 *Emunot*, V, 8.

13 See Maimonides' Commentary on Mish. Sanh., X (following the discussion of the thirteenth Article of Faith). See the same attitude in the *Guide*, III, 51 (p. 384), and especially in Hilkhot 'Akum, 10, 1, and Hilkhot Roẓeaḥ 4, 10.

14 Comm. on Gen. 10.1 (f. 33, col. 4). Citations referring to Abravanel's commentaries on the Pentateuch are marked according to the Warsaw edition of 1862. Cf. '*Iqqarim*, IV, xxviii, 4–6 (according to Husik's translation, Philadelphia, 1930; vol. IV, part I, pp. 267–270).

15 *Or Adonai*, I, Preface (Vienna, 1860, p. 3a).

16 Comm. on Deut. 6.6 (f. 15, col. 2). In opposition to Abraham ben David of Posquières (*Criticisms* on Maimonides' *Code*, Hilkhot Teshubah, III, 7) and Albo ('*Iqqarim*, I, ii, 7) who maintained that one who believed in the corporeality of God in accordance with the plain reading of Scripture was no heretic, Abravanel thought that the "acceptance of a false notion, when a principle of faith is involved, prevents the soul from the attainment of real perfection and from life in the world to come, *even if that acceptance was made without any evil intention*" (*Principles*, p. 14a). Cf. also his view of Gersonides who, according to Abravanel, expressed opinions on the question of Creation, the soul, prophecy and miracles which are "forbidden to hear, let alone to be-

lieve in," since the adherence to such opinions constitutes a "criminal offense" (Comm. on Josh. 11., introd., f. 21, col. 3).

17 *Principles*, p. 29a.

18 Comm. on Mish. Sanh. X (eighth article of faith).

19 See Abravanel's Comm. on Gen., 10.1 (f. 48, col. 4). The corresponding passage in *Happalat ha-Happalah* (Hebrew translation of Averroes' *Destruction of the Destruction*, by Kalonymos ben David ben Todros, Bodleian Library, Michael Collection, Ms. 293, ff. 137b–138a) is somewhat different. Abravanel might have used the other Hebrew translation (MS. in Leyden) of Averroes' work (cf. Steinschneider, *Uebersetzungen*, pp. 333–4).

20 *Opus Majus*, Part II, chaps 5 and 6 (Eng. trans. by Robert Belle Burke, Philadelphia, 1928, vol. I, pp. 47–48) and chapter 14 (vol. I, pp. 64–65). *Ibid.*, part IV, chap. 16 (vol. I, p. 301): "For from the beginning the Hebrews have been very skillful in the knowledge of astronomy; and all nations have obtained this science as well as other sciences from them."

21 Justin Martyr, *Hortatory Address to the Greeks*, xxv–xxvi and xxix–xxxi. Justin, in all likelihood, here follows Philo (cf. H. A. Wolfson, *Philo*, I, 1947, pp. 141–142) and perhaps also Aristobulos (see Eusebius, *Praep. Ev.*, XIII, 12).

22 Clement of Alexandria, *The Miscellanies*, I, 21; II, 18; V, 14.

23 *City of God*, XVIII, 37 (I am quoting Augustine here according to Healey's translation. Most of the other quotations from *De Civitate Dei* are according to the English version of Dods. Citations from other Church Fathers are mostly according to the version of the Ante-Nicene Christian Library).

24 *Khazari*, I, 63; II, 66. Maimonides' position is much more cautious. He says: "Many branches of science . . . were once cultivated by our forefathers, but were in the course of time neglected" by the Jews "in consequence of the tyranny" exercised over them by "barbarous nations" (*Guide*, I, 71). This is a defensive rather than an offensive attitude. See also *Guide*, II, end of Chapter 11. On one occasion, *ibid.*, II, 8 (p. 163), he even stresses the superiority of Greek knowledge.

25 Comm. on Gen. 10.1 (f. 33, col. 1).

26 Comm. on I Kings 3.12 (f. 206, col. 2—f. 211, col. 2).

27 *Principles*, p. 29a.

28 *Guide*, II, 25.

29 Comm. on Gen. 2.1–3 (f. 16, col. 4).

30 Comm. on Deut. 17.8 (f. 35, col. 3).

31 *Salvations*, p. 83b.

32 *Deeds of God* (*Mif'alot Elohim*) and *New Heavens* (*Shamayim Ḥadashim*). Of the former work, I used the Venice edition of 1592; of the latter, that of Roedelheim, 1828.

33 John Elof Boodin, *God and Creation*, New York, 1934, p. 422.

34 *Ibid.*, pp. 422–423.

35 Origen, *De Principiis*, II, 1:4. In repudiating the view that "God could not create anything when nothing existed," Origen supports himself on II Macc. VII, 28: "I ask of thee, my son, to look at the heaven and the earth, and all the things which are in them, and beholding these, to know that God made

all these things when they did not exist." Jerome's "casual mistranslation" of this verse, to which Boodin referred, was therefore made according to Origen's interpretation.

36 Justin Martyr, *First Apology*, LIX; Clement, *The Miscellanies*, V, 14.

37 Irenaeus, *Adv. Haer.*, II, 10:1.

38 *The Miscellanies*, V, 14.

39 *Khazari*, I, 67.

40 *Deeds of God*, p. 3d.

41 *Ibid.*, p. 4c.

42 *New Heavens*, p. 2a.

43 *Milḥamot*, VI, ii.12.

44 Comm. on Josh. 10.12 (f. 21, col. 4).

45 *Or Adonai*, II, iv. 2, 3 (ed. Vienna, 1860, pp. 43b, 45ab).

46 Comm. on Josh. 10.12 (f. 22, col. 1).

47 *Announcer of Salvation (Mashmi'a Yeshu'ah)*, p. 14d.

48 *Deeds of God*, p. 6a. See the identical idea in Albo, *'Iqqarim*, I, xii, 1.

49 *New Heavens*, p. 2b.

50 *Principles*, p. 28b. See also *New Heavens*, p. 2b. For the relationship between this view of Abravanel (i.e., the extraordinary importance he imputed to the Creation principle) and the development of Jewish dogmaticism in the second half of the fifteenth century, see my remarks in *The Marranos of Spain*, p. 136, note 2.

51 *Deeds of God*, p. 53c. According to Abravanel, "the spiritual beings who, like their Creator, possess life and thought as essential parts of their nature, necessarily emanated from the same divine source just as rays emanate from the sun. This is why Scripture denotes these spiritual creatures by the name 'light,' and this is also why the term 'created' or 'made' is not applied here and only the expression 'let there be' — indicating absolute being — is used instead." (The identification of "angels" with the light in the creation story was suggested by Augustine, *City of God*, XI, 9. In his Comm. on Gen. 1.3 [f. 2, col. 3], however, Abravanel rejects it.)

52 For the variations in the concept of the universe in the Middle Ages see *The Legacy of Israel*, edited by R. Bevan and Charles Singer, London, 1927, p. 195.

53 Comm. on Josh. 10.13 (f. 24, col. 1).

54 *New Heavens*, p. 18a.

55 Maimonides, *Sefer ha-Mada*, Hilkhot Yĕsodei ha-Torah, III, 2.

56 This is the Ptolemaic view, which Abravanel adopted. Speaking of Maimonides' astronomical concept, he says: "Maimonides followed the opinion of Ptolemy which is more in accordance with reality" (*New Heavens*, p. 7a). For a summary of Maimonides' view of the universe see *Sefer ha-Mada*, Hil. Yĕsodei ha-Torah, III, 4–5.

57 Comm. on Deut. 4.15 (f. 9, col. 3). Abravanel's most comprehensive exposition of his views on the universe, together with his presentation of other theories on the subject, are found in his Comm. on Exod. 24.18 (f. 47, cols. 2–3); Comm. on I Kings 3.12 (f. 208, col. 4); and *Crown*, pp. 79–82.

58 See below, especially pp. 114–5.

59 *Crown*, p. 36; Comm. on Exod. 24.1 (f. 46, col. 2); cf. Maimonides' *Sefer ha-Mada*, Hil. Yes. ha-Tor. I, 5 and *Guide*, I, 70 (p. 106); II, 1 (p. 151); and the opposing view of Gersonides, *Milḥamot*, V, iii,11.

60 *Guide*, I, 72 (p. 113).

61 Comm. on Exod. 7.8 (f. 12, col. 4) and 24.18 (f. 47, col. 2). By accepting the existence of pure spirits or forms, Abravanel follows Maimonides and Aristotle and differs with Ibn Gabirol who maintained that, like everything else in existence, spiritual substances, including angels, are composed of matter and form (*Fountain of Life*, IV, 2–4, 7). Ibn Gabirol's *Fountain of Life* is mentioned by Abravanel in his Comm. on I Kings 3.12 (f. 209, col. 1).

62 *Guide*, II, 6.   63 *Ibid.*, II, 4, 9.

64 Job, 25.3.

65 Daniel, 7.10.

66 *Crown*, p. 82; Comm. on I Kings 3.12 (f. 209, col. 2).

67 Cf. *'Iqqarim*, II, 12:3.

68 *Deeds of God*, p. 54a; Comm. on I Kings 3.12 (f. 209, col. 2). Cf. Maimonides' *Guide*, II, 6 and St. Thomas' *Summa Contra Gentiles*, III–I, chap. LXXIX. Maimonides, however, while pointing out that "angel" means a divine messenger, subtly turned the argument around by saying that any messenger—i.e., anyone or anything that performs a mission, and not necessarily a spiritual being—is sometimes referred to as "angel" in the Bible. For Maimonides, real angels, that is, "angels through which God rules this world," are only the intelligences that "effect the motion of the spheres" (*Guide*, II, 6).

69 Comm. on I Kings 3.12 (f. 209, col. 3); *Deeds of God*, p. 72d; *Wells*, 44b. As Abravanel himself indicates, he follows here closely in the footsteps of al-Ghazali. On the latter's view on causality as an act of God's will see T. J. De Boer, *The History of Philosophy in Islam*, Eng. trans. by Edward R. Jones, London, 1903, pp. 160–161.

70 See *City of God*, X, 12. Cf. Gilson, *The Spirit of Mediaeval Philosophy*, New York, 1940, p. 374.

71 *Deeds of God*, p. 48a.

72 See *Summa Contra Gentiles*, III–I, chap. LXXX. The influence of Aquinas' angelology on Abravanel is further attested by the fact that he translated the former's work on the spiritual creatures into Hebrew (see M. Almosnino, *Meameẓ koaḥ*, Venice, 1587–88, p. 117a; cf. Jellinek, *Thomas von Aquino in der jüdischen Literatur*, Leipzig, 1853, p. 8). See also A. C. McGiffert, *A History of Christian Thought*, New York, 1932, II, p. 271.

73 Comm. on Exod. 7.8 (f. 12, col. 4).   74 *Guide*, III, 29, 37, 46.

75 *Or Adonai*, IV, 6 (ed. Vienna, 1860, p. 89ab).

76 *'Iqqarim*, III, viii, 2, 4. On the universality of the belief in demons among Jews in the Middle Ages see J. Trachtenberg, *Jewish Magic and Superstition*, New York, 1939, pp. 26–27, 29–31.

77 *City of God*, II, 10; XI, 13, 15; IX, 18; *Summa Theologica*, I., Q. LXIII, Art. 2–3, 7–8.

78 Comm. on Exod. 7.8 (f. 12, col. 4); Comm. on Deut. 18.9 (f. 37, col. 4).

79 Seneca, *Epistulae Morales*, Epis. XLI, 8.
80 *Naturales Quaestiones*, Book I, Preface, 5.
81 Comm. on Gen. 1.26 (f. 14A, col. 2).
82 *Ibid.*, 1.26 (f. 14A, col. 4). In presenting this view of man's symbolic import, Abravanel refers for support to Maimonides (see *Guide*, I, 72; in Pines' Eng. trans. [1963]: pp. 190–191); however, he was doubtlessly also acquainted with earlier proponents of the same theory, like Ibn Ẓaddiq and others (see on these A. Jellinek, introd. to Joseph ibn Ẓaddiq's Microcosm [*Sefer 'Olam ha-Qatan*, Leipzig, 1854, p. x] and S. Fried, in his edition of Isaac Israeli's *Sefer ha-Yesodot*, Drohobycz, 1900, p. 59).
83 Comm. on Gen. 1.26 (f. 14A, col. 2).
84 *Guide*, I, 72; II, 4.
85 Comm. on Gen. 1.16 (f. 12, col. 4).
86 *Ibid.*; *New Heavens*, 17a.
87 *Emunot*, IV, introd. IV, 2.
88 *Guide*, III, 13–14; I, 72; II, 4, 5. The following statement of Maimonides (*ibid.*, III, 13) summarizes his view on the question: ". . . The universe does not exist for man's sake, but . . . each being exists for its own sake and not because of some other thing."
89 *Emunot*, IV, 2. Cf. Henry Malter, *Saadia Gaon*, Philadelphia, 1921, pp. 212–213, note 485.
90 Comm. on Gen. 1.16 (f. 12, col. 4); Comm. on I Sam. 25.29 (f. 128, col. 1).
91 See S. Munk, *Mélanges de philosophie juive et arabe*, Paris, 1857, p. 377.
92 *Summa Theologica*, I, Q. LXX, Art. 3. Among Jewish thinkers Arama is notable for having rejected the same theory (see *'Aqedat Yiẓḥaq*, Warsaw, 1882, chapters 2 and 5). Also Abravanel's parable about the mosquito might have been borrowed from Arama (*ibid.*, p. 76). For other passages bearing close similarity which appear in the works of both writers, see Carmoly, *Ozar Nechmad*, II, 54, and H. J. Polak, introd. to Arama's *'Aqedat Yiẓḥaq*, Warsaw, 1882, 6–7.—As for the original authorship of these statements, it cannot always be unequivocally determined in favor of Arama, as the latter's son, Meir Arama (see his statement published by Gabriel Polak in *Ha-Maggid*, II, No. 25 [30.vi.1858], p. 99), and some later authors, would have it. It appears that Abravanel and Arama used to meet while in Naples and discuss theological and philosophical subjects (*ibid.*), and it is not implausible that a number of ideas, analyzed or formulated in these discussions, could rightly claim the authorship of both writers. It should also be noted that Arama's *'Aqedat Yiẓḥaq*, although originally written perhaps in the eighties, remained unpublished throughout its author's life and certain changes could have been introduced in that work under the influence of Abravanel.
93 *Salvations*, p. 47a. Cf. *Principles*, p. 14b: "God acts at will and is not like the rest of the beings—the *angels*, the spheres, the stars, the elements and what is composed of them—all of which are *ordered to act in a certain way and have neither control over their actions nor desire to do what they are doing.*"
94 *'Iqqarim*, IV, 2; and cf. Arama, *'Aqedat Yiẓḥaq*, chap. 10, p. 130, and *Guide*, II, chap. 7.

95 *Emunot*, VI, 3; *Guide*, I, 70; *Eight Chapters*, I (Eng. trans. by Joseph I. Gorfinkel, New York, 1912): "The human soul is one" (p. 37) "although it has five faculties" (pp. 38–39).

96 *Wells*, p. 47. It must be pointed out, however, that this is only man's initial position, from which he can ascend to a higher status or descend to a lower one (see Comm. on Gen. 1.26 [f. 14A, cols. 2–3]), while according to his highest potentiality man is superior to all created beings. This is also indicated in the "circle of creation," which begins with God, leads downward through the angels, spheres and stars to the lowest of all elements (earth), and rises from this point through the plants, animals and man—the last stage of creation—back to God (*ibid.*, col. 2; *Deeds of God*, p. 48ab). On the "circle" theory see Zimmels, *op. cit.*, pp. 102–103. Cf. Klausner, *Me-Aplaton 'ad Spinoza*, Jerusalem, 1955, pp. 276–278.

97 *Salvations*, p. 37a.   98 Comm. on Gen. 2.4 (f. 15, col. 2).

99 *Ibid.*, 1.26 (f. 14A, cols. 3–4). Cf. *Crown*, p. 32 and *Salvations*, p. 36ab.

100 *Ibid.*, p. 36a: "The human souls are not created at the time of the creation of the bodies in which they reside, for they do not follow from the body's constitution. Like the rest of the spiritual beings which exist individually, they were all created in the six days of creation."

101 *Deeds of God*, p. 54d.

102 *New Heavens*, p. 50b.

103 *Deeds of God*, p. 48bc.

104 Comm. on I Sam. 25.29 (f. 128, col. 3): "The reward of the souls in the world beyond is their ability to attain the true concept of God which is a source of the most wonderful felicity, an attainment impossible for man in this earthly life because of the disturbances on the part of matter." See also Comm. on Deut. 9.25 (f. 20, col. 4) and Comm. on Exod. 24.17.

105 Comm. on Deut. 34.5 (f. 23, col. 4).

106 Comm. on I Sam. 25.31 (f. 128, col. 2).

107 *Ibid.*, 25.31 (f. 128, col. 4).

108 *Salvations*, p. 47a.

109 Comm. on Deut. 25.5 (f. 49, col. 1, 2, 3). Cf. *Salvations*, p. 24b.

110 Comm. on Deut. 25.5 (f. 49, col. 2). Abravanel rejects, however, the view of Plato as well as of Albertus Magnus that human souls are transmigrated also into animal bodies. *Wells*, p. 50a. Cf. Gershom G. Sholem, *Major Trends in Jewish Mysticism*, Jerusalem, 1941, p. 238.

111 *Salvations*, p. 36ab.

112 *Emunot*, VII, 4; Nahmanides, *Sha'ar ha-Gemul*, Warsaw, 1862, pp. 19a, 20b, 21a, 22b.

113 *Wells*, 117b, 118ab; *Announcer*, pp. 14bc, 15a, 47a. Cf. Crescas, *Or Adonai*, III, iv. 2.

114 The title of Abravanel's non-extant work on resurrection—*Zedek 'Olamim*—also conveys this idea. Translated literally it means "Eternal Justice," as well as the "Justice of [Two] Worlds."

115 Comm. on I Sam. 25.31 (f. 128, cols. 3–4).

116 *Sefer ha-Mada*, Hil. 'Akum, XI, 8–9; and see especially Maimonides'

letter to the Jewish scholars of southern France, published by Alexander Marx in *Hebrew Union College Annual*, III, pp. 349–358 (particularly pp. 350–351); see also *Guide*, II, 10, where Maimonides discusses the limits of the spheres' influence upon the earth.

117 *Crown*, p. 32.
118 Comm. on Deut. 4.15 (f. 9, col. 3).
119 *Ibid.*, 4.15 (f. 10, col. 4). Abravanel refers to Aristotle, *Ethics*, III, 10. In all probability he had in mind the passage in *Nic. Ethics*, III, 5 (1113b, 5–14).
120 Comm. on Deut. 4.15 (f. 11, col. 1).
121 *Ibid.*, 4.15 (f. 11, col. 2).
122 *Ibid.*, 4.15 (f. 9, col. 3).
123 *Crown*, p. 32; *Wells*, 20b.
124 Comm. on Deut. 4.15 (f. 10, col. 2).
125 *Ibid.* See also *Wells*, 105b.
126 Comm. on Deut. 4.15 (f. 10, col. 3); cf. *Crown*, pp. 37–38.
127 Comm. on Deut. 18.14 (f. 38, cols. 1–2).
128 *Ibid.*, 18.14 (f. 38, col. 1).
129 According to Abravanel, astrology cannot always be relied upon because providence sometimes decides in opposition to the constellations, and the latter "cannot have any effect against what divine providence decreed" (Comm. on Num. 22.22 [f. 2B, col. 2]).
130 Comm. on I Kings 3.12 (f. 207, col. 3); Comm. on Exod. 24.18 (f. 47, cols. 2–3).
131 *Sefer ha-Mada*, Hil. Yes. ha-Tor. X, 4. According to Maimonides, performance of miracles is no proof for *prophecy* (*ibid.*, VII, 7; VIII, 1) and consequently a prophet has no need to perform miracles (*ibid.*, X, 1). In his Epistle to the Jews of Yemen, however, while stating that Moses' wondrous acts were effected to meet national emergencies and not to make the people believe in him (*Iggeret Teman*, ed. Warsaw, 1837, p. 8a), he maintains nevertheless that one who claims to be a prophet should substantiate the claim by performing a miracle (*ibid.*, p. 8b).
132 *Milḥamot*, VI, ii, 13.
133 *Or Adonai*, II, iv, 2.
134 *Emunot*, III, 4.
135 Comm. on Deut. 18.14 (f. 39, col. 2); *Deeds of God*, p. 91a.
136 *Milḥamot*, II, 6.
137 Comm. on Num. 12.1 (f. 11, col. 3).
138 *City of God*, XI, 2.
139 Thus God spoke to Moses (Comm. on Exod. 19.1 [f. 33, col. 1]; 19.3 [f. 34, col. 1]) and to Samuel (Comm. on I Sam. 3.4 [f. 83, col. 2]). That God communicates speech through a material substratum or a created sound was a view held in the Middle Ages by the Mu'tazilites. "Over none of the Mu'tazilites' innovations did such a violent strife rage as over this—a strife which passed beyond scholastic bounds and made itself felt in everyday life" (Ignaz Goldziher, *Mohammed and Islam*, New Haven, 1917, p. 120).

140 Comm. on Gen. 41, introd. (f. 19B, col. 1).

141 *Ibid.*

142 *Ibid.* introd. (f. 19B, col. 2); *Wells*, pp. 35b–36a. Abravanel's classification of dreams is undoubtedly influenced by that of St. Thomas, *Summa Theologica*, II–II, Q. 95, Art. 6.—For a detailed discussion of Abravanel's views on Prophecy as compared with those of Maimonides, see Alvin J. Reines, "Abravanel on Prophecy in the *Moreh Nebukhim*," in *HUCA*, XXXI (1960), and XXXIII (1962)—XXXVII (1966).

143 Comm. on I Sam. 28.8 (f. 133, col. 1); see *Milḥamot*, VI, pt. II, chap. 14; *Sefer ha-Mada*, Hil. 'Akum, XI, 11: necromancy represents nothing but "deceit" and "nonsense."

144 Comm. on I Sam. 28.8 (f. 133, col. 2).

145 Cf. *City of God*, IX, 21.

146 Comm. on I Sam. 28.8 (f. 133, col. 3).

147 *Summa Theologica*, II–II, Q. CLXXIV, Art. 5 (Reply Obj. 4).

148 *Guide*, III, 37. Cf. *Sefer ha-Mada*, Hil. Akum, XI, 11.

149 See Lynn Thorndike, *A History of Magic and Experimental Science*, II, New York, 1923, pp. 551–552.

150 This, again, is in accordance with Albertus Magnus, who speaks of the "three sciences of magic, necromancy and astrology." See Thorndike, *op. cit.*, II, p. 556.

151 Comm. on Exod. 7.8 (f. 12, col. 4).

152 See James J. Walsh, *The Century of Columbus*, New York, 1914, p. 345; F. A. Scharpff, *Der Kardinal und Bischof Nikolaus von Cusa als Reformator in Kirche, Reich und Philosophie des 15. Jahrhunderts*, Tuebingen, 1871, pp. 311–3.

153 *Khazari*, III, 11.

154 Machiavelli, *Discourses on the First Ten Books of Titus Livy*, II, 2.

155 See Henry S. Lucas, *The Renaissance and the Reformation*, New York, 1934, pp. 5–6.

156 See Ralph Roeder, *The Man of the Renaissance*, New York, 1933, p. 78. Cf. Savonarola, *Spiritual and Ascetic Letters*, edited by B. W. Randolph, London, 1907, p. 96.

157 See Henry S. Lucas, *op. cit.*, p. 153.

158 See Pasquale Villari, *A History of Girolamo Savonarola and his Times*, London, 1863, pp. 64–65.

159 Lynn Thorndike (*op. cit.*, IV, p. 611), in summarizing intellectual conditions in the fifteenth century, says: "Astrological prediction rode high in public favor producing most of the 'best sellers' in the incunabula period and absorbing no small portion of time in the universities."

160 Villari, *op. cit.*, p. 63.

161 *Khazari*, IV, 27.

162 See above, note 116. From Maimonides to Pico it is difficult to find anyone who expressed unqualified opposition to astrology. Even men like Petrarch and Oresme, who seem to have rated astrology as a sham, were not so definite in their views (cf. Thorndike, *op. cit.*, III, pp. 220–221, 416).

CHAPTER TWO

1 Cf. Harry A. Wolfson, "Halevi and Maimonides on Design, Chance and Necessity," in *The Proceedings of the American Academy for Jewish Research*, vol. XI, 1941.

2 "Israel," says Abravanel, ". . . should know and understand the course of the generations from the beginning of creation . . . until the days of the Messiah" (Comm. on Josh., introd. [f. 2, col. 3]). Full and complete historical knowledge, however, embracing not only the general course of development but also all the details, was granted, according to Abravanel, only to Moses. See Comm. on Deut. 27. 14 (f. 4B, col. 3) and Comm. on Exod., 19.1 (f. 32, col. 4).

3 *Guide*, II, 29.

4 Comm. on Lev. 25.1 (f. 8B, col. 4).

5 *Emunot*, I, 1 (First Proof for Creation out of Nothing).

6 *Deeds of God*, p. 45a.

7 *Ibid.*, p. 47a.

8 *Adv. Haer.*, II. x. 3–4; V. xxix. 2; xxxvi. 3; *City of God*, XI, 6; XIV, 13; XX, 16.

9 See Abraham bar Hiyya, *Megillat ha-Megalle*, ed. Berlin, 1924, pp. 5, 10, 13; Nahmanides, Comm. on Gen. 2.3; Lev. 25.1; Abravanel, *Deeds of God*, pp. 47b, 45c; Comm. on Lev. 25.1 (f. 8, col. 4—f. 9, col. 1).

10 That the world has a limited span of life (6000 years) after which it will be destroyed is stated in *Sanh.* 97a; *Rosh ha-Shanah* 31; *'Avodah Zarah* 9a.

11 *Deeds of God*, p. 46a.

12 Origen, *De Principiis*, III, 5.

13 *Adv. Haer.*, V, xxviii, 3.

14 Comm. on Gen. 1.2 (f. 14B, col. 3). For Abravanel's view that God actually created the world in six days, and not at one instant, as Maimonides thought (*Guide*, II, 30), see Comm. on Gen. 1.1 (f. 3, col. 4).

15 Comm. on Lev. 25.1 (f. 8, col. 4).

16 Comm. on Gen. 2.1 (f. 14B, cols. 3–4); see also *Deeds of God*, p. 11ab and *Salvations*, 19b and 20a. More especially, each of the acts of creation alludes to events in the history of Israel; thus, the creation of Adam on the sixth day alludes to the coming of the Messiah in the sixth millenium (Comm. on Gen. 1.26 [f. 14A, col. 2]).

17 See Julius Guttmann's introduction to *Megillat ha-Megalle*, p. XIII.

18 Cf. Abravanel's Comm. on Gen. 2.1 (f. 14, col. 3) and *Deeds of God*, p. 11ab with Abraham bar Hiyya's *Megillat ha-Megalle*, pp. 21–28 and Nahmanides' Comm. on Lev. 25.2 and *Torat Adonai Temimah*, ed. Jellinek, Vienna, 1872, pp. 28–29.

19 See below pp. 219, 223–5.

20 *Deeds of God*, p. 46c; Comm. on Lev. 25.1 (f. 9B, col. 1).

21 *Deeds of God*, p. 47b.

22 *Megillat ha-Megalle*, p. 11.

23 *Crown*, p. 82.
24 *Deeds of God*, p. 47ab.
25 *Ibid.*, p. 45b.
26 Isaiah 66.22.
27 *Deeds of God*, p. 45d.
28 Eccles. 1.9.
29 *Deeds of God*, p. 46a.
30 *De Principiis*, III, 5.
31 *Deeds of God*, p. 49b.
32 *Ibid.*
33 *New Heavens*, p. 49b; *Deeds of God*, pp. 47d, 48c.
34 *Timaeus*, 29-30; *Emunot*, III, introd.; Plato is referred to by Abravanel as the "divine" (Comm. on Exod. 2.10 [f. 4, col. 2]) and as a "pupil of the prophet Jeremiah" (*Deeds of God*, 55b).
35 Cf. *Khazari*, I, 95.
36 Comm. on Gen. 3.1 (f. 20, col. 1) : "The first man was in a state of intellectual perfection ;" 1.26 (f. 14, col. 2) ; 1.16 (f. 12, col. 4).
37 *Ibid.*, 5.3 (f. 26, col. 3).
38 *City of God*, XIII, 20; XIV, 26.
39 Augustine's *City of God* is mentioned by Abravanel in his Comm. on Gen., 2.23 (f. 18, col. 4). In his Comm. on I Sam., 28.8 he refers to Augustine as to "one of the greatest among the Christian scholars."
40 Comm. on Gen. 2.5 (f. 17, col. 1).
41 *Ibid.*, 2.8 (f. 17, col. 4).
42 *Ibid.* This is in accordance with Galen, who thought that old age and death result from the body's inability to reproduce, through the assimilation of food, the exact measure of its natural moistness consumed by the inner heat of the body or by the surrounding air. Cf. *Megillat ha-Megalle*, p. 50. See also Jacob Guttmann, "Ueber Abraham bar Chija's 'Buch der Enthuellung'," in *Monatsschrift fuer Geschichte und Wissenschaft des Judenthums*, 1903, p. 547.
43 Cf. *City of God*, XIV, 26, and Seneca, *Epistulae Morales*, Epis. XC, 18.
44 Comm. on Gen. 2.5 (f. 17, col. 1).
45 *City of God*, XIV, 11.
46 Comm. on Gen. 2.5-7 (f. 17, col. 3): "Ibn Ezra," says Abravanel, "stirred the world by saying that the definite article which precedes the word *Adam* (man) contains a secret. By this he means that if *Adam* were a proper noun, the definite article could not be prefixed, and therefore *Adam* should be understood as a noun designating the genus of mankind, rather than an individual. To this I answer that *Adam* represented a single man and at the same time mankind as a whole, since there was no one else of his kind. This is why the definite article was added."
47 *Ibid.*, 1.27 (f. 13B, col. 1).
48 *Ibid.*, 2.18 (f. 18, col. 1).
49 *City of God*, XIV, 11.

50 According to Abravanel, Comm. on Gen. 3.1 (ed. Venice, 1579, f. 29, col. 3). Saadia's comments on Gen. 3.1, are not extant (Cf. Malter, *op. cit.*, pp. 312-313).

51 Comm. on Gen. 3.1 (f. 19, cols. 3-4).

52 See above p. 115.

53 *Salvations*, p. 47a. See also Comm. on Gen. 2.5 (f. 17, col. 1).

54 *Ibid.*, 3.1 (f. 20, col. 1).

55 *City of God*, XIV, 12.

56 *Ibid.*, XIII, 20; XIV, 14.

57 Comm. on Gen. 2.8 (f. 17, col. 4); *ibid.*, 3.22 (f. 22, col. 3).

58 *City of God*, XIV, 13.

59 Comm. on Gen., 11.1 (f. 34, col. 1).

60 *Ibid.*, 2.8 (f. 17, col. 4—f. 18, col. 1).

61 *Ibid.*, 3.17 (f. 21, col. 1).

62 *City of God*, XIV, 3.

63 Comm. on Gen. 11.1 (f. 34, col. 1).

64 *Guide*, II, 47.

65 Comm. on Gen. 5.3 (f. 26, cols. 3-4). Cf. Comm. on Deut. 14.3 (f. 27, col. 2) and *Wells*, 34a.

66 Comm. on Gen. 6.1 (f. 27, col. 4).

67 *Ibid.*, 6.1 (f. 27, col. 3).

68 *Ibid.*, 6.1; 6.11.

69 *Ibid.*, 6.5 (f. 28, col. 4).

70 *Ibid.*, 4.25 (f. 25, col. 3).

71 *Ibid.*; also 11.1 (f. 34, col. 1). In the desire for luxury, Abravanel sees the symptoms of man's moral sickness: "The natural and essential thing is fully satisfying, while the artificial things provoke desires which can never be satisfied" (*ibid.*, 11.1 [f. 34, col. 4]). On the similarity between the views of Abravanel and Seneca concerning the pursuit of the luxurious and the crafts as an aspect of city life, see Seneca, *Epistulae Morales*, Ep. XC, 19; Cf. Baer, "Don Yizḥaq Abravanel ve-Yaḥaso el Ba'ayot ha-Historia ve-ha-Mĕdina," in *Tarbiz*, VIII (1937), pp. 249-252; and see below, p. 305, note 13.

72 Comm. on Gen. 4.25 (f. 25, col. 3).

73 *Ibid.* As L. Strauss (On "Abravanel's Philosophical Tendency and Political Teachings," in *Isaac Abravanel*, six lectures, ed. by J. B. Trend and H. Loewe, Cambridge, 1937, pp. 109-110, note 2) correctly pointed out, the distinction between the three ways of life (animal, political and contemplative) is based on Aristotle, *Eth. Nic.*, I, 5, (1095b, 17ff), while its application to the three sons of Adam was made by Efodi in his commentary on *The Guide*, II, 30. (Strauss' assertion that the same application was made by Maimonides in the passage referred to is erroneous.) Abravanel, however, was influenced mainly by Albo, who applied the above distinction to the three sons of Adam in a manner much more elaborate and forceful than that of Efodi (*'Iqqarim*, III. xv. 8; ed. Husik, vol. III, pp. 134-135). Cf. Baer, *loc. cit.*, p. 251, note 24. It should also be pointed out that the idea of the three classes of man originates with Plato (*Republic*, IX, 581) who, in addition to Aristotle, may be considered a direct source of influence.

74 Comm. on Gen. 6.1 (f. 27, col. 3). Cf. *ibid.*, 11.1 (f. 34, col. 1).

75 *Ibid.*, 5.3 (f. 26, col. 4). The shortening of man's life is, according to Abravanel, not only a punishment for sin, but also a medium for man's advancement. Thus, he says that even prior to the deluge "it became evident that man could not control his material inclinations, and the longer he lived the more material he became. This is why man's life span was reduced to a maximum of 120 years. It is a sufficient span of life for one who is striving for the perfection of his soul, and as for those who look for luxuries and material benefits, long life would only induce them to greater sin. Furthermore, the proximity of death inspires man with fear and moves him to look to God for mercy. If man would have lived to be a thousand years old, his evil nature would have induced him to postpone repeatedly his concentration on moral perfection and as a result he would have indulged in material passions hopelessly" (*ibid.*, 6.1 [f. 27, col. 4]).

76 Comm. on Deut. 14.3 (f. 27, col. 2).

77 Comm. on Gen. 10.1 (f. 33, col. 1).

78 *Ibid.*, 10.2 (f. 33, col. 2).

79 *Ibid.*, 11.1 (f. 34, col. 2).

80 *Ibid.;* cf. *Khazari*, I, 49; *ibid.*, II, 68.

81 Comm. on Gen. 2.19 (f. 18, col. 2).

82 *Ibid.*

83 *Ibid.*, 2.1 (f. 34, col. 2).

84 *Ibid.*

85 *Ibid.*, 10.1 (f. 33, col. 1).

86 *Ibid.*

87 *Ibid.*

88 *Ibid.*, 11.10 (f. 34, col. 2). The implied definition of nationhood is of great interest. In connection with L. Strauss' remark that in "Abravanel's usage, *nation* often has the meaning of a religious community" (*op. cit.*, p. 110, note 2), I must say that Abravanel differentiates very clearly between religion and nation. As Abravanel sees it, religion is a force which may cement various nations into one national unit (*Wells*, p. 23a); but it is definitely distinct from nation and cannot be identified with it (see below, p. 212).

89 *Khazari*, I, 47, 95.

90 Comm. on Gen. 11.1 (f. 35, col. 1); Cf. Comm. on Exod., introduction. (Like Halevi, *Khazari*, I, 95, Abravanel maintains that Israel is the "core of the human race and the rest of humanity is like its peeling.") The racial unity and the racial selection of Israel are discussed also in *Crown*, pp. 50–51.

91 *Crown*, pp. 37–38; *Principles*, p. 14b; Comm. on Exod. 23.20 (f. 45, col. 1).

92 Comm. on Deut. 14.1 (f. 27, col. 2); cf. *ibid.*, 12.20 (f. 25, col. 1).

93 Comm. on Gen. 11.1 (f. 34, col. 2).

94 Comm. on Exod. 24.17 (f. 47, cols. 3–4).

95 Comm. on Deut. 32.6 (f. 13B, col. 3); *ibid.*, 8.1 (f. 18, col. 3), 33.13 (f. 20B, col. 4); 32.6 (f. 13B, col. 2); Comm. on Exod. 23.20 (f. 45,

cols. 1–2); Comm. on II Kings, 17.34–35 (f. 293, col. 1); Comm. on I Sam. 24.24 (f. 187, col. 3); *Crown*, pp. 44, 46–48. In the selection of Palestine, as in the selection of Israel, Abravanel follows Halevi (*Khazari*, II, 12, 14).

    96 Comm. on Exod. 18.13 (f. 31, col. 4); 24.17 (f. 47, col. 3).
    97 See below, pp. 206–208.
    98 Comm. on Deut. 28.15 (f. 5B, cols. 2–3).
    99 Comm. on Gen. 2.1 (f. 14B, col. 4).
    100 *Salvations*, p. 56a; See also *Announcer*, p. 10a.
    101 Comm. on Isaiah, introduction (f. 3, col. 1); 2 end (f. 9, col. 2, ed. 1641); Comm. on Malachi 3.19 (f. 301, col. 2). Abravanel's view on the two purposes of Resurrection—the establishment of justice (see above, p. 118) and the convincing of all men that "it is God to whom the kingdom belongs" (*Announcer*, pp. 14b, 16c)—might have been borrowed from Crescas, *Or Adonai*, III, iv. 2.

    102 *Announcer*, on Psalm 47. Even then, however, there will be a difference between God's rule over the nations and his rule over Israel; for fully and permanently will His providence be manifested in Israel only (*ibid.*).

    103 Cf. *City of God*, XXII, 30. Comm. on Ezek. 36.26 (f. 203, col. 1).
    104 Comm. on I Sam. 25.29 (f. 128, cols. 2–3); *Deeds of God*, pp. 53d, 55a.
    105 *Ibid.*, p. 56b.
    106 *Ibid.*, p. 56c.
    107 Cf. above, p. 295, note 96; and see A. C. McGiffert, *A History of Christian Thought*, 1932, II, pp. 364–365.

    108 Saadia's theory according to which God's foreknowledge that certain developments will take place is not the cause of these developments is typical of this attempt (*Emunot*, IV, 4 end, 5). Cf. *City of God*, XIV, 11.

    109 See *Inheritance*, p. 95.
    110 Baer, *op. cit.*, p. 245: "Abravanel was the first among the Jews who *added the views of the Renaissance to those of traditional Judaism* and began to see tradition through the illuminating mirror of a *Humanistic historical concept*" (italics mine, B.N.).

    111 Machiavelli, *The Prince*, XV.
    112 *Ibid.*

CHAPTER THREE

    1 Aristotle, *Politics*, I, i. 8–9 (1252b 30—1253a 5).
    2 Augustine, *City of God*, XIX, 12, 15; Irenaeus, *Against Heresies*, V, xxiv. 2.
    3 *Politics*, I. 1.11–12 (1253a 20—1253a 30); II. i.7 (1261b 10ff); III. i.8 (1275b 20); VII. vii.5 (1328b 15ff).
    4 *Against Heresies*, V. xxiv.2; *City of God*, XIX, 15.

5 *Ibid.*
6 Thomas Aquinas, *On the Governance of Rulers* (*De Regimine Principum*), Eng. trans. by Gerald B. Phelan, London & New York, 1938, chap. I, p. 33.
7 *Ibid.*, p. 34.
8 *Ibid.*, p. 35.
9 *Ibid.;* see also *Summa Contra Gentiles,* III–II, chap. LXXXV.
10 *On Governance of Rulers,* p. 39.
11 Comm. on Gen. 11.1 (f. 34, col. 1).
12 *Wells*, 56b.
13 Comm. on Gen. 11.1 (f. 34, col. 2); Baer (*op. cit.* p. 248) and L. Strauss (*op. cit.* pp. 109–110) minimize or disregard the influence of the Church Fathers on Abravanel's view with regard to the origin of the state, and stress the influence of Seneca. In our opinion, greater emphasis should be laid upon the dissimilarity rather than the similarity of the political views of Seneca and Abravanel. According to Seneca, man, even before his nature was corrupted by vice, had some form of government—namely, kingship—in which the "ruler ruled well and the subject obeyed well" (Epis. XC, 4–5), and consequently each man was not a "king unto himself." As for the happiness of man in primeval times, it was, in the view of Seneca, one of innocence only, and not of spiritual perfection in any sense. Therefore, Seneca considered it desirable for man to rise from the primitive state, if he could rise through the urge of progress and not through the corruption of vice. Seneca's view of man in the state of innocence is definitely low. "No matter how excellent and guileless was the life of the men at that age, they were not wise men" (Epis. XC, 44). And again: "It was by reason of their ignorance of things that the men of these days were innocent; and it makes a great deal of difference whether one wills not to sin or has not the knowledge to sin. Justice was unknown to them, unknown was prudence, unknown also self-control and bravery . . . Virtue is not vouchsafed to a soul unless that soul has been trained and taught, and by unremitting practice brought to perfection" (Epis. XC, 46). Contrary to this, Abravanel maintained, as we have seen, that man, in the original state of nature, was not only materially but also spiritually on the highest level he ever reached, and thus civilization, symbolized by the state, represents nothing but a moral decline. Abravanel is, therefore, basically influenced by the Church Fathers and not by Seneca. Or, we should rather say, he accepted Seneca's views only to the extent that the Church Fathers accepted them. Nor should one ignore the possibility of a direct influence by Plato, whose view of primitive society (*Laws*, III, 679) is more favorable than that of Seneca. In 1505, when Abravanel wrote his Comm. on Gen., Plato's *Laws* was already well known in Ficino's Latin translation.
14 *Politics*, I. i.4 (1252a 25—1252a 30); I. ii. 7, 13 (1254a 15, 1254b 15–20).
15 Augustine, *City of God,* XIX, 15; St. Ambrose, *Exhortatio virginitatis,* I.3. Cf. Seneca, Epis. XIV. 2.
16 *City of God,* XIX, 12.
17 Comm. on Gen. 10.1 (f. 33, col. 1); Comm. on Deut. 20.10 (f. 41, cols. 3–4).
18 Comm. on Isaiah, introd. (f. 3, col. 2); Comm. on Exod. 21.2 (f. 40, col. 2). The same view was held by Seneca (*On Benefits*, III, xx. 1), and like

Seneca (*ibid.*, III, xix. 4) Abravanel speaks of the "general aversion to domination" and the "common hatred of being a slave" (Comm. on Deut. 20.10 [f. 41, col. 4]).

19 *Ibid.*, 21.8 (f. 41, col. 2). Thus Abravanel says that "if an Israelite master kills a Canaanite slave he should be punished, not because he committed manslaughter, since such a slave is his personal property [which he is entitled to destroy at will], but because he manifested a degree of cruelty and bad manners" which cannot be permitted in an Israelite.

20 *Politics*, I. i.5 (1252b 8–9).

21 Comm. on Deut. 20.10 (f. 41, col. 4). That "certain races are born to govern, and certain others to be governed and to serve" was a view advocated by Dante, *De Monarchia*, II, 7 (Eng. trans. by F. J. Church, London, 1879, p. 234); see also *ibid.*, II, 3 (p. 216).

22 See Comm. on Deut. 20.10 (f. 41, col. 4); 18.1 (f. 37, col. 2).

23 Cicero, *Laws*, I. 14–16; *Republic*, III, 22.

24 For a detailed discussion of the Roman Law in its application by the Church Fathers, see A. J. Carlyle, *A History of Mediaeval Theory in the West*, I, pp. 102–160.

25 Origen, *Contra Celsum*, V. 40.

26 Thus according to Irenaeus, the "Decalogue consists of natural precepts which from the beginning God implanted in mankind," while the Mosaic Law is just a "yoke" with which He "found it necessary to bridle the desires of the Jews" (*Adv. Haer.*, IV, 15:1). Similarly, St. Ambrose maintained that the Mosaic Law was given to man because he had failed to obey the natural law (*Epis.* LXXIII, 10).

27 Justin Martyr (*First Apology, XIV*), Jerome (*Epis.* CXXX.14), and Augustine (*Epis.*, CLVII,4) are only some of the Church Fathers who reflect definite communistic tendencies. This position was also maintained in the Middle Ages. As Ernest Barker, in his essay on Mediaeval Political Thought, says: "It had been a general doctrine in the Church since the days of St. Augustine that communism was the ideal condition of society" (see *Social and Political Ideas of Some Great Mediaeval Thinkers*, edited by F. J. C. Hearnshaw, London, 1923, p. 24). That Abravanel shared this view is clearly indicated in his Comm. on Gen. 11.1 (f. 34, col. 3).

28 See above, notes 4 and 15.

29 *Guide*, II, 40 (p. 234).

30 *Ibid.*, pp. 232–233.

31 See, for instance, *Politics*, IV, i.2 (1288b 21—28); *ibid.*, IV, ix.9 (1296a 7).

32 *Principles*, p. 12a; Comm. on Exod. 19.1 (f. 32, col. 3).

33 *Principles*, p. 16a; Comm. on Exod. 19.1 (f. 32, col. 3): "The commandments given to Adam and Noah did not represent conventional or natural laws, i.e., laws inherent in man's nature. They were divine. The commandments given to the Fathers were also divine. They were not called laws because they were not given to a mass of people, but were meant to serve as directives of conduct for certain individuals only." See also *ibid.*, 21.2 (f. 40, col. 2), from which it is clear that Abravanel considered the Decalogue as belonging to the

Divine Law in its broader meaning and to the Constitutional Law in its narrower meaning, but not to the Natural Law.

34 *Ibid.*, 19.1 (f. 33, col. 1).
35 *Ibid.* (cols. 1–2).
36 Comm. on Deut. 16.18 (f. 33, col. 4).
37 *Ibid.* See also *ibid.*, 17.14 (f. 37, col. 2).
38 *Ibid.*, 16.18 (f. 33, col. 4).
39 Cf. L. Strauss, *loc. cit.*, p. 124.
40 Deut., 16.18.
41 Comm. on Deut. 16.18 (f. 38, col. 4).
42 Mish. Sanh. I, 1, 4, 6.

43 See for instance Maimonides' "principle of faith" that "there has never been, nor will there ever be, any other divine Law but that of Moses our Teacher" (*Guide*, II, 39). See also *Sefer ha-Mada*, Hil. Yes. ha-Tor., IX, 1 and Comm. on Sanh. X (ninth principle).

44 Comm. on Exod. 19.1 (f. 33, col. 1); Comm. on I Kings, 1.53 (f. 197, col. 1). The problem of the discrepancy between the Mosaic Law and many of the ordinances issued in later times is solved by Abravanel in the following manner: The post-Mosaic decrees were intended to be applied only in certain generations and under certain circumstances. "These too were ordered to Moses on Sinai and submitted by him orally to his successors" (*Principles of Faith*, 18a).

45 Comm. on Deut. 16.18 (f. 33, col. 4). See Mish. Sanh. I, 5.
46 See his Comm. on Deut. 16.18 (ed. Pesaro, 1513/1514).
47 Comm. on Deut. 16.18 (f. 34, col. 1).
48 *De Republica*, I, 10.

49 Comm. on Deut. 16.18 (f. 34, col. 1). "There are kingdoms in which the appointment of judges is in the hands of the king who, as the head of the judicial system, is supposed to be entitled to organize that system. This is the law and custom in the kingdoms of Castile, Aragon and Naples. There are countries, however, in which the appointment of judges is the privilege of the people. This is the case in some domains of the Spanish peninsula, in France, and the entire land of the West [i.e., England]."

50 Comm. on Deut. 17.8 (f. 34, col. 3)
51 Mish. Sanh. I, 6; IV, 3.
52 Comm. on Deut. 17.8 (f. 34, cols. 3–4).
53 *Ibid.*, f. 34, col. 3.
54 *Ibid.*
55 *Ibid.*, f. 35, col. 1.
56 *Ibid.*

57 R. Elazar ben Yaåkov, in *Sanh.*, 46a (שמעתי שבית דין מכין ועונשין שלא מן התורה).

58 Comm. on Deut. 17.8 (f. 34, col. 4); *ibid.*, 17.14 (f. 36, col. 1).
59 *Ibid.*, 17.8 (f. 34, col. 3).

60 See R. W. Carlyle and A. J. Carlyle, *History of Mediaeval Political Theory in the West*, VI, pp. 134, 208–209.

61 On the relations between the cities and the Crown and the procedure by which the former elected their representatives to the Cortes during the reign of Ferdinand and Isabella, see M. A. S. Hume, *Spain*, Cambridge, 1940, pp. 18–21.

62 See his Comm. on Judges, introd. (f. 39, col. 1).

63 *Ibid.*, introd. (f. 39, col. 2). See especially *ibid.*, 17.1 (f. 65, col. 1) and 18.1 (f. 66, col. 1).

64 *Ibid.*, introd. (f. 39, col. 3).

65 *Ibid.* (f. 39, cols. 3–4).

66 *Politics*, IV, xi. 9–21 (1295b 29–1296b 9). The influence on Abravanel of Plato's statements in the *Laws* (III, 693C and VI, 756E) in favor of a government combining monarchic and democratic elements is extremely unlikely. First, Ficino's Latin translation of the *Laws* did not appear before 1484, that is, after Abravanel had written his above-quoted Comm. on Judges and, in all probability, also those parts of his Comm. on Deut. which relate to this discussion (the possibility that he was acquainted with the abridged Latin version of the *Laws* by George of Trebizond is remote). Second, Plato's ideal government in the *Laws* is a restricted monarchy or a controlled democracy, as is evident from the examples he adduces for his scheme (*ibid.*, III, 693, 694, 695, 698), but does not have the definite features of a "mixed government" of the kind we find in Aristotle and Cicero.

67 Cicero, *Laws*, III, v.12.

68 *Ibid.*, III, iii.8.

69 *Ibid.*, III, iii.6.

70 *Ibid.*, III, iii.8.

71 *Ibid.*

72 Polybius, *Histories*, VI, 11–18.

73 To these classical sources we should add, however, the influence of Thomas Aquinas who likewise maintained that a mixed government is the "best form of polity" and, furthermore, that this kind of government was in existence in the Mosaic days. According to St. Thomas, Moses and his successors were like "kings," the seventy elders represented the aristocracy, and the "rulers" the democratic element. See *Summa Theologica*, II–I, Q. CV, Art 1. Similarly, in the wake of Thomas, John of Paris believed that the Jews in the days of Moses and Joshua enjoyed the advantages of a "mixed government"—a combination of kingship, aristocracy and democracy—which he considered the ideal governmental form. See his *Tractatus de potestate regia et papali*, capit. xix (see Jean Leclercq, *Jean de Paris et l'Ecclésiologie du xiiie siècle*, Paris, 1942, pp. 236–237).

74 Comm. on Exod. 18.13 (f. 31, col. 4).

75 See Ibn Ezra's Comm. on Exod., 18.21.

76 *Ibid.* Ibn Ezra applied to this condition the saying from Proverbs 28.2: "For the transgression of the land, many are the princes thereof."

77 Comm. on Exod. 18.13 (f. 31, col. 4).

78 Comm. on I Sam. 8.4 (f. 92, col. 3); Comm. on Deut. 17.14 (f. 36, col. 1).

79 Comm. on Judges, 17.7 (f. 66, col. 2).

80 "The Venetian constitution," writes Horatio Brown, "compelled the envy and admiration of all Italian and numerous foreign statesmen" (*Cambridge Modern History*, I, p. 270).

81 This is the place to point out that the arrangement of four councils for each tribe is already proposed in Abravanel's Comm. on Deut. 1.9 (f. 4, col. 1), and this, in complete opposition to his unqualified stand against tribal institutions in the same Comm. on Deut. (16.18 [f. 33, col. 4]). The glaring contradiction can be explained only if we assume that the remarks in favor of tribal institutions were added by Abravanel when he revised the manuscript of his commentary shortly after his escape from Naples to Corfu (see Comm. on Deut., introd., f. la) while the statement in opposition to tribal institutions was written when Abravanel was still in Spain and somehow escaped revision. In a prolific writer like Abravanel, who wrote his books not always under ideal conditions, such occurrences are understandable.

82 See *Cambridge Modern History*, I, pp. 276–277.

83 Comm. on Exod. 18.13 (f. 31, col. 4).

84 Exodus, 18.24.

85 Deut. 1.13, 15. That the "rulers" were chosen by the people and not by Moses was a view held by Thomas Aquinas who also referred to the above section in Deut. See *Summa Theologica*, II–I, Q. CV, Art. 1.

86 In fact, in the same Comm. on Exod. 19.1 (f. 32, col. 4), Abravanel reaffirms his view regarding the six institutions of the secular and spiritual governments.

87 See above, p. 161.

88 Comm. on Exod. 18.13 (f. 31, col. 4).

89 Comm. on Judges, introd. (f. 39, col. 3); *ibid.* (f. 40, col. 4); Comm. on Deut. 16.18 (f. 33, col. 4).

90 A. J. Carlyle, *A History of Mediaeval Political Theory*, VI, p. 206.

91 Comm. on Deut. 17.14 (f. 36, col. 1).

92 Cf. Dante, *De Monarchia*, I, xiv–xv; "For Wycliffe as for Ockham the necessity of unity in the state is the main proof of the excellence of monarchy" (John Neville Figgis, *The Divine Right of Kings*, Cambridge, 1934, p. 69).

93 This is the view of Aristotle. See *Politics*, III, x.6 (1286a 32ff). Similarly, Abravanel's argument that "if the king is just, it is still better to have a government of many just men" (Comm. on Deut. 17.14 [f. 36, col. 1], and Comm. on I Sam. 8.4 [f. 92, col. 3]) is taken from the *Politics*.

94 Comm. on Deut. 17.14 (f. 36, col. 1); Comm. on I Sam. 8.4 (f. 92, col. 3).

95 Cf. *Wells*, 63ab.

96 On the happiness enjoyed by a self-governing people in comparison with a people ruled by a king, see also Abravanel's Comm. on Judges 18.7 (f. 66, col. 2).

97 It should be pointed out that although military expansionism is for Abravanel a sign of health in a state (cf. *Wells*, 63ab), his preferred policy

for a state is one of peace. See Comm. on Deut. 20.10 (f. 41, col. 3) and below, note 123.

98 *Ibid.* 17.14 (f. 36, col. 1); Comm. on I Sam. 8.4 (f. 92, cols. 3–4). The last two quotations from Abravanel are, with the exception of some revisions, in accordance with the translation of B. Halper, *Post-Biblical Hebrew Literature*, Philadelphia, 1921, pp. 221–224.

99 Comm. on Deut. 17.14 (f. 36, col. 2, 4); Comm. on I Sam. 8.4 (f. 93, col. 3).

100 Comm. on Deut. 17.14 (f. 36, col. 2).

101 Comm. on Judges, introd. (f. 40, col. 2). Cf. Maimonides, *Sefer Shofetim*, Hilkhot Melakhim, IV, 1.

102 *Ibid.*, IV, 9.

103 Comm. on Judges, introd. (f. 40, col. 2); Hilkhot Melakhim, IV, 10.

104 Comm. on Judges, introd. (f. 40, col. 2). Cf. Mish. Sanh. II, 2.5.

105 Comm. on Judges, introd. (f. 40, col. 2); Comm. on I Kings, 1.53 (f. 196, cols. 1–2).

106 I Sam. 8.11–17.

107 Hilkhot Melakhim, IV, 2–7.

108 Comm. on I Sam. 8.9 (f. 94, col. 1). The same view was held by Thomas Aquinas, *Summa Theologica*, II–I, Q. CV, Art. 1, Reply Obj. 5. Cf. *Sanh.* 20b.

109 Comm. on I Sam. 8.12 (f. 94, cols. 1–2).

110 *Ibid.* 8.14 (f. 94, col. 2).

111 *Ibid.*

112 *Politics*, III. ix,4 (1285a 27). Abravanel actually quotes this statement of Aristotle in his Comm. on I Sam. 8.4 (f. 92, col. 2). This is one of the many answers implied in Abravanel's political writings to Baer's questioning whether he read Aristotle's *Politics* (see Baer, *op. cit.*, p. 245).

113 See, for instance, John of Salisbury's *Policraticus*, IV, 1–4; VII, 17 (Eng. trans. by John Dickinson, New York, 1927); Thomas Aquinas, *Summa Theologica*, II–I, Q. CV, Art. 1 (Obj. 5).

114 Quoted by Carlyle, *A History of Mediaeval Political Theory*, VI, p. 136.

115 Comm. on I Sam. 8.4 (f. 93, col. 3).

116 Comm. on Judges, introd. (f. 40, col. 1). Cf. Maimonides' Commentary on Mish. Sanh. II, 2 and Tal. Sanh. 19a.

117 Comm. on Judges, introd. (f. 40, col. 1).

118 Comm. on Deut. 17.14 (f. 36, col. 4).

119 *Politics*, III, x.7 (1286b 8); III, xi.11–12 (1288a 7ff).

120 *The Offices*, I. xxvii.93.

121 Seneca, *De clementia*, I, vii.1: "God is the standard after which a king should model himself."

122 Comm. on Deut. 14.14 (f. 36, col. 4—f. 37, col. 1). Modesty is repeatedly stressed by Abravanel as a king's cardinal virtue. Cf. Cicero's praise of humility in public servants: "The higher we are placed, the more humbly we should walk" (*The Offices*, I, xxvi.90).

123 Comm. on Deut. 14.14 (f. 36, col. 4—f. 37, col. 1); 20.10 (f. 41, col. 3). Abravanel's criticism against practices of cruelty and vengeance by kings is inspired by Seneca whose parable about the king of the bees who has no sting he cites in support of his view (Cf. Seneca, *De clementia*, I. xix.1–3). Abravanel's opposition to military aggressiveness when satisfaction can be obtained by peaceful negotiations and his insistence upon humanitarian practices in war bears a close resemblance to the position of Cicero (*The Offices*, I, xi.35–36). Although Abravanel maintains that overwhelming military strength is the only true assurance for peace (Comm. on I Kings, 11.42 [f. 242, col. 2]), he advocates restraint in military action since "every war involves great risks and therefore should be avoided whenever possible . . . the outcome of wars is often contrary to all logical calculations . . . Sometimes victory is gained by those who initiate the war, but sometimes they are defeated by peace loving people who had no experience in warfare. Therefore it is more proper to choose peace which is real than to rely on victory which is doubtful." (Comm. on Deut. 20.10 [f. 41, col. 3]). On the general clamor for peace in the Middle Ages as expressed in medieval political literature, see Hearnshaw, *op. cit.*, p. 109.

124 Comm. on Judges, 10.14 (f. 54, col. 4). Abravanel's motivation for a king to behave justly and lawfully (Comm. on Deut. 17.14 [f. 37, col. 1]) is taken from medieval and classical literature. His first reason, i.e., that the king is like a mirror for the people, since he offers an example for their moral behavior, is borrowed from Cicero, *Republic*, II, xlii.69 (undoubtedly through an intermediary source, since *The Republic* was non-extant in the Middle Ages), and *Laws*, III, xiv.31. The second argument that the government of a just king is stable and enduring while that of a tyrant cannot last is taken from Seneca, *De clementia*, I, viii, 6; I. x; xi.4, and also from St. Thomas, *On the Governance of Rulers*, chap. 10, pp. 80–81. The third, that the reward of just kings is the heavenly beatitude of the world to come, is again taken from Thomas Aquinas, *ibid.*, chaps. 8–9.

125 Comm. on Judges, 10.14 (f. 54, col. 4). Cf. *Policraticus*, IV, 1.

126 *Ibid.*, introd. (f. 40, col. 1); Comm. on Deut. 17.14 (f. 36, col. 4; f. 37, col. 1). According to Abravanel, the purpose of prohibiting the acquisition of many horses is to restrain the king's ambition for war and conquest, while the prohibition against the accumulation of much money is aimed at preventing the development of greed and avarice which will finally lead the king to acquire possessions by robbery and extortion. Cf. *Policraticus*, VII, 17. Cf. also Thomas Aquinas, *Summa Theologica*, II–I, Q. CV, Art. 1, Reply Obj. 2.

127 Comm. on I Sam. 8.4 (f. 92, col. 3).

128 *Ibid.*, col. 2.

129 *Ibid.*, col. 3; Comm. on Deut. 17.14 (f. 36, col. 1).

130 *Ibid.;* Comm. on I Sam. 8.4 (f. 92, col. 4).

131 *Ibid.*, col. 2.

132 Thomas Aquinas, *On the Governance of Rulers*, VI (pp. 58–59); Stephen C. Tornay, *Ockham, Studies and Selections*, La Salle (Illinois), 1938, p. 81, note 4.—That Occam was studied by Jewish scholastics in the 15th century can be seen, among other things, from 'Ali ben Joseph Ḥabilio's translation of his *Summa logicae* into Hebrew (see MSS. *Codices Hebraici Biblioth. I. B. De-Rossi*, II, Parma, 1803, p. 49 [No. 457.10]; and cf. *ibid.*, I, p. 159 [No. 281]).

133 Comm. on Deut. 17.14 (f. 36, cols. 1–2); Comm. on I Sam. 8.4 (f. 92, col. 4).

134 *Ibid.*

135 Commentary on Aristotle's *Politics*, I, 12 (quoted by Lester K. Born, in the introduction to Erasmus' *The Education of a Christian Prince*, New York, 1936, p. 116). See also *Summa Theologica*, II–I, Q. CV, Art. 1, Obj. 5 (where true kingship, as opposed to tyranny, is praised as the ideal form of government) and I, Q. CIII, Art. 3 ("The best government is government by one").

136 See *City of God*, V. 19 (wherein a differentiation is made between kings and tyrants); V. 24 (dealing with the behavior of a good emperor); and V. 25–26 (wherein Christian emperors are highly praised).

137 See *Announcer*, p. 19a; Comm. on Isaiah 34, epilogue (f. 53, col. 4).

138 See Born, *op. cit.*, p. 103.

139 *Policraticus*, IV, 1, 10, 12.

140 *De monarchia*, I, 7.

141 See Sharwood Smith's essay on "Dante and World Empire" in Hearnshaw's *The Social and Political Ideas of Some Great Mediaeval Thinkers*, pp. 107–138.

142 See A. J. Carlyle, *History of Mediaeval Political Theory*, VI, pp. 136–138.

143 Sanh. 20b.

144 *Sefer Shofetim*, Hilkhot Melakhim, I, 1.

145 See *Emunot*, X, 9. Saadia, who stresses the negative aspects of the usually excessive pride of princes, nevertheless considers the rule of kings beneficial and vital for the social order (מה שזכרוהו מסידור העולם בשמירה ובמשפט ובמנוי, אינו נדחה). He advocates a rule moderated by "wisdom" (which includes consideration of the world to come) for the good of both king and people. Halevi's position on the question of kingship in general (though not in its particular relationship to Israel) is clear from the many passages in which he stresses the resemblance of the Divine rule to kingship, as well as from his various descriptions of royalty (see especially, *Khazari*, IV, 3, pp. 208–209; and IV, 5, p. 213).—As for Ibn Ezra, see his Commentary on Deut. 33.5, in which Moses is regarded as a king, and his Comm. on Gen. 49.10, in which the establishment of kingship in Israel is declared as an improvement on the preceding state of affairs.

146 In his Comm. on Gen. 49.10, Nahmanides speaks of the eternity of the Israelite Kingdom and the inviolable sanctity of the privilege of kingship granted by God. See Gersonides, Comm. on the Pentateuch (Deut. 16.18), Venice, 1547 (f. 224, cols. 1–2), and Albo, *'Iqqarim*, IV, 26.—See also Arama's view in favor of Monarchism in his *'Aqeda*, on Exod., XLIII, p. 134b.

147 Comm. on I Sam. 8.4 (f. 91, col. 2—f. 92, col. 2). See also Comm. on Hosea, 13.11 (f. 238, col. 3). Most of the pro-monarchist authorities in Jewry based themselves on Deut. 17.15 ("Thou shalt set a king over thee") from which they concluded that the establishment of kingship was a command of God. From a theological standpoint, however, they had to solve a great difficulty. They had to eliminate the contradiction presented by Samuel's obviously negative attitude toward kingship. To explain this difficulty away various answers were given, all of which were aimed at proving that it was not the

request for a king as such that angered the prophet, but the immoral motives which prompted that request or the unfair manner in which it was made (see, for instance, Maimonides, *Mishneh Torah,* Hilkhot Melakhim, I, 2). Abravanel convincingly refuted these theories and arrived at the conclusion that the only satisfactory explanation for Samuel's bitter reproach of kingship was the latter's objection to kingship as such. According to Abravanel, then, Samuel's exhortations against kingship constituted the true expression of Judaism on the subject. The discrepancy between the position of Samuel and that in Deuteronomy was, of course, still there. But while the authorities who preceded Abravanel attempted to explain the pronouncements in Samuel so as to coordinate them with the views expressed in Deuteronomy, Abravanel set himself the task of explaining the statement in Deuteronomy so as to agree with the position of Samuel. Abravanel's solution was that the passage in question in Deuteronomy does not contain a *command,* but only a *permission* to establish a kingship. Strangely enough, the idea is borrowed from the pro-monarchist Ibn Ezra (see his Comm. on Deut. 17.15). See also below, note 182.

148 On the economic, political and religious reasons that prompted the Jews of Spain to be essentially pro-monarchic, see Abraham A. Neuman, *The Jews in Spain,* I, pp. 4, 6, 12-16. The relations between the king and the Jews are concisely summarized as follows: "Whatever the temper or disposition of the individual king, wise counsel would generally dictate in his own interest a policy of strengthening the position of the Jews in the land, rendering their existence secure and promoting their prosperity" (p. 4). "In self interest, therefore, the Jews emphasized their obedience to the king's law in contrast to the general law of the nation" (p. 13).

149 F. Baer, *loc. cit.,* p. 256.

150 Desiderius Erasmus, *The Complaint of Peace,* with a digression on the *Folly of Kings in Unlimited Monarchies,* Eng. trans., London, 1795, p. 140. See also his *Praise of Folly,* New York, 1922, pp. 246-250.

151 *The Complaint of Peace,* p. 140.

152 See Machiavelli's *Discourses on the First Ten Books of Titus Livy,* I, 2.

153 *Republic,* V, 473; IX, 580. Monarchical government, although tempered by a democratic attitude, is considered by Plato also in his *Laws* (III, 694, 695) among the best forms of government (and see above, p. 306, note 66).

154 *Politics,* III. ix.10 (1287b 38). I am quoting Aristotle here according to the Ross edition.

155 *Ibid.,* IV. ii.1 (1289a 29).

156 *De Clementia,* I, 2.

157 Plutarch, *A Discourse to an Unlearned Prince,* 3.

158 Cicero, *The Offices,* III, vi.32.

159 *Ibid.,* II. viii.26 and III. vi.32.

160 *Republic,* I. 14: "Monarchy is, in my judgment, far the best of the three simple types of states." See also *ibid.,* I. 35.

161 See *Laws,* III. ii.4, where Cicero speaks favorably of kings, and III. vii.15, where he states that the monarchy was rejected in Rome "not so much through the fault of the kingship as that of the king."

162 Abravanel lauded Alfonso V as an ideal king. See Comm. on Joshua, introd., f. 1a.

163 See introduction to his Comm. on I Kings (f. 188, col. 1) and introduction to his Comm. on Deut., f. 1a. See also introduction to *Wells,* 7b.

164 Comm. on I Kings, introduction (f. 188, col. 2).

165 Comm. on Deut. 17.14 (f. 37, cols. 1, 2). Thus Abravanel completely justifies Solomon's executions of his opponents, including his brother, on the ground that they harbored intentions of revolt (see Comm. on I Kings, 1.22–31 [f. 200, cols. 3–4—f. 201, cols. 1, 2, 3]). Repeatedly Abravanel stresses that no one is permitted to harm his king or to plot against him (see Comm. on I Sam. 24.7 [f. 124, col. 4], and II Sam. I, 14 [f. 139, col. 1]). The same view is expressed with regard to the nations as well as with regard to Israel (see, for instance, his denunciation of the Gibeonites for their unfaithfulness to their king, Comm. on Josh. 10.1 [f. 20, cols. 1–2]). It is stressed, moreover, not only in respect to one's own king, but also in respect to foreign kings in whose service one happens to be. What is more, one should not rebel against a foreign king even when the latter is engaged in war against one's *own* king and nation (see his strong objection to Gersonides' opinion that David requested to join Achish, in his military expedition against Israel, in order to sabotage the latter's activities "which would constitute a conspiracy and extremely ugly conduct"—Comm. on I Sam. 29.5 (f. 135, cols. 1–2). In view of these emphatic statements against anti-monarchist revolutions, I consider Fritz Baer's conjecture (see *op. cit.,* p. 242, and Baer's article on Abravanel in *Encyclopaedia Judaica,* I, p. 585) that Abravanel participated in the conspiracy of the Portuguese nobles against João II—and this despite Abravanel's vehement denials (see, e.g., Comm. on Josh. introd., f. 1, col. 1)—as impossible to accept. A man who had conspired against his king would not have denounced conspirators against kingly rule so unreservedly and unqualifiedly as did Abravanel; nor would he have stressed the sanctity of the king's authority and its inviolability under *all* circumstances.

166 Comm. on Deut. 17.14 (f. 37, col. 2). Similarly Bracton (Bretton), the English writer on law of the thirteenth century, maintained that if the king "breaks the law, it is enough that he await the vengeance of God, for none of his subjects may punish him." See Figgis, *op. cit.,* p. 34.

167 Comm. on I Sam. 8.4 (f. 93, col. 2). See above, pp. 178–9. Cf. *De Monarchia,* III. 16: "The electors do not choose the Emperor, but merely announce God's Choice."

168 According to Abravanel, even the sinful kings of Israel, although not directly selected by God, still came to power by divine will "to punish the offspring of David's house" (Comm. on I Kings, 1.53, supplementary remarks to chapter I, f. 196, col. 3). In discussing the kings of the nations, Abravanel says that they represent some of "God's rule and glory" (Comm. on Deut. 17.14 [f. 37, col. 2]). That all power comes from God was a concept upheld, among others, by Augustine, *City of God,* V. 21.

169 *History of Mediaeval Political Theory in the West,* VI, p. 206.

170 *Policraticus,* VIII, 20: "It is just for public tyrants to be killed" (Dickinson's trans., p. 370). "Nor is blame attached to any of those by whose

valor a penitent and humbled people was thus set free, but their memory is preserved in affection by posterity as servants of the Lord" (pp. 368–369).

171 "The supreme power of the prince is limited by the law of nature and by the positive law common to all nations. If the executive power oversteps the limits of his power, the people may use sword against him," *Dialogue*, II, p. 924m, i.60 (translated by Stephen C. Tornay, *Ockham, Studies and Selections*, p. 81).

172 *On the Governance of Rulers*, VI.

173 *Ibid.*

174 "When the people enthrone a king they solemnly undertake to follow his instructions and carry out his orders. This undertaking is without reservations or conditions. It is an absolute pact (אמנה מוחלטת). This is why rebels against a king deserve the death penalty regardless of whether the king is a villain or a pious man" (Comm. on Deut., 17.14 [f. 37, cols. 1–2]).

175 Hobbes, *Leviathan*, II, 18.

176 See A. J. Carlyle, *Political Liberty, a History of the Conception in the Middle Ages and Modern Times*, p. 16.

177 See, for instance, Baer (*loc. cit.*), pp. 255–256; Strauss (*loc. cit.*, p. 116); Sarachek (*op. cit.*, p. 156).

178 See Ernest Barker's introduction to John Healey's translation of *The City of God*, New York, 1931, p. xxxii and E. Gilson, *The Spirit of Mediaeval Philosophy*, New York, 1940, p. 387.

179 Comm. on I Sam. 8.4 (f. 92, col. 1 and especially f. 93, col. 3); Cf. Comm. on Deut. 17.14 (f. 36, col. 2).

180 Comm. on I Sam. 8.4 (f. 93, col. 4): "The institution of a king was essential for all other nations because they did not have the guidance of divine providence."

181 Comm. on Deut. 17.14 (f. 36, col. 2).

182 Comm. on I Sam. 8.4 (f. 93, col. 2). Comm. on Deut. 17.14 (f. 36, col. 3): "The asking for a king is neither a good deed nor a transgression prohibited by the Law. The establishment of monarchy was not a duty, an obligation imposed upon the people, but a permission, a concession on the part of the law to human weakness and the evil inclination. In other words, this request is far from being praised as a virtue, yet it is no sin either. If it were a full-fledged sin, the Law would not have permitted it." See above, note 147.

183 Comm. on I Sam. 8.4 (f. 92, col. 1): "This shows that the very appointment of a king, of whatever kind, was a great evil and a criminal offense."

184 *Ibid.*, 8.4 (f. 93, col. 3).

185 Comm. on Exodus, 14.1 (f. 32, col. 4). On the dual aspect of Moses' leadership see also Abravanel's Comm. on I Sam. 9.1 (f. 95, col. 1): "Moses was the master of all rulers, the first and foremost among all kings, saviours and lawgivers."

186 Comm. on I Kings, 1.53 (f. 196, col. 4). Abravanel's view that Moses, as the head of both governments, was the source of all authority, spiritual and temporal (*ibid.*), is borrowed from Christian sources. According to Pope Gelasius I (fifth century), "the true and perfect king and priest was Christ

himself" who separated these two offices (A. J. Carlyle, *History of Mediaeval Political Theory*, I, pp. 190–191). The Gelasian view about the two authorities, the secular and ecclesiastical, both of which derived from God and were separated by Christ himself, who alone was both king and priest, was stressed by the twelfth-century canonist Stephen of Tournai (A. J. Carlyle, *op. cit.*, p. 198).

187 Comm. on Deut. 17.8 (f. 34, col. 4): "The assembly of the Synhedrion was divinely inspired. The equality of their number to that of Moses' High Court was to indicate that the spirit of Moses and that of the prophesying elders rested upon them. This is also evident from the place of their meeting—the Chamber of the Hewn Stone of the Temple—for it indicates that the Divine Presence which existed in the House of God was always with them."

188 Comm. on Deut. 17.14 (f. 36, col. 2): "The kings of Judah and Israel were obscurantists (מורדי אור); they led the people away from the path of righteousness, as was the case with Jeroboam, all the rest of the kings of Israel and most of the kings of Judah, and it was for them that the people was impoverished, ruined and exiled. Quite different is the picture we see in the judges and prophets of Israel. All of them were men of courage, God-fearing and lovers of truth. In contrast to the kings, among whom only few escaped the temptation of idolatry, none of the judges deserted God for paganism. All this proves that while the leadership of the judges was good, that of the kings was bad and harmful and dangerous in the extreme." See also *Announcer*, pp. 33b, 35ab. Cf. Thomas' praise of the judges in *Summa Theologica*, II–I. Q. CV, Art. 1, Reply Obj. 1.

189 *Guide*, II, 45.

190 Comm. on I Kings 3.5 (f. 204, col. 3—f. 205, col. 2); *ibid.*, 8.15 (f. 231, col. 2).

191 According to Abravanel, the first three kings, Saul, David and Solomon, were, like the judges (see above, note 188), "God-fearing, men of courage and truth" (Comm. on I Kings, introduction, f. 188, col. 2).

192 See Savonarola's diatribe against princes and his mockery of their claims to "genealogy from the Gods," in Villari, *op. cit.*, p. 171.

CHAPTER FOUR

1 "All the subjects which had given rise to dogmatic controversy in the Christian Church, except some too specifically Christian, were discussed by the *mutakallims*, the dogmatists of the Islam . . . That explains why Catholic and Protestant dogmatists could accuse each other of crypto-Mohammedanism" (Christian Snouck Hurgronje, *Mohammedanism*, New York, 1916, pp. 74–75).

2 Mohammed al-Ghazali, *Alchemy of Happiness*, translated by Henry A. Homes, Albany, 1873, p. 69.

3 *Ibid.*, p. 65.

4 *Ibid.*, p. 69.

5 *Ibid.*, p. 74.

6 On the differences between the view on the Messianic Age of the medieval Church and that of some of the early Fathers, see below, pp. 243–4.

7 For a thorough analysis of the essential features of Jewish Messianism and the differences between it and the Christian messianic concept, see Joseph Klausner, *Toledot ha-Ra'ayon ha-Meshiḥi be-Yisrael*, Jerusalem, 1927, pp. 9, 320–321; *Jesus of Nazareth*, London and New York, 1925, pp. 199–200, 398–400; "Ha-Mashiaḥ ha-Yehudi ve-ha-Mashiaḥ ha-Noẓri," in *Yahadut ve-Enoshiyut*, 3rd ed., Tel-Aviv, 1941, pp. 177–189.

8 *Announcer*, p. 8b.

9 *Or Adonai*, introductions to parts II and III; *'Iqqarim*, I, xxiii.7 (Husik ed. I, p. 186); IV. xlii. 1.3 (vol. IV, part II, page 413–414).

10 *Salvations*, introduction, p. 4a.

11 *Ibid.*; cf. *Announcer*, introduction, p. 2c.

12 *Announcer*, p. 41d.

13 Abravanel discusses this type of Marrano in *Announcer*, p. 6ab.

14 *Ibid.*, p. 42ac. Abravanel defines these Marranos as מורדים ופושעים. A broader treatment of Abravanel's views on the Marranos is found in B. Netanyahu, *The Marranos of Spain*, pp. 177–203.

15 *Ibid.*, p. 6abc, 27c, 33d, 77d.

16 Ezekiel, 20.32–33.

17 *Announcer*, p. 41d.

18 *Ibid.*, p. 77d.

19 Comm. on Deut. 28.49 (f. 6B, col. 4–f. 7B, col. 1).

20 Ezekiel, 20.34.

21 *Announcer*, pp. 41d, 21c: "Once Israel was chosen to be God's people, no Israelite can become a member of another nation. They belong to God's people, even against their will and even if they leave the fold of their religion. Therefore said the prophet: 'When thou passest through the waters, I will be with thee.' This is an allusion to the angry waters of baptism through which pass all those who accept their religion [i.e., Christianity]." Cf. Comm. on Isaiah 43.1–2.

22 Ezekiel, 20.35; see *Announcer*, p. 41d. According to Abravanel, "those who left the fold" will not come to the Land of Israel in a direct way, without obstacles and disturbances, but will wander around from one state to another, through strange lands and foreign nations, and it is to these wanderings that the prophets undoubtedly referred when speaking of the 'wilderness of the peoples'" (*ibid.*, 41d). Furthermore, "the sinful and the rebellious who will hold on to their wickedness and will fail to return to God will die during those wanderings and travails which will take place at the time of the gathering of the exiles" (*ibid.*, p. 42c; see also p. 42a).

23 *Announcer*, pp. 17b, 20d, 22c.

24 *Ibid.*, p. 3b.

25 *Wells*, p. 17a.

26 "I said to myself: now is the time to strengthen the weak and

encourage the stumbling by reminding them of the good promises of God which were expressed by His servants, the prophets, and to look for the time of the end of wonders whose secret is sealed and concealed. I wanted to reveal to the sons of Judah the day of redemption; to announce loudly, with a voice sounding like a golden bell, that their salvation was near, that Israel was not foresaken, and that The Messiah would come soon and would not tarry" (*ibid.*, introd., p. 9a).

27 *Shebet Yehudah,* ed. Wiener, Hannover, 1855, p. 70.

28 See *Milḥemet Ḥovah,* Constantinople, 1710, p. 14ab.

29 *Das apologetische Schreiben des Josua Lorki* (Hebrew and German), ed. L. Landau, Antwerp, 1906, pp. 4-12.

30 These include fourteen major signs, all incorporated in the prophecies of Isaiah (*Announcer,* pp. 32c, 34b), and eight minor signs (*ibid.*, pp. 41a, 52b).

31 *Announcer,* p. 10ab; cf. Comm. on Deut. 28.15 (f. 5B, col. 2).

32 *Announcer,* p. 10b. See also Comm. on Deut. 28.15 (f. 5B, col. 2); Comm. on I Kings 14 (epilogue), f. 249, col. 3; Comm. on II Kings (epilogue), f. 308, cols. 3-4. Abravanel undoubtedly here follows Crescas, *Or Adonai,* III. v.2 (p. 82a).

33 Comm. on Deut. 28.15 (f. 5B, col. 2); *Or Adonai,* III. v.2.

34 *Ibid.; Announcer,* p. 10b; Comm. on I Kings 14 (epilogue), f. 249, cols. 2-3.

35 *Ibid.; Announcer,* p. 10b; Comm. on Deut. 28.15 (f. 5B, col. 2).

36 *Ibid.*

37 *Ibid.; Salvations,* p. 38b; Comm. on II Kings (epilogue), f. 308, col. 4; Comm. on Deut. 28.15 (f. 5B, col. 2): "The gathering of the Jews in the Land of Israel during the period of the Second Temple was in no way different from the concentration of Jews in Beitar after the destruction of the Temple or in Alexandria and other countries." Abravanel goes even to the extreme of saying that "the Temple of the Second Commonwealth was in no way different from the great synagogues of Israel in the Diaspora" (*ibid.*). "Suppose," he adds, "that the Moslem king who now reigns over Jerusalem would permit the Jews living in his domains to go to the Land of Israel and build there a temple on the condition that they remain always subject to him. It would not be surprising if in the course of time they rebelled against him. This is what actually happened in the period of the Second Temple" (*ibid.*). This interesting thought, as well as the general idea that the exile began with the destruction of the First Temple, were borrowed by Abravanel, without acknowledgment, from Crescas, *Or Adonai,* III. v.2 (pp. 81b-82a).

38 *Wells,* 85ab.

39 *Announcer,* introduction, p. 2ab; Comm. on Deut. 28.49 (f. 6B, col. 4); *Wells,* p. 61a. Notable especially is Abravanel's sharp attack against the Jewish scholar Hayyim Galipapa, who, in his *Epistle of Redemption,* declared that Daniel's prophecies refer to the Second Commonwealth, that there is not one prophecy in the Bible that points conclusively to the Messianic Age and that the entire belief in the Messiah is based on tradition only. Cf. Albo's criticism of Galipapa, *'Iqqarim,* IV, 42,6ff (ed. Husik, vol. IV, part II, pp. 418ff).

40 Dan. 2.31-35.
41 Dan. 2.35.
42 Dan. 2.37-44.
43 Dan. 7.2-14.
44 Dan. 7.8.
45 Dan. 7.12.
46 Dan. 7.13-14.
47 Dan. 7.23.
48 Dan. 7.24.
49 Dan. 7.25.
50 Dan. 7.27.
51 Dan. 2.38; 8.20-21; 10.20; 11.2.
52 See, for instance, Irenaeus, *Adv. Haer.,* V. 26:1; Saadia, Comm. on Daniel, 7.7 (Hebrew transl. J. Kapaḥ, Jerusalem, 1981, pp. 128-131).
53 *Wells,* p. 40b.
54 *Ibid.*
55 Dan. 2.44.
56 *Wells,* p. 41ab.
57 Dan. 2.44.
58 *Wells,* 41a. For the same reason Abravanel rejects the Christian interpretation of the "small horn" as referring to anti-Christ. According to the latter view, the Day of Judgment would come after the anti-Christ will have offended and abused Jesus for three and a half years (time, times and half a time). "It is almost fifteen hundred years," Abravanel points out, "that the Moslems in their various lands and nations, which comprise most of the world, and the Israelites as well, repudiate Jesus' religion and expose its absurdity, while the Moslems have even persecuted Christians, fought them without mercy, conquered their countries and expelled them from the Holy Land, so that today the place of his crucifixion and burial, the holiest spot for Christians, is in the hands of the Moslems. And how can it be assumed that their God suffered all this for so many years, and would not exert judgment over all these nations, as he will against what the anti-Christ will speak and do in three and a half years" (*Wells,* p. 68b).
59 See *Milḥemet Ḥovah,* p. 31a.
60 Nahmanides, *Disputation,* ed. Steinschneider, Stettin, 1860, p. 12.
61 *Wells,* p. 41b: "In fact, the beginning of Christianity coincided with the beginning of the Roman Empire as such, since Jesus was born in the days of Octavius."
62 *Ibid.*
63 *Ibid.,* p. 58b.
64 *Ibid.,* p. 64b.
65 *Ibid.,* p. 65a.
66 *Ibid.*
67 *Salvations,* p. 45b.
68 *Wells,* pp. 23a, 40b.

69 "When Constantine the Great accepted the religion of Jesus, he ruled over all of Africa and most of Asia, and he compelled all those who were under his rule to accept the authority of the Christian religion. In this way all the Ishmaelites and the rest of the peoples who were under the dominion of the Romans were regarded as Christians. In this condition they found themselves for close to 500 years until Mohammed, the Moslem prophet, arose, and since he was followed by many nations, all of them succeeded in freeing themselves from the control of the Romans and their faith. Nevertheless, although they had renounced Christianity, many of the principles of Jesus' religion remained rooted in the laws of the Moslems, and for this reason the latter continued to be regarded as part of the Roman kingdom, besides the fact that they were subjected to the Romans for a long time" (*Wells*, p. 23a).

70 *Wells*, p. 63a; see Ibn Ezra, Comm. on Dan. 7.6–7.

71 *Ibid.; Wells*, p. 40b: "Iron and clay cannot mix and cannot form a compound."

72 *Wells*, p. 41a.

73 *Ibid.*, p. 121a; *Salvations*, p. 35a; *Announcer*, pp. 19c, 59b.

74 *Salvations*, p. 10ab.

75 *Ibid.* According to Abravanel, each succeeding kingdom comprises the kingdoms which preceded it. See *Wells*, 20b.

76 *Wells*, p. 40b.

77 *Ibid.*

78 *Ibid.*, p. 17a.

79 *Ibid.*, p. 17ab.

80 Dan. 7.25.

81 Joseph ibn Zaddiq, writing in 1467, gives this date in his *Zēkher Zaddiq* (ed. Neubauer, *Med. Jew. Chron.*, I, 1887, p. 90). According to Abraham ibn Daud (*Sēfer ha-Qabbalah*, ed. Neubauer, *op. cit.*, p. 54), however, the destruction of the Second Temple took place in 3829 (69).

82 *Wells*, p. 77b–78a.

83 Dan. 8.14.

84 See *Sēfer ha-Qabbalah*, I, 49; *Zēkher Zaddiq*, I, 87.

85 *Wells*, p. 86a.

86 Dan. 12.11.

87 *Wells*, p. 121ab. To be exact, from the time the continuous burnt offering was abolished. See a different interpretation of the same figure *ibid.*, p. 125b.

88 *Ibid.*, p. 121ab.

89 *Ibid.*, 121b.

90 Dan. 12.12.

91 *Wells*, p. 121b.

92 *Salvations*, introduction, p. 4a: "And I cleansed the house of Israel from the plague [of defeatism] and moved the people from the valley of despair to the gates of hope."

93 *Ibid.*

94 *Ibid.*

95 Nahmanides, *Disputation*, p. 10.
96 Yehiel of Paris, *Disputation*, ed. Thorn, 1873, p. 2.
97 *Salvations*, p. 17a.
98 Nahmanides, *op. cit.*, p. 8.
99 *Salvations*, introduction, p. 5a; see especially *ibid.*, p. 17ab.
100 San., 97a; Abodah Zarah, 9a.
101 San., 97b.
102 *Shebet Yehudah*, p. 70.
103 *Ibid.*, p. 72.
104 *Salvations*, pp. 11b, 18b.
105 *Ibid.*, pp. 19a, 20a, 21a, 30b.
106 *Ibid.*, pp. 12a, 19a.
107 *Ibid.*, pp. 30b, 31a.
108 *Ibid.*, p. 20a.
109 *Ibid.*, p. 21ab. The theory regarding the definite periods of time in which the Messiah could and could not have appeared is presented also in *Shebet Yehudah*, p. 71, as part of an argument used by Albo in the Tortosa disputation. According to the report of the same disputation published in *Juschurun* (ed. Kobak), VI (1868), pp. 45–51, the last two thousand years of the world's existence form the period in which the Messiah *may* come, while according to Albo's view, as presented in *Shebet Yehudah* (which is also the view of Abravanel), it is the period in which he *must* come. Although Abravanel gave this point special emphasis, and in consequence developed a different conception of both the messianic and pre-messianic periods, the notion in the main had been clearly expressed during the disputation in Tortosa. See Antonio Pacios López, *La Disputa de Tortosa*, II (Actas), Madrid-Barcelona, 1957, pp. 31–32, 35–36, 410–411. And see also Ad. Posnanski, "Le colloque de Tortose et de San Mateo," in *R.E.J.*, LXXV (1922), p. 84.
110 See above, p. 133.
111 Psalms, 90.4.
112 *Salvations*, p. 12b.
113 *Ibid.*, p. 13a.
114 See above, p. 133 and p. 299, n. 16.
115 *Salvations*, p. 13a.
116 San., 97b.
117 *Wells*, p. 123a; *Salvations*, p. 21b.
118 *Salvations*, p. 13a; *Wells*, p. 125b.
119 *Ibid.*, p. 120b; *Announcer*, p. 7a.
120 *Ibid.*, p. 31c.
121 Comm. on Gen. 15.1 (f. 39, col. 4).
122 *Wells*, p. 115b.
123 *Announcer*, p. 48abc; Comm. on Ezek. 38.1; *Wells*, p. 116a. *Salvations*, p. 21b: According to Abravanel, Armilus is the commander of the Christians, Gog—the chief of the Moslems. See also Comm. on Ezek., 38.2 (f. 206,

col. 2); *Wells*, p. 115b. On the Tannaitic, Pseudepigraphic and Midrashic literature dealing with "Gog and Magog," see J. Klausner, *Tolĕdot ha-Ra'ayon ha-Meshiḥi bĕ-Yisrael*, pp. 319-322.

124 *Wells*, p. 115b.

125 *Ibid.*, pp. 107a, 111b-112ab.

126 *Announcer*, p. 60a; *Salvations*, 35b.

127 *Announcer*, p. 37a. *Nozrim* in Jeremiah means "beleaguerers," but a homonym later came to mean Christians. Abravanel applies the term in its post-biblical meaning. See also Comm. on Jeremiah, 31.5 (f. 130, col. 2).

128 *Wells*, p. 115b.

129 *Salvations*, p. 35a; *Announcer*, pp. 59c, 62ab; San., 98b.

130 See above, p. 207.

131 Abba H. Silver, *A History of Messianic Speculation in Israel*, New York, 1927, pp. 56-57: "Abraham ibn Ezra and Meir of Rothenburg seem to be the only men who in the Middle Ages doubted Eldad's story."

131a See Baer, II, p. 385 (document from 1487); A. Neubauer, "'Inyĕnei 'Aseret ha-Shĕvatim," in *Kobez al Yad*, IV (1888), pp. 10-22, 64-69, and other documents relating to the Ten Tribes, including the letter from Jerusalem of R. Obadiah of Bertinoro dating from 1488 (pp. 22-23). See also A. Z. Aescoly, "Yĕhudei Ḥabash ba-Sifrut ha-'Ivrit," in *Zion*, I (1936), pp. 328-329.

132 *Das apologetische Schreiben des Josua Lorki*, pp. 2-3.

133 Jeremiah, 3.14.

134 See above, p. 204.

135 *Wells*, p. 76ab.

136 See *Announcer*, p. 72c: "The prophecy of Zechariah (9.12): 'Return to strength' is not a command but a prediction. It implies that while the Jews in the captivity of the exile lack horses and chariots and weapons of war, they will still return to power and strength [when the day of Redemption comes]'."

137 *Announcer*, p. 62c.

138 *Ibid.*, p. 21b.

139 *Ibid.*, pp. 59c, 61a.

140 *Ibid.*, the final passage on Obadiah.

141 *Wells*, p. 115b; *Announcer*, p. 31d.

142 *Ibid.*, p. 17bc.

143 *Ibid.*, p. 15b.

144 *Ibid.*, p. 31c; cf. *Wells*, p. 116b.

145 *Announcer*, p. 74a.

146 *Ibid.*, p. 44ab.

147 *Ibid.*, p. 14d. Abravanel saw three stages in the battle against Christendom: Constantinople, Rhodes, Rome.

148 *Announcer*, p. 71d: "The prophecy of the destruction of Tyre in Zechariah refers to Venice which was built according to the pattern of Tyre and by the people of Tyre after the latter's destruction." Cf. Comm. on Zechariah 9.2 (f. 289, cols. 3-4).

149 *Announcer*, pp. 17c, 40b, 59a. Abravanel stresses a number of times that Edom was the real enemy and shows a more lenient attitude toward the Moslems (*Announcer*, pp. 7b, 62a, 65c). His hatred for Islam, however, is by no means slight (see *ibid.*, p. 31c).

150 See, for instance, Yeru. Ta'anit, I.1.

151 See, for instance, Ibn Ezra, Comm. on Gen. 27, on the blessing of Esau, and David Kimhi, Comm. on Joel 4.19. And see *'Iqqarim*, IV, 42:18 (ed. Husik, Vol. IV, part II, pp. 428–429).

152 Comm. on Isaiah, 34, end (f. 53, col. 4); *Announcer*, p. 18c.

153 *Ibid.*

154 *Josippon*, ed. Guenzburg, Berditschev, 1896–1913, pp. 5–8; *Announcer*, p. 19abc.

155 Isaiah, 34.6; *Announcer*, p. 17c.

156 *Ibid.*, pp. 14d, 17d, 18a; Comm. on Isaiah 25.2 (f. 34, col. 2).

157 *Announcer*, p. 17d. See *Midrash Tanchuma* (ed. Salomon Buber, Vilna, 1885) on Exod. 7.14 [15].

158 *Announcer*, pp. 17d, 51a.

159 *Ibid.*, pp. 17d, 18a.

160 *Ibid.*, p. 59b.

161 *Ibid.*, p. 44b; cf. Nahmanides, *Disputation*, pp. 11a, 13a. In one place, however, Abravanel says: "It is quite possible that the Messiah will first appear in the land of the Moslems, and who knows whether a king of the Moslems will not accept the religion of Israel and will be the Messiah who will save Israel" (*Salvations*, p. 15a).

162 *Salvations*, p. 50b. Comm. on Isaiah 43, introduction (f. 79, col. 2).

163 *Announcer*, p. 9c.

164 *Ibid.*, p. 10c; Comm. on Zechariah 9.2–4 (f. 289, col. 3).

165 *Announcer*, p. 10c.

166 *Ibid.*, pp. 21d, 22c.

167 See above, p. 118.

168 *Wells*, p. 118a.

169 *Salvations*, p. 56a.

170 *Announcer*, p. 9c.

171 *Ibid.*, p. 27d.

172 *Ibid.*, p. 28b.

173 *Ibid.*, p. 9c.

174 *Ibid.*: "During the days of the Messiah things will be as they were at the beginning of creation, for then the lion was not a killer, nor were killers the other beasts or birds of prey. This is proven by the fact that although all genera were created in single pairs, none of them was missing when they entered Noah's ark."

175 *Ibid.*, pp. 47d, 63a; *Salvations*, p. 69b.

176 *Ibid.*, p. 56a.

177 *Announcer*, pp. 34d, 38bc: "The new covenant mentioned in Jeremiah does not mean a new law, because the Law of Moses will never change or be

substituted by another law at any time. But it means that Israel will now truly fulfill all the commandments of the divine Law and that all of the Israelites — young and old — will know God not through study and investigation, but in a direct and natural way. They will know God just as people know the first axioms about which there is no doubt in their minds."

178 *Salvations,* p. 27a.

179 *Ibid.,* p. 38a. As Abravanel envisions it, however, there will be a tribunal in Jerusalem for deciding international conflicts and controversies. See Comm. on Isaiah 2.4 (f. 7, col. 3).

180 *Salvations,* p. 38a.

181 *Announcer,* p. 34d.

182 Maimonides, *Code,* end.

183 See Silver, *op. cit.,* pp. 6-7.

184 Justin Martyr, *Dialogue with Trypho,* LXXX-LXXXI.

185 Irenaeus, *Adv. Haer.,* V., 28:3; 29:2.

186 *Ibid.,* V.26:1; 15:1-2, 35.

187 Tertullian, *Adv. Marcionem,* III, 24.

188 Henry D. Ward, *History and Doctrine of the Millennium,* Boston, 1840, p. 18.

189 Jerome, Comm. on Ezekiel, 16.46.

190 See Ward, *op. cit.,* p. 21.

191 *City of God,* XX, 7, 9, 13, 16; XXII, 30.

192 See Emile Gebhart, *Mystics and Heretics in Italy,* London, 1922, 70-93.

193 Cf. Ad. Harnack, *History of Dogma,* Eng. trans., London and Edinburgh, 1894, I, 167-169; II, 297-300.

194 For the three major points of Savonarola's prophecies, see Savonarola's "On the Watch Tower of Italy," in Herbert Lucas, *Fra Girolamo Savonarola,* London, 1906, p. 60.

195 "What is Babylon," said Savonarola, "but Rome? Babylon signifies confusion. There is not in the world greater confusion of crime and all sorts of iniquity than that at Rome. Since they have made it a dwelling of harlots, God will make it a stall for swines and horses." I am quoting Savonarola according to John Abraham Herand's *The Life and Times of Girolamo Savonarola,* London, 1843, p. 88.

196 See Pasquale Villari, *Life and Times of Girolamo Savonarola,* 10th ed., London and New York, 1909, 154-155, 214.

197 Isaiah, 34.5; *Announcer,* p. 17c.

198 See Savonarola, *The Triumph of the Cross,* trans. by O'dell Travers Hill, London, 1868, p. 231: "The Jews were not to be converted to Christ till the end of the world," and his statement regarding the approaching conversion of the Jews, quoted by Herbert Lucas, *op. cit.,* p. 62.

199 Hieronymus Savonarola, *Predigten,* German trans. by Hiltgart Schottmueller, Berlin, 1901, p. 86.

200 This is Savonarola's own description of his influence. See Herbert Lucas, *op. cit.,* p. 60.

201 An echo of Savonarola's campaign against official Rome may be heard in the following statement of Abravanel: "All the priests of Rome and her Bishops pursue avarice and bribery and are not concerned with their religion, for the sign of heresy is upon their forehead" (*Salvations*, p. 34a).

202 Graetz, VIII, chap. 14 (p. 324); Jacob Guttmann, *Die religionsphilosophischen Lehren des Isaak Abravanel*, Breslau, 1916, p. 6.

203 For detailed lists of the numerous translations made by Christians of and from Abravanel's works, as well as for the refutations written against him, see J. Ch. Wolf, *Bibliotheca Hebraea*, I, Hamburg and Leipzig, 1715, pp. 627-641; Giovanni Bernardo de Rossi, *Historisches Woerterbuch der juedischen Schriftsteller und ihre Werke* (German translation by Hamberger of *Dizionario storico degli autori Ebrei e delle loro opere*), 2nd ed., 1832, pp. 17-18; A. T. Hartmann, *Abrabanele*, in Ersch and Gruber's *Allgemeine Encyclopaedie*, I, 1818, 151-153; Julius Fuerst, *Bibliotheca Judaica*, Leipzig, 1849, pp. 11-15; Antonio Ribeiro dos Santos, in *Memorias de Litteratura Portugueza*, publicadas pela Academia Real das Sciencias de Lisboa, II, Lisbon, 1792, pp. 287-290. See also M. Steinschneider, "Isaak Abravanel," in *Catalogus librorum hebraeorum in bibliotheca Bodleiana*, II, Berlin, 1931.

204 Hugo Grotius shows knowledge of Abravanel's political views and cites him as a distinguished authority in his *De jure belli et pacis*, Book I, chap. I, § vi; Richard Simon follows in the footsteps of Abravanel in his *Histoire critique du vieux testament*, Rotterdam, 1685, Book I, chap. II, pp. 18-20, and declares that, of all Jewish scholars, Abravanel is the commentator "from whom one can profit most in the understanding of the Bible" (*ibid.*, Book III, chap. VI, p. 380a; and see also pp. 536-537). Johann Buxtorf the younger, although he often argued against Abravanel, was nevertheless among his staunchest admirers, as is evident from the many translations he made of his works (see the full list in Rodríguez de Castro, *Biblioteca española*, I, 1871, pp. 350-351), as well as from his entire attitude toward him. Pierre Bayle speaks of Abravanel in the highest terms in his *Dictionnaire historique et critique*, 1696 (5th edition, Amsterdam, 1734, p. 45). For the attitude of Adrianus Relandus toward Abravanel see his *Analecta Rabbinica*, Utrecht, 1702, pp. 110, 141.

205 Calvin's sharp attack against Abravanel, whom he believed "to excel others in acuteness," was directed against what Calvin considered to be the six major points of Abravanel's messianic theory. It is contained in his Commentaries on Daniel, 4.44, 45 (Eng. trans. pp. 183-186). See Jacobus Alting, *Schilo*, 1662, I.i, c. 9; Buddeus, *Prudentiae civilis rabbinicae specimen*, Jena, 1693, 12; Carpzov, *Introductio in theologiam judaicam* etc., Leipzig, 1687, p. 81; Huet, *Demonstratio evangelica*, Paris, 1679, prop. ix, c. iv, § 14.

206 Constantine L'Empereur wrote refutations of Abravanel's commentaries on Isaiah, 42.13 and 43 (Leyden, 1631); Grossgebauer wrote a refutation of the whole of Abravanel's *Wells of Salvation*, the manuscript remaining unpublished (see Wolf, *op. cit.*, IV, p. 876); Sebastian Schnell wrote against Abravanel's commentaries on Isaiah 34 and Obadiah, which he also translated (Altdorf, 1647); Antonius Hulsius and B. Augustus Varenius wrote against some of Abravanel's interpretations of Daniel, the former in his *Theologia Judaica*, Brede, 1653/4, I, 528, the latter in his *Refutatio decem characterum de Jesu non Messia*, Rostock, 1699.

207 See Julio Bartolocci, *Bibliotheca magna rabbinica*, III, Rome, 1683, 874–876; Rodríguez de Castro, *op. cit.*, p. 346; Louis Moreri, *Le grand dictionnaire historique*, Lyons, 1674 (*Abarbinel*).

208 J. Ch. Basnage, *Histoire des Juifs*, V, Rotterdam, 1707, pp. 1897–1899; Michel de Boissy, *Dissertations critiques pour servir d'éclaircissement à l'histoire des Juifs*, Paris, 1785, I, 23–31, II, 199ff (the ninth dissertation); Auguste-Arthur Beugnot, *Les juifs d'occident*, Paris, 1824, pp. 210–226.

209 For the attitude of Joseph Solomon del Medigo toward Abravanel, whose works he considers as "a gift from God," see his *Iggereth Aḥuz* in Geiger's *Melo Chofnayim*, Berlin, 1840 (Hebrew part, p. 21).

210 See S. D. Luzzatto, "Ueber die angeblichen Plagiate Abravanel's und Moscato's," in Jost's *Israelitische Annalen*, 1840, p. 24.

211 *Salvations*, p. 51b.

212 *Crown*, pp. 82–83. Jacob Guttmann, *op. cit.*, pp. 13, 14, minimizes, in our opinion without justification, Abravanel's admiration for the Cabala.

213 Already in his Comm. on Kings, which was written shortly after the expulsion from Spain, Abravanel justifies the failure of Spain's Jews to return to Jerusalem during the period of the Second Commonwealth by their realization that what took place at that time was no real redemption, which, according to Abravanel, will be recognized by the presence of certain miraculous signs (see Comm. on II Kings, f. 305, col. 2).

BIBLIOGRAPHY

ABOAB, IMMANUEL, *Nomologia,* Amsterdam, 1629.
ABRAVANEL, ISAAC,
  a) Commentaries: On the Pentateuch, Venice, 1579 (Warsaw, 1862)*; on the Former Prophets, Pesaro, 1511/12 (Leipzig, 1686); on the Latter Prophets, Pesaro, 1520 (Amsterdam, 1641).
  b) Messianic Writings: *Ma'aynei ha-Yeshu'ah* (*Wells of Salvation*), Ferrara, 1551; *Mashmi'a Yeshu'ah* (*Announcer of Salvation*), Saloniki, 1526 (Amsterdam, 1644); *Yeshu'ot Meshiḥo* (*Salvations of His Anointed*), Koenigsberg, 1861.
  c) Philosophical Works: *'Ateret Zeqenim* (*Crown of the Elders*), Sabionetta, 1557 (Warsaw, 1894); *Ẓurot ha-Yesodot* (*The Forms of the Elements*), published as addendum to *'Ateret Zeqenim; Shamayim Ḥadashim* (*New Heavens*), Roedelheim, 1828; *Mif'alot Elohim* (*Deeds of God*), Venice, 1592; *She'elot u-Teshuvot le-Shaul ha-Kohen* (*Questions and Answers to Saul ha-Kohen*), Venice, 1574; Commentary on the *Guide,* Prague, 1831/32.
  d) On the fundamentals of Judaism: *Rosh Amana* (*Principles of Faith*), Constantinople, 1505 (Koenigsberg, 1861); *Naḥalat Avot* (*Inheritance of the Fathers*), Constantinople, 1505 (Venice, 1545).
  e) Letters: Letter to the Count of Faro, first published, together with a German translation by Jeanette Schwerin-Abarbanel, in *Magazin fuer die Wissenschaft des Judentums,* xviii (1891), and republished by Joaquim de Carvalho in *Revista de Estudos Hebraicos,* I, Lisbon, 1928; Letter to Yehiel of Pisa, published by E. Carmoly in *Ozar Nechmad,* II (Vienna, 1857); two letters to Yehiel of Pisa, published by David Kaufmann (first letter not fully) in *Revue des Études Juives,* xxvi (1893), and republished (in full) by M. Grossberg as addendum to Abraham ibn Ezra's *Sefer ha-'Aẓamim,* London, 1901.
ABRAVANEL, JUDAH (Leone Ebreo), *The Philosophy of Love* (*Dialoghi d'Amore*), trans. by F. Friedeberg-Seeley & Jean H. Barnes, London, 1937; Hebrew Poems (republished by C. Gebhardt in his *Leone Ebreo,* 1929).
ABRAHAM BAR ḤIYYA, *Sefer Megillat ha-Megalle,* edited by Adolf (Ze'ev) Posnanski, with an introduction by Julius Guttmann, Berlin, 1924.
Acta Eruditorum, Leipzig, 1686, 1710 (contains articles on Abravanel).
ALBO, JOSEPH, *Sefer ha-'Ikkarim,* ed. Isaac Husik, Philadelphia, 1929/30.
AMATUS LUSITANUS, *Centuriae Curationum,* Venice, 1566.
ANTONIO, NICOLÁS, "Isaac Abarbinel," in *Bibliotheca Hispana Nova,* Rome, 1672.
AQUINAS, THOMAS, *Summa Theologica; Summa contra gentiles* (Eng. trans. of the Dominican Fathers); *On the Governance of Rulers,* Eng. trans. of

---

* Editions of Abravanel's works enclosed in parenthesis are those usually cited by the author, although the first editions were always consulted.

De regimine principum by Gerald B. Phelan, London and New York, 1938.

ARAMA, ISAAC, '*Aqedat Yizḥaq*, ed. Ch. J. Polak, Warsaw, 1882; *Ḥazut Qasha*, ed. Polak, Warsaw, 1884.

ARAMA, MEIR, Statement published by Gabriel Polak in *Ha-Maggid*, II (1858), No. 25.

ARISTOTLE, *The Works of*, ed. W. D. Ross, Oxford (Volumes II–III; VIII, IX, X), 1921–1931.

Archivo Histórico Portuguez, I–IV, VI–VIII.

AUGUSTINE, AURELIUS, *The Works of*, Edinburgh, 1871.

BACON, ROGER, *Opus Majus*, Eng. trans. by Robert B. Burke, Philadelphia, 1928.

BAER, FRITZ, *Die Juden im christlichen Spanien*, Berlin, 1929/1936; "Abravanel," in *Encyclopaedia Judaica*, I; "Don Yizḥaq Abravanel ve-Yaḥaso el Be'ayot ha-Historia ve-ha-Medina," in *Tarbiz*, VIII (1937); "Ha-Tenu'ah ha-Meshiḥit bi-Tequfat ha-Gerush," in *Zion*, V, Jerusalem, 5693 (1933); *Galut*, Berlin, 1936 (contains a chapter on Abravanel); *Toledot ha-Yehudim bi-Sefrad ha-Noẓrit*, Tel-Aviv, 1945; second, revised edition, 1959 (Eng. trans. by L. Schoffman, H. Halkin and others: *A History of the Jews in Christian Spain*, 2 vols., Philadelphia, 1961–1966); *Studien zur Geschichte der Juden im Koenigreich Aragonien waehrend des 13. und 14. Jahrhunderts*, Berlin, 1913; *Untersuchungen ueber Quellen und Komposition des Schebet Jehuda*, Berlin, 1923.

BARON, SALO W., *A Social and Religious History of the Jews*, vols. ix, xi, 1965, 1967.

BARTOLOCCI, JULIO, *Bibliotheca magna rabbinica*, III, Rome, 1683 (article on Abravanel).

BARZILAY, ISAAC B., *Between Reason and Faith*, The Hague-Paris, 1967 (chapter on Abravanel).

BASNAGE, J. CH., *Histoire de Juifs*, V, Rotterdam, 1707.

BAYLE, PIERRE, *Dictionnaire historique et critique*, I, 5th ed., Amsterdam, 1734 (article on Abravanel).

BELL, A. F. G., *Portuguese Literature*, Oxford, 1922.

BEMBO, PIETRO, *Della Istoria Viniziana*, I, Venice, 1790.

BERGENROTH, GUSTAV ADOLPH, *Calendar of Letters, Dispatches, and State Papers*, London, 1862.

BERGMANN, J., "Abrabanels Stellung zur Agada," in *Monatsschrift fuer Geschichte und Wissenschaft des Judentums*, 1937.

BERNÁLDEZ, ANDRÉS, *Historia de los reyes Católicos Don Fernando y Doña Isabel*, Seville, 1869; *Memorias del Reinado de los Reyes Católicos*, ed. Manuel Gómez-Moreno and Juan de M. Carriazo, Madrid, 1962.

BERNSTEIN, SIMON, *Shomerei ha-Ḥomot*, Tel-Aviv, 1938.

BEUGNOT, AUGUSTE-ARTHUR, COUNT, *Les juifs d'occident*, Paris, 1824.

Bikkurei ha-'Ittim, 1820 (contains biography of Abravanel).

BOER, T. J. DE, *The History of Philosophy in Islam*, translated by Edward R. Jones, London, 1903.

BOISSY, L. M. DE, *Dissertations critiques pour servir d'éclaircissment à l'histoire des juifs*, Paris, 1785.

BOODIN, JOHN E., *God and Creation*, New York, 1934.
BOUTERWEK, FREDERICK, *History of Spanish and Portuguese Literature*, London, 1823.
BROWN, HORATIO F., *Venice, an Historical Sketch of the Republic*, 2nd ed., London, 1895; *Studies in the History of Venice*, London, 1907.
BURKE, U. R., *A History of Spain*, London & New York, 1895.
BUXTORF, JOHANN (the younger), *Dissertationes philologico-theologicae*, 1662.
CALVIN, JOHN, *Commentaries on Daniel*, Eng. translation by T. Myers, 1852.
CANTERA Y BURGOS, F., "Don 'Ishaq Brauanel'," in *Baron Jubilee Volume* (to be published).
CARANDE, RAMÓN, "Sevilla, fortaleza y mercado," in *Anuario de Historia del Derecho Español*, II.
CARLYLE, R. W. & A. J., *A History of Mediaeval Political Theory in the West*, 6 volumes, 2nd ed., 1927–1936.
CARLYLE, A. J., *Political Liberty*, Oxford, 1941.
CARMOLY, E., "Toledot Don Yiẓhaq Abravanel," in *Ozar Nechmad*, II (1857); "Analecten," in *Israelitische Annalen*, 1839; *Divrei ha-Yamim li-Bnei Yahya*, Frankfort on the Main, 1850.
CARO, GEORG, *Social- und Wirtschaftsgeschichte der Juden im Mittelalter und in der Neuzeit*, Leipzig, 1908–1920; "Die Juden des Mittelalters in ihrer Wirtschaftlichen Betaetigung," in *MGWJ*, 1904.
CARVALHO, JOAQUIM DE, *Leão Hebreu, Filósofo*, Coimbra, 1918.
CASSUTO, U., *Gli Ebrei a Firenze nell' età del rinascimento*, Florence, 1918; "Abravanel" (family in Italy), in *Encyclopaedia Judaica*, I.
CASTRO, RODRÍGUEZ DE, "R. Don Izchaq Abarbanel," in *Biblioteca española*, I, 1781.
CHONES, S., *Toledot ha-Posekim* (contains article on Abravanel), Warsaw, 1929.
CICERO, MARCUS TULLIUS, *De officiis*, with an Eng. trans. by Walter Miller, London, 1947; *De republica, De legibus*, with an Eng. trans. by Clinton W. Keyes, New York, 1928.
CLEMENCÍN, DIEGO, *Elógio de la Réina Católica Doña Isabel*, Madrid, 1821.
CLEMENT OF ALEXANDRIA, *The Writings of*, trans. by William Wilson, Edinburgh, 1867–69.
COMINES, PHILIP DE, *The Memoires*, ed. Andrew R. Scoble, London, 1906.
CORRODI, HEINRICH, *Kritische Geschichte des Chiliasmus*, Frankfort and Leipzig, 1781.
CRESCAS, HASDAI, *Or Adonai*, Vienna, 1860; "Letter to the Jews of Avignon" (supplement to *Shevet Yehudah*, ed. Wiener, Hannover, 1855).
Cronicón de Valladolid, published by Pedro Sainz de Baranda in *Colección de Documentos inéditos para la Historia de España*, XIII.
DANTE, *De Monarchia*, translated by F. J. Church, London, 1879.
DELITZSCH, FRANZ, "Leo der Hebraeer," in *Literaturblatt des Orients*, 1840, nos. 6, 7, 8.
DUBNOW, SIMON, *Weltgeschichte des Juedischen Volkes*, 1927, V–VI.
DUNHAM, S. A., *A History of Spain and Portugal*, New York, 1833.
ERASMUS, DESIDERIUS, *The Complaint of Peace*, Eng. trans., London, 1795; *Praise of Folly*, New York, 1922; *The Education of a Christian Prince*, with an introduction by Lester K. Born, New York, 1936.

FERORELLI, NICOLA, *Gli Ebrei nell' Italia meridionale dall'età Romana al secolo xviii*, Torino, 1915.

FIGGIS, JOHN NEVILLE, *The Divine Right of Kings*, Cambridge, 1934.

FINKELSCHERER, HERBERT, "Quellen und Motive der Staats- und Gesellschaftsauffassung des Don Isaak Abravanel, in *MGWJ*, 1937.

FINN, S. J., *Kenesseth Israel* (contains article on Abravanel), Warsaw, 1886.

FOAKES-JACKSON, F. J., *The History of the Christian Church*, 1924.

FREIRE, ANSELMO BRAAMCAMP, "Maria Brandoa," in *Archivo Histórico Portuguez*, VI; "As conspirações no reinado de D. João II, in *Arch. Hist. Port.*, I–II.

FÜRST, JULIUS, *Bibliotheca Judaica*, I, Leipzig, 1849.

GANZ, DAVID, *Ẓemaḥ David*, Warsaw, 1878.

GABISHON, ABRAHAM, *'Omer ha-Shikhḥa*, Leghorn, 1748.

GEBHARDT, C., *Leone Ebreo*, 1929 (Bibliotheca Spinozana, III).

GEIGER, ABRAHAM, *Melo Chofnajim*, Berlin, 1840.

GERSONIDES, LEVI, *Milḥamot Adonai*, Leipzig, 1866; Commentary on the Pentateuch, Venice, 1547.

GHAZZALLI, MOHAMMED AL-, *Alchemy of Happiness*, trans. by Henry A. Homes, Albany, 1873.

GIANNONE, PIETRO, *Civil History of the Kingdom of Naples* (Eng. trans. by James Ogilvie of *Istoria civile del Regno di Napoli*), London, 1731.

GILSON, ÉTIENNE, *Reason and Revelation in the Middle Ages*, New York, 1935; *The Philosophy of St. Thomas Aquinas*, Cambridge, 1929; *The Spirit of Mediaeval Philosophy*, New York, 1940.

GINZBERG, LOUIS, "Isaac Abravanel," in *Jewish Encyclopedia*, I.

GOLDZIHER, IGNAZ, *Mohammed and Islam*, New Haven, 1917.

GROTIUS, HUGO, *De jure belli et pacis*, Paris, 1625.

GRUENBERG, S., *Eine Leuchte der Bibelexegese um die Wende des Mittelalters*, Berlin, 1928.

GRAETZ, H., *Geschichte der Juden*, viii–ix, Leipzig, 1864–1866, 1891.

GUICCIARDINI, FRANCESCO, *The Historie of Guicciardin* (Eng. trans. by Geffray Fenton of *Storia d'Italia*), 3rd. ed., London, 1618.

GUTTMANN, JACOB, *Die religionsphilosophischen Lehren des Isaak Abravanel*, Breslau, 1916; "Ueber Abraham bar Chijjas 'Buch der Enthuellung'," in *MGWJ*, 1903; *Das Verhaeltniss des Thomas von Aquino zum Judenthum und zur juedischen Literatur*, Goettingen, 1891.

GUTTMANN, JULIUS, *Die Philosophie des Judenthums*, Munich, 1933 (Eng. trans. by D. W. Silverman: *Philosophies of Judaism*, New York, 1964).

HALPER, B., *Post Biblical Hebrew Literature*, Philadelphia, 1921.

HARNACK, ADOLPH, *History of Dogma*, Eng. trans., London & Edinburgh, 1894.

HARTMANN, [A. T.], "Abrabanele," in Ersch and Gruber, *Allgemeine Encyclopädie*, I, 1818.

HEARNSHAW, F. J. C. (editor), *Social and Political Ideas of Some Great Mediaeval Thinkers*, London, 1923.

HEINEMANN, ISAAK, "Abravanels Lehre vom Neidergang der Menschheit," in *MGWJ*, 1938.

HERAND, JOHN A., *The Life and Times of Girolamo Savonarola*, London, 1843.
HERBEN, JAN, *Huss and his Followers*, London, 1926.
HESCHEL, ABRAHAM, *Don Jizchak Abravanel*, Berlin, 1937.
HESQETO, BARUCH UZZIEL, Introduction to *Ma'aynei ha-Yeshu'ah*, Ferrara, 1551.
HOBBES, THOMAS, *The Leviathan*, Oxford, 1946.
HORODEZKY, S. A., "Don Isaak ben Jehuda Abravanel," in *Encyclopaedia Judaica*, I.
HUETIUS, P. D., *Demonstratio Evangelica*, Paris, 1679.
HURGONJE, CHRISTIAN S., *Mohammedanism*, New York, 1916.
HUSIK, ISAAC, *A History of Mediaeval Jewish Philosophy*, New York, 1916.
IBN DAUD OF TOLEDO, ABRAHAM, *Sefer ha-Qabbalah*, in A. Neubauer's *Mediaeval Jewish Chronicles*, I, Oxford, 1887.
IBN EZRA, ABRAHAM, Commentary on the Pentateuch (ed. *Miqraot Gedolot*), Warsaw, 1860/61; Comm. on Daniel (same edition), Warsaw, 1864.
IBN GABIROL, SOLOMON, *Meqor Ḥayyim* (Hebrew trans. of *Fons vitae* by J. Bluestein, ed. by A. Zifroni with introd. by J. Klausner), Tel-Aviv, 1926.
IRENAEUS, *The Writings of*, Edinburgh, 1868/9.
ISAAC BEN MOSES (Profiat Duran), Commentary on the *Guide*, ed. Bendet Kohen, Berlin, 1925.
JABEZ, JOSEPH, *Or ha-Chajim*, Zolkiew, 1848.
JACOB, U. F., "Some Notes on Occam as a Political Thinker," in the *Bulletin of the John Rylands Library*, Manchester, XX.
JEHIEL OF PARIS, *Disputation* (in Hebrew), Thorn, 1873.
JELLINEK, ADOLPH, *Thomas von Aquino in der jüdischen Literatur*, Leipzig, 1853.
Jeshurun, ed. Kobak, VI, Bamberg, 1868.
JOËL, MANUEL, *Don Chasdai Creskas' religionsphilosophische Lehren*, Breslau, 1866.
JOHN OF SALISBURY, "Frivolities of Courtiers and Footprints of Philosophers" (the first three books of the *Policraticus*), trans. by Joseph B. Pike, London, 1938; *Policraticus* (without the first three books), trans. by John Dickinson, New York, 1927.
JOSEPH BEN ẒADDIQ OF AREVALO, *Zekher Ẓaddiq*, in A. Neubauer's *Mediaeval Jewish Chronicles*, I, Oxford, 1887.
JOSEPH BEN JACOB IBN ẒADDIQ, *'Olam Qatan*, ed. Jellinek, Leipzig, 1854.
JOSEPH HA-KOHEN, *'Emeq ha-Bakha*, ed. Letteris, Cracow, 1895; ed. Wiener (in German translation), Leipzig, 1858.
Josippon, ed. David Guenzburg, Berditschev, 1896–1913.
JOST, J. M., *Geschichte des Judenthums*, III, Leipzig, 1859.
JUDAH HA-LEVI, *Kitab al-Khazari*, translated from the Arabic with an introduction by Hartwig Hirschfeld, London, 1916.
JUSTINUS MARTYR, *The Writings of J. M. and Athenagoras*, Edinburgh, 1867.
KAPSALI, ELIAHU, *D'Bei Eliahu*, ed. M. Lattes, Padova, 1569; Excerpts from *D'Bei Eliahu*, published by S. D. Luzzatto as supplement to Wiener's German version of Joseph ha-Kohen's *'Emeq ha-Bakha*, Leipzig, 1858.
KAUFMANN, DAVID, "La famille de Yehiel de Pise," in *Revue des études juives*, xxvi (1893); "Don Isaac Abravanel et le commerce des épices avec Calicut," in *Revue des études juives*, xxxviii (1899).

KAYSERLING, M., *Geschichte der Juden in Portugal,* Leipzig, 1867; "Isaac Abravanel" (biography), in *The Jewish Encyclopedia,* I; *Biblioteca Española-Portugeza-Judaica,* Strasbourg, 1890; *Christopher Columbus,* New York, 1928.

KELLNER, M. M., English translation (with introduction) of Isaac Abravanel's *Rosh Amana (Principles of Faith,* Rutherford, 1982); ed., with introduction, *Rosh Amana,* Jerusalem, 1993.

KLAUSNER, JOSEPH, *Jesus of Nazareth,* London and New York, 1925; *Toledot ha-Ra'ayon ha-Meshihi be-Yisrael,* Jerusalem, 1927; *Yahadut ve-Enoshi-yut,* Jerusalem, 1955.

KONFORTE, DAVID, *Qore ha-Dorot,* ed. Cassel, Berlin, 1846.

LEA, HENRY CHARLES, *A History of the Inquisition of the Middle Ages,* London, 1922; *A History of the Inquisition of Spain,* New York, 1906.

LEMOS, MAXIMILIANO DE, *História de Medicina em Portugal,* I, Lisbon, 1899.

LEVY, S., *Isaac Abravanel as a Theologian,* London, 1939.

LINDO, E. H., *The History of the Jews of Spain and Portugal,* London, 1848.

LLORENTE, J. A., *Histoire critique de l'inquisition d'Espagne,* Paris, 1817/18.

LOEB, ISIDORE, "Abravanel," in *La Grande Encyclopédie,* I (1886).

LÓPEZ, PERO, AYALA DE, *Crónica del Rey Don Enrique Tercero,* in *Crónicas de los Reyes de Castilla,* II, Madrid, 1780.

LOPEZ, ISAAC, *Kur Mazrēf ha-Emunot u-Marēh ha-Emet,* Metz, 1847.

LORKI, JOSHUA, *Das Apologetische Schreiben* etc. (German and Hebrew), ed. L. Landau, Antwerp, 1906.

LUCAS, HENRY S., *The Renaissance and the Reformation,* New York, 1934.

LUCAS, HERBERT, *Fra Girolamo Savonarola,* London, 1906.

LUZZATTO, SAMUEL DAVID, "Ueber die angeblichen Plagiate Abravanel's und Moscato's," in Jost's *Israelitische Annalen,* 1840.

MACHIAVELLI, NICCOLO, *The Historical, Political and Diplomatic Writings of,* trans. by Christian E. Detmold, Boston, 1882.

MAIMONIDES, MOSES, *The Guide for the Perplexed,* translated from the original Arabic text by M. Friedlaender, 2nd ed., London, 1904 (new Eng. translation by Sh. Pines, *The Guide of the Perplexed,* 1963); *Eight Chapters,* Eng. tran. by Joseph I. Gorfinkel, New York 1912; *Mishneh Torah,* Leipzig, 1862; Commentary on the Mishnah, Venice, 1606; *Iggeret Teman,* Warsaw, 1837.

MALTER, HENRY, *Saadia Gaon,* Philadelphia, 1921.

MARGULIES, S. H., "La famiglia Abravanel in Italia," in *Rivista Israelitica,* III (1906).

MARX, ALEXANDER, *Studies in Jewish History and Booklore,* New York, 1944; "The Expulsion of the Jews from Spain," in *Jewish Quarterly Revue,* 1908.

MAI, J. H., *Dissertatio historico-philologica de origine, vita atque scriptis Don Isaaci Abrabanielis,* Altdorf, 1708.

MCCOWN, CHESTER CARLTON, *The Promise of His Coming,* A Historical Interpretation and Evolution of the Idea of the Second Advent, New York, 1921.

MCGIFFERT, ARTHUR CUSHMAN, *A History of Christian Thought,* New York, 1932.

Ha-Meassef, 1784, ed. Letteris, 1862 (contains a biography of Abravanel).

MENAHEM BEN ZERAH, Ẓēdah la-Derekh, Sabbioneta, 1567-8 (?).
MENASSEH BEN ISRAEL, Conciliator, Amsterdam, 1633.
MERRIMAN, ROGER B., The Rise of the Spanish Empire, New York, 1925-6.
MINKIN, JACOB S., Abarbanel and the Expulsion of the Jews from Spain, New York, 1938.
MORÉRI, LOUIS, "Abarbinel," in Le grand dictionnaire historique, Lyons, 1674.
MUNK, S., Mélanges de philosophie juive et arabe, Paris, 1857.
NAHMANIDES, Sha'ar ha-Gemul, Warsaw, 1862; Commentary on the Pentateuch, Pesaro, 1513/14; Disputation, ed. Steinschneider, Stettin, 1860.
NAVÉ, P., "Leone Ebreo's Lament on the Death of his Father," in Romanica et Occidentalia (Études dédiées à la mémoire de Hiram Peri [Pflaum], ed. M. Lazar), 1963, pp. 56-69.
NETANYAHU, B., The Marranos of Spain, New York, 1973[2]; Toward the Inquisition, Ithaca and London, 1997 (includes article on Samuel Abravanel); The Origins of the Inquisition in Fifteenth Century Spain, New York, 1995.
NEUMAN, ABRAHAM A., The Jews in Spain, Philadelphia, 1942.
NEUMARK, DAVID, Toledot ha-'Iqqarim be-Israel, II, Odessa, 5679 (1919).
NICKERSON, HOFFMAN, The Inquisition, New York, 1932.
O'NEILL, JOHN, Cosmology, London, 1923.
ORIGEN, The Writings of, Edinburgh, 1869/72.
PACIOS LÓPEZ, ANTONIO, La Disputa de Tortosa, Madrid-Barcelona, 2 vols., 1957.
PALENCIA, ALONSO DE, Crónica de Enrique IV, trans. by D. A. Paz y Melia, Madrid, 1904.
PFLAUM, HEINZ, Die Idee der Liebe; Leone Ebreo, Tuebingen, 1926.
PINA, RUY DE, Crónica de D. Afonso V, Lisbon, 1790.
PLATO, The Dialogues of, trans. by B. Jowett, 5 volumes, 3rd ed., London, 1924.
PLUTARCH, Moralia, with an Eng. trans. by Frank C. Babbit, New York, 1927.
POLYBIUS, The Histories, Eng. trans. by E. S. Shuckburgh, 2 vols., London, 1889.
POSNANSKI, ADOLF, "Le colloque de Tortose et de San Mateo," in Revue des études juives, lxxiv-lxxvi; Schiloh, Leipzig, 1904.
PRESCOTT, W. H., History of the Reign of Ferdinand and Isabella (ed. American Publishers Corporation), New York, n.d.
REINES, ALVIN J., "Abravanel on Prophecy in the Moreh Nebukhim," in HUCA, XXXI (1960), XXXIII (1962)-XXXVII (1966).
RELAND, HADRIAN, Analecta rabbinica, Utrecht, 1702.
RESENDE, GARCIA DE, Cancioneiro Geral, Coimbra, 1910.
RIBEIRO DOS SANTOS, ANTONIO, "Memoria da Litteratura Sagrada dos Judeos Portuguezes desde os primeiros tempos da Monarquia até os fins do Seculo XV," in Memorias de Litteratura Portugueza, publicadas pela Academia Real das Sciencias de Lisboa, II, Lisbon, 1792, pp. 287-307 (on Abravanel).
RÍOS, JOSÉ AMADOR DE LOS, Historia social, política y religiosa de los Judios de España y Portugal, Madrid, 1876.
ROEDER, RALPH, The Man of the Renaissance, New York, 1933.

Rosenthal, Erwin I. J., "Don Isaac Abravanel: Financier, Statesman and Scholar," in *Bulletin of John Rylands Library*, XXI.

Rossi, Giovanni Bernardo de, *Historisches Wörterbuch der juedischen Schriftsteller und ihre Werke* (German trans. by Hamberger of *Dizionario storico degli autori Ebrei e delle loro opere*), 2nd ed., 1832.

Rossi, Azariah de, *Meor Einayim*, Wilno, 1863-1865.

Roth, Cecil, *The History of the Jews in Italy*, Philadelphia, 1946; *History of the Marranos*, Philadelphia, 1932; *The Jews in the Renaissance*, Philadelphia, 1959; *Venice*, Philadelphia, 1930.

Ruiz, Gregorio, *Don Isaac Abrabanel y su comentario al libro de Amos*, Madrid, 1984.

Saadia, Gaon, *Sefer ha-Emunot ve-ha-Deot*, Cracow, 1880.

Sanceau, Elaine, *The Land of Prester John*, New York, 1944.

Santillana, Iñigo Lopez de Mendoza, *Letter of the Marquis of Santillana to Don Peter*, Oxford, 1922.

Sanuto, Marino, *La Spedizione de Carlo VIII in Italia*, Venice, 1873.

Sarachek, Joseph, *Don Isaac Abravanel*, New York, 1938; *The Doctrine of the Messiah in Medieval Jewish Literature*, New York, 1932; *Faith and Reason; the Conflict Over the Rationalism of Maimonides*, Williamsport, Pa., 1935.

Savonarola, Girolamo, *Spiritual and Ascetic Letters*, ed. by B. W. Randolph, London, 1907; *The Triumph of the Cross*, trans. by O'dell Travers Hill, London, 1868; *Predigten*, German trans. by Hiltgart Schottmueller, Berlin, 1901.

Schaefer, H., *Geschichte von Portugal*, Hamburg, 1839.

Scharpff, F. A., *Der Kardinal und Bischof Nikolaus von Cusa*, 1871.

Schipper, Ignaz, *Anfaenge des Kapitalismus bei den abendlaendischen Juden*, Vienna and Leipzig, 1907; *Toledot ha-Kalkalah ha-Yehudit*, Tel-Aviv, 5697 (1937).

Schmueli, E., *Don Yiẓḥaq Abravanel ve-Gerush Sefarad*, Jerusalem, 1963.

Scholem, Gershom G., *Major Trends in Jewish Mysticism*, Jerusalem, 1941.

Schwab, Moïse, "Abravanel et son époque," in *Archives Israélites*, 1863 (xxiv) and 1864 (xxv).

Schwerin-Abarbanel, Jeanette, "Ein Brief Don Isaac Abarbanels in portugiesischer Sprache," in *Magazin f. die Wissenschaft des Judentums*, 1891.

Segal, M. Z., "Yiẓḥaq Abravanel betor Parshan ha-Miqra," *Tarbiz*, viii (1937).

Seneca, Lucius Annaeus, *Ad Lucilium epistulae morales*, with an Eng. trans. by Richard M. Gummere, London, 1917; *Minor Dialogues*, together with the Dialogue on Clemency, translated by A. Stewart, 1889; *On Benefits*, translated by A. Stewart (Bohn's Classical Library), 1887.

Serrano y Sanz, Manuel, *Orígenes de la dominación española en América* (Nueva Biblioteca de Autores Españoles), Madrid, 1918.

Silver, Abba Hillel, *A History of the Messianic Speculation in Israel*, New York, 1927.

Simon, Richard, *Histoire Critique du Vieux Testament*, Rotterdam, 1685; *Critique de la Bibliotheque des Auteurs Ecclesiastiques*, ed. Elies Du-Pin, III, Paris, 1730.

Singer, C. and D., "The Jewish Factor in Medieval Thought," in *The Legacy of Israel*, Oxford, 1928.

SOUSA, ANTONIO CAETANO DE, *Provas da história genealógica da casa real portugueza*, I, Lisbon, 1739.
STEIN, EDMUND (MENAHEM), *Dat vĕ-Da'at*, pp. 174-183 (articles on Abravanel).
STEINSCHNEIDER, M., "Isak Abravanel," in *Catalogus Librorum Hebraeorum in Bibliotheca Bodleiana*, II, Berlin, 1931; *Die hebräischen Uebersetzungen des Mittelalters*, Berlin, 1893.
STRAUSS, L., "On Abravanel's Philosophical Tendency and Political Teaching," in *Isaak Abravanel*, ed. by Trend and Lowe, Cambridge, 1937.
SUÁREZ FERNÁNDEZ, LUIS, *Documentos acerca de la Expulsión de los Judíos*, Valladolid, 1964.
TAYLOR, HENRY OSBORN, *The Mediaval Mind*, London, 1930.
TERTULLIANUS, QUINTUS SEPTIMIUS FLORENS, *The Writings of*, 3 volumes, Edinburgh, 1869/70.
THORNDIKE, LYNN, *A History of Magic and Experimental Science*, New York, 8 vols., 1929-1958.
TORNAY, STEPHEN C., *Ockham, Studies and Selections*, La Salle (Illinois), 1938.
TRACHTENBERG, J., *Jewish Magic and Superstition*, New York, 1939.
TREND, B., AND LOEWE, H. (editors), *Isaac Abravanel* (six lectures), Cambridge, 1937.
URBACH, E. E., "Die Staatsauffassung des Don Isaak Abrabanel," in *MGWJ*, 1937.
USQUE, SAMUEL, *Consolaçam ás Tribaçoens de Israel*, Coimbra, 1906-8 (Eng. trans. by Martin A. Cohen, *Consolation for the Tribulations of Israel*, Philadelphia, 1965).
VERGA, SOLOMON IBN, *Shebet Yehudah*, Adrianopol, 1554; ed. Wiener, Hannover, 1855; ed. Baer-Shochet, Jerusalem, 5707 (1947).
VERRILL, ALPHEUS HYATT, *The Inquisition*, New York and London, 1931.
VILLARI, PASQUALE, *The History of Girolamo Savonarola and His Times*, London, 1863.
WALSH, W. T., *Isabella of Spain*, New York, 1930.
WARD, HENRY D., *History and Doctrine of the Millennium*, Boston, 1840.
WEDEL, T. O., *The Mediaeval Attitude Toward Astrology*, Yale University Press, 1920.
WOLF, J. CH., *Bibliotheca Hebraea*, I, Hamburg and Leipzig, 1715; IV, Hamburg, 1733 (contains articles on Abravanel).
WOLFSON, HARRY AUSTRYN, "The Double Faith Theory," in *JQR*, 1942; "Halevi and Maimonides on Design and Necessity," in *Proceedings of AAJR*, XI (1941); *Philo*, I-II, Cambridge, Mass., 1948.
YAHYA, GEDALYAH IBN, *Shalshelet ha-Qabbalah*, Venice, 1586.
YAHYA, JOSEPH BEN DAVID IBN, *Torah Or*, Bologna, 1538.
YAHUDA, A. S., "Don Isaac Abravanel, homme d'état et érudit," in *La Revue Juive de Genéve*, Novembre-Decembre, 1937.
YEATS, JOHN, *The Growth and Vicissitudes of Commerce*, New York, 1878.
ZACUTO, ABRAHAM, *Sefer Juchassin*, ed. Filipowski, London and Edinburgh, 1857.
ZIMMELS, B., *Leo Hebraeus*, Breslau, 1886; *Leone Ebreo* (Neue Studien), Vienna, 1892.
ZURITA, GERÓNIMO, *Historia del rei Don Hernando el Catholico* (Anales de la Corona de Aragon, V), Saragossa, 1670.

INDEX

Abarbanel, Henrique Fernandez, 262, 269
Abarbanel, Jacob, 262
Abel, 139, 140
Abner, convert. *See* Alfonso of Valladolid
Aboab, Immanuel, 261, 278
Aboab, Isaac, 52, 278
Abot, Commentary on. *See Inheritance of the Fathers*
Abraham, patriarch, 143, 224
Abraham bar Ḥiyya, 128, 132, 133, 134, 149, 217, 245, 300
Abraham ben David of Posquières, 292
Abraham ben David of Toledo, 266, 320
Abraham ben Solomon of Torrutiel, 283
Abravanel, variations in spelling and meaning, 261–263
Abravanel, Isaac, family background and biographical data, 3–11, 265–268; studies and early literary efforts, 12–17, 268–269; at court of Portugal, 18–26, 270–272; relations with Braganzas, 23–24, 271, 314; position on Portuguese-Spanish war, 24; A. and conspiracy against João II, 28–31, 34–36, 263–264, 274, 314; at the court of Spain, 38–40, 50–53; efforts to avert expulsion of Jews from Spain, 54–56, 58, 279–280; at the court of Naples, 62–69, 283–284; in Sicily, 69–71, 284; in Corfu, 71–74, 285; in Monopoli, 74–81, 285, 288; in Venice, 82–91, 288–290; A. and medieval thought, 96–97, 128–129, 148–149; his attitude toward Renaissance thinking, 148; toward humanism, 183–184; view of Bible, 101–102, 292; of Revelation, 99–101; creation *ex nihilo,* 103, 107; nature, 110; miracles, 110; angels, 110–111, 115, 295; demons, 111, 124, 295; the universe, 109–111; man, 115–117, 297; transmigration of souls, 117–118, 297; dreams, 123, 299; necromancy, 123–124, 299; astrology, 119–120, 298; magic, 124; resurrection, 118, 145, 238–239; providence, 120, 145, 304; prophecy, 121–123; general conception of history, 131–133, 147–148; view of the first generations of man, 139; first language, 141–142; symbolism of Adam's three sons, 139–140, 302; of Noah's, 142; sin and punishment, 137–138, 142–143, 303; slavery, 154, 306; luxury, 140–141, 151, 302. A.'s political theory in relation to that of Church Fathers, 152–154, 305; of Aristotle, 153–154; of Maimonides, 155–156; of Seneca, 305; conception of dual authority: human and divine, 159; of judicial system, 160–166, 172; mixed government, 165, 308; Social Contract, 178–179, 188, 315; view of kingship, 173–177, 311–312; compared with medieval political tradition: (a) Jewish, 182, 312; (b) Christian, 184, 186–188, 314–315; compared with Graeco-Roman tradition, 184–185, 313; conception of messianic age, 226–234, 238–242; attitude toward messianic prophecies, 204–205; new interpretation of alleged messianic allusions, 206, 213–214, 318; prediction of "end," 216–226; attitude toward Christendom, 227, 233–234, 236–237; toward Islam, 238; anticipated struggle between Christendom and Islam, 236–237; opinion of Jewish condition in Spain, 49, 89, 276; complex attitude toward Marranos, 201–203; nationalism and religion, 143, 212, 303; A. as courtier, 24–25, 51, 59, 67–69, 271–272; as financier, 18, 25, 39–40, 50, 51, 52, 59, 83–84, 88, 90; as leader of Jews, 18, 25, 52, 54–56,

·337·

88–90; as thinker, 126, 128, 148, 193, 247–249, 251; A.'s historic influence (a) in Christendom, 251–253, 325–326; (b) in Jewry, VII–VIII, 254, 255, 326. For more detailed indications, *see under* Creation; Sin; Universe, etc. For his writings, *see* Bibliography, 327 and under individual titles
Abravanel, Isaac, of Saloniki, 289
Abravanel, Isaac, grandson of Isaac Abravanel, 289
Abravanel, Jacob, nephew of Isaac, 79, 262, 287
Abravanel, Joseph, ancestor of Isaac, 4
Abravanel, Joseph, son of Isaac, 25, 74, 80, 272, 290; erroneously called Isaac II, 285
Abravanel, Joseph, nephew and son-in-law of Isaac, 35, 50, 51, 73, 79, 80, 84, 269, 281, 282, 287; death sentence by João II, 35–36, 261, 263, 274
Abravanel, Judah, father of Isaac, 3, 9, 10, 13, 14, 17, 268, 269, 270
Abravanel, Judah, great-grandfather of Isaac, 3, 265
Abravanel, Judah (Leone Ebreo), son of Isaac, 16, 25, 60, 66, 69, 70, 79, 80, 85, 86, 254, 268, 270, 289; and spelling of family name, 262; and João II's sentence of death on Isaac Abravanel, 264; ref. to works by, 264, 268, 278, 281, 285, 287, 288, 289, 290; philosophical concepts compared with father's, 288
Abravanel, Samuel (Juan Sanchez de Sevilla), 3, 4, 5, 6, 265, 266, 267, 269, 270
Abravanel, Samuel, son of Isaac, 25, 69, 76, 272
Abravanel, Samuel, brother of Isaac, 51
Abravaniel, Don Yuda, 265
Absolutism, 162, 188
Achish, 314
Acosta, Uriel, 202
Adam, first man, 139, 141, 157, 225, 300, 302, 306; meaning of name, 301
Adriatic Sea, 169, 235
Aescoli, A. Z., 322
Africa, 229, 320
Aguilar, Alfonso de, 70
Ahab, 176

Alami, Solomon, 17
Albalag, Isaac, 37
Albarrazín, 277
Albertus Magnus, 124, 297, 299
Albo, Joseph, 97, 110, 112, 115, 182, 201, 291, 292, 294, 302, 312, 318, 321
Alcalá de Henares, 52, 278, 279
Alexander the Great, 184, 216
Alexander VI, Pope, 69, 236, 245
Alexandria, 288
Alfonso V, of Aragon, 64
Alfonso II, of Naples, 62, 63, 64, 68, 69, 70, 71, 72, 185, 246, 284
Alfonso V, of Portugal, 10, 11, 12, 13, 16, 18, 19, 20, 21, 22, 24, 25–26, 27, 28, 29, 46, 72, 268, 269, 270, 271; anti-Jewish legislation by, 269; relations with Isaac Abravanel, 185, 270, 271–272; lauded by Abravanel, 313
Alfonso VI, of Castile, 7
Alfonso X, of Castile, 4, 266
Alfonso XI, of Castile, 267
Alfonso, Count of Barcellos, first Duke of Braganza, 11, 12, 27
Alfonso, Count of Faro, 23, 27, 271
Alfonso of Valladolid, 37
Algarve, 7
Alghazali (al-Ghazali). *See* Ghazali
Aljubarrota, battle of, 6, 7, 8
Almeida, Lope de, 19, 20
Almosnino, Moses, 295
Alshekh, Moses, 254
Alting, Heinrich, 251, 325
Alvaro, Count of Olivença, 27, 35
Ambrose, St., 305; on Mosaic Law, 306
Anabaptists, 244, 245
Andalusia, 40, 267; expulsion of Jews from, 48, 277
Angels, 109, 110, 111, 112, 115, 116, 139, 294, 295, 296, 297
Announcer of Salvation, 78, 86, 206, 285, 286; ref. to, 294, 297, 304, 312, 316, 317, 318, 320, 321, 322, 323, 324; quoted, 317
Anti-Semitism, German, medieval parallelism to, 44, 45, 47
Apocalyptic wars, 232–238
Apocalyptic writings, 209–216, 231, 242
Apulia, 74, 77

Aquinas, Thomas, 38, 95, 96, 97, 108, 111, 112, 115, 116, 124, 135, 151, 152, 179, 180, 187–188, 295, 299, 305, 308, 309, 310, 311, 316. *See also Summa*
Arabia, 197
Aragon, 7, 39, 40, 48, 64, 180, 276, 277, 279, 307; Inquisition in, 278
Arama, Isaac, 276, 296
Arama, Meir, 261, 296
Aristobulos, Hellenistic Jewish philosopher, 293
Aristotle, 14, 15, 17, 66, 95, 104, 105, 107, 108, 109, 110, 114, 115, 116, 119, 130, 147, 151, 152, 153, 154, 155, 156, 165, 176, 177, 184, 185, 187, 249, 254, 295; influence on Abravanel, 298, 302, 308; ref. to work by, 304, 309, 310, 312, 313
Armilus, 228
Arrayolos, Portugal, 31, 32
Articles of Faith, 97, 98, 291
Arzilla, Morocco, 18, 268
Ashkenazi, Saul ha-Kohen. *See* Saul ha-Kohen Ashkenazi
Asia, 236, 237, 320
Assyria, 207
Astrology, 15, 118–121, 122, 123, 128, 298, 299
Astronomy, medieval concept, 134
Atienza, Spain, 51
Augustine, St., 38, 95, 96, 97, 100, 104, 110, 112, 122, 132, 135, 136, 137, 138, 149, 151, 152, 180, 190, 196, 244, 245, 305; ref. to work by, 293, 294, 301, 304, 305, 306, 314; Abravanel's opinion of, 301. *See also City of God*
Averroes, 14, 17, 86, 95, 96, 100, 293
Avicenna, 14, 109
Ayala, López de. *See* López de Ayala, Pero
Axarquis, 39

Babel, Tower of, 141, 142, 143, 144, 145
Babylon, 25, 207, 209, 211, 212, 214, 216, 231, 245, 324
Bacon, Roger, 96, 100
Badajoz, 32
Baer, F. Y., 183, 261, 262, 263, 265, 266, 267, 269, 273, 274, 275, 276, 277, 278, 279, 280, 281, 282, 302, 304, 305, 313, 314, 315, 322
Balkans, 233
Barcelona, 213
Bar-Kokhba, Simon, 224
Bari, 74, 79
Barker, Ernest, 306, 315
Barletta, Italy, 79, 80
Baron, Salo W., 281
Bartolocci, Julio, 252, 263, 266, 326
Basle university, 128
Basnage, Jacob Christian, 252, 326
Bayle, Pierre, 251, 261, 325
Bell, A. F. G., 268, 271
Bembo, [Cardinal] Pietro, 285
Benavente, Duke of, 267
Bergenroth, G. A., 276
Bernáldez, Andrés, 275, 277, 279, 280, 281, 283
Bernstein, Simon, 286
Beth Joseph, 289
Bettar, 318
Beugnot, Auguste-Arthur, Count, 252, 326
Bible, 99, 100, 101, 102, 103, 107, 160, 205, 206, 208, 221, 233, 252; Abravanel's commentaries, 25, 36–37, 38, 86. *See also* under individual books
Black Sea, 235
Bodin, Jean, 162
Boer, T. J. de, 295
Boissy, L. M. de, 252, 326
Bologna, 174
Bonaventura, St., 116
Boniface VIII, Pope, 159
Boodin, John E., 103, 104, 293, 294
Born, Lester K., 312
Bouterwek, Frederick, 268
Bracton (Bratton), Henry de, 314
Braganza, Duke of. *See* Alfonso, Count of Barcellos; Ferdinand I and Ferdinand II, Dukes of Braganza
Braganza, Princes of, 11, 12, 13, 23, 24, 27, 28, 30, 31, 40, 84, 264, 271, 274
Brindisi, 74
Brown, H. F., 288, 309
Buddeus, Johann Franz, 251; ref. to work by, 325
Burghers, attitude toward Jews, 8, 11, 41–42, 43, 46, 62, 64, 164, 275
Burgos, Bishop of. *See* Paul of Burgos
Burgos, Spain, 57

Burke, U. R., 276
Buxtorf, Johann, the younger, 251, 325

Cabalists and Cabala, 17, 66, 111, 117, 134, 254–255, 269, 326
Caballeria, Alfonso de la, 276, 279
Cadiz, 277
Cadiz, Marquis of, 54
Caesar, Gaius Julius, 184, 214
Cain, 139, 140, 141
Calabria, 70, 71, 74
Caligula, 214
Calvin, John, 127, 251; attacks Abravanel, 325
Canaan, 142
Cape of Good Hope, 288
Capsali, Elijah, 268, 276, 277, 279, 280, 281, 282, 283, 284, 290
Carande, Ramón, 267
Çarfati, Abraham, 52, 287
Carlyle, A. J., 187, 306, 308, 309, 315, 316
Carlyle, R. W., 308, 310
Carmoly, Eliakim, 272, 284, 285, 296
Caro, Georg, 275
Carpzov, Johann Benedikt II, 251, 325
Cartagena, Spain, 282
Carvalho, Joaquim de, 262, 263, 269, 270, 271
Cassuto, U., 269, 287
Castile, 3, 4, 6, 7, 8, 14, 16, 21, 24, 32, 35, 39, 46, 51, 54, 164, 268, 270, 274, 276, 278, 307
Castro, Rodriguez de, 252; ref. to work by, 325, 326
Catalonia, 281
Cathari, the, 275
Causality, Abravanel's view of, 110; al-Ghazali's influence, 295
Cephalonia, 78, 235, 236
Cerfati, Muser, 287
Cerignola, battle of, 80
Chajun, Joseph, 261
Chapters of R. Eliezer, 225
Charles V, 276
Charles VIII, of France, 67, 68, 69, 70, 186, 235, 246, 247
Chiliasm. *See* Millenarianism
Christianity, Christendom, 95, 96, 197, 200, 201, 206, 208, 212, 213, 214, 215, 216, 221, 223, 228, 229, 232, 233, 234, 235, 236, 237, 238, 244, 249, 254; and Islam, 316, 320; Christian interest in Abravanel, 251–253. *See also* Conversions; Messianism
Christiani, Pablo, 213
Church, the, 153, 154, 159, 182, 183, 190, 196; attitude toward Jews, 42, 43, 44, 62, 275. *See also* Clergy
Church Fathers, 102, 104, 132; influence on Abravanel, 13, 248, 305; and Roman Law, 306; and Mosaic Law, 306; view of man, 153–154; society and civilization, 152–153, 305; origin of State, 151–152; attitude toward kingship, 180; messianic concept, 317; millennial concept, 243, 245
Cicero, 13, 38, 154, 165, 166, 173, 177, 185, 187, 249, 306, 308, 310, 313
Cities, Spanish, relations with Crown, 41–43, 164, 308
City of God, by St. Augustine, ref. to, 294, 295, 298, 299, 300, 301, 302, 304, 305, 312, 314, 324
Civil law, 154, 155
Clemencín, Diego, 280
Clement of Alexandria, 100, 104; ref. to work by, 292, 293, 294
Clergy, attitude toward Jews, 19, 41, 44
Columbus, Christopher, 236
Columbus, Diego, 236
Comines, Philippe de, 64, 69, 82, 283, 284, 288
Commonwealth, First, 208, 218
Commonwealth, Second, 145, 160, 161, 163, 172, 181, 205, 206, 207, 208, 216, 218, 219, 228, 229, 318, 326
Communism, 306
Complaint Against Fate, by Judah Abravanel, 264, 278, 281, 287, 288
Constantine the Great, 320
Constantinople, 71, 85, 169, 219, 234, 235, 322
Conversions, 5, 6, 42, 43, 44, 59–60, 68, 199–200, 201, 203, 230
Conversos. See Marranos
Copernicus, 126
Cordova, Gonsalvo de. *See* Gonsalvo de Cordova
Cordova, 4, 265, 277
Corfu, 71–74, 78, 285, 286, 309; Abravanel criticized Jews in, 283

Corinth, Gulf of, 235
Cortes of Toledo (1480), 275
Cortes of Valladolid (1293), 266
Cosmology, 80, 107, 240–242
Council of Rome in 373, 243
Court, in Israel, (a) Higher, 161, 162, 163, 164, 165, 167, 171, 316; *see also* Synhedrion. (b) Lower, 160, 161, 164, 166, 167, 170, 172
Cracow, University of, 128
Creation, as philosophical concept, 78, 101, 102–108, 125, 133, 134, 293–294, 296, 300
Crescas, Hasdai, 99, 106, 112, 122, 201; ref. to work by, 266, 297, 299, 304; influence on Abravanel, 318
Crimea, 235
Cromwell, Oliver, 244
Crown (in Portugal, Spain and Naples), attitude toward Jews, 8, 12, 20–21, 28, 30, 40, 41, 42, 46, 62, 64, 65
Crown of the Elders, 17, 37, 261; ref. to, 268, 269, 270, 285, 292, 294, 295, 297, 298, 301, 303, 326
Crusades, 230, 236
Cycle theory of history, 134–135
Cyprus, 82
Cyrus, 219

Daniel, Book of Daniel, 86, 88, 109, 110, 209, 210, 211, 212, 213, 228, 318; Commentary on, *see Wells of Salvation*
Dante, 108, 180, 306, 309, 312
David, House of David, 181, 192, 207, 238, 241, 266, 314, 316
David ibn Yahya, 285
Day of Judgment, 117–118, 196, 197, 198, 211, 237, 239, 259, 319
Days of the World, 65–66, 75, 85
Death, theories on, 195–196, 300; Abravanel's concept of, 301–303
Decalogue, view of Church Fathers on, 306; view of Abravanel on, 306
Deeds of God, 66, 80, 293; ref. to, 294, 295, 297, 298, 300, 301, 304
Defensor Pacis, by Marsilius of Padua, 159
Demons, 111, 112, 124, 125; Jewish belief in, 295
De officio regis, by John Wycliff, 159

Determinism, 119, 130, 131, 147, 148, 244, 247
Deuteronomy, Commentary on, 17, 18, 73, 75, 85, 158, 160, 163, 167, 170, 171, 185; ref. to, 261, 274, 276, 284, 285, 293, 294, 295, 297, 298, 300, 303, 305, 306, 307, 308, 309, 310, 311, 314, 315, 316, 317, 318
Dias, Bartholomeu, 288
Diaspora, 65, 208, 318
Discourses on the First Ten Books of Titus Livy, by Machiavelli, 189, 313
Disputationes adversus astrologiam, by Pico della Mirandola, 128
Divine Right of Kings, 186–189. See also Monarchism
Dreams, 123, 299
Duarte, King of Portugal, 9, 10, 11, 16, 21, 27
Dubnow, S., 278, 282
Dunham, S. A., 271
Duran, Simon, 250
Duran, Profiat (Efodi), 302

Ebreo, Leone. *See* Abravanel, Judah, son of Isaac
Eckhart, Meister, 147
Edict of expulsion from Spain. *See* Expulsion from Spain
Edom, 233, 234, 246, 323
Education of a Christian Prince, by Erasmus, 184
Edward I, of England, 41
Efodi. *See* Duran, Profiat
Egypt, 82, 93, 142, 145, 207, 228, 229, 233, 235, 288
El'azar ben Ya'akov, R., 307
Eldad ha-Dani, 229, 322
Elizabeth, wife of Alfonso V, of Portugal, 11
Emanations, theory of, 103
Empereur, Constantine l', 251, 325
Empedocles, 132
Emunot ve-Deot, by Saadia, ref. to, 291, 292, 296, 297, 298, 300, 301, 304, 312
England, 41, 180, 307
Enlightenment, 251
Enoch, 140
Enrique II, of Castile, 267
Enrique III, of Castile, 3, 267
Ephodi. *See* Duran, Profiat

· 341 ·

Epistulae morales, by Seneca, 302, 305
Erasmus, Desiderio, 127, 183–184; ref. to works by, 312, 313
Esau, 143
Eschatology, 132, 133, 134, 145–146, 200, 209–216, 237–242, 243. *See also* Messianism
Espina, Alfonso de, 275
Este, Dukes of, 61
Eternal Justice, 65–66, 69, 85
Etheridge, I. W., 282
Ethics of the Fathers. *See Inheritance of the Fathers*
Eusebius, 293
Evil. *See* Sin
Evora, 11, 31
Evora, Bishop of, 35
Exile. *See* Diaspora
Exodus, Commentary on, 158, 167, 170; date of completion, 290; ref. to, 294, 295, 297, 298, 299, 300, 301, 303, 305, 306, 307, 308, 309, 315
Expulsion from Spain, 48, 49, 53–60, 63, 277, 279–283
Ezekiel, 52, 202, 315, 316; Commentary on, date of completion, 289; ref. to, 203, 304, 321

Faith, as philosophical concept, 95, 96, 97, 98, 99, 125, 126, 291, 292. *See also* Reason
Faro, Count of. *See* Alfonso, Count of Faro
Federigo, King of Naples, 79, 287
Fenton, G., 282
Ferdinand, King of Aragon, 27, 30, 38, 39, 40, 42, 46, 47, 48, 49, 50, 51, 53, 54, 55, 56, 57, 59, 64, 67, 68, 77, 164, 185, 186, 268, 276, 277, 278, 281; and expulsion of Jews from Spain, 53–57, 280, 281
Ferdinand III, of Castile, 3, 4
Ferdinand of Naples. *See* Ferrante I
Ferdinand I, Duke of Braganza, 23, 24
Ferdinand II, Duke of Braganza, 23, 24, 28, 29, 30, 31, 32, 35; and conspiracy against João II, 30, 34, 263–264, 273
Fernando IV, of Castile, 3, 265
Fernando, Infante, 3, 10, 14
Ferorelli, Nicola, 261, 262, 283, 286, 287

Ferrante I, King of Naples, 62, 63, 64, 65, 67, 185, 283
Ferrante II, King of Naples, 70, 71, 73, 77, 79, 284, 288
Ferrara, 61
Feudalism, 169
Ficino, Marsilius, 128; ref. to work by, 305, 308
Fifth Kingdom, 209, 210–211, 212, 213, 214, 215, 216, 228, 243
Fifth Monarchy Men, 244
Figgis, John Neville, ref. to work by, 309, 314
Fita, Fidel, 277
Flanders, 17, 269, 270
Florence, 61, 66, 128, 174, 183, 235, 246, 247
Former Prophets, Commentary on, 72
Forms of the Elements, 17, 269
Fourth Kingdom, 213, 214, 228, 243
France, 42, 67, 69, 70, 73, 74, 75, 77, 79, 80, 235, 246, 307; Maimonides' letter to Jewish scholars in, 298
Freire, Anselmo Braamcamp, ref. to work by, 263, 269, 270, 271
Fried, S., 296
Friedländer, M., 291
Fuerst, Julius, 325

Galba, Servius Sulpicius, 214
Galen, ideas on old age and death, 301
Galipapa, Ḥayyim, criticized by Abravanel, 312
Gama, Vasco da, 82, 288
Gebhardt, Carl, ref. to work by, 261, 262, 263, 264, 265, 269, 270, 271, 273, 274, 278, 281, 283, 284, 287, 288, 289, 290
Gebhardt, Emile, ref. to work by, 324
Geiger, Abraham, 289, 290, 326
Gelasius I, Pope, 315
Genesis, Commentary on, date of completion, 86, 289; ref. to, 292, 293, 294, 295, 297, 299, 300, 301, 302, 303, 305, 306, 321
Genoa, 61, 63, 69, 174, 238
George of Trebizond, work by, 308
Germany, 77
Germany, Nazi, medieval parallelism in Jewish situation, 45, 47, 63, 227
Gersonides, 86, 106, 108, 121, 122, 123,

128, 182, 244, 292, 314; ref. to work by, 295, 312
Ghazali, Mohammed, 100, 115, 197, 295, 316
Giannone, Pietro, ref. to work by, 284
Gibeon, 106
Gibeonites, 314
Gibraltar, 83
Gilson, Étienne, 95, 291, 295, 315
Gog, 228, 321, 322
Gomorrah, 250
Gonsalvo de Cordova, 70, 71, 79, 80, 236, 286, 287
Gorfinkel, Joseph I., 297
Graetz, Heinrich, 262, 266, 267, 268, 269, 271, 272, 275, 278, 280, 282, 283, 284, 285, 289, 290, 325
Granada, 39, 48, 53, 235, 237
Greece, Greeks, 71, 82, 142, 169, 207, 211, 212, 214, 215, 216
Greek philosophy, 97, 100, 104, 113, 268, 292. See also under names of individual philosophers
Gregory the Great, Pope, 188
Grimani, Antonio, 74
Grossberg, M., 269, 273
Grossgebauer, Theophilus, 325
Grotius, Hugo, 251; cites Abravanel, 325
Guadalajara, Spain, 52
Guadalupe, 59
Guadiana, 32
Guicciardini, Francesco, 68, 71, 128, 276, 284, 285, 288
Guide, Commentary on, 25, 52, 85, 87, 272, 279, 286, 289, 290
Guide for the Perplexed, by Maimonides, ref. to, 291, 292, 293, 295, 296, 297, 298, 299, 300, 302, 306, 307, 316
Guinea, 21
Guttmann, Jacob, ref. to work by, 266, 272, 286, 289, 290, 301, 325, 326
Guttmann, Julius, 300

Habilio, 'Ali b. Joseph, 311
Habravanel. See Abravanel, Isaac
Ha-Kohen, Joseph, 282
Ha-Kohen, Saul. See Saul ha-Kohen Ashkenazi. See also Questions of and Answers to Saul ha-Kohen
Halevi, Judah, 96, 97, 100, 105, 126, 128, 141, 143, 182, 303, 304; views on Monarchism, 312
Halper, B., 310
Ham, 141, 142
Ha-Meassef, 270
Harnack, A., 324
Hartmann, A. T., 325
Hasmonean dynasty, 181, 207
Ḥayat, Judah, 283
Ḥayyim ibn Musa, 269
Hearnshaw, F. J. C., 311, 312
Heavenly bodies, 108, 109, 111, 114, 115, 119, 120, 124, 134
Hebrew language, 141–142
Henry of Gascogne, 7
Henry VII, King of England, 26
Henry, the Navigator, 21
Herand, J. A., 324
Herzl, Theodore, 250
Hesqeto (Forti), Baruch Uzziel, 265, 267, 272, 283, 284, 288, 289, 290
Hirschfeld, H., 291
History, philosophical concept of, 37, 65, 130–148, 244, 247, 300
Hobbes, Thomas, 188; ref. to work by, 315
Holy League, the, 69
Hosea, Commentary on, 312
Huesca, Spain, 53
Huet (Huetius), Pierre Daniel, 251; ref. to work by, 325
Hulsius, Antonius, differs with Abravanel, 251, 325
Humanism, 66, 96, 183, 184, 304
Hume, M. A. S., ref. to work by, 308
Hungary, 235
Hurgonje, Christian Snouck, work by, quoted, 316
Husik, Isaac, 291, 292, 302, 318
Hussite Movement, 244

Ibn Caspi, Joseph, 37
Ibn Ezra, Abraham, 128, 168, 169, 182, 215, 252, 269, 273, 308, 312, 313, 320, 322; on the word "Adam," 301
Ibn Gabirol, Solomon, concept of spiritual substances, 295
Ibn Musa, Ḥayyim, 17, 269
Ibn Yaḥya. See Yaḥya
Ibn Zaddiq, Joseph ben Jacob, 296

Iqqarim, ref. to, 292, 295, 296, 302, 317, 318, 323
Imitatio Christi, 127
Immortality, Abravanel's concept of, 116, 297
India, 21, 82, 83
Inheritance of the Fathers, 72, 76, 85, 285; ref. to, 285, 286, 289, 304
Inquisition (Spanish), The, 5, 40, 42, 44, 45, 46, 47, 48, 49, 53, 54, 57, 58, 64, 239, 250, 275, 276, 277, 280, 281; compared with medieval inquisition, 275
International disputes in messianic age, 322
Irenaeus, 98, 104, 132, 133, 243, 292, 306; ref. to work by, 294, 299, 303, 319, 324
Isaac, patriarch, 143
Isabella, Queen, 27, 38, 39, 40, 42, 46, 49, 50, 51, 55, 56, 57, 59, 164, 268, 276, 277, 280
Isaiah, 134, 228, 232, 233, 234, 240, 246, 286, 318; Commentary on, 71, 72, 73, 78, 85, 286, 304, 305, 317, 323, 324
Isidore of Seville, 133, 149, 180
Islam, 95, 196, 197, 214, 215, 216, 228, 232, 234, 235, 238, 254, 291, 316, 321, 323. *See also* Moslems
Israel, 120, 143–145, 240, 241, 250, 303, 304, 317
Israeli, Isaac, 296
Italy, 59, 60, 61, 62, 66, 67, 68, 69, 71, 73, 77, 80, 82, 85, 158, 166, 170, 171, 180, 183, 233, 235, 236, 237, 245, 246, 247, 282. *See also* under individual cities and city-states

Jabez, Joseph, 272
Jacob, patriarch, 143
Jaen, Spain, 4, 277
James II, King of Aragon, 265
Japheth, 141, 142
Jellinek, A., 295, 296, 300
Jeremiah, 229, 233; Commentary on, ref. to, 282, 322; date of completion, 289
Jeroboam, 316
Jerome, St., 38, 104, 243, 294, 305, 324

Jerusalem, 160, 171, 209, 225, 229, 232, 240, 243, 324, 326
Jesebel, 176
Jesus of Nazareth, 197, 199, 200, 205, 206, 208, 211, 212, 213, 221, 222, 223, 224, 243, 250, 319, 320
Jethro, 170
Joachim of Flora, 244
João I, of Portugal, 3, 8, 9, 11, 20, 21, 27, 62, 64, 274
João II, of Portugal, 26, 27, 28, 29, 30, 31, 32, 33, 34, 35, 50, 58, 62, 64, 185, 229, 261, 263, 270, 272, 274; Isaac Abravanel and the revolt against, 263–264, 273, 314
João, Marquis of Montemor, 27, 28, 30, 35
Job, Book of, 109
John Hyrcanus, 181
John of Paris, 308
John of Salisbury, 180, 187; ref. to work by, 310
Joseph ben Zaddiq of Arevalo, 261, 267, 320
Joseph ha-Kohen, 282
Joseph ibn Shraga, 269
Joseph ibn Yahya, grandson of courtier, ref. to work by, 271
Josephus, 233
Joshua, 106, 308
Joshua, Book of, Commentary on, ref. to, 270, 271, 272, 273, 274, 290, 293, 294, 314; date of completion, 36, 274
Juan I, of Castile, 267
Judarias, 10, 11, 12, 275
Judges, 162, 165, 166, 167, 175, 177, 192, 307
Judges, Book of, Commentary on, 36; ref. to, 274, 308, 309, 310, 311
Judgment, Day of. *See* Day of Judgment
Justin Martyr, 100, 104, 243; ref. to work by, 293, 294, 306, 324

Kalonymos ben David ben Todros, ref. to work by, 293
Kanczug, Poland, 235
Kapsali, Elijah. *See* Capsali, Elijah
Katzenellenbogen, Meir, 290
Kaufmann, David, 261, 269, 288

Kayserling, Meyer, 261, 267, 268, 269, 271, 272, 274, 275, 276, 278, 280, 284
Khazari, Kitab al-, by Judah Halevi, ref. to, 291, 293, 294, 299, 301, 303, 312
Kimḥi, David, 206, 323
Kimḥi, Joseph, 212, 213
Kings. *See* Monarchism
Kings, Book of, Commentary on, 65; ref. to, 274, 278, 279, 280, 281, 282, 283, 290, 292, 293, 294, 295, 298, 304, 307, 310, 311, 314, 315, 316, 318, 326
Klausner, Joseph, 297, 317, 322
Koran, 99
Kush, 142

Laemmlein, Asher, 254
Laguardia, Spain, 53
Lahaqat Neviim. See Vision of God
Landau, L., 318
Languages, theory of, 141–142
Languedoc, Inquisition in, 275
Latter Prophets, Commentary on, 86, 289
Law, divine, 155, 156, 157, 158, 306–307
Law, human, 155, 156, 157, 158
Law of nations, 154, 155
Lemos, Maximiliano, 262, 268
Leon, Judah Messer, 66
Leon, Kingdom of, 164
Lepanto, 78, 235
Levita, Elijah, 261
Leviticus, Commentary on, ref. to, 300
Light of God, by Crescas. *See Or Adonai*
Lindo, E. M., 282
Lisbon, 3, 11, 269
Llorente, Juan Antonio, ref. to work by, 280
Lombardy, 276
López de Ayala, Pero, 265, 267
Lopez, Fernam, 14
López, Isaac, ref. to work by, 289
Lorki, Joshua, 206, 230, 318
Louis XI, King of France, 27
Louis XII, King of France, 79
Louis XVI, King of France, 188
Lucas, Henry S., 299
Lucas, Herbert, 324
Lucca, 61, 174

Lusitanus, Amatus, ref. to work by, 262
Luther, Martin, 127
Luzzatto, Samuel David, 254, 282, 283, 291, 326
Lyons, 243
Lyra, Nicholas de, 38, 233

Magog, 322
Machiavelli, Niccolò, 47, 126, 127, 148, 184, 189; ref. to work by, 299, 304, 313
Madrid, 278
Magic, 124, 127, 299
Maimonides, 17, 25, 37, 52, 78, 86, 87, 96, 97, 98, 99, 101, 104, 105, 106, 108, 109, 111, 112, 113, 114, 115, 116, 117, 119, 121, 122, 123, 124, 128, 131, 135, 138, 147, 155, 156, 157, 175, 182, 192, 242, 252; compared with Thomas Aquinas, 291; Abravanel on Maimonides' *Articles of Faith,* 291, 292; ref. to work by, 292, 293, 294, 295, 296, 297, 298, 300, 302, 307, 310, 313, 324. *See also Guide for the Perplexed*
Malachi, Commentary on, 304
Malaga, ransom of Jews in, 280
Malter, H., 296, 302
Man, as philosophical concept, 112–118, 135–137, 295, 296; and the universe, 118, 125, 126; as a political animal, 151, 152, 153; natural equality of, 153–154, 157
Man, Fall of. *See* Sin
Manilius, 128
Manasseh ben Israel, 252
Mantua, 61
Manuel (Manoel) I, King of Portugal, 289
Marranos, 5, 6, 8, 43, 44, 45, 46, 47, 48, 49, 57, 201, 202, 203, 204, 266, 275, 276, 281, 289, 317
Marsilius of Padua, 159
Marx, Alexander, 261, 276, 278, 279, 280, 287, 298
Marx, Karl, 250
Maximilian I, Emperor, 290
Mazzara, Sicily, 68, 69, 284
McGiffert, A. C., 295, 304
Media, 216, 231
Medici (family), 61, 183

Medicine, 14–15
Medigo, Elijah del, 66, 86
Medigo, Joseph Solomon del, 254, 290, 326
Medinaceli, Duke of, 54
Mediterranean Sea, 233, 235
Meir of Rothenburg, 322
Melamed, Meir, son-in-law of Abraham Senior, 54, 59, 279, 281
Menahem ben Zerah, 261, 266
Mendoza, Cardinal, 54, 59
Menz, Judah, 290
Messiah, 198, 199, 201, 204, 205, 206, 216, 317, 318, 325
Messianic calculations, 145, 205–215, 216–226, 289, 300
Messianic prophecies, 250–251
Messianic tribulations, 204, 219, 232
Messianism, vii, 77, 78, 85, 86; Jewish concept, 145, 195, 198, 199, 200, 202, 205–215, 222, 224–226, 238–242, 253; Christian concept, 195, 198, 200, 205, 221, 223, 253; Abravanel's influence, 251, 254
Messianic trilogy. *See* Announcer of Salvation, Salvations of His Annointed, Wells of Salvation
Messina, 70, 71, 72, 73, 74, 79, 284, 285
Milan, 61, 67, 69, 235
Milḥamot Adonai, ref. to, 294, 298
Millenarianism, 237–242, 243, 244, 245, 246, 247, 249, 250, 253. *See also* Eschatology
Miracles, 106, 107, 110, 122, 125, 127–128, 144
Mirandola, Pico della. *See* Pico della Mirandola
Modena, 61
Mohammed, 197, 212, 213, 224, 250, 320
Moldavia, 235
Molina, 52
Molkho, Solomon, 254
Monarchism, 162, 164, 165, 166, 173–179, 180, 184, 185, 186, 188, 190, 191, 193, 305, 309, 310, 311, 312, 313, 314, 315, 316. *See also* Divine Right of Kings
Monopoli, Isaac Abravanel in, 74–81, 85, 90, 285, 286, 288
Montemor, Marquis of. *See* João, Marquis of Montemor

Moors. *See* Moslems
Morea, the, 78
Moreri, Louis, 252; ref. to work by, 326
Mosaic Law and Constitution, 158, 160, 161, 167, 190, 193, 292, 306, 307, 323
Moses, 99, 102, 116, 153, 158, 160, 162, 163, 167, 168, 170, 191, 192, 298, 300, 307, 308, 309, 312, 315, 316
Moslems, 4, 5, 7, 48, 232, 235, 236, 237, 238, 319, 320
Munk, S., ref. to work by, 296
Murcia, Spain, 41, 52
Mutakallims, 315
Mu'tazilites, views of, 298
Mysticism, 15–16, 52–53, 78, 90, 111, 217, 242, 254

Naboth, the Jesreelite, 176
Naḥalat Abot. See Inheritance of the Fathers
Nahmanides, 118, 132, 133, 138, 149, 161, 182, 213, 217, 222, 245, 312; ref. to work by, 297, 300, 319, 323
Naples, 62–71, 72, 73, 74, 75, 77, 79, 85, 87, 89, 183, 186, 235, 246, 268, 283, 284, 285, 286, 289, 296, 309; Abravanel in, 61–80
Narboni, David ben Joseph, 37
Nasi, Joseph, Duke of Naxos, 256
Natural law, 154, 155, 156
Naturales quaestiones, by Seneca, 296
Nature, as philosophical concept, 105–106, 110, 111, 130
Navia, Juan Alonso de, 276
Nebuchadnezzar, 184, 187, 209, 225
Necromancy, 123–124, 299. *See also* Magic
Neo-Platonism, 66, 80
Nero, 214
Neubauer, A., 266, 320, 322
Neuman, Abraham A., 275, 313
New Christians. *See* Marranos
New Heavens, 78, 80, 286; ref. to. 293, 294, 296, 297, 301
New Testament, 99
Nicholas of Cusa, 126, 176, 180, 251
Nimrod, 141
Nobility, attitude toward Jew, 8, 9, 41
North Africa, 18, 21, 59
Numbers, Commentary on, 298

Obadiah, 233, 322
Obadiah of Bertinoro, 322
Ockham, William, 179, 187, 309, 311
Octavian (Gaius Julius Caesar Octavianus), 214
Odemira, Count of, 23, 271
Or Adonai, by Crescas, ref. to, 112, 294, 295, 298, 304, 317, 318
Ordinances of Alfonso V, 10
Oresme, 299
Origen, 104, 132, 134, 243; ref. to work by, 293–294, 300, 306
Otho, Marcus Salvius, 214

Pacios López, Antonio, 321
Padua, 87, 290
Palencia, Alonso de, 271, 275, 277, 278
Palermo, 69, 70
Palestine, 181, 229, 232, 237, 238, 240, 241, 256, 304, 318
Papacy, attitude toward Jews, 62, 214. *See also* under individual popes
Papal states, 62
Paracelsus, 128
Passover Sacrifice, 75, 76, 85, 296; ref. to, 267, 269, 270, 271, 272, 278, 279, 283, 284, 285, 290
Paul of Burgos, 38, 207, 230, 233
Peace, medieval yearning for, 311
Pedro, Don, of Portugal, 10, 11, 12, 13, 16, 21, 23, 27
Pentateuch, Commentary on, 17, 37, 86
Petrarch, 299
Persia, Persians, 209, 211, 212, 214, 216, 231, 234
Pflaum (Peri), H., 278, 283, 287, 288
Philip the Fair, 42
Philo, 102, 293
Philosophy and Faith, Jewish concept, 96, 97; Abravanel's attitude, 96–97, 100, 102
Pico della Mirandola, Giovanni, 66, 128, 299
Pines, S. 292
Pisa, 19
Plasencia, 33, 273, 274, 278, 279, 282, 287
Plato, 66, 80, 100, 103, 104, 116, 117, 128, 132, 135, 184, 249; influence on Abravanel, 301, 302, 305, 308; ref. to work by, 313

Plotinus, 103
Plutarch, 185, 187; ref. to work by, 313
Polak, H. J., 296
Poland, 128, 235
Polignano, Italy, 285, 288
Polybius, 166; ref. to work by, 308
Pontano, Giovanni, 66, 284
Portugal, 3, 5, 6, 7, 8, 9, 11, 12, 13, 14, 18, 21, 25, 33, 34, 36, 39, 41, 46, 50, 51, 58, 65, 73, 83, 84, 85, 87, 89, 185, 263, 264, 267, 269, 271, 272, 273, 274, 281, 285, 287, 289; royal attitude toward Jews, 7–10, 12, 22, 26, 28, 30
Prescott, W. H., 276, 283, 284
Prester, John, 229
Prince, The, by Machiavelli, 47, 184, 189
Principles of Faith, 73, 85, 266, 285; and Maimonides' Creed, 291; ref. to, 292, 293, 296, 303, 307
Priuli, Venetian diarist, cited, 288
Prophecy, 85, 121–123, 202–203, 216, 217, 219, 220; Maimonides' concept of, 298
Prophets, Commentary on, 17, 86
Protestantism, 253
Providence, 120, 145, 207, 208, 298, 304, 315
Ptolemies, the, 228
Ptolemy, 108, 109, 294
Put, 142
Pythagoras, 104, 117

Questions of and Answers to Saul ha-Kohen, 87; ref. to, 261, 268, 269, 272, 283, 284, 286, 288, 290

Racism, 42, 44, 306
Rationalism, attitude of Isaac Abravanel, 15, 16, 37–38; Jewish attitude, 140, 143, 217, 221
Reason, as philosophical concept, 95, 96, 97, 98, 99, 101, 291, 292
Redemption, 75, 77, 78, 80, 87, 88, 145, 204, 205, 225, 229, 231, 322. For date, *see* Messianic calculations
Reformation, 159, 244, 249, 251, 252, 253
Reggio, Calabria, 285
Regiomontanus, 128
Reines, A. J., 299

Reland, Adrian, 251; ref. to work by, 325
Renaissance, 64, 67, 97, 126, 127, 129, 148, 149, 169, 184, 248, 249, 304
Repentance, 117
Republic, by Cicero, 185
Requena, Spain, 51
Requesens, Admiral, 69–70
Resende, Garcia de, 28, 261, 272
Resurrection, 117–118, 145, 226, 238–239, 242, 243, 297, 304
Reubeni, David, 254
Revelation, 95–103, 105, 107, 125, 156, 292
Revenge, as messianic concept, 226, 227–228, 232, 234, 239
Reward and punishment, 138, 140, 141, 142–143, 144, 145, 147
Rhodes, island of, 233, 235, 322
Rios, Amador de los, José, 267, 275, 278
Roeder, R., 299
Roman Empire and beginnings of Christianity, 320
Roman Empire, Eastern, 219, 234
Roman Law and the Church Fathers, 306
Roman Republic, 165, 172, 185
Rome, Romans, 68, 142, 169, 172, 174, 193, 207, 211, 212, 213, 214, 215, 216, 219, 226, 228, 229, 233, 234, 235, 237, 238, 245, 246, 276, 313, 322, 324, 325
Rosh Amanah. See Principles of Faith
Ross, D. W., 313
Rossi, Azariah de, 254
Rossi, Giovanni Bernardo de, 266, 283, 311, 325
Roth, Cecil, 275, 282
Rousseau, Jean Jacques, 147, 179, 188, 248

Saadia, 96, 97, 98, 104, 114, 115, 118, 122, 131, 132, 135, 136, 137, 182, 217, 245, 302, 304, 312, 319
Saloniki, 69, 72, 76, 284
Salvation, 113, 117, 196, 197, 198, 202, 204, 255
Salvations of His Annointed, 78, 286; ref. to, 285, 291, 292, 293, 296, 297, 300, 302, 304, 317, 318, 319, 320, 321, 323, 324, 325, 326
Samaria, 231
Samuel, prophet, 123, 124, 175, 176, 191, 298, 312, 313
Samuel, Book of, Commentary on, 36, 158, 185, 272; ref. to, 296, 299, 301, 304, 308, 309, 310, 311, 312, 315
Sanchez, Juan Sanchez de Sevilla. *See* Abravanel, Samuel
Sancho IV, of Castile, 265, 266
Santangel, Luis de, 59, 276
Santarem, 12
Santiago, Archbishop of, 267
Santillana, Marquis of, 268
Sanuto (Sanudo), Marino, ref. to work by, 261, 284, 285
Santos, Ribeiro dos, 271, 325
Sapienza, 78
Sarachek, J., 291, 315
Saragossa, 52, 277
Sarco, Joseph, 269
Saul, King, 123, 124, 181, 316
Saul ha-Kohen Ashkenazi, 86, 87, 268, 284, 285. *See Questions of and Answers to Saul ha-Kohen*
Savonarola, 127, 193, 242, 245, 246, 247, 249, 250, 251, 316, 324; ref. to work by, 299, 324, 325
Savoy, 61
Schaefer, H., 271, 272
Scharff, F. S., 299
Schipper, I., 274, 281, 282
Schnell, Sebastian, 251, 325
Scholasticism, 96, 101, 102, 249
Scholem, G. G., 269, 297
Schwerin-Abarbanel, Jeanette, 271
Scotus, Duns, 96
Second Temple. *See* Temple, Second
Secret of the Guide, 290
Segura de la Orden, 33, 38, 273, 274, 278, 279
Seleucids, the, 228
Seminara, Italy, 71, 73
Senarega, B., 283
Seneca, 13, 112, 177, 184, 185, 249, 295, 301; influence on Isaac Abravanel, 302, 305, 306, 310, 311
Senior, Abraham, 50, 52, 54, 55, 56, 59, 276, 278, 279, 281
Serrano y Sanz, Manuel, ref. to work by, 278, 281
Seth, 139, 140, 143

Setubal, 35, 84
Seville, 3, 4, 5, 264, 266, 267, 270
Sezira, João, 19, 20, 270
Sforza, Ludovico, 67
Shabbethai Zevi, viii, 254
Shalshelet ha-Qabbalah, by Gedaliah ibn Yaḥya, ref. to, 280, 283
Shebet Yehudah, ref. to, 261, 266, 270, 271, 283, 318, 321
Shem, 141, 142, 143
Sicily, 235, 284; Isaac Abravanel in, 68–71
Siena, 61, 174
Siger of Brabant, 96
Silver, Abba H., 322, 329
Simancas, 281
Simon b. Mattityahu, 181
Simon, Richard, 251, 325
Sin, philosophic concept of, 125, 136–138, 139, 140, 141, 144, 147, 151, 152, 196, 197, 303
Singer, Charles, 291, 294
Singer, D., 291
Sixtus IV, Pope, 19
Slavery, 153, 154, 155, 305–306
Smith, Sharwood, 312
Sodom, 250
Solomon ha-Levi of Burgos. *See* Paul of Burgos
Solomon, King, 192, 314, 316
Soul, as philosophical concept, 115–116, 117, 118, 125, 297
Sousa, Antonio Caetano de, ref. to work by, 261, 265, 267, 271
Spain, 3, 4, 5, 6, 40, 41, 42, 44, 45, 46–49, 50, 51, 52, 53, 54, 57, 59, 60, 61, 62, 63, 65, 69, 70, 72, 76, 77, 79, 80, 87, 89, 91, 158, 161, 164, 171, 180, 185, 186, 200, 201, 227, 230, 234, 235, 236, 237, 242, 262–263, 266, 268, 272, 274, 275, 276, 277, 278, 280, 281, 282, 285, 309, 326. *See also* Expulsion
Spice trade, 82
Spinoza, Baruch, viii
State, concept of, 151–170, 302; Venice as the ideal, 166–170. *See also* Monarchism, Theocracy
Steinschneider, M., 289, 293
Stephen of Tournai, 315
Strauss, L., 302, 303, 305, 307, 315
Suárez Fernández, Luis, 273, 277, 281

Summa contra gentiles, by Thomas Aquinas, ref. to, 295, 305
Summa theologica, by Thomas Aquinas, ref. to, 295, 296, 299, 308, 309, 310, 311, 316
Synhedrion, 162, 163, 164, 165, 166, 171, 172, 173, 192, 241, 315

Taborites, 244, 245
Tagus, 32
Talmud, 222, 223, 225, 226, 233
Tangier, 9, 21
Tanusi, Eliezer, 72, 285
Tarazona, Aragon, 40, 50
Taylor, A. O., 291
Temple, First, 145, 219
Temple, Second, 181–182, 208, 214, 219, 224; date of destruction, 320
Ten Tribes, 207, 322; and Messianism, 229–232, 238
Tertullian, 243; ref. to work by, 324
Theocracy, 189–194, 241–242, 245
Theology, Christian, 97, 98, 99, 101, 104, 112, 113, 136
Theology, Jewish, 97, 98, 101, 104
Theology, Moslem, 98, 99, 100, 104
Thomas à Kempis, 127
Thomists, 95, 96
Thorndike, L., 299
Tiberius, Claudius Nero, 214
Toledo, Spain, 164, 278
Tornay, Stephen C., 311, 315
Tortosa, disputation at, 206, 222, 321
Torquemada, Tomás, 277
Trachtenberg, J., 295
Transmigration of souls, 117, 118, 297
Tribal institutions, Abravanel's views on, 171–172, 309
Tristan de Leon, 276
Trujillo, Spain, 275
Turkey, Turks, 59, 71, 72, 73, 74, 77, 78, 82, 169, 216, 219, 234, 235, 236, 254, 289
Turkish-Venetian War, 78, 79

Universe, philosophical concept, 101, 105, 108–112, 114, 115, 126, 132, 134, 195, 294; and man, 118–125; destructibility of, 131–132, 133, 300
Usque, Samuel, ref. to work by, 261
Vespasian, 214

Villa Velha, Portugal, 32
Villa Viçosa, Portugal, 32
Villari, Pasquale, ref. to work by, 299, 316, 324
Villena, Spain, 51
Vision of God, 25, 85, 272
Vitellius, Aulus, 214
Viterbo, Fra Egidio da, 66

Waldenses, 275
Walsh, James J., 299
Walsh, W. T., 276
Ward, H. D., 324
Wars, attitude to, 24, 311
Wells of Salvation, 77, 78, 209, 219, 220, 228, 286; ref. to, 265, 266, 272, 279, 280, 283, 286, 295, 297, 298, 302, 303, 305, 309, 314, 317, 318, 319, 320, 321
Will, Divine, 125, 130, 131, 135, 146, 147
Will, Free, as philosophical concept, 115, 124, 136, 147, 148, 292
Wolf, Johann Christoph, 261, 283, 325

Woman, A's view of, 136, 137, 139
Wycliff, John, 159, 309

Yahya, David ibn, 72, 285
Yahya, Gedaliah ibn, 22
Yahya, Joseph ibn, 22, 271
Yahya, ibn, family, 28
Yeats, John, 288
Yehiel of Pisa, 18, 19, 20, 29, 268, 269, 270, 273, 285
Yehuda, Don, of Cordova, 265
Yemen, 231; Maimonides' letter to Jews of, 298
Yosippon, 233, 323

Zacuto, Abraham, ref. to work by, 261, 267
Zechariah, Commentary on, ref. to, 261, 265, 322
Zedeq 'Olamim, 297
Zerah ben Nathan, 290
Zimmels, B., 278, 283, 297
Zurita, Gerónimo, ref. to work by, 261, 281, 288, 289
Zwingli, 127